Rock & Roll
in Kennedy's America

Rock & Roll
in Kennedy's America

A CULTURAL HISTORY
of the
EARLY 1960s

Richard Aquila

Johns Hopkins University Press
Baltimore

Johns Hopkins University Press
2715 North Charles Street
Baltimore, Maryland 21218
www.press.jhu.edu

Library of Congress Cataloging-in-Publication Data

Names: Aquila, Richard, 1946– author.
Title: Rock & roll in Kennedy's America : a cultural history of the early
    1960s / Richard Aquila.
Other titles: Rock and roll in Kennedy's America
Description: Baltimore : Johns Hopkins University Press, 2022. |
    Includes bibliographical references and index.
Identifiers: LCCN 2021062979 | ISBN 9781421444987 (hardcover) |
    ISBN 9781421444994 (ebook)
Subjects: LCSH: Rock music—United States—1961–1970—History and criticism. |
    Rock music—Social aspects—United States—History—20th century.
Classification: LCC ML3534.3 .A76 2022 | DDC 781.660973/09046—dc23
LC record available at https://lccn.loc.gov/2021062979

A catalog record for this book is available from the British Library.

Special discounts are available for bulk purchases of this book. For more information, please contact Special Sales at specialsales@jh.edu.

For Marie

Contents

Introduction. "Only in America"   1

Part 1
NEW DIRECTIONS FOR EARLY 60s ROCK & ROLL

Chapter 1. "It's Now or Never": Rock & Roll Enters a New Decade   11

Chapter 2. "What Does a Girl Do?" The Girl Group Revolution of the Early 60s   35

Chapter 3. "Heat Wave": Motown's Hot Sounds for Young America   63

Chapter 4. "Surfin' Safari": Surf Music, Car Songs, and the Mythic West   96

Part 2
OLD STYLES ROCK ON

Chapter 5. "On Broadway": R&B Rock Takes Center Stage   135

Chapter 6. "Let's Have a Party!": Rockin' the Country   164

Chapter 7. "A Teenager in Love": Veteran Pop Rockers in the Early 60s   199

Chapter 8. "Take Good Care of My Baby": Pop Rock's Second Wave   227

Chapter 9. "Wild Weekend": Top Tunes, News, and Weather   270

Part 3
ROCKIN' ON THE NEW FRONTIER

Chapter 10. "God, Country and My Baby": Rock & Roll and the Culture of the Cold War   307

Chapter 11. "This Magic Moment": Rock & Roll in Kennedy's America   330

Acknowledgments   341

Interviews   343

Notes   345

Index   387

Rock & Roll
in Kennedy's America

Introduction

"Only in America"

Jay and the Americans' "Only in America" appeared on the pop charts at the height of President John F. Kennedy's popularity. It peaked at number 25 on *Billboard's* Top 100 just weeks after Martin Luther King Jr. delivered his "I Have a Dream" speech at the March on Washington on August 28, 1963. Composed by legendary songwriters Jerry Leiber, Mike Stoller, Barry Mann, and Cynthia Weil, the upbeat song was a perfect fit for the optimistic, patriotic mood of the nation. The lyrics about young love were set against a red, white, and blue backdrop that portrayed America as a land of freedom and equality where anyone could strike it rich or grow up to be president. Even the song's message about young love plugged into American exceptionalism. With trumpets blaring, the lead singer proclaims, "Only in America, land of opportunity, would a classy girl like you fall for a poor boy like me."[1]

Ironically, the story behind the 1963 hit reveals a darker side of the American experience. Producers Leiber and Stoller initially recorded the song with the Drifters, a talented R&B rock group best known for their number 1 hit, "Save the Last Dance for Me" (1960). Given racial tensions of the day, the Drifters' Atlantic label refused to release a record that featured a Black group singing about equal opportunity. Leiber and Stoller went back into the studio and overdubbed new vocals by a white group, Jay and the Americans. "Given their name, we figured Jay and the boys would have no problems with 'Only in America,'" explains Leiber. "It changed from a satirical social protest song into a flag-waving piece of patriotism. And, wouldn't you know it—the damn thing took off like a rocket."[2] The Drifters' original recording and Jay and the Americans' subsequent

Top 30 hit illustrate the connections—sometimes obvious, sometimes not—between rock & roll and life in the early 60s.

Rock & Roll in Kennedy's America offers a fresh look at the early 1960s through the prism of rock & roll. The book revisits all the memorable hits and misses heard on *American Bandstand* and Top 40 radio stations across the country. Although playlists were dominated by rock & roll, they also included traditional pop, folk music, novelty records, country songs, and other records that targeted young audiences. The diverse music provided a rock & roll soundtrack for millions of teenagers in high school between 1960 and 1964. But this book isn't just about music. The backstory involves the first baby boomers in high school, a ubiquitous Cold War culture, a booming economy, a blossoming civil rights movement, signs of rising feminism, and ultimately the tragic death of a handsome young president.

Despite the quality and cultural importance of early 1960s rock & roll, the music was soon forgotten. The coming of the Beatles changed rock & roll forever. Among the casualties of the British Rock Invasion of 1964 were most of the American rock stars who had dominated the charts since the 1950s. Early 60s rock & roll fell by the wayside as musical styles changed to keep pace with the political and social turmoil of the late 60s and early 70s. Subsequently, the early 60s were swept into the dustbin of rock & roll history. Relatively few performers from that era have been inducted into the Rock & Roll Hall of Fame, and many critics and fans now dismiss the early 60s as a low point for rock & roll. Not everyone agrees. "There was a lot of great music in the early 60s," insists Bobby Vee, who had 11 hits on the Top 40 charts in those years, including a number 1 record, "Take Good Care of My Baby." "But, people just sort of forgot about it because it was sandwiched in between two major eras—the coming of Elvis in the 1950s and the Beatles in the mid-1960s."[3]

As the 1970s dawned, both early 60s rock & roll and Kennedy's America were just distant memories of a more innocent time. A new common wisdom took hold, insisting that rock & roll was on the decline in the early 60s and would not bounce back until the Beatles arrived on the scene in the mid-60s. Don McLean's 1971 record "American Pie" went even further. It pinpointed "the day the music died"—tracing it back to a plane crash in a snowy Iowa cornfield on February 3, 1959, that took the lives of rock & roll stars Buddy Holly, Ritchie Valens, and the Big Bopper. The tragic tale about rock & roll's demise sounds plausible at first. Problem is, it just isn't true.

THE DAY THE MUSIC DIDN'T DIE

Although some experts and fans realize that quality rock & roll existed in the early 60s, the myth of rock & roll's passing has become reality for too many casual observers. One of the goals of this book is to set the rock & roll record straight. Contrary to popular opinion, the music did not die on that cold February morning in 1959. Not only was rock & roll alive and kicking in the early 60s, but it was thriving. It didn't fade until after 1963, when it became a casualty of the same cataclysmic forces that overwhelmed the rest of America during the tumultuous decade known as the *sixties*.

This book reclaims the lost history of early 60s rock & roll. The dramatic tale stars talented country rockers like Elvis Presley, Brenda Lee, and Roy Orbison; innovative R&B rock artists such as Ray Charles, Smokey Robinson, Mary Wells, Sam Cooke, and the Shirelles; outstanding pop rockers like Dion, Connie Francis, the Beach Boys, Lesley Gore, Del Shannon, and the 4 Seasons; and hundreds of other singers and musicians, including pop artists and folk singers who earned hit records with songs aimed at young audiences. The soundtrack features many of rock & roll's greatest hits, including the Shirelles' "Will You Love Me Tomorrow," Dion's "Runaround Sue," U.S. Bonds' "Quarter to Three," and the Kingsmen's "Louie Louie," as well as more obscure rock gems like Wanda Jackson's "Let's Have a Party" and the Lafayettes' "Life's Too Short."

Operating behind the scenes are music business executives like Motown's Berry Gordy and Atlantic Records' Ahmet Ertegun, as well as talented song writers and/or producers such as Leiber and Stoller, Carole King, Gerry Goffin, Phil Spector, and Holland, Dozier, and Holland. The audience, comprised mostly of baby boomers, plays an equally important part in the story. These teenagers weren't just passive observers. They helped determine which singers and songs would make it and which would not. They adapted lyrics and rock styles to fit their own needs. And, they danced creatively to the beat at record hops or while watching *American Bandstand*.

By the time the curtain closes on this musical drama, the truth is obvious. The music didn't die on February 3, 1959 as myth has it. Instead, rock & roll survived in grand fashion. The early 60s became one of the most important and innovative eras in rock history.

ROCK & ROLL AND BABY BOOMERS IN KENNEDY'S AMERICA

This book revisits all the memorable songs that teenagers were listening to in the early 60s, including rock & roll, pop, country, folk, and other music aimed at young audiences. In each case, it asks the same question: What does the artist or record reveal about the times? This historical approach not only demonstrates the diversity and vitality of the music, but it offers new details about teenagers and everyday life in Kennedy's America.

The first wave of baby boomers entered high school in the fall of 1960. That freshman class boasted almost half a million more students than the previous one, an upward trend that continued every year of JFK's presidency. Ultimately, the years 1960 through 1964 witnessed approximately three million more high school students than in the previous four years.[4]

America had never experienced a cohort like this one. The baby boom was the largest generation in the nation's history, and its future looked brighter than anything that had come before. From day one, baby boomers were pampered by doting parents, early childhood educators, and Dr. Spock. They were given all the opportunities and consumer goods that their parents didn't have growing up during the Great Depression and World War II. Baby boomers were the first generation raised on television. They stayed in school for more years than previous generations. And, they lingered between childhood and adulthood for a longer time. Their youth was celebrated in a postwar era that glorified technology and new products and dismissed anything old as obsolete. Baby boomers functioned more freely than members of earlier generations due to more disposable income, a new car culture, and the breakdown of communities and nuclear families. Every generation thinks it's unique, but baby boomers had the numbers and evidence to prove it.[5]

Rock & roll became the popular music of the baby boom generation. Like pop music of earlier generations, it facilitated group identity. Popular music is "concerned with participation, with dances, parties, outings, demonstrations, and any other social gatherings where camaraderie and simple shared emotions are important," explains British writer Richard Mabey. "The music, in fact, acts as a further binding force on the group, and the observed responses of the other members are a way of clarifying your own."[6]

Throughout the early 60s, rock & roll marked the boundaries of the rising youth culture. It offered baby boomers a distinct music that was ideal for a generation that saw itself as unique. Baby boomers knew rock & roll when they heard it. Regardless of whether the specific type of rock & roll was influenced by rhythm & blues, country music, pop, or some other style, it didn't sound like traditional pop music. Rock & roll showcased youthful voices, electric guitars, drums, saxophones, piano triplets, and a big beat perfect for dancing. Lyrics addressed teenage interests, including young love, school, dancing, cars, fads, and fashions.

Rock & roll wasn't just about lyrics and sound, however. Arguably, the musical medium was the message. Rock & roll was the music of youth, and most of the performers were about the same age as their fans. That fact gave the music, at the very least, the appearance of being a folk form. Listeners assumed the performers were speaking directly to and for them because they all seemed to be sharing similar experiences and values. "When we had our first hits, we were just high school kids ourselves," explained Dion, a rock & roll pioneer who found success both as the lead singer of Dion and the Belmonts and as a solo artist. "We knew exactly the kind of music our friends liked."[7]

Rock & roll offered a means to generational solidarity. The music provided a public arena for adolescent voices and concerns. It gave baby boomers their own special songs, dance steps, musical heroes, and shared experiences, which set them apart from adults. Only teenagers could tell you who wrote the Book of Love or who put the bomp in the bomp bomp bomp bomp bomp. Only they could talk knowingly about the Beach Boys, the Ronettes, or deejays like Dick Biondi. Only they could identify *Bandstand* regulars such as Bunny Gibson, Bob

The 1960s began with the promise of a better future—a "New Frontier." It ended with a pessimistic country polarized by the Vietnam War and issues involving race, gender, and the counterculture. Yet, the high hopes of the early 60s were never forgotten. For "one brief shining moment," anything seemed possible for both President Kennedy and young people across the country. This book revisits that unique era through rock & roll. This is history you can dance to!

Part 1

NEW
DIRECTIONS
for
EARLY 60s
ROCK & ROLL

1

"It's Now or Never"

Rock & Roll Enters a New Decade

On March 3, 1960, an airplane carrying Sergeant Elvis Presley landed at McGuire Air Force Base in New Jersey. All 79 soldiers onboard were scheduled to be discharged from the army. As soon as Elvis stepped off the plane, 200 fans and onlookers began cheering and screaming. A few minutes later, Elvis told journalists, "I will never abandon [rock & roll] as long as people keep appreciating it." In the audience, several of Elvis's friends and business associates, including his manager, Colonel Tom Parker, and RCA producer, Steve Sholes, smiled. The next day Sholes wrote a publicity piece for *D.J. Digest*. "Yesterday . . . Elvis returned to the United States after his tour of duty in Germany for the army," reported Sholes. "Elvis looked wonderful . . . we are hoping to set up a session at a studio near to his home, very soon."[1]

Two weeks later the recording session took place in Nashville. Presley was joined by old bandmates, guitarist Scotty Moore and drummer D.J. Fontana, as well as his favorite backup singers, the Jordanaires. As the session began, Colonel Parker and others watching from the control booth wondered if Elvis could still sing and whether he'd be able to come back after a two-year hiatus in the army. No doubt, Presley had similar fears. Did he still have *it*? The answer was a resounding yes! Elvis ran through six songs without a hitch. One of the recordings, "Stuck on You," was released as Presley's first post-army single, and it rocketed to number 1 on the *Billboard* pop charts.[2]

Elvis's second session took place on April 3 and produced his next single, "It's Now or Never." The operatic song was new territory for the King of Rock & Roll. It was based on the well-known nineteenth-century Italian song, "O Solo Mio." Elvis had always loved the melody and jumped at the chance to record a new version with a different title and lyrics. "This was pure pop music, delivered with both superb musical command and the highest level of professionalism," says music scholar Ernst Jorgensen. "And, it all represented exactly Colonel Parker's dreams and hopes for Elvis's new artistic direction."[3]

"It's Now or Never" gave Elvis his second straight number 1 hit. The title was a fitting description of Elvis's situation in 1960. When he was drafted in 1958 he feared his fans "aren't going to know me when I get back."[4] Now, the moment of truth had arrived.

In retrospect, the notion that "it's now or never" could also have been applied to rock & roll's position at the beginning of the 1960s. Like Elvis, rock & roll was facing major challenges. Many of the music's biggest stars had left the stage by the end of the 1950s. Even worse, rock & roll had to cope with a payola scandal that threatened its very survival. Unless the music business acted quickly, the rock & roll sounds that had dominated the pop charts since Elvis's arrival in 1956 could soon disappear.

PROBLEMS FACING ROCK & ROLL

Rock & roll was at a crossroads in 1960. Many rock & roll pioneers were no longer around, and the future of the music's biggest superstar was in question. Despite Elvis's assurances that he'd never stop singing rock & roll, there were troubling signs. When Presley got out of the army, his legendary sideburns, greasy hair, and flashy clothes gave way to a professionally styled hairdo with trimmed sideburns and fashionable clothes better suited to businessmen than rock & roll rebels.

Even Elvis's approach to music seemed to be tacking toward the middle-of-the-road. Two of his first three post-Army hits, "Fame and Fortune" and "It's Now or Never," were traditional pop songs, and Presley's first scheduled singing appearance was on a Frank Sinatra TV special, which featured the erstwhile King of Rock & Roll singing a duet with the legendary Chairman of the Board. Ed Sullivan, who had hosted the wild rockabilly singer on his TV show in 1956, was stunned by Elvis's subdued performance. Presley "teams up with Sinatra," reported Sullivan, "with Frank singing alternate bars of 'Love Me Tender,' while Elvis warbles phrases of [Sinatra's] 'Witchcraft.'"[5]

Presley's goal to become a serious movie star added to fans' fears that he was abandoning rock & roll. Just days after his discharge from the army, he told reporters, "I have three pictures in a row to do. I hope they won't be rock and roll pictures 'cause I have made four already and you can only get away with that for so long." Clearly, Elvis had a plan, but it was less certain how rock & roll fit into it. "I want to become a good actor, because you can't build a whole career on just singing," he explained. "Look at Frank Sinatra. Until he added acting to singing he found himself slipping downhill."[6]

The first film Presley made after getting out of the army, *G.I. Blues,* demonstrated that the movie Elvis was no James Dean. "Elvis Presley . . . is the smiling All-American Boy in his first post-service picture," noted reviewer John L. Scott. "Most mature theater-goers will welcome the change in Presley. Now as to his squealing teen-age fans—it is hoped they also will go along with the metamorphosis." Scott's description of Elvis's new singing style undoubtedly did little to calm rock & roll fans: "[Elvis] has reduced that old rock and roll wiggle to a rhythmical shaking of knees," said Scott. "He doesn't leer, and his formerly oily mop of hair is no more."[7]

Presley's return from the army sparked more questions than answers about his future on the rock & roll stage. Was Elvis still the once and future King of Rock & Roll? Or, was the King gone for good? Fans feared the alarming cover story in the June issue of *Movie Mirror* might be true: "The King of Rock 'N' Roll is Dead!"[8]

While the verdict was still out on Elvis, there was no doubt about the fate of other rock & roll pioneers. By 1960, Jerry Lee Lewis was shunned for marrying his 13-year-old cousin. Little Richard traded in his rock & roll shoes for a new career as a preacher. Chuck Berry was arrested in 1959 and charged with transporting an underage female across state lines for immoral purposes. He was convicted in 1961 and spent the next 18 months in federal prison. Other rock & roll stars also disappeared from the record charts, including Bill Haley, Eddie Cochran, Gene Vincent, and Carl Perkins. Nobody made a more dramatic exit from the rock & roll stage than Buddy Holly, Ritchie Valens, and the Big Bopper. Their final scene began in early 1959 with a whirlwind Winter Dance Party

When news leaked that the Harris committee was dispatching investigators nationwide to collect information about payola activities, ABC ordered all disc jockeys to sign the affidavit and divest themselves of all music-related businesses or else. Dick Clark, who had myriad interests in record companies, performers, and other music-related activities, likened ABC's ultimatum to somebody putting a "shotgun to your head." Clark admitted he had made a ton of money in music-related activities, but insisted he had done nothing illegal. Nonetheless, he agreed to give up all his holdings rather than leave *Bandstand.* ABC claimed that Clark's prompt action demonstrated his integrity. They allowed him to write up his own watered-down affidavit, which merely stated that Clark had never taken cash to play specific records.

Alan Freed refused to comply with ABC's demands. Worried that signing an affidavit might lead to perjury charges, he assured the network that his radio show had never been compromised by payola. He pointed out that his principles would not allow him to sign an affidavit or give up outside interests, explaining that ABC was aware of his business interests when they hired him. ABC responded by firing him just before Thanksgiving in 1959. Shortly thereafter, Freed was removed from his television dance party on New York's WNEW-TV.[15]

Radio stations across the country followed ABC's lead. Resignations and firings swept across the country like a tidal wave. Before the purge ended, hundreds of disc jockeys were removed. Steve Labunski, who managed a Top 40 station in Minneapolis, felt that deejays and rock & roll had been unfairly attacked: "The whole thing was about resentment of the music. If they were paying people to put Glenn Miller on the radio, they would never have stepped in. The payola scandal let people get off their chests their resentment of youth and their music, and Blacks."[16]

Meanwhile, the various payola investigations moved forward. The House committee opened its official hearings on February 8, 1960. Chairman Harris explained they were investigating payola due to nationwide complaints that "material sent over the airwaves has been influenced by undisclosed economic inducements." For maximum media coverage and dramatic effect, the committee called in witness after witness, starting with small-time individuals and ending with Alan Freed and Dick Clark. Appearing before the committee in late April, 1960, Freed appeared tense and overwrought. The more he proclaimed his innocence, the guiltier he looked.[17] The fact that Freed was followed to the stand by the young, clean-cut Dick Clark did not help. Clark performed much better in front of the committee, parrying payola charges confidently and effortlessly. He insisted he had never taken bribes to play records. While he admitted that he did make a considerable amount of money from his investments in record companies, pressing plants, and other music-related activities, he argued forcefully and correctly that none of those activities was illegal. Clark emerged from the hearings almost unscathed. His boy-scout image may have been tarnished a bit, but Dick Clark kept his job as host of *Bandstand* and retained the loyalty of friends and fans.[18]

While Clark survived the payola scandal, others were not as fortunate. The New York City District Attorney's Office subpoenaed records and accounts from numerous disc jockeys and over 50 record companies and distributors. A grand jury then indicted Alan Freed and four other deejays, one program director, and two other station employees for violating New York's commercial bribery statute. Not to be outdone, the New York State Attorney General proceeded with his own payola investigation. The Federal Communications Commission likewise continued its attack, requiring every radio and TV station in the country to submit a sworn statement indicating how they had dealt with payola and what they had done to ensure payola would not be a problem in the future. The Federal Trade Commission pushed forward on another front, assigning 40 staffers to investigate payola nationwide. When the information they collected suggested that an "exceedingly high percentage" of the nation's 481 record labels and 256 distributors used payola, they swung into action. Over 100 record companies and distributors were charged with using payola to promote products. All were required to sign forms acknowledging that even if they had not committed crimes, they would cease and desist payola activities in the future. In addition, FTC investigations determined that at least 255 disc jockeys or other station employees had taken payola. Lacking jurisdiction, the Federal Trade Commission handed the files over to the Federal Communications Commission, the Internal

Revenue Service, and the Harris committee for further action. The Internal Revenue Service promptly began its own investigations, auditing the tax returns of deejays who had neglected to report payola earnings as gifts.[19]

Alan Freed became public enemy #1 for payola abuse. After being fired from radio and TV shows in New York City, he became a target of probes by Congress, New York State's Attorney General, the New York City District Attorney's Office, the Federal Communications Commission, Federal Trade Commission, and Internal Revenue Service. The former deejay slipped deeper and deeper into alcoholism as he watched his woes and legal fees pile up. In 1962 a broken and beaten Freed pleaded guilty in a New York criminal court to charges that he had accepted payola. He received a $500 fine (later reduced to $300 because he did not have the money to pay) and a six-month suspended jail sentence. In 1964 he was indicted again, this time for tax evasion of payola received between 1957 and 1959. On January 20, 1965, Freed died of uremic poisoning related to kidney failure. *Cashbox* magazine viewed him as a martyr, noting Alan Freed "suffered the most and was perhaps singled out for alleged wrongs that had become a business way-of-life for many others."[20]

By the spring of 1960 the payola scandal and most of the investigations had run their course. All that remained were a few trials and government proceedings that dragged on into the early 60s. In 1961 the chairman of the Federal Trade Commission proudly declared that payola had been "pretty well stamped out."[21]

The payola scandal produced mixed results. Congress amended the Communications Act of 1934, making payola illegal and punishable by a $10,000 fine and/or a year in jail. Federal government agencies such as the Federal Communications Commission, Federal Trade Commission, and Internal Revenue Service cracked down on offenders and issued new regulations to stop payola in the future. The individual careers of hundreds of disc jockeys were either ruined or temporarily interrupted. Some wound up paying fines or serving time in jail, but most were simply shamed in the court of public opinion. In most cases the record companies or distributors who offered payola were never punished because they received immunity in return for testimony. The deejays who took payola became the fall guys.[22]

In the end, there was no end. Despite the pronouncements of victory in the war against payola, commercial bribes continued after 1960, albeit in different forms. Even BMI and rock & roll—the two unofficial targets of the payola investigations—were not stamped out. If critics of rock & roll had hoped the scandal would put an end to the new teenage music, they were disappointed. When the smoke cleared, rock & roll was still standing.

Over the years, numerous writers and critics have suggested that the payola scandal gutted rock & roll, resulting in a watered-down version of the music in the early 60s.[23] In reality, rock & roll not only survived on Top 40 radio, but it thrived. In 1960—the year the scandal peaked and then subsided—there were actually far more Top 10 hits by Black artists, rockabilly artists, and pop rockers than back in 1958 before the scandal hit. By 1963 baby boomer demand for rock & roll sent record sales skyrocketing to all-time highs.

The early 1960s would witness the rise of new rock & roll sounds and styles. As many rock & roll pioneers faded from view, a second generation of talented artists arrived on the pop charts. These newcomers along with the veterans still on the scene would pump new energy into the music. Their creativity and innovations would take rock & roll to even greater heights. The first sign of the changing times occurred on August 1, 1960 when Chubby Checker's "The Twist" debuted on *Billboard*.

THE TWIST AND OTHER THINGS THAT
WENT BUMP IN THE NIGHT

The Twist certainly was not the first rock & roll dance craze. Back in the 1950s fads were sparked by hits such as the Diamonds' "The Stroll" (1957) and Johnny Otis's "Willie and the Hand Jive" (1958). But Chubby Checker's "The Twist" (1960) was in a class of its own. Dick Clark called it the "biggest dance in the history of popular music." The original version by Hank Ballard and the Midnighters was a hit on the R&B charts in 1959. The following year Checker's cover skyrocketed to number 1 on the pop charts. When Chubby's record was rereleased in 1961, it once again became a number 1 hit. Hoping to take advantage of the new craze, hundreds of other Twist records appeared between 1960 and 1963. By the time the phenomenon ended, millions of people in America and worldwide knew how to Twist.[24]

Chubby Checker's First Album (Courtesy of the Rock & Roll Hall of Fame and Museum)

The fad began innocently enough. Dick Clark saw some African American teenagers doing strange-looking dance steps on *American Bandstand*. They explained they were doing "the Twist," a new dance described on Hank Ballard and the Midnighters' R&B song. Clark balked at playing the record because Ballard had a reputation for recording risqué R&B material. But, he grasped the Twist's potential when other *Bandstand* dancers began copying the steps. Dick convinced his friend Bernie Lowe (who owned Philadelphia's Cameo-Parkway Records) that a cover would sell. So, Lowe recorded an almost identical version by Chubby Checker in June, 1960.[25]

Dick Clark was pleased with both the singer and sound. Checker, whose real name was Ernest Evans, came from South Philly like Frankie Avalon and Fabian, who frequently appeared on *Bandstand*. Evans was discovered while working part-time at a local poultry store. The owner was impressed when he heard the outgoing 18-year-old sing for customers, so he introduced him to

Lowe and his partner Kal Mann, who signed Evans to a recording contract. One day Clark and his wife Barbara dropped by the Cameo-Parkway studio to talk to Bernie about making a musical Christmas card featuring imitations of famous singers doing "Jingle Bells." Evans, an African American, took a seat at the piano and began copying Fats Domino. Amused, Barbara cracked, "He's cute. He looks like a little Fats Domino—like a *chubby checker*." Not only did the name stick, but Chubby Checker wound up doing Clark's musical Christmas card, which served as the basis for Checker's first Top 40 hit, "The Class" (1959).[26]

Chubby hit it big the following year with his cover of "The Twist." According to Cameo's A&R man, Dave Appell, Chubby was selected because "he came pretty close to the original record. We figured we'd do [the] record with a kid, and then we would at least be on the Clark show." Appell wasn't the only one who thought the cover sounded like the original. Hank Ballard vividly recalls the first time he heard Chubby's version. He was relaxing at a swimming pool at a Miami hotel when suddenly "The Twist" came on the radio. "I actually thought it was me," he says. "They went and did a clone of my record."[27]

Checker's version took off like a rocket and climbed all the way to number 1, eclipsing Ballard's original. "Most of the country first saw it done on *American Bandstand*," notes Clark. "Part of the promotion of Chubby was purely visual," he explains. "He was young, good looking, and a born ham whose hip-wiggling version of the dance often looked more like a tricky exercise. Chubby sold the dance as he sold the song. It was an incredible event for all of us." Even though Chubby Checker became synonymous with the Twist, he always acknowledged Clark's important role. "I may have started the whole nation Twisting," said Checker, "but I couldn't have done it without Dick Clark and *American Bandstand*."[28]

Almost overnight, the Twist became the hottest fad in the country. The innovative dance was perfect in an era when marketers were offering consumers lots of "new and improved" products. The daily exposure on TV sold "The Twist" to baby boom viewers. The easy-to-learn dance steps helped. "It's like putting out a cigarette with both feet, and coming out of a shower and wiping your bottom with a towel to the beat of the music," explained Chubby. "It's that simple." The more popular the Twist became, the more adults complained. "If [the dancers] turned off the music," joked Bob Hope, "they'd be arrested."[29]

The fact that many adults thought the Twist was sexually suggestive made it that much more appealing to teenagers. The new dance picked up momentum throughout 1960 and 1961. Other Twist records such as Fabian's "Kissin' and Twistin'" (1960) and Danny & the Juniors' "Twistin' U.S.A." (1960) hit the charts. Checker became a fixture on TV, Twisting in the spotlight as he lip-synched to the record. To celebrate the one year anniversary of his original hit, Chubby recorded "Let's Twist Again (Like We Did Last Summer)," which became a Top 10 hit in 1961 and won a Grammy Award. With no end in sight for the dance craze, Cameo-Parkway reissued "The Twist" in November. To everyone's amazement, the record again shot up to number 1.

Something unexpected happened the second time around, though. Suddenly, teenagers were no longer the only ones dancing. Adults across America were jumping—or more accurately, Twisting—on Chubby's musical bandwagon. As the reissue of "The Twist" headed toward the top of the charts in early 1962, it was joined by two more Twist hits, Gary "U.S." Bonds' "Dear Lady Twist" and Joey Dee and the Starliters' "The Peppermint Twist, Part 1." The latter, recorded live at New York City's Peppermint Lounge, had the biggest impact. En route to becoming a number 1 hit, it transformed the Twist into an adult dance craze.

The Peppermint Lounge, a seedy little club on West 45th Street, quickly became the city's hottest night spot. Tom Wolfe reported in *The New York Herald Tribune* that high society types were "laying fives, 10s and 20-dollar bills on cops, doormen and a couple of sets of maitre d's to get within sight of the bandstand and a dance floor the size of somebody's kitchen." Chubby Checker was delighted that celebrities were now flocking to the Peppermint Lounge to Twist the night away. "God bless Zsa Zsa Gabor," he proclaimed. "She did the Twist at the Peppermint Lounge . . . The columnist, Earl Wilson, was there. . . . Earl wrote about it, and suddenly everyone in the world was doing the Twist."[30]

Throughout 1962 new Twist records appeared almost daily, including the Isley Brothers' "Twist and Shout," Chubby Checker's "Slow Twistin'," Gary U.S. Bonds' "Twist, Twist Senora," and Jimmy Soul's "Twistin' Matilda." The older generation also tried to capitalize on the new fad. Count Basie and His Orchestra released "Basie's Twist," while Frank Sinatra recorded a strange, pop-sounding record called "Ev'rybody's Twistin'."

In addition to the flurry of Twist records, there were Twist-related products like Twist sneakers, fringed Twist dresses, Twist jewelry, and how-to-Twist kits that included instructions and a diagram. The Twist was spotlighted on *The Dick Van Dyke Show*, *The Flintstones*, and other TV programs. Chubby Checker, the undisputed King of the Twist, even performed it in the film, *Don't Knock the Twist* (1962).

The craze was unstoppable. Throughout 1962 and into 1963 the dance was a must at social gatherings across America, including record hops, weddings, church socials, and senior citizen soirees. Twist parties were even held at the White House. *The Washington Star* described one such event in February 1962: "Anyone who still had any misgivings about the current dance craze simply hasn't seen it done the way Mrs. Kennedy, who looked lovely in a long white satin sheath, and [Secretary of Defense] Robert McNamara, frequently called 'the brain' of the cabinet, performed it," wrote society reporter Betty Beale. "It was rhythmic, fun and peppy, and more restrained than the good old Charleston."[31]

During Kennedy's administration, as the nation held its collective breath over the Bay of Pigs, the Vienna Summit, and the Cuban Missile Crisis, many Americans young and old found escape Twisting the night away. The new dance became one of America's most popular exports of the Cold War era. Twist records were the rage throughout Europe, as well as in Latin America, Australia, and Asia. Of course, not everyone welcomed the new fad. The Soviet Union banned the Twist, linking it to American decadence.

The Twist phenomenon unleashed other novel dances. Chubby Checker led the way with "The Hucklebuck" (1960), "Pony Time" (1961), "The Fly" (1961), and "Limbo Rock" (1962). Others followed, including the Dovells' "Bristol Stomp" (1961), Little Eva's "Loco-Motion" and Dee Dee Sharp's "Mashed Potato Time" (1962), and Major Lance's "The Monkey Time" (1963). There were also hits about dancing in general such as the Flares' "Foot Stomping" (1961), Contours' "Do You Love Me" and Chris Montez's "Let's Dance" (1962), and Chris Kenner's "Land of 1000 Dances" (1963).

Just as presidential candidate John F. Kennedy energized America by promising "to get the country moving again," the Twist and other fast dances got teenagers rockin' again. The dynamic dances were the perfect antidote to rock

& roll's doldrums in the wake of the payola scandal. Decades later Chubby Checker explained the Twist's enduring appeal: "I think that people are addicted to simplicity. Keep it fun. Keep it stupid. Make sure it's a little sexy . . . 'The Twist' has all of these elements."[32]

The dance fads that captured America's fancy in the early 60s had a lasting impact. "The Twist changed the dance floor," insists Chubby Checker, "and it gave us 'dancing apart to the beat,' dancing together but not touching." Fast dances like the Bop soon gave way to the Twist and other dance steps that no longer required couples. Not everyone was pleased, as evidenced by Gabriel and the Angels' 1962 record, "Don't Wanna Twist No-More," which featured Gabriel refusing to Twist "because I never get to hold my baby." The fact that "The Twist" sold millions, while "Don't Wanna Twist No-More" didn't even chart, suggests that most teenagers loved the new dances that allowed them to do their own thing either alongside a partner or by themselves. Some of the new dances were done as fast as possible. Others were slower and more sensual. In both cases, suggestive movements allowed individuals to express themselves in ways that anticipated the sexual revolution of the late 1960s and 70s.[33]

Even though new dances like the Twist, Pony, and Shimmy were no longer just for young people, rock & roll dancing was still primarily a teenage domain. The success of these dance fads reveals much about America and baby boom culture of the early 60s. It demonstrates the power of media and marketing to sell products. Fads of the 1950s such as Crockett-mania and Hula-Hoops were early indications that profits could be had marketing products to the young generation. Early 60s dance crazes built on that foundation. With *Bandstand* pointing the way, mass media and advertisers profited enormously by promoting new dance crazes relentlessly and shamelessly.

Baby boomers eagerly adopted fresh dances, which suggests that they bought into the era's consumer culture as much as adults. Teenagers acquired new dance fads as readily as their parents purchased the latest cars, fashions, and other products. But there was a new "twist." Unlike most earlier youth fads, which had been created by adults and marketed to kids, early 60s' dance crazes began with young people and then spread to grown-ups. The Twist signaled American culture was beginning to tilt toward youth.

New dances were linked to other economic and cultural trends. They demonstrate that African American culture was gaining a higher profile in Kennedy's America. Numerous hits spotlighted Black performers singing about dances that often originated in Black neighborhoods. These records suggest that racial and cultural integration were occurring years before landmark legislation such as the Civil Rights Act of 1964.

The spread of the Twist and other dances to countries around the world underscores the United States' economic and cultural leadership after World War II. During the early 1960s American products dominated world markets. Rock & roll dances contributed by exporting American culture, introducing millions of people worldwide to American music, products, and notions of the American Dream. Even the Beatles were inspired. When John, George, Paul, and Ringo made their first visit to the United States in 1964, one of the first things they did was go to the Peppermint Lounge. Ringo immediately rushed out onto the dance floor to Twist with an eager young lady.[34]

THE RISE OF NEO-DOO-WOP

Along with introducing new dances, early 60s rock & roll reshaped doo-wop. The distinct harmony sound, which featured voices singing nonsense syllables, had roots in R&B and 1950s rock & roll. The Silhouettes' number 1 hit from 1958, "Get a Job" is a perfect example: "Yip yip yip yip yip yip yip yip / Bum bum bum bum bum bum . . . get a job," sings the group.[35] By the end of the 1950s, both Black rock & roll groups like the Silhouettes and white groups such as Dion and the Belmonts were recording excellent doo-wop records. The Dell-Vikings, Crests, and Impalas included both Black and white singers. The popularity of doo-wop suggests that integration was becoming more common not just in rock & roll but in America of the 1950s.

The doo-wop sound was firmly established by the time the 1960s began. Several doo-wop classics charted again when they were reissued in 1960, including the Five Satins' "In the Still of the Nite" and the Heartbeats' "A Thousand Miles Away." New songs by veteran groups also became hits. Little Anthony and the Imperials, who hit it big with "Tears on My Pillow" (1958), earned a Top 30 hit in early 1960 with "Shimmy, Shimmy, Ko-Ko-Bop." The provocative record featured doo-wop harmonies, a big beat, and suggestive lyrics that pushed the limits of sexual propriety. It begins with a guy sitting in a jungle hut. Suddenly, a beautiful native woman enters and begins to dance seductively. He jumps up and joins her in the erotic dance. As the music builds to a climax, his spine begins to "tingle" as he sings passionately, "Held her tight and close to me, man I'm glad I'm single."[36]

New doo-wop groups also hit the charts in 1960. Kathy Young and the Innocents earned a number 3 hit with "A Thousand Stars," a heartfelt ballad that viewed romance from the vantage point of a teenage girl. The Safaris' Top 10 hit, "Image of a Girl," offered a boy's perspective about lying in bed at night longing for true love.

Doo-wop picked up momentum in late 1960 with the release of Maurice Williams and the Zodiacs' "Stay." The record debuted in October, and within a month it was number 1. The song sounded remarkably fresh, even though the group was recycled. The African American singers started out in the 1950s as the Gladiolas and scored a hit with "Little Darlin'" (1957). After changing their name, they found greater success with "Stay." The record featured a catchy tune, solid dance beat, and suggestive lyrics. As Maurice urges his girl to stay "just a little bit longer," the Zodiacs provide backup through monosyllabic words, doo-wop sounds, and an urgent falsetto that kicks the request into high gear.

"Stay" was soon joined on the charts by another doo-wop song with a fresh sound. In December 1960 an Italian American group named the Capris released "There's a Moon Out Tonight," which peaked at number 3 in February 1961. The ballad described a teenage couple out for a romantic stroll on a beautiful moonlit night. It featured lyrics about young love, a prominent beat perfect for slow dancing, tight doo-wop harmonies, and a soaring falsetto that guided the song to a memorable climax. By injecting new energy into the old doo-wop style, songs like "There's a Moon Out Tonight" and "Stay" set the stage for a phenomenal hit that would spark a "neo-doo-wop" craze.

In March 1961 the Marcels exploded onto the rock & roll scene with an outrageous doo-wop version of the Rodgers and Hart pop standard, "Blue Moon." The record opens suddenly with a barrage of nonsense syllables: "Bomp baba bomp / Ba bomp ba bomp bomp / Bomp ba bomp ba bomp / Dang a dang dang / Ding a dong ding." The lead vocalist then blasts the song into the rock & roll stratosphere with a supercharged rendition of the original lyrics. Backup singers inject added energy through creative doo-wop sounds. The rock & roll world was stunned by this sonic marvel of doo-wop delight. Kids couldn't get enough of it and sang the nonsense refrain repeatedly, trying to figure out how many "bomps," not to mention "ding a dong dings," there were.

Many adults hated the Marcels' desecration of the pop classic, but that only made teenagers love it more. The doo-wop rendition of "Blue Moon" highlighted the dividing line between the adult world and baby boom culture. The Marcels had magically transformed the pop standard into a rock & roll anthem for young ears only. If kids were attracted by the sound and beat, they understood intuitively that the group represented other types of change. Unlike most vocal groups, the Marcels featured three Blacks and two whites. If some onlookers were put off by the racial mix, others understood that the group and "Blue Moon" were on the cutting edge of the musical and cultural changes taking place in Kennedy's America.

The Marcels' number 1 hit opened the floodgates to a tsunami of doo-wop records. The neo-doo-wop craze of 1961–63 produced hits like the Tokens' "The Lion Sleeps Tonight," Edsels' "Rama Lama Ding Dong," Echoes' "Baby Blue," and Curtis Lee's "Pretty Little Angel Eyes" in 1961, Gene Chandler's "Duke of Earl" and Ernie Maresca's "SHOUT! SHOUT! (Knock Yourself Out)" in 1962, and the Earls' "Remember Then" in 1963.[37]

Maresca's "SHOUT! SHOUT!" was arguably the wildest doo-wop hit on the *Billboard* charts. The Top 10 record had it all: an exciting sound, big beat, teen-oriented lyrics, and the promise of rock & roll salvation. The fast-paced song offers a whirlwind tour of youth culture. Ernie's uninhibited vocal describes a raucous party that's just begun. There's a boy all alone who wants to be kissed, and a girl's in the corner doing the Twist. Maresca implores someone to play "Runaround Sue" (which he cowrote with Dion) and alludes to other hits like "Quarter to Three" and "School is Out." He urges partygoers to crank up the jukebox and do dances like the Fly with their hands in the sky. Doo-wop backup singers add support, egging on the lively crowd to shout, scream, and "put another dime in the record machine."[38] Maresca responds by unleashing one of the greatest screams in rock & roll history. Although Ernie Maresca never had another hit, rock & roll fans never forgot his glorious song about teenage fun on a Saturday night.

Even minor hits attracted attention. The Rivingtons stepped into the rock & roll spotlight in 1962 with one of the weirdest songs in music history, "Papa-Oom-Mow-Mow." Teenagers didn't know whether to laugh or just gasp for air when the group shouted out their absurd doo-wop lyrics. "Pa pa pa pa, papa oom ma mow mow," intoned a singer with a staccato voice that sounded like a magpie on steroids. Somewhere in the lyrics was buried a story about a nameless man with a senseless message that made people want to "stomp and shout."[39] But it didn't really matter. All teenagers cared about were the outrageous doo-wop sounds. Although the record stalled at number 48 on the charts, it became a cult classic and inspired the Trashmen's "Surfin' Bird," a number 4 hit in 1964. The Rivingtons added to their irreverent rock & roll legacy with two more minor hits in 1963, "Mama, Oom, Mow, Mow" and "The Bird's the Word."

Neo-doo-wop offered audiences a sound that was at once old and new. Little Caesar and the Romans' 1961 hit, "Those Oldies But Goodies (Remind Me of You)," underscored the importance of earlier songs. The record's nostalgic lyrics and familiar street-corner-harmonies created the perfect bridge between rock & roll's past and present. Little Caesar laments how earlier songs bring back memories of lost love. "Forever they will haunt me but what can I do," he asks his ex-girlfriend. "Those oldies but goodies . . . reminds me of you." English teachers recoiled at the grammatically incorrect line, but high school kids loved the song, sending it all the way up to number 9.[40]

If neo-doo-wop echoed the past, it also introduced innovations that were perfect for a baby boom generation that considered itself unique. Neo-doo-wop hits were often more pop-oriented than 1950s doo-wop. The Crests earned hits in 1960 with "Step by Step" and "Trouble in Paradise," written by Billy Dawn Smith, who also wrote pop songs for Perry Como and Nat "King" Cole. Other neo-doo-wop hits written by Brill Building composers featured pop-oriented lyrics and arrangements. Even pop singers scored rock & roll hits with songs written and/or produced by Brill Building professionals. Steve Lawrence, for instance, found success in 1960 with faux doo-wop hits like "Footsteps" and "Pretty Blue Eyes."

Neo-doo-wop helped introduce another innovation to rock & roll: folk music. By the late 1950s folk was gaining popularity among young listeners through the music of the Weavers and Kingston Trio. One of the teenagers who fell in love with folk music was 16-year-old Jay Siegel. "I was listening to the radio one day, and I heard this great piece of music by the Weavers at Carnegie Hall with Pete Seeger," he explained. "They were singing this song called 'Wimoweh.' I loved it. The whole lead vocal was done in falsetto. I just loved the melody, the whole idea of it. And I realized that I was able to sing that falsetto."[41]

By 1961 Jay Siegel was a member of the Tokens. Shortly after they earned a Top 20 hit with the doo-wop influenced "Tonight I Fell in Love," they switched to the RCA label and were assigned to producers Hugo Peretti and Luigi Creatore. Siegel convinced his bandmates (Hank Medress, Phil Margo, and Mitch Margo) that they should play "Wimoweh" for Hugo and Luigi. The producers were intrigued, but questioned the folk song's commercial appeal, so they hired Brill Building songwriter George Weiss to compose new pop-oriented lyrics. The resulting record, "The Lion Sleeps Tonight," listed Weiss, Hugo, and Luigi as composers, but the Tokens also deserved credit. "We kinda gave them the demo . . . of Wimoweh without the lyric," explains Phil Margo. "We pretty much laid down the feel of it, the bongo drums etc." The group didn't see Weiss's lyrics until the day of the recording session. "We were supposed to sing the lyric to the melody line of the chant ("Wimoweh"), but it got boring . . . repeating the same thing over and over again," says Margo. "So we went over to the piano and . . . actually wrote a new melody to go with the lyrics. We unfortunately never got credited or paid for that."[42]

The recording session for "The Lion Sleeps Tonight" went smoothly, and the group nailed the song on the third take. Still, the producers didn't think a song about a lion in Africa would sell. Neither did most of the Tokens. "Three . . . of the four guys in the group said, no, they didn't even want it to be released," explains Siegel. "They thought it was too weird for the time . . . but I thought it had a shot." When Jay played a dub for his longtime friend, songwriter Carole King, her eyes widened and she said excitedly, "This is a . . . smash record."[43]

Both Siegel's hunch and King's assessment were understatements. The record started out as a regional hit in New England, but then exploded onto the national charts. "The Lion Sleeps Tonight" was two minutes and thirty-five seconds of pop perfection. The memorable melody framed a magical tale that hinted at life and death in an exotic land. "In the jungle, the mighty jungle, a lion sleeps tonight," sang Jay Siegel while the rest of the group called out "a-wimo-weh, a-wimo-weh." A reoccurring timpani drum powered the song forward as the chants continued. Soaring above everything was Siegel's amazing falsetto, enhanced by a beautiful female voice singing an operatic counterpoint.

The recording "was a group effort, and we all contributed," says Siegel. "We actually coproduced the record with [Hugo and Luigi]. We knew what to do vocally. What they did do, which was important, is that they hired Sammy Lowe as arranger." The veteran orchestra leader came up with several great ideas. "He's the one who did that great rhythmic drum figure, plus that soprano saxophone in the middle," notes Siegel. "And Sammy Lowe was responsible for getting Anita Darian who was with the Metropolitan Opera." She sang "this really high soprano part an octave higher than what I sang." The Tokens didn't know what to expect when she first entered the studio. "We thought it was pretty strange to have an opera singer sing on the record and we shook our heads and said, 'what's that all about?'" recalls Siegel. "But I have to credit our producers because they were right."[44]

By the time the recording session was over, the Tokens, Hugo and Luigi, and Sammy Lowe had concocted a fresh rock & roll blend of doo-wop, pop music, opera, R&B, and folk. The multilayered sounds created a musical mosaic unlike anything audiences had heard before. Within weeks of its release, "The Lion Sleeps Tonight" shot up to number 1 on the charts. It sold three million copies in the United States and millions more overseas when it became number 1 in 36 countries. Even the timing of the record's release was serendipitous. The song's popularity may have been helped by the fact that the Tokens' rock & roll rendition of an African song came out just as Kennedy's Peace Corps was getting young Americans interested in developing nations in Africa and elsewhere. The connection between "The Lion Sleeps Tonight" and JFK was reinforced the following year when African singer Miriam Makeba performed her version at the president's birthday celebration in Madison Square Garden.

"The Lion Sleeps Tonight" resonated with audiences partly because it was more than just doo-wop. The song "had no category," insists Jay Siegel. "There really was nothing like it." The group's record company promoted the Tokens as a new "folk and rock" act, and over 80 percent of their appearances were on college campuses, where folk music was extremely popular. "We did a lot of folk music at our concerts," recalls Siegel. "We'd mix in traditional folk songs with rock & roll, doo-wop, and songs we wrote. We even had a guy that played the banjo."[45] "The Lion Sleeps Tonight" turned out to be one of the most innovative rock & roll hits of the early 60s, as well as one of the most creative songs in pop music history. Arguably, the Tokens' rock & roll folk tale blazed a trail for what would later be called "folk-rock" in the mid-1960s and early 70s.

Most listeners in the early 1960s, however, were not aware of the song's troubling back story. The man who wrote the original piece, which later morphed into the Weavers' "Wimoweh" and the Tokens' "A Lion Sleeps Tonight," never received the recognition or royalties he deserved. Initially titled "Mbube" (Zulu for lion), the song was written in 1939 by a Zulu named Solomon Linda, who recorded it that year with his South African group, the Evening Birds. The folk song was simple, yet captivating. It featured Linda's remarkable falsetto sung above Zulu chants about a lion hunt. The recording "achieved immortality only in its dying seconds," suggests South African writer Rian Malan, "when Solly took a deep breath, opened his mouth and improvised the melody."[46]

Linda's recording eventually wound up in the hands of folklorist Alan Lomax, who forwarded it to Pete Seeger in the hope that the folksinger would record it for posterity. Seeger instantly fell in love with the strange sound. Amazed by the ethereal falsetto and haunting chants, Pete transcribed the sometimes indecipherable words from the scratchy 78 record. Although he mistakenly wrote down "awimoweh" every time the backup group sang "uyimbuge," he managed to capture the essence of the song. Seeger and the Weavers recorded it in 1952 and featured it in live concerts. "'Wimoweh' [became] just about my favorite song to sing for the next forty years," said Pete.[47]

Linda was not listed as the songwriter on the Weavers' record or any of the subsequent versions, because the artists all assumed the song was in the public domain. When Seeger found out about the composer, he immediately instructed his music publisher to pay Linda a share of the profits. Years later Pete learned that Linda had received only a small percentage of the money, so he sent him a personal check for $1000.[48]

Although Solomon Linda died a pauper in 1962 without proper credit or compensation for "Mbube," his musical legacy lived on with more than a little help from the Tokens. The phenomenal success of "The Lion Sleeps Tonight," which reworked both Linda's original and the Weavers' 1952 rendition, secured Linda's place in music history. "'The Lion Sleeps Tonight' gets played every day somewhere on a radio station all over the world," says Jay Siegel. "When it was featured in *The Lion King*, RCA re-released it and it became a worldwide hit for the second time. We then acquired a brand-new audience of 5-year-old kids."[49] Although the Tokens' version became the signature hit, Solomon Linda's important contribution is undeniable. Somewhere in the jungle, the cosmic jungle, Linda's original falsetto can still be heard wailing above the Zulu chants of "uyimbuge," or as the Tokens and Weavers would say, "a-wimoweh, a-wimoweh."

"The Lion Sleeps Tonight" demonstrates how innovative early 60s doo-wop could be. Not only was the sound different from 1950s doo-wop, but neo-doo-wop was aimed at a new generation of rock & roll fans. Several records focused on neo-doo-wop's distinct sound, which created an obvious boundary between baby boomers and adults. The best example is Barry Mann's Top 10 hit from 1961 "Who Put the Bomp (In the Bomp Bomp Bomp)." The brainchild of Brill Building composers Mann and Gerry Goffin, the song poked fun at the outrageous style. If youngsters laughed with the song, adults laughed at it, as Mann posed such urgent musical questions as "Who put the dip in the dip da dip da dip?" With cliché doo-wop sounds blasting in the background, Mann adds he'd like to shake that guy's hand because "he made my baby fall in love with me," punctuated by a deep voice exclaiming "YEAH!"[50]

Neo-doo-wop hits that showcased romance, dancing, and other topics of interest to baby boomers added to generational solidarity. Jimmy Charles and the Revelletts' "A Million to One" (1960), for instance, defended young lovers from the slings and arrows of outrageous parents. Teenagers could also relate to the persecuted protagonist on Gabriel and the Angels' 1962 record "That's Life (That's Tough)." His frustration grows as adults and friends simply reply "that's tough" to each of his troubles involving romance, school, taxes, and the draft. By the song's end, the young guy can't take it anymore. "Won't anybody ever listen to me," he cries out. "You're all against me all of you."[51]

Neo-doo-wop mirrored other aspects of daily life, including the era's patriotism and attitudes toward marriage, gender, and race. The music, for instance, offers evidence of increasing racial equality. Hit records mixed Black and white styles and were often written, produced, and performed by Blacks and whites. In addition, Black and white solo artists and doo-wop groups rode the same tour buses and appeared together on stage in front of mixed audiences. White pop rock singer Bobby Vee remembers the inter-racial camaraderie that developed: "You throw 50 guys and gals on a bus for 30 days and they pretty much work out their differences, color or otherwise," he explains. "Over the course of 30 days . . . they become good friends." Beverly Lee of the Shirelles has similar memories of friendships that developed on integrated tours like Dick Clark's Caravan of Stars: "We were a family unit and we looked out for one another," she says. "Dick was like a big brother to us."[52]

No doo-wop record better reflected changing racial attitudes than Gene Chandler's "Duke of Earl." Chandler originally recorded the song with his group the Dukays. When their record label refused to release it, the master was sold to Vee Jay Records, which then issued the Dukays' record using only the lead singer's name. The quintessential neo-doo-wop ballad rocketed to number 1 in early 1962 and made the Black singer a star. The song's optimistic view of the future resonated with listeners witnessing the rising civil rights movement. Suddenly, the dapper Gene Chandler, dressed formally in black tails, a top hat, and cape, and carrying a walking stick, seemed to be everywhere. He performed the song in the movie *Don't Knock the Twist*, and made numerous TV appearances singing confidently about his future. "Nothing can stop me now," proclaims the African American singer, "'cause I'm the Duke of Earl."[53]

The neo-doo-wop craze was like a shooting star in the rock & roll universe. It burst on the scene in 1960, burned brightly in 1961, and tailed off by the end of 1963. Of course, doo-wop never disappeared completely. It inspired many singers of the late 60s and beyond. To this day, the distinct sound remains etched in the collective memory of all those who grew up in Kennedy's America.

2

"What Does a Girl Do?"

The Girl Group Revolution of the Early 1960s

The Shirelles' "What Does a Girl Do?" debuted on the *Billboard* charts on September 7, 1963. The record is a good example of the era's popular "girl group" sound. Powered by a solid dance beat, the lead singer delivers an impassioned vocal that condemns established courtship rituals. Backup singers cheer her on with classic doo-wop harmonies. Why, asks the young woman, are boys the only ones who can make the first move? They ask girls for dates and phone numbers. They stand on street corners and whistle when girls go by. And only boys get to propose marriage. But, what happens if the girl wants to start the relationship? "Somebody tell me," she sings desperately, "what does a girl do?"[1]

The Shirelles led a girl group revolution that transformed rock & roll in the early 1960s. They earned twelve Top 40 hits, including two number 1 records, "Will You Love Me Tomorrow" (1961) and "Soldier Boy" (1962). Their spectacular success blazed a path for women singers, including Black and white girl groups and solo artists. Hits by the Shirelles and other girl groups offered creative blends of rock & roll, rhythm and blues, gospel, and pop. Many featured sophisticated arrangements and innovative sounds, including violins, cellos, and horns.

The girl group phenomenon offers fresh information about social change in Kennedy's America. Their songs targeted the first wave of baby boomers, a new generation of teenagers that flooded into high schools in the early 1960s. The numerous hits by the Shirelles and other African American girl groups demonstrate gains in racial integration. Not only were these groups integrating the pop charts, but their records often were collaborations between Black singers and diverse production teams that included Black and white producers, song-writers, and musicians.

The spike in the number of girl groups on the pop charts also suggests that women were making gains in Kennedy's America. Girl group songs introduced female perspectives into rock & roll on a large scale, as evidenced by the Shirelles' "What Does a Girl Do," which came out the same year as Betty Friedan's path-breaking book, *The Feminine Mystique*. Both planted seeds for the modern women's rights movement, which would blossom in the 1970s and 80s. Just as Friedan's book became a click moment for an older generation of women, the Shirelles' proto-feminist song offered a wake-up call to a new generation unwilling to accept the status quo. The songs and styles of groups like the Shirelles helped baby boom girls figure out what it meant to be a young woman in the early 1960s.

GIRL GROUPS TAKE THE STAGE

Female harmony groups were common on the pop charts long before rock & roll came along. The Andrews Sisters, Boswell Sisters, and similar groups were popular in the 1930s and 40s. The 1950s welcomed the McGuire Sisters and Chordettes. Girl groups became even more popular with the advent of 1950s rock & roll acts like the Teen Queens, Poni-Tails, Chantels, and Shirelles.

The Shirelles—Shirley Owens, Beverly Lee, Doris Coley, and Addie "Micki" Harris—would take the girl group sound to new heights in the early 1960s. The four teenagers from Passaic, New Jersey, earned a minor hit in 1958 with "I Met Him on a Sunday." Two years later they cracked the Top 40 with "Tonight's the Night." But the best was yet to come. In 1961 the Shirelles became the first African American girl group to earn a number 1 hit when "Will You Love Me Tomorrow" made it to the top of the charts. The song was written by two young white composers who worked in New York's Brill Building district. Eighteen-year-old Carole King came up with the melody and string arrangements, while her 21-year-old husband, Gerry Goffin, wrote the lyrics. Released on November 21, 1960, the record reached number 1 on January 30, 1961 and remained in the Top 10 for seven weeks. Over the next three years the Shirelles earned ten more Top 40 hits, including another number 1 record, "Soldier Boy" (1962).

The Shirelles (Richard Aquila Collection)

The Shirelles' unique sound contributed to their success. Their innocent yet intimate vocals made them seem vulnerable, while their untrained voices and simple harmonies created a pristine sound that gave the records authenticity. The girls crafted a rock & roll hybrid that combined R&B, doo-wop, gospel, and pop. Luther Dixon, one of the few Black producers at a white record company, added innovative touches, including violins, cellos, keyboards, even timpani. "Luther was wonderful as a producer, because he had an ear for music," says Beverly Lee. "He knew what to get out of us and how to get it out of us."[2]

The best Shirelles records had a great sound, memorable lyrics, and solid beats. Ballads such as "Soldier Boy" were tailor-made for slow dancing, while upbeat songs like "Boys" were perfect for fast dancing. When the legendary Bo

Diddley was asked to name his favorite song from the 1950s and early 60s, he didn't choose a fast-paced rock & roll or blues song. The R&B rocker just smiled and said, "the Shirelles' 'Soldier Boy,' of course."[3]

Young audiences loved the group's sound and style. The four attractive singers, just out of high school themselves, swayed seductively to the beat as they sang lyrics aimed at baby boomers. Teenagers "could relate to our songs," explains Beverly Lee, "because we were kids and we were singing about things that kids were doing."[4] One of the things that high schoolers were doing was thinking a lot about romance. Not surprisingly, the Shirelles' hits usually focused on young love.

Two of the group's more memorable songs—"Tonight's the Night" (1960) and "Will You Love Me Tomorrow" (1961)—took teenage relationships a step further. Both featured lyrics that, given the time period, were explicit in their treatment of a subject that was front and center in many baby boomer brains— sex. "Tonight's the Night" spotlighted a young couple discussing whether to go all the way. The guy promises that tonight he's going to kiss her, turn the lights down low, and make her "feel all aglow." The girl is reluctant, but finally gives in. The Shirelles' follow-up, "Will You Love Me Tomorrow" (1961), offered a more subtle yet sensual approach to the ultimate question facing teenagers. The number 1 hit was told from the perspective of a girl about to have sex for the first time. As she marvels at the "magic" of his size (which appears as "sighs" on the written lyrics), she wonders if she's doing the right thing for "just a moment's pleasure." She asks her boyfriend one last time, "Will you still love me tomorrow?"[5]

The Shirelles' career was aided by changing racial attitudes. As the civil rights movement picked up momentum, the group became an obvious symbol of the opportunities for African Americans. Not only were they the first Black girl group to have a number 1 hit, but the Shirelles were also the first to perform at all-white colleges in the South. The road to success wasn't an easy one in an era of segregation. The Shirelles had to cope with racism as well as segregated concerts, restaurants, and hotels. At some stops, even water fountains were segregated: "We had 'colored' on the one fountain and 'white' on the other fountain," recalls Shirley Owens, "and you can't touch the 'white' . . . because you can be arrested. I've been there."[6]

The year 1963 marked the beginning of the end for the Shirelles. First, they lost an integral part of their creative team when African American producer and songwriter Luther Dixon left for a new job with Capitol Records. Shortly thereafter the assassination of President Kennedy altered the mood of the country. Suddenly the Shirelles' innocent sound was out of step with baby boomers' serious concerns. Within weeks of JFK's death the Shirelles—like many American performers—became casualties of the British Rock Invasion.

After 1963 the Shirelles never had another Top 40 hit. But, before their impressive run on the charts was over, the group changed the rock & roll landscape. Along with pointing the way for other female singers, they offered a fresh sound and perceptive lyrics that reflected social change, particularly for women, Blacks, and baby boomers. The Shirelles' place in music history was guaranteed in 1996 when they were inducted into the Rock & Roll Hall of Fame.

The Shirelles paved the way for other African American girl groups.[7] The Chiffons were one of the most successful. The four young women from the Bronx earned a number 1 hit in 1963 with "He's So Fine," a wistful ballad that featured Shirelle-like vocals and lyrics geared to young women. The song was written by the group's manager, Ronnie Mack, and produced by the Tokens, who earned a number 1 hit the previous year with "The Lion Sleeps Tonight." Recording engineer Johnny Cue offered one crucial piece of advice. The Tokens' Hank Medress explains, "Our engineer, suggested that we use 'doo-lang, doo-lang, doo-lang,' the catchy little figure the girls sing later in the record, in the beginning of the record as well." The result was irresistible. Listeners loved the melody and got hooked on the "doo-langs." Many teenage girls could relate to the lead singer's desire to attract a handsome guy with wavy hair, and cheered when she said, "I don't know how I'm gonna do it, but I'm gonna make him mine."[8]

The Chiffons' follow-up, "One Fine Day," was equally sensational. The number 5 hit opens suddenly with quick drum beats and a frantic piano riff. The group jumps in with a doo-wop riff —"Shooby dooby dooby dooby do wah wah"—and then launches into an upbeat tale about young love that won't be denied. In retrospect, the record offers insights about the changing times. "One

Fine Day" demonstrates that racial integration was becoming more common. The song was recorded by an African American girl group, written by white composers Carole King and Gerry Goffin, and produced by the Tokens, a white doo-wop group. So, was it Black music, white music, or both? "To me, that was just pop music of the day," says the Tokens' Jay Siegel. "It was a great mix [of Black and white music]. It was a big hit on the R&B charts, and it was a number 1 record on the Top Pop charts . . . It was multicultural."[9]

The hit record also suggests that women's perspectives were becoming more important in the early 60s. Although the song was not consciously a feminist anthem, it featured a confident young woman with a plan. The determined girl assures her ex-boyfriend, "One fine day, you're gonna want me for your girl." The song's hopeful message tapped into the nation's upbeat mood. By the early 60s the lethargy of Eisenhower's America had been replaced by the excitement and promise of Kennedy's "New Frontier." "One Fine Day" echoed the nation's optimism. Just as Martin Luther King Jr.'s "I Have a Dream Speech" predicted "that one day this nation will rise up and live out the true meaning of its creed," the Chiffons promised "one fine day" would arrive for the couple in the song. But the record wasn't just reflecting the times, it was anticipating them. It became a hit in June 1963, two months before King's seminal speech at the March on Washington.[10]

Not all African American girl groups tried to copy the Shirelles. The Jaynetts offered a sound unlike anything else heard on Top 40 radio. They scored a number 2 hit in 1963 with the eerie "Sally, Go 'Round the Roses." Written by Zell Sanders and Lona Stevens and arranged by Artie Butler, the record features ambiguous lyrics that tell a shadowy story about a woman and an unfaithful lover. The singers create a hypnotic effect as they assure Sally that it's okay to "go 'round the roses," which can't hurt her or tell her secret.[11]

Artie Butler explains how "Sally" came about. "I was hired by Abner Spector, the guy who owned the [Tuff] record label. He brought me the song and explained that . . . he would like me to listen to it to see what I could come up with." A few days later Artie reported back with a "concept and feel" for the record. At Spector's request, he then created the musical arrangement. "I went to Broadway Recording Studios in the old Ed Sullivan Theater Building . . . I played all of the instruments on the record except the guitar parts," recalls Butler. "I was going for a very different sound. I recorded in mono one instrument at a time. Each time I added another layer, I went to another tape machine. I used two Ampex 350 tape machines @ 7½ IPS. I kept going from one machine to the other and changed the EQ and the reverb . . . on each layer to give it the strange sound. Each time I added another layer, the sound kept getting more distant sounding due to the tape hiss. That is why I changed the EQ and the reverb on each layer. It let the new layer 'speak' over the previous layer. There was not much of a song to begin with, so I felt I had to create something that would make it its own thing. I had this sound in my mind before I started on the project.[12]

When Artie was done he played the track for Spector. "He *hated* it. I mean *hated* it," says Artie. "He told me I wasted his money . . . I tried to explain that it was a different sounding record. He was furious with me. He referred to it as 'a different sounding piece of crap.'" The stunned Artie sought advice from his friends Jerry Leiber and Mike Stoller. They loved the recording and volunteered to buy the master. Their reaction gave Spector second thoughts, and he quickly released the record, which rocketed toward the top of the charts. Although the record label credited Butler with arranging and conducting the music, Spector never paid him for his efforts and creativity. "Not one dime," says Artie. "I never worked with the man again, and the Jaynetts never had another hit. It's a real shame because I had some good ideas for the group."[13]

Although listeners weren't sure what to make of the weird-sounding record or its cryptic lyrics, they were intrigued by the overall effect. Ever since, rock & roll fans have been arguing about the record's meaning. Some suggest it's about suicide, a mental breakdown, a religious experience, an unwanted pregnancy, or lesbian lovers. Others claim that the song sounds spooky because the studio was either haunted or the recording equipment was not working properly. Still others insist that sometimes a song about a guy cheating on a girl is just a song about a guy cheating on a girl. Artie Butler just shakes his head at the theories: "Since I made the record, I have heard so many strange tales about it. Everything from secret messages from Saturn in the lyric, ghosts etc.," he explains. "There was nothing wrong with the equipment in the studio either." Even though Artie never made money from his work on "Sally," the innovative hit launched his career. He later became a successful arranger, composer, and conductor, and worked with numerous top artists, including the Drifters, Neil Diamond, and Dionne Warwick.[14]

The tremendous popularity of African American girl groups set the stage for white girl groups.[15] The Angels were one of the most successful. Shortly after the Shirelles scored a number 1 hit with "Will You Love Me Tomorrow," the Angels earned their first hit record with "Till" (1961), followed by another Top 40 hit, "Cry Baby Cry" (1962). The New Jersey group—Peggy Santiglia, Phyllis "Jiggs" Allbut, and Barbara "Bibs" Allbut—came back even stronger in 1963 with "My Boyfriend's Back." The song, originally intended for the Shirelles, was written by Bob Feldman, Jerry Goldstein, and Richard Gottehrer. They hired the Angels to record a demo, but it turned out so well that the group's record label released it as a single.[16]

When "My Boyfriend's Back" became a number 1 hit, Ed Sullivan booked the Angels for his popular TV show. Teenage girls in the audience could relate to the Angels' style as well as the song's message, which was in keeping with the era's gender expectations. The three pretty young women, dressed in modest crew-neck dresses with long sleeves, sang joyfully about rejecting unwanted advances from a guy. "My boyfriend's back," declared lead singer Peggy Santiglia, "he's gonna save my reputation."[17] Although the Angels never had another Top 10 hit, they continued to tour and earned several other hits that appealed to teenage girls.

The Angels weren't the only successful white girl group on the early 60s pop charts. The Paris Sisters—Albeth, Sherrell, and Priscilla—racked up three impressive hits with the help of producer Phil Spector. The trio initially patterned themselves after the Andrews Sisters, wearing identical dresses and singing three-part pop harmonies. They made the transition to rock & roll after signing with Lester Sill's Gregmark Records. Sill and his protégé, Phil Spector, were looking for girl groups to record. (Spector's first taste of success came in 1958 when he and his group, the Teddy Bears, scored a number 1 hit with "To Know Him, Is To Love Him.") "Phil came to our home and sat with us and interviewed us," recalls Sherrell Paris. "He had us sing separately and listened to each voice. Priscilla had the softest voice, which he preferred for the records. And that was it, we started recording with him."[18]

The Paris Sisters' first hit was "Be My Boy" (1961). The intimate ballad resonated with young listeners. Teenage boys were attracted to Priscilla's sensual lead vocal, while girls identified with the lyrics about a young woman praying that the boy of her dreams would return her love. The group's follow-up was the sensational "I Love How You Love Me," which became a number 5 hit in 1961. Spector arranged and produced the recording to achieve the exact sound he wanted. The result was one of the most erotic songs in rock & roll history. "I loved the song because it was a chance for me to sing in a soft sexy voice, which I had never done before," explains Priscilla Paris. "I don't think 'I Love How You Love Me' was teenage music at all. I was 15, but nobody knew it. Walter Winchell said it was the sexiest sound he'd ever heard. I didn't try to sing sexy. I didn't realize what I was doing. It just turned out to be one of the sexiest—without being vulgar—records there ever was."[19]

The Paris Sisters' last Top 40 hit came in early 1962 with "He Knows I Love Him Too Much." Produced by Spector and written by Carole King and Gerry Goffin, the song featured a passive teenage girl who, in keeping with traditional gender roles, was all too willing to forgive her boyfriend's rude and abusive behavior.[20]

The three hits not only brought success to the Paris Sisters, but they established Spector's reputation as a producer extraordinaire of girl group records. He would soon kick the girl group phenomenon into high gear with a series of innovative records for two African American girl groups, the Crystals and Ronettes.

GIRL GROUPS AND PHIL SPECTOR'S WALL OF SOUND

Prior to the Paris Sisters' Top 40 hits, Phil Spector produced outstanding records such as Ray Peterson's "Corinna Corinna," Curtis Lee's "Pretty Little Angel Eyes," and Gene Pitney's "Every Breath I Take," all in 1961. His success with the Paris Sisters convinced him to stay on the girl group band wagon.

Spector's work with girl groups in the early 1960s made him one of rock & roll's most creative forces. More often than not he aimed at an R&B sound that evoked the music he loved as a kid growing up in 1950s Los Angeles. Longtime friend Russ Titelman recalls that Spector always had "the most incredible records," including Ray Charles, Larry Williams, and "all this stuff most white kids didn't hear."[21]

With the help of partner Lester Sill, Spector established Philles Records in 1961. Like pioneer movie directors D. W. Griffith and John Ford, Spector saw himself as the real artist who controlled the entire production. Auteur rock & roll producer Spector put together a stock company of singers, musicians, arrangers, and engineers and micromanaged them to create the exact sound he wanted. Phil wrote or chose the songs, and he decided who would sing, regardless of whether they were members of the group listed on the record label. Singers and session players weren't always pleased: "Years ago . . . we were little Stepford singers, interchangeable, one from column A, two from column B," notes the Ronettes' Ronnie Bennett (who later married Spector). "We were seen as employees, not artists."[22]

Darlene Love, who sang on numerous Spector records, offers a different perspective. "Phil Spector was a recording genius," she insists. "Everybody back in those recording days . . . went into the studio together, and . . . did everything at the same time. Spector was one of the first who did the music first, then the background singers and then he would put my lead on." Darlene adds, "He knew exactly what he wanted . . . He would tell even the background singers how he wanted them to sing. He did the same thing with the lead singing. He would say, 'Darlene, I want you to sing a certain way so stay on my melody. Don't deviate.'"[23]

Spector's big break came in 1961. While Philles Records was getting started, Phil landed a position with Hill and Range Music Publishers. The loosely defined job allowed him to hang out at the Brill Building where he could find new songs, new talent, and produce some records for the Big Top label owned by Hill and Range. Unbeknownst to his employer, Spector was simultaneously scouting talent and material for his Philles label. One of the groups Spector auditioned for Hill and Range was the Crystals, five high school girls from the Bronx who looked and sounded like the Shirelles. When Spector heard lead singer Barbara Alston and the others perform an original song called "There's No Other (Like My Baby)," he secretly recorded them for Philles Records. Soon after, the record was released and became a Top 20 hit in early 1962. Hill and Range executives were shocked by Spector's duplicity. "We were very angry because we felt [the Crystals] were Big Top artists," explains Hill and Range's John Bienstock. "There was no question about the fact that [Spector] was just rehearsing them for Big Top—hell, he rehearsed them for weeks in our offices. And then he just stole them right out of here." Hill and Range immediately fired Spector. "He was talented," said Bienstock, "but he was just a piece of shit."[24]

Unrepentant and unfazed, Spector plotted a course to make the Crystals the biggest girl group in rock & roll. In early 1962 he brought them into the studio to record "Uptown," written by Barry Mann and Cynthia Weil. The record featured a musical ambience similar to the one found on Leiber and Stoller's production of "Spanish Harlem" (cowritten by Spector and Leiber). The song opens with lead vocalist Barbara Alston singing about her guy who gets up every morning and goes to work downtown, where he does menial jobs as bosses yell and order him around. The sound of a guitar playing a simple Spanish-sounding melody adds to the sad mood. Suddenly, the song kicks into high gear as Barbara and the rest of the Crystals sing joyously about how the man is rejuvenated at the end of a hard day when he returns to his home "uptown where he can hold his head up high" and his woman is there to make him whole again. The moving lyrics—powered by rock & roll guitars, drums, and the dramatic sounds of cellos, violins, mandolins, and castanets—resonated with audiences at a time when civil rights messages were commonplace.[25]

By the time "Uptown" peaked at number 13 on the charts in May 1962, Spector was already plotting his next move. With the help of Liberty Records' A&R man Snuff Garrett, Phil landed a job with the West Coast label to produce records in New York City. The new position, like the previous one with Hill and Range, allowed him to hang out in the Brill Building district looking for new songs and talent. A clause in the contract allowed Phil to continue making records on his own Philles label. The potential conflict of interest inherent in Spector's arrangement with Liberty would soon be realized.

Looking for new material, Spector visited the New York office of music publisher Aaron Schroeder. When Schroeder played him a demo of a Gene Pitney composition, "He's a Rebel," Phil's jaw dropped. Mesmerized by the sound and lyrics, he knew it would be a surefire hit for the Crystals. "[Spector] was still with Liberty and that's where the fun began," explained Pitney. "He may have been there on a fishing trip for Liberty, but he knew he was gonna cut it himself."[26] When Spector learned that Snuff Garrett, who got him the job with Liberty, was going to record "He's a Rebel" with pop singer Vikki Carr, Phil sprang into action. He resigned from Liberty under the pretense that he was tired and needed time off from record producing. He then flew out to LA and set up a recording session. When the Crystals refused to fly to California, Spector panicked. Lester Sill suggested they use a local R&B trio named the Blossoms as replacements. He pointed out that the group's lead singer, Darlene Love, had an emotional, gospel-influenced voice that would be perfect for Pitney's powerful lyrics. "With the song we got," said Sill, "these girls are better than the Crystals."[27]

Spector loved the idea. Not only would it allow him to produce the record immediately, but the product would sound better. The plan would also mean more money for Spector and Sill. Since Philles Records owned the rights to the Crystals' name, the record label could list the Crystals as the artists to take advantage of the group's success. However, the profits would go to Spector and Sill, since they hired the Blossoms as session singers at a flat rate and didn't pay a cent to the real Crystals. Spector's decision to pawn the Blossoms off as the Crystals was unethical but not illegal. The same can be said of Spector's scheme to record "He's a Rebel" before Garrett could complete Vikki Carr's version. Carr later explained what happened: "Snuff and I were recording the song. We took a break and in the studio next to ours we heard 'He's a Rebel.' Phil had gone in and rushed to record it," she said. "Snuff . . . called the president of the company and said, 'Look, Phil took my song . . .' The president said, 'If you think your version is as good, then go ahead and release it.'" The Liberty version was rushed out, but went nowhere fast. Snuff just shook his head and said, "Ours crashed and burned on takeoff."[28]

Music critics and fans might argue about the ethics of how Spector came to record "He's a Rebel," but one thing is certain: the difference between Garrett's pop version and Spector's rock production is like day and night. Phil's dynamic record begins explosively as drums and a piano establish a shuffling beat, later punctuated by guitars, horns, and handclaps. Gospel-influenced voices then tell a dramatic tale about a teenage rebel with a cause. The guy's proud girlfriend defends him when people say he's no good . Others write him off as a rebel, but she knows the truth: "He is always good to me, good to him I'll try to be, 'cause he's not a rebel, no-no-no . . . to me."[29] The musical riffs and syncopated lyrics play off each other like a point-counterpoint, creating a sensational sonic blend of multitracked vocals, memorable melody, and insistent beat. The innovative sound and defiant lyrics rocketed "He's a Rebel" all the way up to number 1 in the fall of 1962.

Spector was just getting started. The year 1963 witnessed more smash hits by the Crystals—or at least what audiences thought were the Crystals. The upbeat "He's Sure the Boy I Love" peaked at number 11 in January. Although the label listed the Crystals as the artists, the song was actually performed by the Blossoms. When Darlene Love first heard the record played on the radio, she felt betrayed because Spector had assured her the record would be released under her name. "I had a fit," she explained. "I figured this was going to be my record . . . all the records that were number one records were by the Crystals. The Darlene Love records never went higher than Top 20 . . . even though it was the same voice."[30]

Spector's next two Crystals releases did even better. "Da Doo Ron Ron (When He Walked Me Home)" and "Then He Kissed Me" were both cowritten by Phil Spector, Ellie Greenwich, and Jeff Barry and featured La La Brooks, a recent addition to the Crystals' lineup, on lead. Actually, Darlene Love sang lead on the first few takes of "Da Doo Ron Ron," but Spector wasn't satisfied with the sound, so he switched to Brooks without informing Darlene. When the record was released in the spring of 1963, it climbed all the way to number 3. The song explodes out of the speakers with horns and handclaps sounding like the roar of an oncoming train. A drum roll leads into the high energy vocals: "I met him on a Monday and my heart stood still, da do ron-ron-ron, da do ron-ron," sing the Crystals excitedly. "Somebody told me that his name was Bill, da do ron-ron-ron, da do ron-ron."[31] The song never lets up. The multitracked lead vocal is encouraged ever onward by backup singers clapping their hands and shouting "da do ron-ron," while music at full throttle adds a sense of urgency to the teenage tale about love and lust at first sight. The pressure builds and builds until the record is brought to a climax, after just 2 minutes and 6 seconds of pure, unadulterated rock & roll.

The Crystal's follow-up, the equally sensational "Then He Kissed Me," made it to number 6. The romantic lyrics are the ultimate expression of young love. They describe a boy and girl meeting at a dance. When he walks her home, they kiss under the stars. They date, fall in love, and then kiss in a way that they "want to be kissed forevermore." Finally, he takes her home to meet his mom and dad. Then he proposes. "I felt so happy I almost cried," she says, "and then he kissed me."[32] The sentimental lyrics are counterbalanced by powerful music. The opening guitar chords establish a hypnotic riff later reinforced by pounding drums, clicking castanets, blasting horns, and soaring violins. The impressive sound climbs higher and higher, yet it remains anchored by insistent guitar riffs that seem to proclaim the eternal power of young love and rock & roll. Fans had never heard anything like this before. The potent mix of R&B, rock, pop, and classical music was rock & roll on steroids.

The Crystals' trilogy—"He's a Rebel" (1962), "Da Doo Ron Ron" (1963), and "Then He Kissed Me" (1963)—epitomizes what came to be known as Spector's Wall of Sound. To create the total sound experience, the inventive producer took basic rock beats and instruments and then overdubbed layer upon layer of sounds, including multitracked vocals, handclaps, harpsichords, pianos, horns, violins, cellos, violas, castanets, cowbells, and any other sounds needed to get the desired effect. Add in large doses of echo, bring up the heat to a rock & rolling boil, and the "Wall of Sound" is done. To get the full effect, these songs must be played in monaural, as Spector originally intended. Otherwise, the "total sound" of the musical mosaic, which Spector so carefully crafted, crumbles into individual pieces since stereo and digital remixes tend to isolate instruments and voices. "The records are built like a Wagnerian opera," explains Spector. "They start simply and they end with dynamic force, meaning, and purpose." Ellie Greenwich, who cowrote "Da Doo Ron Ron" and "Then He Kissed Me," wasn't surprised. "Wagner was [Phil's] idol," she says. "Wagner was power and bigness and heavy and all that and I think he was going after that in his records."[33]

At the same time that Spector was orchestrating the Crystals' hits, he was also producing Top 40 records by other artists on the Philles label. Among the most successful were Bob B. Soxx and the Blue Jeans' R&B rock version of the Disney classic "Zip-a-Dee-Doo-Dah" (1962), and Darlene Love's "(Today I Met) The Boy I'm Gonna Marry" (1963) and "Wait 'Til My Bobby Gets Home" (1963).

By early 1963 Spector was focusing on the Ronettes, three attractive, multi-racial young women from New York City. The group included Veronica (a.k.a. Ronnie) Bennett, her sister, Estelle, and cousin, Nedra Talley. Phil signed the teenagers to a Philles contract after he saw them dance professionally at New York's Peppermint Lounge. The Ronettes' first hit, "Be My Baby," shot all the way up to number 2 in 1963. The phenomenal record featured Ronnie's dynamic lead vocal enhanced by Spector's Wall of Sound. Ronnie recalls the first time she heard the finished product: "The Ronettes were on tour . . . We were lying in bed watching Dick Clark's *American Bandstand* when he said, 'This is going to be the record of the century.' And it was us."[34]

The Ronettes quickly became the hottest girl group around. The trio had an exotic look, distinct sound, lively performance style, and obvious rock & roll attitude. Unlike most girl groups who looked and sounded like the "good girls" they were, the Ronettes came across as "bad girls." They sang and danced seductively and wore heavy makeup, beehive hairdos, and tight dresses with slits down the side. Ronnie explained that the Ronettes' image was designed to set them apart from all the other girl groups. "We lived in Spanish Harlem . . . I'd see the Spanish girls, and the Puerto Rican girls, and the Black girls, and that was the look I wanted. I wanted to look street tough, because I wasn't, and neither were the other Ronettes," says Ronnie. "I'd see these [neighborhood] girls with their eyeliner and teased hair, and the Black girls—the way they walked and held their cigarettes. It was like, 'Wow, that's what I want to look like.' So the three of us went on stage like that, but we were actually very innocent and pure, and had parents who told us what to do and what not to do." Ronnie still laughs when she thinks about the fringed dresses their aunt made for them to wear on stage when they sang and danced for the first time at the Apollo Theater: "When we turned our backs to the audience and shook," she says, "the crowd would go nuts."[35]

If the Ronettes were hoping to attract attention by their sexy look and style, they weren't disappointed. "We called [the Ronettes] the bad girls of the '60s,"

The Ronettes (Richard Aquila Collection)

explains Darlene Love. "They had the really, really short skirts and they had big, big, big hair. Most of the Black entertainers of the '60s didn't look like that." The Ronettes' image worked. "You had a lot of girl groups out there," notes Ronnie. "We weren't better than them, we were just different. We'd go out individually and dance, we had a different look."[36]

The Ronettes' sound was also unique. Ronnie Bennett sounded as hot as she looked. Her intense vocals cut like a knife, releasing a range of emotions from sheer joy to utter despair. Arguably, no syllables in rock & roll history are more iconic than those found on the Ronettes' signature hit "Be My Baby." Toward the end of the song, everything stops for a moment. Then come a few drum beats pushing the momentum forward again. The Ronettes join in, pleading "Be my baby, be my little baby" several times. Ronnie hums along and finishes with an ecstatic "wha-oh-oh-oh-oh." "All the session players loved my voice," says Ronnie. "My voice was like a cannon to the musicians, like 'Boom!'"[37]

"Be My Baby" became the Ronettes' biggest hit. The million-seller offered a reassuring message about young love and showcased Ronnie's incredible voice backed by Spector's incomparable "Wall of Sound." She later explained how Phil created that loud, full sound: "Everything was done double . . . I mean where most people have one guitar or one drummer we had two of everything, so that's what made that wall of sound." Teenagers across the country were in awe of the amazing sound and the group's seductive style.[38]

Subsequent releases by the Ronettes didn't fare as well. "Baby, I Love You" debuted on the charts in December 1963, and stalled at number 24. The trio earned three final Top 40 hits in 1964: "(The Best Part of) Breakin' Up," "Do I Love You," and "Walkin' in the Rain." The hits stopped when musical styles changed dramatically after the Beatles hit it big in 1964. In 2007 the Ronettes were inducted into the Rock & Roll Hall of Fame.

The Ronettes were shooting stars in the rock & roll universe. Phil Spector would flame out not long afterward. Like many American artists and producers, Spector found it difficult to keep up with the changing times after Kennedy's assassination and the British Rock Invasion. After 1964 the innocent teenage themes featured on Spector's hits of the early 60s no longer fit the mood of the youth culture as the nation struggled with urban unrest, racial violence, antiwar protests, and the emerging counterculture. Spector produced or coproduced only a few more major hits, including the Righteous Brothers' "You've Lost That Lovin' Feelin'" (1964), George Harrison's "My Sweet Lord" (1970), and John Lennon's "Imagine" (1971).

By the end of the 1970s most of Spector's glory days were behind him. His disastrous marriage to Ronnie ended in 1974, and Phil's behavior became more bizarre as he worried about his personal life and place in the record business. His obsessive personality, lack of moral compass, and eccentric behavior eventually led to his downfall. On February 3, 2003, police were summoned to Spector's mansion in Alhambra, California. When they arrived they found him rambling about how a woman he had picked up that night in a bar had accidently shot herself with his pistol. When the unruly Spector refused to take his hands out of his pockets, the police tasered him and placed him under arrest. He later was charged with the murder of Lana Clarkson. After the first trial ended in a mistrial, Spector was tried again in 2009 and found guilty of second-degree murder.[39]

Spector's personal demons always lurked in the shadows of his career. Jerry Leiber, who gave Phil his first big break in New York, remembers Spector as smart but also annoying, ungrateful, and untrustworthy. "He wore his ambition like a topcoat," said Leiber. "It was all over him." After Spector grabbed Lester Sill's share of Philles Records, his former partner noted that Leiber and Atlantic Records' Jerry Wexler had tried to warn him about Spector's duplicity: "He's a snake," they said, "he'll stab his own mother in the back to get ahead." Singer Gene Pitney, who wrote "He's a Rebel," insists that Spector was just "kinda screwy." "Maybe there's a flipside to all that [genius] stuff," he suggests. "Perhaps that's what makes them different and allowed the records they made to be so unique."[40]

In any case, Phil Spector's contributions to girl groups and early 60s rock & roll are undeniable. He produced some of the era's most innovative hits. They showcased great vocals by artists such as Darlene Love and Ronnie Spector. They also featured topnotch music provided by some of the finest studio musicians in the business, including Jack Nitzsche (percussion), Hal Blaine (drums), Larry Knechtel (keyboards), Leon Russell (piano), and guitarists Glen Campbell and Billy Strange, to name just a few. Ultimately, Spector's records were always about more than just the music. They struck a responsive chord with listeners because they spoke directly to baby boomers' hopes and dreams. Spector was the first record producer who consciously tried to turn rock music into an art form. "People made fun of me, the little kid who was making rock 'n' roll records," he explains. "But I knew. I would try to tell all the groups, we're doing something very important. Trust me. And it was very hard because these people didn't have that sense of destiny. They didn't know they were producing art that would change the world. I knew."[41]

Phil Spector was inducted into the Rock & Roll Hall of Fame in 1989. His official Hall of Fame biography reads: "On a string of classic records released between 1961 and 1966 on his Philles label, he elevated the monaural 45 rpm single to an art form. 'Little symphonies for the kiddies,' he called them, and they were indeed dramatic pop records possessed of a grandeur and intimacy theretofore uncommon in rock and roll." Spector died in prison on January 16, 2021.[42]

GIRL GROUPS AND KENNEDY'S AMERICA

No list of rock & roll's greatest hits would be complete without girl group classics like the Shirelles' "Will You Love Me Tomorrow," the Crystals' "He's a Rebel," or the Ronettes' "Be My Baby." Those records featured exceptional vocals and melodies, outstanding dance beats, first-rate production values, and folk-quality lyrics that expressed teenagers' hopes and fears. But quality music wasn't the only reason for the girl group phenomenon of the early 60s. The dynamic hits offered a perfect soundtrack for social and cultural changes sweeping across America.

At the very moment when African American girl groups were integrating the pop charts, freedom riders were heading south to protest segregation, and Martin Luther King Jr. was leading protest marches in Selma, Birmingham, and Washington, DC. Many Black girl groups experienced racial tensions firsthand. The Shirelles' Beverly Lee explains: "I remember doing the first integrated show in Alabama. After we landed, they told us we could not go out of the motel . . . The Ku Klux Klan had marched just before we had gotten there." She adds, "They did not want to rent space to us to perform anywhere. So they found this field, and the people brought their own chairs."[43]

Despite racial problems, girl groups—like the civil rights movement itself—would not be denied. Just as Jackie Robinson broke baseball's color barrier in 1948, Black girl groups helped desegregate the music business, the national pop charts, and concert venues in the early 60s. These singers were living proof of the growing status of Blacks in Kennedy's America. Their frequent media appearances helped raise the national profile of African Americans, which in itself was a victory for civil rights. These girl groups chipped away at racial prejudice, which decreased as increasing numbers of white fans began identifying with

Black singers. White teenagers danced to girl groups' music at record hops and cheered the singers at integrated concerts. And, millions of white teenagers purchased records by Black girl groups and played them in the privacy of their homes, which, ironically, were often located in neighborhoods where African Americans weren't allowed.

Record album covers offer glimpses of changing racial attitudes. At first, record companies were reluctant to advertise the artists' race. The Shirelles' 1961 album *Tonight's the Night* featured only a photograph of a table with a framed picture of a boyfriend (who was white), with a pink strapless prom dress on the floor along with other items such as white gloves, red roses, and a diary. "They didn't put our pictures on the cover on purpose because . . . [they] told us that . . . a lot of people wouldn't want their children to have albums sitting around the room with pictures of Black artists on them," explains the Shirelles' Shirley Owens. "I understood that. We understood it."[44]

Most record companies did not include photographs of Black girl groups on album covers until after the civil rights movement gained momentum. Even then, companies had to tread lightly. The Crystals' 1962 album *Twist Uptown* showed the group dressed in knee-length, pastel summer dresses with white gloves and heels, standing in front of a family-friendly, white station wagon. The Shirelles' 1963 album *Foolish Little Girl* had smiling group members wearing styled, bouffant hairdos and black sequin cocktail dresses. By 1964 the cover of the Ronettes' debut album could be more daring. It featured the group's lead singer in the center, sporting teased hair and lots of makeup. While she peers suggestively over her bare shoulder, the other two Ronettes strike alluring poses in tight blue dresses and beehive hairdos.[45]

The girl group phenomenon was a sign of racial progress in Kennedy's America. Black groups such as the Shirelles, Chantels, Cookies, Ronettes, Crystals, and Chiffons worked closely with diverse production teams that included Black and white songwriters, musicians, and producers. Songs like "Uptown" (1962) by the Crystals and "My Block" (1963) by the Four Pennies (a.k.a. Chiffons) spotlighted issues involving race, poverty, and hope for a better future. And, girl group music brought people of all races together at the grassroots level long before the March on Washington (1963), the Civil Rights Act of 1964, or the Voting Rights Act of 1965 had an impact at the national level. "The music is what touched everyone. I think that's a big part of desegregating things," insists Shirley Owens. "We played the colleges, no problems. Clubs, no problems. Everyone seemed to be happy that we were there. We were working on hit records. They were happy to have us."[46]

Even the tour buses that transported Black and white performers to one-night stands across the country contributed to racial progress. These tours were basically integrated communities on wheels. Problems related to segregation often were no match for the bonds of friendship that developed between Blacks and whites on tour. Bertha Barbee-McNeal of the Velvelettes, an R&B rock group, recalls a troubling moment that occurred on one of Dick Clark's Caravan of Stars bus tours in the South. As Black and white performers walked into a restaurant, they noticed Dick arguing with the man behind the counter. "Dick Clark was not the type of person to argue," she explains. "So to see him riled up . . . you could tell he was upset." Suddenly, Clark motioned for all the performers to get back on the bus. As they pulled away, Dick explained the situation. When the restaurant owner refused to serve Blacks, Clark told him, "Then you can't serve any of us." Barbee-McNeal was impressed. "We performed for Blacks and whites together in the audience," she said. "When someone treats you with respect . . . you don't forget that. [Dick] could've treated us in a different way, but he treated everyone the same. We loved that man."[47]

Some African American girl groups stood their ground against discrimination. When one of Clark's tour buses broke down near a segregated tavern in rural Virginia, the Crystals were in desperate need of a restroom. At first the white owner refused to let them use the tavern's facilities, but when the four teenage girls threatened to relieve themselves in the parking lot he reluctantly gave in with the proviso that they could not eat in the restaurant. Shortly thereafter two carloads of angry whites arrived on the scene. As the men walked menacingly toward them, the Crystals sang out, "My eyes have seen the glory of the coming of the Lord," after which they shouted defiantly at the armed men. Luckily, police cars arrived and defused the dangerous situation.[48]

Other girl groups also took stands against racism. On August 5, 1963, the Shirelles joined Martin Luther King Jr., writer James Baldwin, and singers Ray

Charles, Nina Simone, Johnny Mathis, Clyde McPhatter, and Ella Fitzgerald for a special event, "The Salute to Freedom, 1963." Held at Miles College, an historically Black college in Alabama, the concert raised money to support King's upcoming March on Washington. Despite threats by the Ku Klux Klan and attempts by local officials, police, and business leaders to undermine the show, 13,000 Blacks and whites attended and contributed over $10,000 for civil rights activists to travel to the March on Washington. Afterward, New York Senator Jacob Javits praised the integrated event. "Congratulations to all those participating," he wrote in a telegram. "My warmest praise goes out to you for this inspiring show which deserves the support of all America interested in freedom and human dignity."[49]

African American girl groups were often too close to the action to grasp their contributions to the civil rights movement. "We weren't aware of the importance of what we were doing," admits the Shirelles' Beverly Lee. "We just wanted to make records. We were young and we were excited, and we felt blessed by God to be able to sing." Not until years later did Lee fully comprehend the Shirelles' significance. "Fans [now] tell me, 'you made history.'"[50]

The girl group phenomenon suggests that the times were also changing for women. Although the women's rights movement would not blossom until the late 1960s and 70s, the seeds were planted in Kennedy's America. By 1960, twice as many married women were working outside the home than in 1940, and 40 percent of all women over the age of 16 were employed. More women than ever were attending college. And, numerous professional women were gaining recognition in fields traditionally dominated by men. Women also gained more control over sex, relationships, and career planning after the Food and Drug Administration (FDA) approved the Pill in 1960.

Kennedy's election added momentum to the women's rights movement. In 1961 the new president established the Commission on the Status of Women (PCSW). Initially chaired by Eleanor Roosevelt, it issued a report in 1963 that recommended ways to improve the social, political, legal, and economic status of American women. That same year Kennedy signed the Equal Pay Act, which banned gender discrimination in the workplace. The president's wife, the

31-year-old Jacqueline Bouvier Kennedy, became a popular icon for the era's new woman. Jackie's intelligence, beauty, youth, athleticism, and refined tastes made her a role model for baby boom girls. Across the country, teenage girls were soon wearing a variety of Jackie-inspired fashions, including sophisticated bouffant hairdos, pillbox hats, and long white gloves. Mrs. Kennedy "is becoming the nation's number 1 fashion influence," reported *Life* magazine in 1961, "a deserved compliment to a very young and very poised First Lady."[51]

Images of determined women dominated pop culture. There were bestsellers such as Helen Gurley Brown's *Sex and the Single Girl,* and self-assured young women were featured in movies like *Cleopatra* and TV programs such as *The Many Loves of Dobie Gillis.* Talented young females were also fixtures on the record charts. The spike in the number of girl groups in the early 1960s mirrored the rise of women in American society. In 1959 only two Top 40 hits were recorded by girl groups or groups fronted by a female singer. By 1963 the number had risen to 24. "It was time," explained the Shirelles' Shirley Owens. "It was a male-dominated industry, and it was just time."[52]

Of course, it wasn't easy being a trailblazer. Female rock & rollers had to put up with sexual harassment and often didn't get the same pay or respect as male counterparts. Peggy Santiglia of the Angels recalls the problems she and her group ran into when they toured in 1963 to promote their number 1 hit, "My Boyfriend's Back." "Generally, there'd be one female group appearing in this big lineup. It wasn't easy being a young girl and traveling with all those men," said Santiglia, who was only 19 at the time. "I was the recipient of a lot of unwanted sexual advances. Looking back, they could have been arrested." The Angels ran into other problems. "We had no idea we weren't going to get [the money] we were owed," explained Santiglia. "We kept thinking, 'Oh, it will work out.'" The Angels also had no say in the selection of material. "It wasn't our choice what song came out [after 'My Boyfriend's Back']. We disagreed vehemently with the producers" said Santiglia. "But, that was that."[53]

Despite gender discrimination, girl groups persisted. The girl group phenomenon empowered young women, giving voice to their interests and concerns. Hit songs such as the Shirelles' "Twistin' in the U.S.A." (1962) and the Murmaids'

"Popsicles and Icicles" (1963) spotlighted teenagers' daily activities. Girl groups also became role models. Most of their performance styles showed teenage girls how to be alluring without being overly sexy. And, their look offered fashion tips about hairstyles and clothes. Sherrell Paris remembers that the Paris Sisters wore modest dresses that followed popular fashions. "Well, the empire line was in at the time," she says. "It came up under the bust line, and gathered."[54]

The Ronettes and a few other groups opted for a more daring look that included lots of makeup and tight outfits. But most girl groups understood the dangers of acting or dressing too seductively. The Angels' Peggy Santiglia knew from experience that fashion choices mattered. Her first group, the Delicates, wore tight red dresses: "The funny part is we thought we were hot stuff, but we were still quite innocent and proper wearing our short red gloves." She made it clear that it wasn't easy for young females "to be in show business in the early stage of rock and roll." She added, "most of us . . . were trying to look older and act sophisticated, but for the most part we were innocent kids and at times the door opened to trouble, at least it did for me."[55]

Most songs zeroed in on a topic of particular interest to teenage girls and boys—romantic love. Hit records like the Angels' "Till" (1962) and the Chantels' "Eternally" (1963) glorified love. Other hits, including the Shirelles' "Boys" (1961) and the Girlfriends' "My One and Only Jimmy Boy" (1963), showcased teenage girls' obvious interest in teenage boys. Of course, wanting to interact with boys and knowing how to interact were two different things. Many girls didn't have a clue and desperately needed advice, as evidenced by the Percells' "What Are Boys Made Of" (1963). The lead singer wants to know why boys act mean, do inexplicable things, and if they ever cry. "Oh, won't you tell me?" she pleads.[56]

Girl group songs were often rock & roll equivalents of "Dear Abby" columns. They dished out advice about gender relationships, providing listeners with tactics and ammo for the teenage battle between the sexes. Like the dominant culture, baby boom culture usually portrayed boys as the leaders and girls as the followers. In high school boys asked girls for dates and asked them to dance (unless, it was a "ladies' choice"), and boys became the star athletes while girl cheerleaders offered support from the sidelines. Most songs followed that lead, depicting girls as the weaker sex. The Angels' "My Boyfriend's Back" (1963) features a teenage girl telling a boy who has been harassing her that he's in serious trouble, because her big, strong boyfriend's back in town. "If I were you," she says triumphantly, "I'd take a permanent vacation." Other records showcased dependent females nurturing young males. The eager-to-please young woman on the Four Pennies' 1963 hit "When the Boy's Happy" explains she'll do "most anything to make him feel just like a king," because "when the boy's happy, the girl's happy too."[57]

Unfortunately, female subordination sometimes went too far. Several records show that teenage girls were aware of the problem. The Cookies' 1962 hit "Chains" spotlights a young woman who complains that her boyfriend has her locked up in chains. "They ain't the kind that you can see," she explains. "It's chains of love got a hold on me." Other records such as the Shirelles' "Baby, It's You" (1961) and the Angels' "I Adore Him" (1963) featured young women willing to take anything their boyfriends dished out.[58]

A few songs crossed the line into sexual abuse territory. Two recordings by the Crystals were particularly troubling. Both were written by Carole King and Gerry Goffin and produced by Phil Spector. "Please Hurt Me" (1962) featured a young woman telling her boyfriend that she's willing to be his plaything: "So darlin', if you gotta hurt somebody, please hurt me." The other song, "He Hit Me (and It Felt Like a Kiss)" (1962) was even darker. The female singer notes proudly, "If he didn't care for me, I could have never made him mad, but he hit me, and I was glad." The negative reaction to the song was immediate. "We absolutely hated it," insists the Crystals' Barbara Alston. "Still do." Spector's partner, Lester Sill, was equally appalled. "I got into a big fight with [Phil] over it," he says. "I thought it was a terrible fucking song." When radio stations and fans across the nation refused to play the controversial record, Spector pulled it from circulation, although the song remained on the group's popular album released in 1963.[59]

At the same time, girl group records provide evidence that teenage girls were not as passive as common wisdom suggests. Hits such as the Chantels' "Look in My Eyes" (1961) and the Marvelettes' "Beechwood 4-5789" (1962) featured young women willing to take the lead in relationships. The girl on the Ribbons' "Ain't Gonna Kiss Ya" (1963) dumps her unfaithful boyfriend, telling him, "I ain't gonna kiss you no more . . . ain't gonna tell you I'm yours, for sure."[60]

Some songs boldly went where others had never gone before, guiding young women through the uncharted territory of sex. The Shirelles' "Tonight's the Night" (1960) and "Will You Love Me Tomorrow" (1961) assured teenage girls it was okay to have sex if it was true love. The Cookies' "Girls Grow Up Faster Than Boys" (1963) offered advice on how to attract an older boy. To prove she's no longer a kid, the girl in the song boasts she's now everything a girl should be—"36-21-35." Other records, including the Paris Sisters' "I Love How You Love Me" (1961) and Crystals' "What a Nice Way to Turn Seventeen" (1963), made it clear that young women were eager participants in the era's nascent sexual revolution.[61]

Several records took a more conservative approach. The Starlets' Top 40 hit "Better Tell Him No" (1961) countered the permissive message about pre-marital sex found on the Shirelles' "Tonight's the Night." The teenager on the Starlets' song asks her mother what she should do if a boy tells her that "tonight's the night." The mother replies emphatically, "unless he's got a preacher in his plan, tell him no." The Charmettes' "Please Don't Kiss Me Again" (1963) advised girls they could stop unwanted advances by simply telling boys not to kiss them again, because "one kiss leads to another."[62]

The ultimate warning about the pitfalls of premarital sex can be found on the Bobbettes' "I Shot Mr. Lee," which came out in 1960, the same year as the Shirelles' suggestive "Tonight's the Night." The record was a belated sequel to the group's 1957 hit, "Mr. Lee," which featured a handsome rascal (supposedly based on the Bobbettes' teacher). At one point, the lead vocalist sings suggestively to her lover, "Come on, Mr. Lee, and do your stuff, 'cause you're gonna be mine 'til the end of time." Evidently the affair didn't go as planned, because the Bobbettes are singing a different tune on the 1960 record: "Whoa, we should've never . . . oh no." The scorned girlfriend picks up a gun and goes to Mr. Lee's home. "Shot him in the head, boom boom, whoa oh," she sings joyfully over and over as the song ends. The bizarre teenage tale was a revealing glimpse at sex, violence, and retribution in the early 1960s. Not surprisingly, "I Shot Mr. Lee" got less airplay than the original hit, but the lyrics still resonated with enough young listeners to make the record a modest hit.[63]

Girl group hits frequently offered advice about heartbreak. The Shirelles' "The Dance is Over" (1960), "Big John" (1961), and "Foolish Little Girl" (1963) warned young women to be careful when playing the game of love. The Caravelles' "You Don't Have to Be a Baby to Cry" (1963) provided catharsis for girls who lost at love. The Shirelles' "Stop the Music" (1962) suggested a more assertive approach. Unlike the girl in Lesley Gore's 1963 hit "It's My Party (And I'll Cry if I Want To)," the young woman on the Shirelles' record was more forceful. During her party she marches over to where her boyfriend is dancing with a flirtatious girl. "I can't take it no more," she declares. So, turn off the music and turn on the lights. "The party's over for tonight."[64]

Most girl group songs emphasized that love and romance were just way stations on the road to marriage. In Kennedy's America, marriage was the ultimate goal of most couples. In 1960 the average male got married at age 22, and the average female at 20. Numerous records glorified marriage. In 1963 alone there were songs such as Patti LaBelle and the Blue Belles' "Down the Aisle," the Girlfriends' "My One and Only, Jimmy Boy," and the Secrets' "The Boy Next Door." In the spring of 1964—just as the first baby boomers were graduating from high school—the Dixie Cups chimed in with "Chapel of Love." The number 1 hit opened with the girl group singing sweetly, "We're going to the chapel and we're gonna get married." They add with youthful optimism, "Today's the day we'll say 'I do,' and we'll never be lonely anymore."[65]

The ubiquitous songs about marriage suggest that teenagers were in step with America's Cold War culture. The heightened tensions between the USA and the Soviet Union in the early 1960s contributed to a mainstream culture that viewed marriage, the family, patriotism, religion, and other traditional values as bulwarks against communism. Along with songs about marriage, there were hits such as the Shirelles' "Mama Said" (1961), which idealized parents and the family. Other records demonstrated teenage girls' patriotism and willingness to support the troops. The Shirelles' number 1 hit "Soldier Boy" (1962) is a perfect example. It debuted on the charts just a few months after the USA and Soviet Union almost came to blows during the Berlin Crisis. The singer tells her boyfriend in the army, "Take my love with you to any port or foreign shore," and assures him, "I'll be true to you." Hit records also glorified religion. The Paris Sisters' "Be My Boy" (1961) and Shirelles' "Dedicated to the One I Love" (1961) both featured teenagers praying to God for romantic help.[66]

Girl groups offered fresh sounds, styles, and perspectives that changed rock & roll's trajectory. The girl group fad facilitated the rise of Motown Records, which profited greatly from the success of the Marvelettes, Martha & the Vandellas, and Supremes. It paved the way for later groups like the Shangri-Las and created opportunities for solo artists such as Mary Wells, Lesley Gore, and Little Eva. Equally important, girl groups reflected and shaped baby boom attitudes, actions, fantasies, and fears. "What we have here is a pop culture harbinger in which girl groups . . . anticipate women's groups, and girl talk anticipates a future kind of women's talk," notes media professor Susan J. Douglas, who came of age in the 1960s. "The consciousness-raising groups of the late sixties and early seventies came naturally to many young women because we had a lot of practice. We had been talking about boys . . . for ten years."[67]

The Shirelles' lead singer, Shirley Owens, vividly recalls an incident, which underscores the tremendous musical and cultural impact that girl groups had on teenage girls of the early 1960s. Sometime around 1990 Shirley was in a Newark, New Jersey hospital and met a young woman wearing a pretty ring with the initial "S" on it. When the two began to talk, Shirley learned that the young woman was named "Shirelle," because her mother loved the group and their music so much. "I never told her [who I was]," said Shirley, "I never said a word. I just smiled."[68]

3

"Heat Wave"

Motown's Hot Sounds for Young America

Martha & the Vandellas' "Heat Wave" begins with a bang. The drummer instantly establishes the beat. Other members of the Motown studio band jump right in. The frenetic sound blends guitars, bass, piano, sax, and horns with handclaps as it drives the fast-paced rhythm and insistent beat forward. Twenty-nine seconds in, lead singer Martha Reeves unleashes a frantic vocal. "Whenever I'm with him, something inside starts to burning and I'm filled with desire," she sings with a mix of excitement and fear. "It's like a heat wave burning in my heart."[1]

The high-energy song made listeners want to jump up and dance. Released in 1963 on Berry Gordy's Detroit-based label, "Heat Wave" peaked at number 4 on *Billboard*'s Top 100. Decades later Martha still vividly recalled the night she recorded the song. "At Motown we used to do Christmas parties . . . or other parties, and I was asked to leave one to go into the studio, which was just next door," she explains. "The music was already there . . . So, we put my voice down. I knew it was a hit."[2]

"Heat Wave" epitomizes the "Motown Sound" that emerged in the 1960s. It was powered by infectious melodies, unforgettable hooks, danceable beats, and lyrics about young love. The record was Martha & the Vandellas' first Top 10 hit, setting the stage for later smashes such as "Dancin' in the Streets" (1964) and "Nowhere to Run" (1965). "Heat Wave" became the first Motown record to earn a Grammy nomination. Although it lost out in the R&B category to Ray Charles's "Busted," the hit served notice that Motown had arrived. Throughout the early 60s Motown's hot new sounds spread across America like a heat wave, sizzling with innovations for rock & roll and lessons for young America.

Martha & the Vandellas (Courtesy of the Rock & Roll Hall of Fame and Museum)

BEGINNINGS

The Motown story begins with Berry Gordy Jr. Born in Detroit in 1929, he was the seventh child in a large African American family. His parents got married in Georgia just after World War I. In 1922 they and their first three children, Fuller, Esther, and Anna, moved to Detroit. The Gordys were part of a larger migration of African Americans from the South who headed northward in search of better lives during and after the war. Over the next few years the family expanded to include five more children: Loucye, George, Gwen, Berry Jr., and Robert.[3]

The parents were excellent role models. "Pop" worked hard, learned a trade, and launched a plastering business. "Mother" was equally ambitious. She took business classes, worked in family businesses, and earned money through part-time jobs. By 1936 the Gordys had saved enough to make a down payment on a commercial property on Detroit's Eastside. The building included four store-fronts: the largest became a grocery store, the remaining three housed a print shop and other businesses run by family members. The Gordys lived in two flats on the second floor. The property provided resources to make it through the Depression. The parents were living proof that anyone could succeed in life with hard work, determination, and an entrepreneurial spirit. "As a family we were taught to operate as one," said Gordy. "'There is strength in unity' Mother always used to say." In 1949 the family's accomplishments were spotlighted in a *Color Magazine* article entitled "America's Most Amazing Family: The Famous Gordys of Detroit Have What It Takes."[4]

As a child, Berry loved listening to the radio, particularly music programs. He took piano lessons from his uncle and began writing melodies. The young Gordy also was a boxing fan; his hero was heavyweight champion Joe Louis, whose victory over Max Schmeling in 1938 inspired many African Americans, including the 8-year-old Berry. "All of a sudden, it wasn't so bad to be black," explained Berry. "In that moment a fire started deep inside me; a burning desire to be special, to win, to be somebody."[5]

By the time Gordy was in high school, he was determined to become a professional boxer. He trained daily in a local gym and launched his career. Ten wins, three losses, and two ties later, Berry realized that his first love, music, offered an easier route to fame, fortune, and glory. In 1950 he gave up boxing and became a songwriter. His new career got knocked out when he was drafted into the army. By the time he was discharged in 1953, he had a new plan to enter the music business. Following his parents' example, he started his own business; Berry was positive his record store would succeed. Convinced that "jazz was the only pure art form," he stocked the store almost exclusively with jazz records. Business started slowly and got slower as the weeks progressed.[6]

One afternoon a friend stopped by the store accompanied by two young ladies. When Berry was introduced to Thelma Coleman, he felt an immediate attraction. They began dating and a few months later were married. By the end of 1956 they were the proud parents of three children.[7]

While Gordy's personal life was thriving, his record store floundered. He soon realized that people in his neighborhood wanted nothing to do with jazz. They loved blues and R&B. With the store on the brink of collapse, Berry began stocking records customers wanted. It was too little too late. His venture went belly up in 1955. The failed business drove home advice Pop had given him years before: "The customer is always right." Berry also came away with an appreciation of blues music. "There was an honesty about it," he said, "it was just as pure and real as jazz." He added, "this important lesson came too late to save the store, but would not be too late to make a difference in my songwriting."[8]

After the store closed Gordy took a series of low-paying jobs to support his wife and kids. Eventually, he wound up at a Lincoln-Mercury assembly plant, putting finishing touches on cars that came by on a conveyor belt. The work was tedious but paid well. It also gave him a chance to compose songs in his head as cars rolled slowly by. Still, the aspiring songwriter felt trapped as he listened to coworkers talking about how many more years they had until retirement. His deteriorating home life made the situation worse. As debts and in-law problems piled up, his marriage began to unravel. Gordy felt like he was getting nowhere fast.[9]

Like the legendary bluesman Robert Johnson, Berry Gordy was at a crossroads. He took the path toward music and never looked back. His wife and in-laws were upset when he quit his job to write songs on spec, but Gordy refused to back down. He spent his days writing songs and nights checking out Detroit's hottest clubs. His favorite hangout was the Flame Show Bar, where two of his sisters worked. Gwen owned the photo and cigarette concession and Anna helped out. "The two of them were . . . glamorous, with business in their blood and love in their hearts," said Berry. "Everyone adored them and seemed pleased to meet me, their brother, the songwriter."[10]

One night, Gwen introduced Berry to the bar's owner, Al Green, who also managed singers LaVern Baker and Jackie Wilson. Green took a liking to the young songwriter and invited him to drop by his office at the Pearl Music Publishing Company. When Berry showed up the next day, Green was nowhere to be found. But, Gordy did meet a fellow African American songwriter, Roquel

Davis. The two hit it off, began writing together, and sold some songs to Al Green.[11]

Just when Gordy's songwriting career was taking off, his personal life crashed and burned. In 1957 Thelma filed for a divorce. Berry was devastated and worried about how the divorce might affect his kids. He turned to Gwen for help. Collapsing at a piano in her apartment, he began plunking out a sad tune. Suddenly out of nowhere came a moving ballad that lifted his spirit. "To be loved," he sang with tears in his eyes, "oh what a feeling to be loved."[12]

THE ROAD TO MOTOWN

Music was Berry Gordy's salvation. He and Roquel cranked out song after song. Several were recorded by well-known R&B artists, including Jackie Wilson who earned a minor hit with "Reet Petite" (1957). The following year he made the Top 30 with Gordy's "To Be Loved." Wilson recorded additional Gordy-Davis compositions, including "Lonely Teardrops," which became a number 7 hit in 1959. The songwriters, however, received few royalties. When Wilson's manager refused to negotiate, they quit. Roquel and girlfriend Gwen Gordy formed Anna Records, while Berry went off on his own.[13]

Berry Gordy's plan was to become an independent producer and songwriter. A good starting place involved a promising vocal group that he had met in the office of Pearl Music Publishing. The Matadors were there auditioning for Nat Tarnopol, who took over the company when Al Green died. When Tarnopol rejected them, Gordy approached the five African American singers out in the hall to tell them he liked their singing. He became more intrigued when he learned that their lead singer wrote their songs. The vocalist introduced his band mates: Ronnie White, Pete Moore, Bobby Rogers, and Bobby's cousin, Claudette Rogers. His name, he said, was William Robinson "but they call me Smokey." That was the beginning of a beautiful and profitable friendship. The older Berry became Smokey's mentor. "I had a great teacher in Berry Gordy," said Smokey. "He was the one who showed me how to turn my songs into little stories."[14]

In January 1958, the 18-year-old Smokey auditioned his latest composition for Gordy. "Got a Job" was the answer song to the Silhouettes' recent number 1 hit, "Get a Job." Berry loved it. He added finishing touches and then brought the Matadors into a recording studio. On Gordy's advice, the group changed their name to the Miracles. Shortly thereafter, Gordy negotiated a contract with End Records and "Got a Job" was released. Although the song didn't chart nationally, it sold well in Detroit and launched Gordy's career as a producer and manager.[15]

Not long afterward, Gordy was hanging out in his office with Smokey when a letter arrived with Gordy's payment for producing "Got a Job." When Gordy tore open the envelope, neither he nor Smokey could believe their eyes. The total amount was $3.19. "You might as well start your own record label," joked Smokey. "I don't think you could do any worse than this." Berry realized his protégé was right. On January 12, 1959, he borrowed $800 from his family to launch Tamla Records. Knowing it was important to own rights to songs, he also formed Jobete Music Publishing and signed Smokey as his first writer.[16]

Tamla was now open for business. In early 1959 Gordy arranged a recording session for local R&B singer Marv Johnson. Berry loved Johnson's singing style and helped him write "Come to Me," a high-energy rocker that blended an R&B sound with teen-oriented lyrics. The song became the first record released on the Tamla label. Local deejays loved it, but Gordy didn't have the means to distribute the record nationally, so he sold the master to United Artists and it became a Top 30 hit. In 1960 Gordy cowrote and produced two more United Artist releases for Johnson: "You Got What It Takes" and "I Love the Way You Love." Both became Top 10 hits.[17]

Gordy's success with Marv Johnson added to his reputation as a songwriter and producer. Equally important, it provided working capital for Tamla. The next step forward came when Smokey showed up at Gordy's apartment excited about his latest composition, "Bad Girl." After the two friends reworked some chords and lyrics, Gordy arranged a recording session for the Miracles. "The record came out so great I decided to use it to launch another label," explained Berry. He chose the name "Motown" to spotlight his hometown's reputation as the "Motor City."

In 1959 "Bad Girl" was issued on the Motown label (which made the Miracles the first artists on the new label). Since Berry still lacked resources to distribute nationally, he cut a deal with Chess Records to reissue the song. The Miracles soon had their first national hit, albeit a minor one. The doo-wop ballad introduced a wider audience to Smokey's unusual tenor voice and clever lyrics about an independent young woman who was labeled a "bad girl because she wants to be free." The musical tale reflected the era's double standard, which maintained that women were supposed to be dependent on men. "Bad Girl" was just the beginning for the Miracles and Motown.[18]

HITSVILLE, U.S.A.

When the 1960s began, Berry Gordy was on a roll. His failed marriage was behind him, and he had a new love interest, Raynoma Liles. "Ray" was a talented singer and musician who shared his commitment to making Motown a success. In addition, Gordy was writing and producing hits for the Miracles, Marv Johnson, and others. Plus, Motown Records had just relocated to 2648 West Grand Boulevard in Detroit. Family and friends pitched in to convert the residential home into Motown headquarters, complete with a lobby, recording studio, control room, offices, and upstairs apartment for Berry, Ray, and their two children. When the no-frills makeover was complete, Berry draped a huge banner over the picture window that proudly proclaimed "Hitsville U.S.A." A friend laughed when he heard the name. "That's the only name I can think of that expresses what I want it to be," replied a confident Gordy, "a hip name for a factory where hits are going to be built."[19]

Although the bright blue banner was more aspirational than true, it nonetheless offered a succinct mission statement for the new company. Gordy devised an action plan that would make his dream a reality. Remembering that his first business venture failed because he stubbornly tried to sell jazz records to customers who demanded blues and R&B, Gordy was now determined to give customers what they wanted. "On Motown's first day there were five people there," recalls Smokey Robinson. "[Berry] sat us down and said: 'I'm gonna start my own record label and we're not just gonna make Black music. We're gonna make music that everybody can enjoy. We're always gonna have great beats and great stories and we're always gonna make quality records.'"[20]

Gordy built on other lessons learned along the way. "One of the reasons Berry started Motown was because [record companies and distributors] didn't pay," noted Smokey. Motown got started "so everybody could get paid." Even Gordy's auto factory job shaped his vision for a record company. Eventually, Motown, like Henry Ford's assembly lines, would rely on division of labor. Songwriters, singers, musicians, and producers would create the records. Focus groups would provide quality control. An artist development program would teach performers dance steps, public speaking, etiquette, posture, and personal grooming. And, packagers, distributors, and sales people would market the product.[21]

One of Gordy's first moves was to hire William "Mickey" Stevenson as his A&R man "in charge of all the creative activities of producing a record." Stevenson helped Gordy assemble an impressive team of singers, songwriters, musicians, and producers. By the early 1960s Motown's roster included talented artists such as the Miracles, Marvelettes, Martha & the Vandellas, Mary Wells, Marvin Gaye, and Little Stevie Wonder, as well as gifted songwriters and producers like Smokey Robinson, Brian Holland, Lamont Dozier, and Eddie Holland.[22]

Camaraderie developed quickly as everyone worked together to crank out topnotch records in the close quarters at 2648 West Grand Boulevard. Everyone took part: "Artists sang background on each other's sessions, or played the tambourine or clapped their hands; any employee who could carry a tune or keep a beat was used," said Gordy.[23]

The same studio band played on most Motown hits. Years later, Gordy recalled how Mickey Stevenson recruited the group. "He went on the lookout for great musicians, combing even the seediest of bars and hangouts," explained Berry. "If they could play, Mickey would bring 'em in, putting together the greatest house band that anyone could ever want. They called themselves the Funk Brothers." The core included drummer Benny Benjamin, bass player James Jamerson, guitarist Robert White, and keyboardists Earl Van Dyke and Joe Hunter. Additional talent was hired as needed to play horns, strings, or other instruments.

The resulting sound was an innovative mix of rock & roll, pop, gospel, and R&B layered over a base of pure jazz. "Many of these guys came from a jazz background," noted Gordy. "I understood their instincts to turn things around to their liking, but I also knew what I wanted to hear—commercially." If they improvised too much, Gordy reined them back in. One day James Jamerson's inventive jazz licks went too far. The angry Gordy halted the session and glared at Jamerson. "Look man," he said with barely controlled fury, "I've told you over and over again this ain't no fuckin' jazz session. You've got to stay on the . . . downbeat." When they resumed, the unrepentant bass player stuck mostly to the script, but occasionally adlibbed just to make a point. "[Jamerson] knew I loved what I'd just heard and everyone else knew it too," admitted Berry. "They also knew he had gotten me."[24]

The Funk Brothers' innovative sounds propelled rock & roll into uncharted territory. "All of the music was jazz. The musicians were very accomplished and worked out rhythms and bass lines right there on the spot," explains Martha Reeves. They "had the intellect and ability to perform the music in the styles of the artists," she adds. "If the music was played for the Miracles, Temptations, or Supremes, they played a different way. My music does not sound like Smokey's. It doesn't sound like the Supremes or Mary Wells. It sounds like Martha Reeves. Same musicians, same producers, but they treated everyone with their own flavor."[25]

The Motown team included more than just talented artists, songwriters, and producers. Gordy understood that a record company needed quality people to promote artists, sell records, and keep track of finances. Not surprisingly, he turned first to trusted family members: Mother and Pop became virtual house parents at 2648 West Grand Boulevard. His sisters pitched in: Esther and her accountant husband, George Edwards, took care of finances; Loucye supervised pressing and shipping records, billing, and collection; Gwen and Anna helped with artist development. Gordy's brothers also got involved. Robert became a recording engineer. George and Fuller initially spent most of their time working for Pop's construction business and print shop, but they, too, took part in the Motown enterprise. Berry's girlfriend Ray (who became his second wife) worked with Motown artists and was in charge of Jobete Music Publishing.

In time Gordy added secretaries and staffers from the outside. In 1959 he hired 18-year-old Al Abrams (Motown's first white employee). Initially, Abrams was responsible for record promotion, but his portfolio later expanded to include publicity and press relations. "In those very first days . . . music was always getting categorized—R&B or pop, black or white," explains Martha Reeves. "It was [Al's] efforts that got us through the doors that were always shut to us."[26]

The name "Hitsville U.S.A." became a reality and not just an empty boast when Motown scored its first big hit in the spring of 1960. Foreshadowing things to come, it was called "Money (That's What I Want)." The upbeat record was two minutes and twenty-four seconds of sheer rock & roll bliss. As the raucous band plays on, singer Barrett Strong makes it clear that love's a thrill, but doesn't pay bills. With drums still pounding and music blaring at the song's end, Barrett tells listeners one last time what he wants: "All the lean greens . . . Give me money!"[27]

Strong's unapologetic ode to capitalism became a Top 30 hit. Not only did the dynamic sound and danceable beat appeal to baby boomers raised on rock & roll, but the materialistic message struck a responsive chord in an era known for consumerism and conspicuous consumption. Initially, "Money" was released on Tamla, but orders came in so fast Gordy couldn't meet the demand, so it was reissued on Anna Records, the nationally distributed label co-owned by his sister Gwen. When the song became a hit, Gordy was happy yet disappointed. "On my next record I knew I had to go for it myself," he said, "national all the way."[28]

WAY OVER THERE

Berry Gordy soon discovered the perfect song to make Motown a national label. Smokey Robinson's "'Way Over There' had great feeling, great melody, and great lyrics," said Gordy. Convinced of its potential, Gordy brought the Miracles into the studio to cut a record. He then made arrangements to promote and distribute it across the country.[29] When the record started getting airplay in major cities in March 1960, Gordy should have been ecstatic. Instead, he second-guessed his production technique and became convinced the record could be an even bigger hit if he added strings. So, he rushed the Miracles back into the studio to rerecord the song. "The Drifters had come out then, and they were using violins on all their records," explains Smokey. "Everybody started jumping on the violin bandwagon. So, Berry did, too." The "new, improved" version stalled at number 93 on the national charts. "The first version . . . had an honesty and raw soul," Gordy later admitted. "The second was a copy." Even though the reissue failed, Berry looked at the bright side. "After many tries, I had finally done it," he said. "I had gone national. Motown had now entered the music scene."[30]

Neither Berry Gordy nor the Miracles had to wait long to make it big. The times were changing in ways that helped Motown. In October 1960, Democratic candidate John F. Kennedy asked a judge in Atlanta to release Martin Luther King Jr., who had been jailed for leading a protest march. The following month Kennedy picked up 70 percent of the Black vote, enabling him to defeat Richard Nixon in a close election. Initially, President Kennedy moved slowly on civil rights because he did not want to alienate southern Democrats who favored segregation. But, the movement for civil rights would not be denied. Grassroots protests continued throughout 1961, and in May the Congress of Racial Equality (CORE) organized "Freedom Rides" to challenge segregated facilities along interstate highways in the South. The surging civil rights movement provided a perfect backdrop for the rise of Motown. At a time when African Americans' quest for social justice made daily headlines, Gordy's record company was featuring Black artists and music aimed at integrated audiences.

On the same day that Kennedy was sworn in as America's 35th president—January 20, 1961—the Miracles reached number 2 on the charts with "Shop Around." Written by Smokey Robinson and Berry Gordy, the song became Motown's first million-seller. The record begins with a young guy describing a conversation with his mother. She warns him about the dangers of early marriage. "My mama told me, 'you better shop around'" sings Robinson. The colorful tale shows that Smokey had taken Gordy's advice that a song had to tell an interesting story. "It is the kids who are buying the records," said Smokey. "This is the people you're trying to reach."[31]

If "Shop Around" was aimed at baby boomers, it hit the target. The humorous story appealed to young listeners, while the upbeat music was perfect for fast dancing. As an added bonus, Robinson's expressive falsetto and the group's unique harmonies put a new spin on the popular doo-wop style. "Claudette [who married Smokey] was the key to our harmonies," says her cousin and fellow group member, Bobby Rogers. "I sang under her, Ronnie [White] was the baritone and Pete [Moore] is a bass-baritone. But we all sang a little higher trying to reach her voice." Claudette and Smokey "would almost sing the same note, which gave him a lot of leeway, because he could sing something different and that note would still be in the background." "That was the essence of our sound," adds Pete Moore. "It gave our backgrounds a feminine quality."[32]

"Shop Around" appealed to baby boomers for other reasons. The lyrics hit home with teenagers trying to cope with young romance at a time when the median age for marriage was 22.8 for males and 20.3 for females. The song's references to parents, gender, and capitalism also resonated. In a Cold War culture that idealized the family unit, most teenagers knew what it was like to get advice from a parent. And given the era's gender stereotypes, many listeners agreed it was acceptable for young men to try their luck with numerous women, whereas young ladies had to be more circumspect. Even the song's message reflected the era's consumer culture. Teenagers understood perfectly when the mother in the song said, "Try to get yourself a bargain son, don't be sold on the very first one."[33]

"Shop Around" made the Miracles rock & roll stars. The number 2 hit also gave Berry Gordy the motivation and resources to upgrade the Motown operation. He noted, "If I had been able to put together a strong in-house sales department sooner, that record might have gone to #1." Gordy solved the problem in 1961 by hiring veteran record distributor Barney Ales as head of sales, distribution, and collection. Ales became the first white, top-level executive at Motown. Gordy was convinced that Barney's outgoing personality, important business connections, and skin color would enable him to open doors previously closed to Motown. Ales more than met the boss's expectations. He became Gordy's right-hand man for business affairs and put together a topnotch staff that successfully promoted Motown records.[34]

The Ales hire was one of several important changes made to the business side. The Miracles' success and the potential of other Motown acts convinced Berry that he needed a special unit to manage artists' careers. He appointed his sister, Esther, to head International Talent Management Inc. (ITMI), charged with arranging performances and offering career guidance. Motown's physical plant also expanded to keep pace with company needs: Gordy bought the house next door to provide office space for the growing number of employees. He also purchased other nearby buildings, causing Ales to joke that Hitsville was "the only high-rise that went sideways." As departments proliferated, Gordy hired additional employees and mandated weekly meetings for each unit. But Gordy retained ultimate control, coordinating all activities and making sure each department was meeting company goals.[35]

The creative side of Motown was also transformed. "The success of 'Shop Around' had sent waves of enthusiasm throughout the whole company," says Gordy. "Up until now I had been the only producer. But just as I realized that I couldn't manage all the artists myself, I knew I couldn't produce all of them either." So, he appointed new producers, starting with Smokey Robinson, Mickey Stevenson, and Brian Holland.[36]

Gordy scrambled to keep pace with Motown's expansion. Inspired by his experience in an auto factory, he set up a system for quality control. Every Friday Gordy would lead a discussion, which included producers, songwriters, musicians, singers, and other Motown employees. He'd play potential releases and ask the group which ones had the best chance of becoming hits. These meetings "were exciting, the lifeblood of our operation," explained Gordy. "That was when we picked the records we would release."[37]

Out of one of those product-evaluation meetings in 1961 came Motown's first number 1 hit, "Please Mr. Postman." "[It] was a cute, catchy little tune by a brand-new group called the Marvelettes," noted Gordy. "It was a bouncy track with a clever lyric that had [the lead singer] begging the postman to: *Deliver de letter de sooner de better.*" Given the enormous popularity in 1961 of the Shirelles and other girl groups, Gordy was convinced the Marvelettes could make it big.[38]

The Marvelettes' original members were Gladys Horton, Katherine Anderson, Juanita Cowart, Georgia Dobbins, and Georgeanna Tillman. The five teenagers auditioned for Motown producers Brian Holland and Robert Bateman in the spring of 1961 and were told to come back when they had original material. After Dobbins cowrote "Please Mr. Postman" with a friend, the girls returned for a second audition. "The producers and musicians . . . increased the tempo, added a new beat and made it more up to date," explains Katherine. Motown then offered a recording contract. Since all five girls were still in high school, parent signatures were required. When Georgia's father refused to sign, Wanda Young replaced her.[39]

Motown rushed the reconstituted group into the studio. As soon as Gordy heard the recording, he knew it was a hit. The record begins with one drum beat followed quickly by handclaps and the Marvelettes shouting desperately "Wait!" Lead vocalist Gladys Horton sings, "Oh yes, wait a minute Mr. Postman," as backup singers continue chanting, "wait, wait." Then the fun begins as the girls interact playfully to tell a heartbreaking tale about a frantic girl waiting day after day for the postman to deliver a letter from her boyfriend that never comes. All the while, the house band offers up a funky dance beat, powered by the prominent drumming of the still unknown Marvin Gaye. The record's irresistible sound and catchy lyrics appealed to millions of young listeners, particularly teenage girls who knew what it was like to wait desperately for letters or phone calls from boys. "Please Mr. Postman" became one of the biggest hits of 1961, establishing the Marvelettes as one of the hottest girl groups around.[40]

Not everything Motown touched in 1961 turned to gold. After "Shop Around" not one of the Miracles' next three releases made it higher than number 49. Records by future Motown stars also stalled. Mary Wells's two releases failed to make the Top 30 charts, while the Supremes did worse, recording two songs that went nowhere.

Both Motown and the civil rights movement experienced growth in 1962. Throughout the year the Southern Christian Leadership Conference (SCLC) and other groups pushed for reforms. Demonstrators were scorned, beaten, and jailed in the Deep South, but they kept their eyes on the prize and used every means of direct action available, including voter registration, sit-ins, lawsuits, and mass rallies. Their actions led to several victories, including the court-ordered admission of James Meredith, a Black veteran, into the all-white University of Mississippi.

With the civil rights movement constantly in the news, the public was eager to learn more about African American culture. Motown obliged by offering authentic sounds of Black singers, songwriters, and musicians from the streets of Detroit. In 1962 Mary Wells became the company's newest star when she scored two Top 10 hits. The 19-year-old's first big hit, "The One Who Really Loves You," was written and produced by Smokey Robinson. The record's unique sound hooked many listeners within seconds. It opens with an hypnotic calypso beat. Mary then unleashes a sensuous vocal that is at once submissive yet aggressive. In contrast to familiar hits by girl groups, the backup singers on this song are males not females. Not only does the switch offer a distinct, grittier sound, but it underscores that the woman is in charge. Wells initially pleads with her man not to leave her for another woman. Then she makes an abrupt U-turn. She might as well be telling her boyfriend that he's stupid when she points out that he's falling for insincere girls who are just using him: "So, love, you better wake up, yeah, before we break up," she threatens, "and you lose me . . . the one who really loves you." Young listeners were wowed by the sound and fury. Teenage girls could relate to the female singer for standing up to her wayward boyfriend, while male listeners focused on her suggestive vocal.[41]

Years later Smokey Robinson explained how "The One Who Really Loves You" came about. "Mary always had this hoarse quality to her voice," he noted, "a little raspy thing that was very *sexy*." Smokey hit on a perfect way to showcase her vocal style. "As a kid growing up, one of [the] people that I loved . . . was Harry Belafonte," said Smokey, who was impressed by Belafonte's use of "the bongos, the shakers, and all that." Robinson decided to use that approach with Mary. "I'm gonna have her sing the kind of music that we sing," he explained, "but I'm going to make it calypso-sounding." The gamble paid off. Baby boomers loved the record's irresistible beat and implicit sexuality, sending it all the way up to number 8.[42]

Wells' follow-up, "You Beat Me to the Punch," featured the same sexy vocal style, male backup singers, and syncopated beat found on her previous hit. This time around, though, the female protagonist triumphs over the troublesome man. Initially, the shy girl adheres to accepted dating practices. She hesitates to make the first move, so the boy approaches her, asks her out on a date, and establishes a steady relationship. However, she takes charge when she realizes he's a playboy. Launching a preemptive strike, she breaks up with him: "This time, I'll beat you to the punch," she proclaims proudly. "Yes I will."[43] Teenagers loved the sound, but probably took away different messages depending on gender. Girls were far more likely than boys to appreciate a song that spotlighted an independent young woman dumping her boyfriend.

The Contours added to Motown's success in 1962 with their number 3 hit, "Do You Love Me." Written and produced by Berry Gordy, the song showcased popular dance fads. The record begins slowly with the lead singer explaining that his girlfriend broke his heart because he couldn't dance. But, now he's back to let her know he's got all the moves. "Do you love me," he screams in a gravelly voice, "now that I can dance?" To prove his point, he shouts, "Watch me now!" The Contours then take listeners on a wild ride that includes the Twist, the Mashed Potato, and suggestive phrases like "work it out, baby" and "do you like it like this?" As the vocals careen up and down like an out-of-control rock & roller coaster, entranced listeners could only gasp and hold on tight.[44]

Young listeners loved the record's energy and sound, not to mention the vindication that came from learning all the latest dance steps. The Contours' fame was short-lived, though. They never had another big hit—at least not for another 26 years. Lightning struck again when the Contours' original version of "Do You Love Me" was featured in the 1987 film *Dirty Dancing*. Afterward, the record shot up to number 11 on the charts, thereby earning the Contours the dubious honor of becoming a "one hit wonder" twice with the same song.

Other Motown artists had more consistent success. The Marvelettes earned three Top 40 hits in 1962. "Twistin' Postman" linked their famous mailman to Chubby Checker's dance craze. The group's next release, "Playboy," featured women joining together in solidarity to warn off a young lothario who treats girls like playthings. The Marvelettes' final hit, "Beechwood 4-5789," scored another victory for women's equality by encouraging girls to take charge of relationships with boys. The brash young woman on the bouncy song tells the guy not to be shy and assures him that he can dance with her, hold her hand, and even whisper the kinds of words she loves to hear. Tired of waiting for him to act, she says aggressively, "my number is Beechwood 4-5789. You can call me up and have a date any old time."[45]

While the Marvelettes were advocating new gender roles for women, other Motown artists found success with more traditional approaches. The Miracles earned Top 40 hits with "What's So Good about Good-Bye" and "I'll Try Something New," while Eddie Holland's "Jamie" made it into the Top 30. Shortly thereafter Holland gave up singing to compose songs with his brother Brian and

Lamont Dozier. The Holland-Dozier-Holland team went on to write and produce many of Motown's greatest hits, including songs by the Supremes, Marvin Gaye, and Martha & the Vandellas. When the trio was inducted into the Rock & Roll Hall of Fame in 1990, their biography read: "In their behind-the-scenes roles as staff producers and songwriters, Holland-Dozier-Holland were as responsible as any of the performers for Motown's spectacular success."[46]

Two other Motown acts destined for greatness, Marvin Gaye and the Supremes, scored their first hits in 1962. Gaye began his rock & roll career as a member of Harvey Fuqua's Moonglows. When that doo-wop group disbanded, Fuqua moved to Detroit to work on Gwen Gordy's Anna label and brought Gaye along. The two men were soon drawn into the Gordy orbit, even becoming family members when Fuqua married Gwen and Gaye married her sister, Anna. Fuqua became involved in management, while Marvin found work as a studio musician. However, Gaye's real goal was to become a crooner like Frank Sinatra. Berry Gordy agreed to give him a shot. In 1961 he brought Marvin into the studio and produced an entire album of pop standards, including "My Funny Valentine" and "Witchcraft." Entitled *The Soulful Moods of Marvin Gaye*, the album's liner notes billed Gaye as "one of the nation's great jazz vocalists" (even though few people had ever heard of him). The album flopped.[47]

Despite the failure, Gaye was determined to be a jazz singer and repeatedly refused to record more commercial material. "Marvin was the most stubborn guy around," said Gordy. "That's exactly what [Mickey] Stevenson and my brother George decided to write about." The resulting record featured Gaye's expressive vocal, supported by the Funk Brothers' soulful sounds and backup vocals by Martha & the Vandellas. Although it reached only number 46 on the pop charts, Gordy noted, "Having turned from crooning to grooving, the aptly named song, 'Stubborn Kind of Fellow,' catapulted [Marvin Gaye] into hit status."[48]

The Supremes—Diana Ross, Florence Ballard, and Mary Wilson—struggled even more than Marvin Gaye. When Motown signed the group in 1961, they were called the Primettes. Gordy's faith in them never waned even though their early records went nowhere. Their luck began to turn when they recorded "Your Heart Belongs to Me," written and produced by Smokey Robinson. Although the pretty ballad stalled at number 95 on the national pop charts, it was a moral victory because the Supremes had finally cracked the Top 100.[49]

As 1962 came to a close, Motown's future looked bright. The company earned five Top 20 hits, three more than the previous year, and in October Berry Gordy launched the first Motortown Revue. Patterned after earlier rock & roll bus tours, it featured established Motown acts, as well as up-and-coming performers. Thomas "Beans" Bowles, who worked in management and as a studio musician, went along as tour manager and band member. The support team also included an emcee, a touring band, and chaperones.[50]

Esther Gordy put together the itinerary and rented a bus, which would be accompanied by several cars. Just before the convoy pulled out, she reminded everyone to mind their manners and follow all the rules, because they were representing Motown. They then hit the road bound for Washington, DC, and a one-week engagement at the Howard Theater. After that the convoy would head off for a series of one-nighters in the South, followed by a ten-day stint at New York's Apollo Theater.[51]

At first everything went smoothly. The artists played to audiences in DC that loved the music and cheered the Black performers. Things got rougher as the convoy with Michigan plates drove deeper and deeper into the South. Some whites assumed the passengers were Freedom Riders and hurled racial insults and rocks at them. Most of the artists were shocked by the hotels and restaurants that refused service, not to mention racists who threatened their lives. In Alabama a sniper opened fire on the Motown bus, riddling it with bullet holes. One bullet just missed Marvin Gaye who was sitting in a window seat. Berry Gordy was about to cancel the tour when Beans Bowles convinced him that the shooting was just an isolated incident. The Motortown Revue continued, and the situation improved considerably as soon as the tour headed north for their final engagement at the Apollo Theater in Harlem.[52]

Despite the problems encountered in the South, Gordy was pleased with the overall results. The Motortown Revue made a lot of money, garnered a ton of publicity for Motown acts, and was a valuable learning experience for all. The seemingly endless one-night stands became a baptism by fire for Motown performers. On stage night after night, they learned the hard way what worked with audiences and what didn't. By the tour's end most of the acts had improved.[53]

Still, Gordy realized changes were needed. For years Gwen and Anna had been pestering their brother to set up an artist development unit. He finally agreed when Bowles returned from the Motortown tour with troubling stories about some of the performers' unprofessional and crude behavior. Gordy realized that Motown artists wouldn't make it in mainstream pop unless they cleaned up their acts. Following his sisters' advice, he established a special department to improve behavior on and off the stage. He chose Harvey Fuqua to head the new unit. Fuqua was responsible for polishing the performers' stage acts, while Gwen and Anna took charge of the singers' looks, costumes, and deportment. Both sisters were proud graduates of Maxine Powell's Modeling and Finishing School in Detroit, so they recruited their former teacher to work with certain acts. These Motown artists came from "humble beginnings . . . some of them from the projects, some of them were using street language, some were rude and crude," noted Mrs. Powell. "I was turned loose to do whatever was necessary to make the artist look first-class."[54]

Fuqua's small operation couldn't keep pace with Motown's rapidly growing roster of artists, so Gordy hired Maxine Powell full-time in 1964 to set up a finishing school for the singers. Along with teaching etiquette, manners, and interview skills, Mrs. Powell gave lessons on fashions, grooming, how to walk, and how to talk. The following year Gordy expanded the curriculum to ensure the artists would look as professional on stage as they did off. He brought in Cholly Atkins (of the Coles and Atkins dance team) to teach choreography. He also named Maurice King music director and put him in charge of band arrangements and teaching groups how to sing harmony.[55]

The artist development program was a big success. Mrs. Powell viewed the performers as "diamonds in the rough and they just needed grooming and needed to find out who they were . . . [and] believe that they could be successful." She was gratified by the results: "I'm very proud of them, they're class today." Berry Gordy was equally proud that Motown took unsophisticated kids off the streets and molded them into polished performers.[56]

Not all Motown artists were on board. Marvin Gaye, for instance, insisted he did not need a charm or finishing school. But, most performers and staffers were happy to get with the program. Martha Reeves insisted the program changed her life. "Our introduction to Mrs. Powell was the best thing that ever happened to us," explained Reeves. "She said to us, you're not the most beautiful women in the world and you're not the most talented people in the business but when I finish with you, you'll all have the charm and class that will take you all over the world and make you presentable to kings and queens, presidents, anyone in the world, you'll be accepted because of what I'm going to teach you. And she was absolutely right."[57]

Over the years, Smokey Robinson and others have suggested that Motown was the first to have an artist development program. Actually, Hollywood provided similar training for movie stars decades earlier, and Bob Marcucci of Chancellor Records created a prototype for rock & roll in the late 1950s when he supervised how Frankie Avalon and Fabian would dress and act. But, even if Motown's program was not the first, it was a huge success. Not only did it teach performers how to succeed in the music business, but the program provided Black youths from the streets of Detroit with the skills and confidence needed to achieve the American Dream. Maxine Powell saw a connection between her work and the civil rights movement. "All my life I was thinking of things that would help my race become outstanding and I thought of class and style," she said, "two things that would be accepted around the world."[58]

When 1963 began, both Motown and the civil rights movement were picking up momentum. In April Martin Luther King Jr. led a march on Birmingham to protest segregation. Most Americans watched in horror as TV news showed police using clubs, water cannons, and vicious dogs against nonviolent demonstrators. The situation in Alabama worsened in June when two African Americans tried to enroll in the state's flagship university. Segregationist Governor George Wallace stood in the "schoolhouse door" to block their admission, so President Kennedy sent in troops to enforce the students' rights. JFK followed up with a nationally televised speech that called for major civil rights legislation.

The racist attacks, growing violence, and hope for change made civil rights workers even more determined to achieve liberty and justice for all. In August more than 250,000 people joined the March on Washington, where Martin Luther King Jr. delivered his "I Have a Dream" speech. The following month Blacks rioted in Birmingham after four African American girls were killed when a bomb exploded at a Baptist church. Kennedy condemned the violence and reiterated his support for civil rights legislation.

The calls for racial justice and harmony spilled over into popular culture. With national attention riveted on African Americans, *Lilies of the Field* became one of the most popular films of 1963. One movie poster spotlighted the film's African American star, Sidney Poitier, and depicted a Catholic nun describing Poitier's character: "He is not of our faith nor of our skin. But he is a man of greatness." The movie garnered four Oscar nominations, including best picture and best actor. When Poitier won he became the first Black to win the best actor award. African American rock & roll singers also took center stage. Ray Charles earned a Grammy for "Busted" and 6 of the 20 songs that reached number 1 on *Billboard*'s pop charts were performed by Black artists, including Little Stevie Wonder's "Fingertips—Pt 2."

Although Stevie was the only Motown artist to score a number 1 hit, many others enjoyed success. Mary Wells began 1963 with her biggest hit yet, "Two Lovers." Written and produced by Smokey Robinson, the song opens with ominous horns setting the mood. Then comes Mary's stunning revelation: "I've got two lovers and I ain't ashamed." The intimate confession immediately caught listeners' attention. After all, teenagers, like society as a whole, understood the difference between "good girls" and "bad girls." Wells's seductive vocal and the swaying melody driven by an insistent bass added to the sensuous sound. Mary describes her first lover as a sweet and kind guy, and she admits shamelessly that she's willing to do "everything" to show her love. Her second lover mistreats her, makes her sad, even makes her cry. Still, she loves him and once again is willing to do everything to prove it. Just when listeners are shaking their heads not knowing whether to pity this young woman or condemn her immorality, Mary goes on offense. She insists she's not unfaithful and the problem isn't her. Speaking directly to her boyfriend, she says "Darling . . . you're a split personality and . . . both of [my lovers] are you." The surprise ending, sexy sound, and great dance beat helped the record become a Top 10 hit.[59]

Mary Wells did even better in early 1964. She earned a number 1 record with "My Guy," which turned out to be her last Motown hit. Shortly thereafter she signed a more lucrative contract with 20th Century Fox Records. She never had another hit. "It really was a big shame," said Smokey, "because I think had she stayed at Motown she could have been around always."[60]

Mary Wells wasn't the only Motown veteran to have a good year in 1963. Smokey Robinson and the Miracles scored two Top 10 hits. The R&B influenced "You've Really Got a Hold on Me" made the charts first and climbed to number 8. Influenced by Sam Cooke's "Bring It on Home to Me" (1962), it featured the same slow beat, call-and-response pattern, and expressive duet between the lead vocalist and a male backup singer. The group earned another number 8 hit later in the year. Unlike the mournful "You've Really Got a Hold on Me," the ebullient "Mickey's Monkey" was a bouncy dance number powered by handclaps, lively singing, and a fresh sound that blended a classic Bo Diddley beat with jazz-influenced horns, guitars, and drums.

Over the next several years Smokey Robinson and the Miracles would earn more than 20 additional Top 40 hits, including a number 1 record, "The Tears of a Clown" (1970). Smokey also found success as a solo artist with Top 10 hits like "Being With You" (1981). Robinson was inducted into the Rock & Roll Hall of Fame in 1987, and in 2012 the entire group was inducted. Smokey also received three Grammys, including a Lifetime Achievement Award, as well as Kennedy Center Honors and the National Medal of Arts Award. He was inducted into the Songwriters Hall of Fame, and in 2016 he was awarded the Library of Congress's prestigious Gershwin Prize for Popular Song.

One of Smokey's closest friends at Motown was Marvin Gaye. Robinson remembers him as a "complex man" with diverse interests, a wonderful sense of humor, and tremendous musical talent. Marvin hit it big in 1963 with three Top 30 hits: "Hitch Hike," "Pride and Joy," and "Can I Get a Witness." Gaye's expressive vocals, influenced by R&B, gospel, jazz, and pop, contributed greatly to his success. "He was one of the greatest singers ever," insists Smokey. "I used to tell

Smokey Robinson and the Miracles. Claudette Rogers Robinson left the group in 1964.
(Courtesy of the Rock & Roll Hall of Fame and Museum)

him all the time, 'You Marvinized my song, man,' because he would do stuff vocally that I had never even dared to dream could be a part of the song."[61]

Other factors contributed to Gaye's success. His three hits in 1963 were well
written and superbly produced, Motown's studio band added depth to the sound
by mixing jazz, R&B, and pop, and Gaye's sexy performance style caused fans to
go wild. Berry Gordy recalls one concert: "Marvin was a show stopper that night.
Before he even opened his mouth the women in the audience went nuts."[62]

By the end of the 60s Gaye was tacking toward soul music and socially relevant songs such as his number 2 hit "What's Going On" (1971). What twists
and turns his career might have taken will never be known. In 1984 he was shot

and killed by his father after a violent argument. Three years later Marvin Gaye was inducted posthumously into the Rock & Roll Hall of Fame.

Two new Motown acts hit the pop charts in 1963—Martha & the Vandellas and Little Stevie Wonder. Martha Reeves initially was hired as a secretary. She got her big break when she filled in for Mary Wells at a recording session: "When that music started, she took her shot," said Berry Gordy, "surprising everyone with her powerful, soulful voice, wailing like there was no tomorrow." Afterward, Gordy paired Martha with Rosalind Ashford and Annette Beard to form the Vandellas.[63]

Martha & the Vandellas' first hit, "Come and Get These Memories," debuted in early April. Written by Holland, Dozier, and Holland, the bittersweet ballad about love gone wrong peaked at number 29. Their follow-up, "Heatwave" (also written by H-D-H), made Martha & the Vandellas stars. Berry Gordy wasn't surprised. "Martha was soul personified. Her movements were understated, but soulful and sexy," he noted. "I loved the way she could stand there, cool, feet planted, and pulsating to the music, as she and the Vandellas . . . captivated the audience."[64] Dressed in stunning outfits, the three pretty young women sang and danced with exuberance. Martha & the Vandellas went on to become one of Motown's most successful groups with smash hits such as "Quicksand" (1964), "Dancing in the Street" (1964), "Nowhere to Run" (1965), and "Jimmy Mack" (1967). In 1995 the group was inducted into the Rock & Roll Hall of Fame.

Joining Martha & the Vandellas on the pop charts in 1963 was another new Motown artist destined for the Hall of Fame. Little Stevie Wonder (born Steveland Hardaway Judkins) was signed by Motown when he was just 11 years old. Gordy remembers the day he met the boy. An excited Mickey Stevenson rushed into his office and urged him to come to the studio. "I hurried down . . . and found a young blind kid that Ronnie White from the Miracles had brought in for us to hear," recalled Gordy. "He was singing, playing the bongos and blowing on a harmonica . . . Something about him was infectious." Gordy dubbed him "Little Stevie Wonder" and signed him to a contract. Motown promoted him as a musical genius—a younger version of Ray Charles. Stevie's early releases went nowhere. Then something unexpected happened. In early 1963 Gordy recorded him live at a concert in Chicago's Regal Theater. When Gordy heard the tape, he knew he had caught rock & roll lightning in a bottle. He quickly produced the master and released the record—"Fingertips—Pt 2."[65]

Within weeks Little Stevie Wonder was a star. Just as President Kennedy was calling for civil rights legislation and public attention was focused on the struggle for Black equality, the talented, young African American singer took the nation by storm. Teenagers across the country couldn't believe their ears the first time they heard the dynamic sounds blasting out of their radios. "Fingertips—Pt 2" begins suddenly with a boyish voice screaming, "Everybody say, yeah!" The live audience shouts back, "Yeah!" The young singer and enthusiastic crowd trade familiar calls and responses. Stevie: "Say yeah." Crowd: "Yeah." The exchange quickens: "Say Yeah" ("Yeah"); "Yeah" ("Yeah"). Stevie yells frantically, "Yeah, yeah, yeah," followed by an explosive musical riff powered by his blaring harmonica and Motown's funky backup band. Little Stevie implores the excited audience to clap their hands louder. Just a little bit louder, he urges. The musical riff explodes again, pulling the exuberant crowd along. As the audience claps rhythmically and continues to scream and shout in response to the young, charismatic officiant, the uninhibited performance soars higher and higher. After a minute or so Little Stevie tells the crowd softly that he'll be leaving but if they want him to, he'll sing the song one more time. He plays a few bars of "Mary Had a Little Lamb," causing the crowd to laugh and cheer wildly. The show's emcee then comes out and tells Stevie to take a bow, as the backup band for the next act begins to set up. Unexpectedly, Little Stevie whips out his harmonica and starts jamming again. The replacement bass player is totally lost and yells frantically "what key, what key?" All the musicians jump back in, blasting out the musical riff while the crowd screams its approval. Little Stevie sings repeatedly, "Good-bye, good-bye, good-bye" as the drummer pounds out a beat and the band repeats the riff. Finally, the emcee brings the frantic rock & roll revival to a close, shouting "How about it . . . Stevie Wonder." The record then ends as suddenly as it began.[66]

"Fingertips—Pt 2" became the first live recording ever to become a number 1 hit on *Billboard*'s Top 100. Little Stevie's exciting record captured not just the power of rock & roll, but also what Motown called "the sound of young

America." The stunning performance expressed the energy and optimism of African Americans and baby boomers in Kennedy's America. Stevie went on to become one of the most successful artists in music history. He would earn numerous hits, including number 1 records such as "Superstition" (1973), "You Are the Sunshine of My Life" (1973), and "I Just Called to Say I Love You" (1984). He'd win 25 Grammys, a Lifetime Achievement Award, and an Oscar. In 1983, he was inducted into the Songwriters Hall of Fame, and in 1989 into the Rock & Roll Hall of Fame, which called him a "true musical pioneer."[67]

THE SOUND OF YOUNG AMERICA

After Motown's breakthrough with the Miracles' "Shop Around" (1961), the hits just kept on coming. Company publicist Al Abrams came up with a marketing slogan to describe the reason for the records' success: Motown, he said, is "The Sound of Young America." The clever catchphrase reflected Berry Gordy's insistence that Motown was not just making Black music. It was producing pop songs that would appeal to young people everywhere regardless of race, ethnicity, gender, class, religion, or country.

Although Abrams correctly identified the link between Motown and baby boomers, that connection only partly explains why the company became one of the largest and most profitable independent record companies in history. First and foremost, Berry Gordy was the visionary and talented administrator behind Motown's success. He was the quintessential common man with uncommon ability. He rose to the top through a potent combination of talent, ambition, energy, hard work, and luck. Smokey Robinson is quick to point out that Detroit was not the only city in America with excellent singers, songwriters, and musicians, but it had something that other places lacked. "We had Berry Gordy, a music man at the helm with great ideas," says Smokey. Gordy's plan from day one was to have hit records on the pop charts that everyone could enjoy. He didn't care if the music was labeled rhythm & blues, country, jazz, rock & roll, or anything else. "My music is pop," he insisted. "Pop means popular. If you sell a million records, you're popular."[68]

To accomplish his goal, Gordy brought in talented singers, songwriters, musicians, producers, and engineers. They consistently produced a quality product aimed at the teenage market. They hit the mark repeatedly with relevant lyrics about romance and upbeat music perfect for dancing. Some songs evoked the familiar sounds of girl groups and doo-wop, while others offered innovative approaches influenced by rock & roll, jazz, gospel, R&B, and pop. The resulting "Motown Sound" featured expressive vocals, great melodies and lyrics, relentless dance beats, and topnotch music powered by Motown's inventive house band.

The Hitsville recording studio also played a role. The small size of the room and ingenious use of basic recording equipment contributed to Motown's identifiable sound. In 1971 *Rolling Stone* writer Jon Landau praised Motown's "trebly style of mixing that relied heavily on electronic limiting and equalizing (boosting the high range frequencies) to give the overall product a distinctive sound, particularly effective for broadcast over AM radio."[69]

Despite the innovative sounds and commercial success, Motown was not as revolutionary as some music experts and fans suggest. The Rock & Roll Hall of Fame notes: "In its Sixties heyday, Motown's parade of hits revolutionized American popular music. After Motown, Black popular music would never again be dismissed as a minority taste."[70] The statement is misleading because it implies that Gordy's accomplishments were unique. Obviously, Motown did produce innovative Black pop music that had an organic folk quality. It was written, performed, and produced by talented African Americans, most from Detroit's Black neighborhoods, and it resonated with baby boomers across the country. However, Gordy was neither the first nor the only one to offer excellent Black pop music to mainstream audiences. In the 1950s Chuck Berry, Fats Domino, the Coasters, and many others integrated the national pop charts with hits aimed at teenagers. In the early 60s—when Motown was just getting started—established African American producers like Luther Dixon and Dave Bartholomew, as well as talented Black artists such as Ray Charles, the Shirelles, and Sam Cooke were already racking up hit after hit on the pop charts. Nevertheless, Gordy and his company produced some of the most creative and compelling records on the early 60s pop charts. Motown hits—along with those by non-Motown artists—made Black pop music more mainstream than ever.

Berry Gordy understood that creativity was just one of the ingredients necessary for success. He also needed an excellent support team to manage the business side of things. Talented people were hired to take care of the books and ensure success in music publishing, artist development, management, booking, marketing, publicity, distribution, and, of course billing and collection. As the company grew in size Gordy tried his best to maintain a sense of community. "We were a family," insists Smokey Robinson. "We went to each other's houses . . . we went on picnics together." All that, says Smokey, "was instilled by Berry Gordy."[71]

The Motown family reminded Berry of his own experience "growing up in the Gordy family—fierce closeness and fierce competition and constant collaboration." That camaraderie contributed to the overall success. "Hitsville had an atmosphere that allowed people to experiment creatively and gave them the courage not to be afraid to make mistakes," he explained. Gordy furthered solidarity through weekly meetings, parties, and other gatherings. He even had Smokey compose a company song, which everyone would sing at the start of meetings and events. "It goes something like this," recalls Martha Reeves, "'We are a very swinging company working hard from day to day nowhere will you find more unity than at Hitsville, USA.' And we'd all sing it and just love it . . . as if we were in school or college. I feel like I'm a graduate of the Motown University, cum laude."[72]

In the early 1960s Motown had all the ingredients for success: inspired leadership, talented singers, songwriters, producers, and musicians, excellent morale, and a first-rate business staff. Equally—if not more—important, the times were right for Motown to make it big. The economy was booming, providing capital for start-ups and disposable income for record buyers. Not coincidentally, Motown found success just as the first wave of baby boomers hit high school. Gordy offered this huge teenage cohort fresh sounds that were perfect for a new generation seeking its own identity.

The blossoming civil rights movement provided fertile ground for Motown's growth. As the movement raised the profile of Blacks nationwide, public interest in African American culture expanded. Motown offered white audiences Black music, albeit in a polished form that made artists and songs more acceptable to the general population. Gordy knew he had to tread carefully. "I used to talk to Barney [Ales], about this," he explained. "I was too white for the Black people and too black for the white people." Gordy found ways around the problem. "I hired a white salesman to go to the South," he said. "I didn't have pictures of Black artists on the record covers until they became big hits."[73]

Prior to 1964 Motown artists and songs did not deal explicitly with civil rights, but their success proved that integration and racial equality were expanding. Significantly, Motown wasn't just reflecting social change. "Motown and R&B music broke down a whole lot of racial barriers," insists Smokey Robinson. Early Motortown Revues encountered many problems in the segregated South, but things changed once racially mixed audiences developed a shared love of Motown music. "We'd go back and not only would they be dancing together, or sitting together, or being together, you'd see white boys with black girlfriends and black boys with white girlfriends," says Smokey. Motown crossed the racial divide in other ways. Whites accounted for 70 percent of Motown's record sales. Berry Gordy noted the "main connection" that many whites had to "Black culture" was through Motown's music. He was equally proud of Motown's impact on African Americans. The Supremes, he says, personified upward mobility with their beautiful gowns, finishing school charm, and pursuit of excellence. "All that," insists Gordy, "was to give Black people things to dream about."[74]

Motown advanced civil rights in other ways. Berry Gordy donated money to civil rights groups and his company issued spoken word albums to promote the cause. The records were the result of a 1963 meeting with Martin Luther King Jr. "Dr. King told me that my music was really about social integration while he was trying to bring about intellectual and political integration," said Gordy. "He wanted me to join him in his movement, and he wanted to be a part of Motown." In 1963 Motown released an album, *The Great March to Freedom*, which included speeches by King and other civil rights leaders at a Detroit rally. Later that year Motown issued a second album, *The Great March on Washington*, which featured King delivering his famous "I Have a Dream Speech" on the steps of the Lincoln Memorial. "I saw Motown much like the world Dr. King was fighting for," said Gordy, "with people of different races and religions, working together harmoniously for a common goal."[75]

Motown scored many little victories for racial equality. "We saw every magazine cover, every front-page article, not just as a breakthrough for . . . [Motown artists] but as a breakthrough in the civil rights struggle," explains publicist Al Abrams. Even Motown's slogan—"The Sound of Young America"—implied equality. Abrams's wife later noted that he crafted that particular wording because "he wanted to push diversity."[76]

Motown had a direct impact on Detroit's Black community. Most of the performers, producers, songwriters, and engineers were local products, and whenever the company needed staff it asked a local all-Black business school to send over applicants. Many young people approached Motown directly. "The house at 2648 West Grand Boulevard [became] known as a place where dreams could be turned into realities," says Gordy. "Local kids would line the sidewalk and front lawn, trying to get discovered or just hoping to get a glimpse of one of the stars," he explains. "They tried everything to get inside. Some succeeded, getting jobs as secretaries, office helpers, even janitors." Motown also had a positive impact on race relations. "In Detroit you could not go into the white areas unless you proved you worked for somebody," recalls Smokey Robinson. "But the kids in those areas would write us letters: 'We love your music . . . but our parents don't know we have it, because they'd make us get rid of it.'" The situation soon changed. "A year or so down the line, we're getting letters from the parents: 'Our kids turned us on to your music. We're so glad you're in business; your music is so uplifting.'"[77]

Detroit took notice when Berry Gordy bought a local landmark in 1963. "I'd never dreamed as a kid that I'd be able to buy the Graystone Ballroom, where black people were only allowed in on Monday nights," explained Gordy. The purchase didn't surprise Mickey Stevenson. "Motown was a very strong backer of Martin Luther King's total program," he said. "Berry felt that our job in Detroit was to make blacks more aware of their culture, of the problems and some of the ways out of the problems." Stevenson added, "We'd showcase our artists . . . at the Graystone Ballroom and it gave us a chance to get the youngsters off the street and see what our image was about . . . Motown was a tremendous avenue of escape and hope.[78]

Berry Gordy personified the civil rights movement's call for Black economic power. He became one of the nation's leading African American entrepreneurs as he transformed his tiny start-up label into a huge American success story. "In the creative world there were a lot of [Black] singers. There weren't a lot of [Black] owners. This guy owned the company," says singer Lionel Richie. "This man took no shit."[79]

Another reason for Gordy's success is that Motown was as adept at making myths as it was hit records. Despite all the hoopla, Motown was neither the first all-Black record label nor even the first record company to market Black R&B singers on the predominately white pop charts. Back in the 1950s and continuing into the early 60s, Black owned and operated companies like Vee-Jay and Duke-Peacock had numerous crossover hits on the pop charts. Years before Motown was founded independent labels owned by whites, such as Atlantic Records, Chess Records, and Imperial Records also had success promoting Black R&B on the pop charts.

Even the notion that Motown was entirely an African American record company is misleading at best. Between 1959 and 1963, Motown released several records by white artists, including Nick and the Jaguars, the Valadiers, Mickey Woods, Debbie Dean, Don McKenzie, and Mike & the Modifiers. Most flopped, although a few like Nick and the Jaguars' proto-surf instrumental, "Ich-i-bon #1" (1960) and Mike & the Modifiers' pop rocker, "I Found Myself a Brand New Baby" (1962) deserved a better fate. The business side of Motown Records was almost entirely white: financial affairs were handled by Sidney and Harold Noveck (the chief accountant and tax attorney), and sales and promotion were directed by Barney Ales. Many African Americans complained when Gordy hired whites. "They said, black people are having trouble getting jobs, and you're hiring white people," noted Gordy. "I'd say, 'well I hire the best person for the job.'"[80]

Even though both Blacks and whites were responsible for Motown's success, the notion of a Black owned and operated company was far more compelling in an era of civil rights. Realizing that perception is often more important than reality, the company promoted the popular image. During the early 1960s Motown became *the* symbol of African American excellence. A large part of the Motown legacy "is its symbolic power to black America," says writer Nelson George. "To that repressed American minority, Motown is the ultimate myth of black capitalism, one that says . . . 'Yes, it can happen. The odds can be beaten.'"[81]

WHERE DID OUR LOVE GO?

In the summer of 1964 the Supremes hit it big with their first number 1 hit, "Where Did Our Love Go," written by Holland-Dozier-Holland. Over the next two and a half years the Supremes earned 10 additional number 1 records. Their spectacular success ushered in a "golden age" for Motown. Between 1964 and 1971 the company earned 90 Top 10 hits, including 25 number 1 records. Leading the way were new superstars such as the Supremes, Four Tops, Temptations, and Jackson 5, as well as established acts like the Miracles, Marvin Gaye, Martha & the Vandellas, and Stevie Wonder. All of them would later be inducted into the Rock & Roll Hall of Fame, along with Berry Gordy, songwriters Holland-Dozier-Holland, and two members of Motown's house band, drummer Benny Benjamin and bassist James Jamerson.

Motown's phenomenal success after 1963 reflected the changing times. Following President Kennedy's assassination, many teenagers felt adrift, and the Beatles—with their fresh sound, upbeat approach, and different look—offered the perfect diversion. Ironically, while the British Invasion pushed many American rock & rollers off the charts, Motown artists thrived because they—like the Beatles—offered fresh sounds, upbeat images, and a different cultural identity. Motown's success was also linked to growing public awareness of the civil rights movement and the rise of Black power. Motown became an obvious symbol of changing racial attitudes. Berry Gordy personified Black success, while Motown performers were living proof of upward mobility. Motown offered a conduit for whites to connect with African American people and culture.

If the Supremes' first hit, "Where Did Our Love Go," launched the period of Motown's greatest success, the title also foreshadowed the company's demise. As the operation grew larger and richer, the family atmosphere that permeated early Motown declined. By the late 1960s some artists chafed at Gordy's paternalism and more than a few believed the owner played favorites. Jealousy drove wedges between artists. Several alleged that Motown's one-sided contracts hindered their careers and deprived them of royalties. Some sued Gordy and Motown. Eventually, many members of the original Hitsville "family" either left the

Motown nest or were pushed out, including Mary Wells, the Marvelettes, Mickey Stevenson, and Holland, Dozier, and Holland.[82]

In 1968 Berry Gordy moved the company's iconic headquarters from 2648 West Grand Boulevard to a new downtown Detroit location. Four years later Motown relocated to Hollywood so Gordy could turn his attention to non-music projects, including movies like *Lady Sings the Blues* (1972), which starred Diana Ross. In 1988 Gordy sold Motown to MCA for $61 million, and later sold Jobete Music Publishing to EMI for an estimated $312 million. Not bad for a guy who started Motown with an $800 loan from his family.

Berry Gordy set out to make records with mass appeal. He accomplished that and more. Motown's total revenues from 1959 to 1988 are estimated to be $1 billion, but the company's legacy isn't just about record sales, singers, and songs. The real magic of Motown is its close connection to the times. "Motown shaped the culture and did all the things that made the 1960s what they were," says civil rights leader Julian Bond. "So, if you don't understand Motown and the influence it had on a generation of black and white young people, then you can't understand the United States, you can't understand America."[83]

4

"Surfin' Safari"

Surf Music, Car Songs, and the Mythic West

The Beach Boys' 1962 hit "Surfin' Safari" begins with three short lines destined to reshape youth culture and rock & roll. First, the group shouts out "Let's go surfin' now!" The invitation for young listeners to try the new surfing craze resonated in post–World War II America, which valued new cars, new products, new fashions, and new experiences. Without missing a beat, the Beach Boys serve up the next line "Everybody's learnin' how," which made perfect sense to school-age listeners accustomed to new activities and latest dance steps. Then comes the clincher: "Come on a safari with me."[1] The invitation to have fun with other teenagers was appealing in itself, but the word *safari* added mystery, re-calling exotic movies like *Tarzan the Magnificent* (1960) and *Hatari* (1962). Teen-agers were intrigued by this new rock group urging them to join a rock & roll safari in search of adventure and romance in California—a land of endless summer.

Even the Beach Boys' name suggested fun in the sun. Their fresh sound in-troduced millions of baby boomers to a new world of woodies and boards with promises of shooting the pier and walking the nose. Most listeners were white, middle-class teenagers from cities, suburbs, and rural areas across the country, so they did not always understand the surf lingo. But, it sounded cool: young people were enjoying wild times surfing in exotic-sounding places like Malibu, Laguna, and Doheny, too.

Powered by youthful harmonies and a driving rock & roll beat, "Surfin' Safari" became the Beach Boys' first big hit, reaching number 14 on the charts. It helped popularize a new musical style—surf music—which captured the excitement of surf culture on the California coast. By the early 60s millions of Americans had headed west to California seeking economic opportunities and the promise of eternal happiness in an enchanted land. Surf music offered a soundtrack for the California Dream.

The innovative surf music that emerged in Kennedy's America included the dynamic vocal style of groups like the Beach Boys and Jan & Dean, as well as the explosive instrumentals of bands such as Dick Dale and the Del-Tones, the Chantays, and Surfaris. Both approaches offered fresh sounds and quality records that spotlighted surfing, car culture, and teenage lifestyles in California. The upbeat music captured the optimistic mood of a confident nation. Surf music's take on the California Dream demonstrated that many young people subscribed to the notion of American Exceptionalism and shared the dominant culture's attitudes toward the pursuit of happiness, consumer goods, and the promise of a better life in the mythic West.

ROCK & ROLL VISIONS OF THE MYTHIC WEST

The California surf culture was the latest iteration of one of America's most enduring myths—the legendary American West. "More than other American regions, the West eludes definition because it is as much dream as a fact," write scholars Frank Bergon and Zeese Papanikolas, "and its locale was never geographical. Before it was a place, it was a conception."[2]

The West evokes numerous images in the American mind. Foremost is the West as a Garden of Eden. There are several variations on this theme. The American West is often portrayed as a land of opportunity where one can find economic, political, and social contentment, as well as personal happiness and individual freedom. The West is also viewed as a faraway, exotic land—a place of adventure and excitement, replete with natural and man-made dangers. A land of legendary beauty, the West was home to heroes like Buffalo Bill and Wyatt Earp, who rode across wide open spaces fighting a never-ending battle against villains and varmints. By the end of the nineteenth century, images of the West as a Garden of Eden and an exciting land of enchantment were well established in the American mind. The mythic West and its connection to traditional values and the notion of American Exceptionalism gained even greater popularity in the twentieth century when the United States was challenged by two world wars, the Great Depression, the Cold War, and other historical forces that threatened the American way of life.

Not surprisingly, the American West in all its glory proved to be an ideal subject for popular culture. It became the setting for early frontier tales, dime novels, and Wild West shows, as well as later Western movies, novels, and TV shows. During the 1950s and early 60s, while adults were watching television Westerns like *Gunsmoke* and popular movies such as *The Searchers* (1956) and *Cimarron* (1960), teenagers were listening to rock & roll hits about colorful Western characters. Cowboys were showcased on Marty Robbins's "El Paso" (1959) and the Ramrods' "(Ghost) Riders in the Sky" (1961), and Indians were featured on hits such as Johnny Preston's "Running Bear" (1960) and Larry Verne's "Mr. Custer" (1960).

The rise of the surfing craze turned the rock & roll spotlight on the mythic West as a Garden of Eden. The 1959 movie *Gidget* helped transform surfing from an obscure sport into a teenage craze. The popular film starred Sandra Dee as Gidget, a pretty teenage girl interested in surfing, romance, and fun on California beaches. The box office smash led to other pop culture products about surfing. John Severson promoted the sport through *Surf Fever* (1960) and other short films, as well as his *Surfer* magazine. A photo essay in a 1961 issue of *Life* magazine raised the national profile of the new sport: "The Mad Happy Surfers, A Way of Life on the Wavetops" showcased California's exciting surf culture. "If you're not a surfer," said one high schooler, "you're not in."[3]

Several beach party movies starring Frankie Avalon and Annette Funicello did even more to promote surf culture and the promise of eternal bliss in California. A movie poster for the first film, *Beach Party* (1963), depicts surfers riding a wave in the background while in the foreground a smiling Annette (in a revealing bathing suit) balances on a surfboard. Directly behind her, an eager Frankie admires her obvious talent as he kneels on a surfboard. At the bottom of the poster are throngs of couples frolicking on the beach. The banner at the top offers a provocative description of a California beach party: "It's what happens when 10,000 kids meet on 5000 Beach Blankets!"[4]

Dismayed by the inaccurate images of surfers in ephemeral movies like *Beach Party* and *Gidget*, California filmmaker Bruce Brown decided to set the record straight. In 1963 he and two of his surfer buddies set off on an odyssey in search of the perfect wave. The resulting documentary, *The Endless Summer*, became a cult hit. The movie and its ubiquitous advertising poster, which depicted three young men holding their surfboards with a bright sun as a backdrop, added to the myth that connected California surfers to the pursuit of happiness.[5]

Surfing was not just a pop culture creation, though. The first West Coast surfboard championship was staged in 1959, the same year *Gidget* debuted. The movie gave surfing a higher profile, but innovative technology made the sport possible. Prior to the mid-1950s, most surfboards were made of solid wood—some were over 20 feet long. By 1961 companies were mass-producing shorter, lightweight boards coated with fiberglass. "We went from giant log boards . . . that were about 20' tall to 12' boards, and then down to even lighter ten footers," says Dick Dale, an avid surfer and surf music pioneer. The new boards made the sport easier to learn, and they could be hauled around almost as easily as beach umbrellas and volleyball equipment. In 1963 *Time* magazine estimated that every weekend about 100,000 surfers were riding the waves at California beaches.[6]

The rise of surf music was also linked to new technologies. The invention of more powerful guitars, amplifiers, and transformers gave surf music pioneers like Dick Dale the means to convey the thunderous sounds of surfing to eager young audiences. The power of his music, says Dale, came "from the ocean, which we re-created with the Fender Dual Showman amplifiers, those were the first power amps in the world."[7] With Dick Dale and the Del-Tones pointing the way, other California garage bands cranked up their amps and unleashed surf music—an innovative rock & roll style that captured the excitement and feel of the new California beach culture.

SURF MUSIC PIONEERS

The growing popularity of surfing gave rise to a California beach culture that glorified the sport. When aspiring filmmakers such as Bruce Brown, Walt Phillips, and Bud Browne first began exhibiting their short silent surfing films in bars, surf shops, and high schools throughout southern California, they would narrate them and play snippets from instrumentals by Duane Eddy, the Ventures, and other rock & roll bands as background music to capture the excitement on the screen.[8]

By 1961 several California bands were experimenting with innovative sounds that grafted rock & roll onto the developing surf culture. Although most of these pioneering surf groups didn't chart nationally, regional hits such as the Gamblers' "Moon Dawg" (1960), Belairs' "Mr. Moto" (1961), and the Mar-Kets' "Surfers' Stomp" (1961) promoted the emerging surf sound on the West Coast. No one played a more important role in the birth of surf music than Dick Dale and the Del-Tones. Although Dale only had a few hit singles and albums on the national charts, his explosive guitar style and dynamic live performances helped launch surf music.[9]

Dick Dale (a.k.a. Richard Anthony Monsour) was born in 1937 in Boston, Massachusetts. He grew up listening to all types of music, including big bands, country, and the ethnic songs played by his Polish White Russian mother and Lebanese father and uncles. In 1954 the high school senior moved with his parents to southern California. The new lifestyle just "totally blew me away," he says. "I got to California and I saw my first bleached blonde [and] somebody wearing bright red lipstick. I couldn't believe the fast pace of the people." In 1955 he joined a car club at school and bought a Harley. He also purchased a cheap guitar and began hanging out at the beach in Balboa. "That's where it all started," he says. "I started living at the beach and surfing every day."[10]

In 1955 Dick Dale met a man who would change his life—guitar inventor Leo Fender. The brash Dale introduced himself, said he had no money or guitar to speak of, and asked for Fender's help. "He took a liking to me," says Dale. Fender handed him a brand-new Stratocaster and asked him to play it. "He started laughing," recalls Dale, "because I started playing it upside down backwards . . . because the book I learned with didn't say 'string it the other way, stupid,' 'cause you're left-handed.'" When Leo regained his composure, he told Dale, "take this guitar and amplifier. Beat it to death. Then, tell me what you think." From that point on Dick became Fender's personal guinea pig, testing the Stratocaster, the Rhodes piano, the Contempo organ, the Precision bass, and other Fender products. Leo always told him to push the instruments to the limit.

"If an instrument can withstand Dick Dale's barrage of punishment," he said, "it is then fit for human consumption."[11]

Working together, Dale and Fender revolutionized early 60s rock & roll. Inspired by the thunderous sounds he heard when surfing, Dick was determined to replicate that in his music, but he needed Leo's help to pull it off. "Leo Fender was the Einstein of making guitars and amplifiers," insists Dale. Early on, Leo created the Telecaster guitar for country musicians like Chet Atkins. Because of their picking style, they didn't need a lot of volume, so the 21-watt amplifier and 8- to 10-inch speaker that came with the Telecaster worked just fine. "When I came along, I wanted to get the sound of Gene Krupa's tribal drumming," says Dale. "When I started doing that I was pushing too much voltage through the amplifier, which would blow out tubes, blow out speakers . . . speakers would even catch fire sometimes." Leo just shook his head and told him not to play so loud. Dale insisted his music had to be loud and convinced Leo to experiment. "That was the birth of getting bigger and bigger [sound]," says Dick. "We finally created the ultimate in 1958 or 59—a 15-inch B130F-Lansing, made by JBL based on specs by Fender and Dale. It never blew out again."[12]

Fender then made a new transformer "which favored highs, mids, and lows," explains Dale. "Transformers didn't do that. They only favored one or the other. But I wanted a round, fat, thick punching sound with a crisp edge to it like a punch going through a wall. So, Leo created an 85-watt upward transformer . . . it would peak at 100 watts." Two weeks later Dick decided to put two speakers in the same cabinet, so Fender went back to the drawing board. "[Leo] had to create a larger output transformer, which was the first 100-watt upward transformer, peaking at 180 watts," says Dale proudly, "and that's when Dick Dale made people's ears bleed."[13]

Dale's innovative sound introduced new elements into rock & roll. "It's a focus on power and energy," he explains, "derived from the equipment and also by the way I play—the staccato, the picking, the style." His approach was almost mystical. "In a Buddhist temple, they will not even let you touch the skin of a drum . . . until you can tongue [the sound] you play," says Dale. "So, if you're going 'ticketty tochetty, ticketty tocketty, ticketty tah,' that means that the sound comes from your brain and will go right down your arms and every part of your body first." He adds, "Gene Krupa was one of the first to do that, and that's how I got that percussion sound . . . I play like I'm choppin' down a tree with just an energy source."

Dick Dale's dynamic sound eventually came to be known as surf music. It blended the sounds of ocean waves with rock & roll beats often punctuated by primal screams or animal sounds. "I got my energy from surfing but also training lions and tigers [which he kept as exotic pets]. I'd be surfing and the roar of my lions would sound exactly like the roar of the ocean." Dick adds, "I'd surf with about 15 of my buddies and I'd go Wow, that's a great and powerful sound and feeling. It was the energy I'd get, so when I got on stage I'd take my guitar and just rip down the strings that I used. So, everybody started calling me 'King of the Surf Guitar.'"[14]

Dick Dale and the Del-Tones became the first surf band to score a hit on the national pop charts. Their instrumental "Let's Go Trippin'" debuted on November 27, 1961, and peaked at number 60 in early 1962. By the time that record appeared Dale was already a surf music legend in southern California. In 1960 he and his group became the regular band at the Rendezvous Ballroom on the Balboa Peninsula. Every week they would play to capacity crowds of almost 4000 young people eager to dance the surfer's stomp to Dick Dale and the Del-Tones' dynamic sounds. Right from the start Dale had a close bond with the audience. "When I get done playing, I always sit on the edge of the stage immediately," he says, "and sign autographs and [talk] for the next two and a half hours." Like his fans, Dick was an avid surfer and enjoyed loud, rhythmic music. Speaking in the third person, he says, "Dick Dale connected with the audience the first time he played, because Dick Dale always . . . plays to the grassroots people."[15]

Dale attributes his signature surf sound to the Fender guitar he played. "The Stratocaster was made for one and only one reason—pure power rock and roll." It was a solid wood guitar, because Fender believed "the thicker the wood, the bigger and purer the sound." Dale vehemently disagrees with music experts who define "surf music" as a wet, splashy sound created by reverb and a vibrato or "whammy" bar to mimic the sensation of riding the crest of a huge wave. Reverb had nothing to do with it, insists Dale. He and Leo initially created reverb to add more vibrato to his vocal performances, not instrumentals. "At home I had this Hammond Organ and inside was this reverb tank. We . . . took out the tank, made a separate encasing with tubes and wiring and I plugged it in a Shure Dynamic Birdcage microphone . . . and that's what I sang through." It worked so well that Dale later plugged his guitar into it for added reverb, but that came much later. When his first album, *Surfers' Choice*, was released in 1962, Dale was already known as the "King of the Surf Guitar." Yet, not one song on that album had reverb on it.[16]

Even "Miserlou," recorded in 1962 and later featured in Quentin Tarantino's 1994 film *Pulp Fiction*, did not use reverb, says Dick Dale. He simply used his Stratocaster to mimic the sounds he heard while surfing. Surf music, he explains, "is . . . the sounds of the waves . . . I'd take my strings and go *weeeeeeer* up high and then you get that rumble just before you're going to be flung over, you know right before you're going to go over the fucking falls and get slammed down, all that rumbling and all that stuff like that they associated the heavy Dick Dale staccato picking *tk-tk-tk-tk-tk-tk* on those strings, it sounded like the barrel of a goddamn wave."[17]

Young fans loved the charismatic Dale's high-octane sound and exciting performances. "Kids came to see Dick Dale and dance," he says. And they were never disappointed. Dick developed a close connection with his audience by playing loud, rhythmic, grassroots music for them not at them. "I make my guitar scream with pain or pleasure or sensuality," he told NPR. "It makes people move their feet and shake their bodies." Dale cranked out powerful surf music and other authentic rock & roll for over six decades. "When I die, it's not going to be in a rocking chair just rocking back and forth with a beer gut," he predicted in 1998. "It'll be on stage with one big explosion and it'll probably be in body parts." When Dick died at the age of 81 on March 16, 2019, he was still touring and had new concerts booked for later that year.[18]

Dick Dale, aided and abetted by inventor Leo Fender, energized rock & roll in the early 1960s. Not only did Dale kick the volume up a notch, but he pointed the way for other bands to try their hand at surf music. The Pendletones from Hawthorne, California, would become the most famous surf group of them all—after they changed their name to the Beach Boys.

THE BEACH BOYS AND THE CALIFORNIA DREAM

If Dick Dale was surf music's original innovator, the Beach Boys were its great-est promoters. By coincidence or design, they linked rock & roll with the California Dream and traditional images of the West as a Garden of Eden. All five members of the group were born and raised in southern California. Brian Wilson wrote, arranged, and produced most of the songs. He also played bass, shared lead vocals, and contributed the distinct falsetto that soared above the layered harmonies. Brian's youngest brother, Carl, played lead guitar and sang backup with occasional lead vocals, while middle brother Dennis was a charismatic drummer and sometime singer. Older cousin Mike Love cowrote many of their biggest hits and usually sang lead. Rounding out the lineup was Brian's buddy from Hawthorne High School, Al Jardine, who played guitar and sang backup. Jardine left the group just before they hit it big and was replaced by the Wilsons' neighbor, David Marks, who played rhythm guitar. When Marks quit in 1963 Jardine rejoined the group.

The Beach Boys got their start like hundreds of other garage bands. The teenagers simply enjoyed getting together to sing songs they heard on the radio. Brian emerged as their leader. "Nobody structures harmonies and chord progres-sions and melodies better than Brian," insists Mike Love. The harmony sound of the Four Freshmen, Hi-Lo's, and Four Preps inspired Brian to create similar arrangements for the Beach Boys. The group loved the Everly Brothers and early doo-wop, says Mike, "but the Four Freshmen really . . . distinguished the Beach Boys' harmonies . . . from so many other groups."[19]

The Wilsons' father became their manager. "Murry was rough," recalls Mike Love. "But . . . he was a genius when it came to promotion." He booked the young band anywhere he could—radio stations, record hops, school dances. Usually, they played for free or just expenses. In 1961 Al Jardine landed them an audi-tion with Hite Morgan and his wife Dorinda of Guild Music Publishing. The Morgans were impressed and encouraged the boys to come back when they had original material. Brian spent the next few days plunking out tunes on his pi-ano, but nothing clicked until one of his brothers made a suggestion. "Dennis told me surfing was popular and why didn't I write some songs about it?" re-calls Brian.[20]

Even though Dennis was the only member of the group who surfed, Brian and Mike were intrigued by the idea. "I began noodling around the piano, sing-ing 'surfin', surfin', surfin',"" recalls Brian. "It sounded stupid, but then Mike sang 'bom-bom-dip-di-dip.' He was fooling around trying to spark a new idea with the same bass sounds he'd sung countless times." Brian worked out a simple mel-ody and basic harmonies, while Mike chimed in with lyrics. They titled the song "Surfin'." To reinforce the image, Brian and his bandmates decided to call themselves the Pendletones, inspired by the Pendleton woolen shirt worn by surfers on chilly nights.[21]

Armed with an original song and a new name, they returned to Guild Pub-lishing and auditioned "Surfin'." The Morgans loved it and arranged a recording session. The demo was sold to Candix Records, which changed the group's name to the Beach Boys and released "Surfin'" as a single in 1961. Initially, the record went nowhere, but when it was reissued in early 1962 it climbed to number 75 on the pop charts. Sales were good enough for Candix to ask for a follow-up. Brian quickly wrote and taped several new songs, but Candix passed on all of them. Undaunted, Murry Wilson sold the demos to Capitol Records. Two of the songs, "Surfin' Safari" and "409," were then released as the group's first single on their new label.[22]

Both sides of the record attracted young listeners. "Surfin' Safari," cowrit-ten by Brian Wilson and Mike Love, reached number 14. The flip side, "409" (a car song composed by Brian and Gary Usher), also charted. The songs estab-lished the Beach Boys' formula for success. Their distinctive sound featured tight harmonies, solid rock & roll beats, and lyrics about surfing, cars, and California youth culture. Although the group set out to make records about teenage inter-ests, their music ultimately tapped into one of America's most enduring myths—the legendary American West. This time around the California Dream did not include prospectors seeking gold or brave pioneers hoping for a better life. Instead, it showcased teenagers on a quest for eternal happiness, romance, and adventure in the warm California sun. Brian created "a whole world at the piano," insists

Carl. "There was an awe connected to California and the way we lived. But, it wasn't the real California so much as the California in Brian's songs."[23]

By the time "Surfin' Safari" peaked on the Top 20 charts on October 13, 1962, the Beach Boys had sparked a national surf music craze and were one of the hottest groups in the country. Capitol Records rushed them into the studio to record their first album. Entitled *Surfin' Safari* to capitalize on their hit, it debuted on *Billboard*'s Top Pop Albums chart on November 24. The picture on the front cover was worth way more than a thousand words. The five Beach Boys in all their iconic glory look like rock & roll versions of the Lewis and Clark expedition. Dressed in matching blue-plaid Pendleton board shirts and perched on a woody, the intrepid rock & rollers peer out at the Pacific Ocean. Behind them is the jagged California coast. In front is the deep blue ocean with an endless horizon. One member of the group sits on the woody's hood and points out to sea. His bandmates are mesmerized by the sight. Two of them sit on top of the vehicle, clutching a surfboard as they look westward. The others sit below, also fixated on the possibilities that lie ahead. The message is clear: the perfect wave if not eternal happiness and adventure can be found in California and the West.

The back of the album cover introduces this unusual group. Photographs at the bottom depict band members singing and playing instruments. Unlike most rock & rollers of the early 1960s, these guys do not have their hair slicked back in pompadours and aren't wearing coats and ties or fancy sweaters. In keeping with the casual California lifestyle, their hair is windswept and they're wearing T-shirts or loose-fitting plaid shirts, baggy pants, and either sandals or loafers with no socks. The liner notes at the top explain: "Here, then . . . are the rockin', rollin' kids who have made the biggest splash along the Pacific shores since the sport of surfing was discovered . . . The dynamic Beach Boys!"[24]

The album was a creative mix of surf music, classic rock & roll, doo-wop, and pop, powered by electrifying guitar licks, solid beats, and inspired harmonies. The twelve tracks mapped out the musical terrain the Beach Boys would explore over the next several years. There were songs about surfing, cars, and other teenage interests. Regardless of subject, the subtext was always young

surfin' safari
THE BEACH BOYS
SURFIN' SAFARI • 409 • SURFIN' • SUMMERTIME BLUES • COUNTY FAIR
HEADS YOU WIN - TAILS I LOSE • CUCKOO CLOCK • MOON DAWG
THE SHIFT • TEN LITTLE INDIANS • CHUG-A-LUG • LITTLE MISS AMERICA

Beach Boys' first album, 1962 (Richard Aquila Collection)

love—with a hint of sex. That was the reason for going on a surfin' safari, driving a car with a big 409 engine, or winning a stuffed toy for a girl at the county fair.

The Beach Boys' next single, released in the spring of 1963, adhered to the formula that earned them their first two-sided hit. A song about surfing ("Surfin' U.S.A.") was the A-side, backed with a song about cars ("Shut Down"). "Surfin' U.S.A." shot up to number 3 and established the group's signature sound. "We developed a stylish sound, the high sound became our sound," explains Brian. "It was the first time we had ever sung our voices twice on one record . . . Sing it once, then sing it again over that, so both sounds are perfectly synchronized. This makes it much brighter and gives it a rather . . . magical sound without using echo chambers. It makes it sound spectacular, so much power."[25]

"Surfin' U.S.A." blended Four Freshmen–style pop harmonies with classic rock & roll. When Brian was composing the song, he kept humming the tune to a Chuck Berry hit from 1958. "I thought to myself, 'what about trying to put surf lyrics to the "Sweet Little Sixteen" melody,'" explains Brian. The record's concept was similar to Chubby Checker's "Twistin' U.S.A.," says Brian, because "they're doing this in this city, they're doing that in that city." So, he called the song "Surfin' U.S.A." The Beach Boys' record became a rock & roll anthem that glorified the new sport and transformed youth culture and the California Dream. Suddenly, teenagers across America began wearing baggies, clam diggers, sandals, and bushy blond hairdos. And, they longed to be surfing in exotic California from Santa Cruz to Doheny way. Thanks to the Beach Boys, baby boomers and other music fans discovered a new path to eternal happiness in the mythic West. "Everybody's gone surfin'," sing the Beach Boys, "surfin' U.S.A."[26]

The record's flip side, "Shut Down," made it clear that the Beach Boys weren't just a surf band. Cowritten by Brian Wilson and local deejay Roger Christian, the fast-paced song transports listeners to a drag race between a super-stock Dodge Dart with a 413 engine and a fuel-injected Sting Ray driven by the song's hero. It begins on a lonely California road. Both cars rev up their engines and at the count of one they accelerate. The 413 takes the lead, but the Sting Ray driver remains cool. When he power shifts, the Sting Ray blasts forward and closes the gap. The Dodge Dart is hot, admits the Sting Ray driver, but his fuel-injected engine is hotter. In a flash, the race is over. The victorious Sting Ray driver then trash-talks his opponent, telling him to shut off his engine because "I shut you down."[27]

When the hot-rod song made it to number 23, it expanded the Beach Boys' appeal and their musical vision of the California Dream. Their mythic West included not only surfing and pretty girls on the beach, but also a red-hot California car culture. Young listeners loved the solid rocker, the frenetic beat, and the hip slang about drag racing. "People liked the competitive lyrics," explains Brian. "We were born and raised around Los Angeles . . . where I had access to a lot of the current word jargon . . . and I used it in my lyrics."[28]

In the spring of 1963 Capitol Records released the Beach Boys' second album, which shot up to number 2. Although the 12 songs covered the same subjects found on earlier Beach Boy records, they demonstrated that the group's sound and style were evolving. "This album showcased our voices," explains

Brian. "We were just kids, but we were serious about our craft." The album marked Brian's arrival as the group's undisputed leader. He took charge of writing, selecting, producing, and arranging all the songs. Boldly going where no one had gone before in rock & roll history, Brian had total control of the Beach Boys' records. His main adviser was Chuck Britz, the recording engineer on most of the group's records made between 1963 and 1966. "Britz was the person in the booth that Brian trusted to help him make the records that were in his head," notes music writer David Leaf.[29]

One of the most important musical developments that occurred on the *Surfin' USA* album involved Brian's falsetto. He began rethinking his harmonic approach after he heard Frankie Valli singing lead on 4 Seasons' hits like "Sherry" (1962). "In the early '60s the 4 Seasons were my favorite group," says Brian. Their fantastic harmonies and excellent records inspired Brian. "I went to the piano thinking I could top their music," he explains. Picking up on the 4 Seasons' approach, Brian began experimenting with his own high voice. He introduced his falsetto on the album's title song, "Surfin' U.S.A." Although Mike Love sings lead, Brian's distinct falsetto in the refrain is what captures the listener's ear.[30]

Brian's falsetto took center stage on three other album tracks that moved the Beach Boys' sound in new directions. "'Farmer's Daughter' was my first chance to fully prove I had a good falsetto voice," says Brian. His expressive falsetto also powered "Lana," an infectious rocker about perfect love and eternal bliss in the mythic West. The young guy in the song implores the lovely Lana to join him in a faraway, heavenly land that promises happiness, silver, and gold. Another track, "Lonely Sea," takes listeners to a totally different place. It opens with Brian's plaintive falsetto, foreshadowing trouble ahead. Like legendary '49ers who headed west with "California or bust" written on the sides of their Conestogas, Brian and his bandmates come face-to-face with the realization that the West has the potential to crush their hopes and dreams. "Lonely Sea" features an uncaring Pacific Ocean that never stops for anything or anybody in its path. Brian's emotional vocal makes it clear that the girl of his dreams—like the lonely sea—eventually will move along. In contrast to most Beach Boy songs, which celebrated the mythic West, "The Lonely Sea" offers a glimpse of the dark side of the California Dream.[31]

The *Surfin' USA* album shows that the Beach Boys' music was evolving. Carl Wilson's creative guitar licks, influenced by both Chuck Berry and Dick Dale, energized songs such as "Shut Down," "Lana," and "Surfin' U.S.A." Other tracks introduced new sounds to the group's repertoire. A happy organ was featured on "Surfin' U.S.A." A honking sax added to the frenetic pace of "Shut Down." A driving piano set the tempo for "Lana" and "Finders Keepers." A xylophone popped up on "Noble Surfer." Five of the twelve songs were instrumentals that showcased the band's musical talents. With lead guitarist Carl pointing the way, the Beach Boys covered Dick Dale's "Let's Go Trippin'" and "Misirlou." They also did two original instrumentals, "Stoked" (written by Brian) and "Surf Jam" (by Carl).

In the summer of 1963 the Beach Boys released their next single, which followed the same surf song/car song formula used on their previous two-sided hits. "Surfer Girl" made it all the way to number 7, while "Little Deuce Coupe" peaked at number 15. "Surfer Girl" offered an innovative approach to surf music. Unlike their previous up-tempo hits about the sport, this one was a slow ballad that captured the feel of teenage love and California surf culture. "The melody was sweet and had a little rise and fall like waves," explains composer Brian Wilson.[32] The song underscored the strong connection between the Beach Boys' version of the California Dream and the mythic American West. The wistful ode to a beautiful girl on the beach was almost a mystical experience. The striking lyrical images and soft harmonies allowed listeners to imagine her lovely face, sun-tanned body, and long hair blowing gently in the ocean breeze. The emotional impact connected the song to the mythic notion that eternal happiness could be found in the fabled lands of the West. At the same time, "Surfer Girl" offered a fresh take on the old myth. It tapped into the post–World War II emphasis on California, as well as the nation's burgeoning consumer culture. The surfing craze was a perfect new product for adolescents seeking fun and romance on sunny California beaches.

The flip side of the "Surfer Girl" record, "Little Deuce Coupe," demonstrated that cars were an integral part of the California Dream. Car songs were not new to rock & roll, but the Beach Boys showcased a new California car culture that linked perfect machines to idyllic life in the Golden State. They made it clear that bold guys, hot women, and fast cars equaled fun in the California sun. "Little Deuce Coupe" begins with a disclaimer by lead singer Mike Love. He's not bragging, he tells his girl, *but* he's got the fastest car in town. Mike proves size does matter, as he describes his car's big engine and other attributes. He tells her she doesn't realize the equipment he's got. Using catchphrases and words known only to car enthusiasts, he explains his powerful car has a "flat head mill" and "lake pipes." "There's one more thing," he says, "I got the pink slip, daddy."[33]

Many young listeners had no clue what the Beach Boys were singing about. Obviously, it was about a fast car, but what exactly was a "deuce coupe," and what the heck was a "pink slip"? Roger Christian, who cowrote the song with Brian, explained that the song was about a 1932 Ford coupe (called a "deuce" because of the 2 in the model year). "Everyone wanted one because deuce coupes had great lines, and you could make street rods out of them," he notes. "If you saw *American Graffiti*, you saw a beauty. The yellow hot rod . . . That was a deuce coupe." Brian made one change in Christian's lyrics. He added the line about the "pink slip" to make the song more California-specific. Many teenagers across the country assumed it was a decorative part on the car. However, music writers Bob Shannon and John Javna point out, "In California, the pink slip is the ownership paper." Even though most listeners didn't understand the nuances about pink slips or 1932 Ford deuces, they knew instantly that "Little Deuce Coupe" was a very cool-sounding song about a hot car.[34]

The Beach Boys rode a creative wave throughout the rest of 1963. Their new *Surfer Girl* album released in the fall climbed all the way to number 7. They also scored another two-sided hit with songs aimed at teenagers: the raucous high school anthem "Be True to Your School," and the introspective "In My Room." The latter, written by Brian Wilson and Gary Usher, underscores the authenticity of the Beach Boys' music. They weren't just singing contrived pop songs about youth culture. Their music echoed their own experiences, which gave it a folk quality. Brian later explained the story behind "In My Room." As kids, the Wilson brothers shared the same bedroom. "One night I sang the song 'Ivory Tower' to them and they liked it," recalls Brian. "I proceeded to teach them . . . how to sing the harmony parts to it . . . We then sang this song night after night. It brought peace to us." Later, when they recorded "In My Room," it was just Brian, Dennis, and Carl singing on the first verse. "We sounded just like we did in our bedroom all those nights," says Brian.[35]

The Beach Boys' sound and style were a perfect fit for the upbeat mood of Kennedy's America. Then, everything suddenly changed. On November 22, 1963, a CBS special bulletin interrupted the popular TV soap opera *As the World Turns*. "Three shots were fired at President Kennedy's motorcade in downtown Dallas," reported Walter Cronkite. "The first reports say that President Kennedy has been seriously wounded." As a nation waited in horror, the news grew darker. Finally, Cronkite returned with a somber update: "President Kennedy died at 1 p.m. Central Standard Time—2 o'clock Eastern Standard Time—some 38 minutes ago."[36]

The nightmarish reality of the young president's assassination unleashed forces that eventually would overwhelm the optimism of early 60s America, as well as the innocence of the baby boom generation. "When the shooting happened," said Brian, "I called Mike and he asked me if I wanted to write a song about it. I said sure. It seemed like something we had to think about, and songs were the way I thought about things." It took just 45 minutes to write "The Warmth of the Sun," which was released in early 1964. "Some of the best songs come pretty quick," says Brian. "They're the most divinely inspired." The pensive ballad never mentions JFK or the assassination directly. Instead, it uses teenage heartbreak as a metaphor. Brian's aching falsetto and the group's soothing harmonies assured young listeners there's always hope. "The melody was so haunting, sad, melancholy, that the only thing that I could think of lyrically was the loss of love," explains Mike Love. "I wanted to have a silver lining on that cloud so I wrote the lyrics from the perspective of, 'Yes, things have changed and love is no longer there, but the memory of it lingers like the warmth of the sun.'"[37]

As a nation mourned the death of a young president, the Beatles (who were the hottest rock group in the United Kingdom) began getting airplay on American radio. Significantly, prior to 1964, no British group or artist had ever achieved sustained success in American rock & roll. The Beatles' "I Want to Hold Your Hand" debuted on the *Billboard* charts on January 18, 1964. By February 1, it was the number 1 hit in the United States. Before the year was out the Beatles racked up fourteen more Top 20 hits, including five additional number 1 records. Their phenomenal success threw open the doors of the American pop charts to other British groups, including the Dave Clark Five, Searchers, and Rolling Stones. These British performers found success on the US charts because they offered fresh sounds, distinctive styles, and alternative fashions for American youths desperate for a new beginning.

While many American rock & rollers were overwhelmed by the British Rock Invasion, the Beach Boys withstood the onslaught. Like the Beatles, Brian Wilson and his bandmates had a sound, style, and look that fit the times. Both groups produced excellent rock & roll records that offered listeners hope in the midst of despair. The Beatles boasted the songwriting talents of Lennon and McCartney, but the Beach Boys had Brian Wilson—singer, songwriter, arranger, and producer extraordinaire. While the Beatles promoted new hairstyles, different fashions, and a novel style associated with a foreign land, the Beach Boys countered with an appealing casual look and fresh California sound.

Even though the Beatles offered an intriguing alternative for American youth seeking literal or figurative escape from the nation's troubles, the Beach Boys' rock & roll version of the California Dream was hard to beat. After all, the image of the West as a land of happiness, hope, and rejuvenation was firmly entrenched in the American mind. Both before and after Kennedy's assassination, the quickest route to the California Dream was through the Beach Boys' music. Not only did their utopian vision of California and the West resonate with young listeners seeking escape and hope after November 22, 1963, but the Beach Boys' sound was as fresh as ever. Equally important, the group was determined to defend American rock & roll against the Beatles.

Brian Wilson and his bandmates had always been competitive, as evidenced by their songs about drag racing, high school rivalries, and surfing. The Beach Boys even took on rival rock & roll groups. "Surfers Rule," a track on their 1963 album *Surfer Girl*, featured the California group bragging that their surf sound trumped the music of their East Coast rivals, the 4 Seasons. In the last verse Mike Love proclaims, "surfers rule," as the rest of the group chimes in with "4 Seasons, you better believe it." Brian then unleashes an hilarious falsetto that mimics Frankie Valli's voice on "Walk Like a Man." The Jersey boys got revenge by whacking a surfer girl on their next album. "No Surfin' Today," written by Bob

Gaudio and Bob Crewe, showcased the 4 Seasons singing about a none-too-bright surfer girl who ignores a warning sign and paddles out into the stormy ocean. Copying the Beach Boys' harmony style, the four Jersey boys sing with mock sadness about the deadly undertow that drags the surfer girl to her death.[38]

The Beach Boys viewed the Beatles as a bigger threat. "The Beatles invasion shook me up an awfully lot," admits Brian. "They eclipsed a lot of what we'd worked for." He and Mike Love huddled together and wrote a bold song that proved the Beach Boys were not about to surrender to either the Beatles or the post-JFK assassination malaise that overwhelmed America's youth culture. They came out fighting with "Fun, Fun, Fun," which debuted on the *Billboard* charts on February 15, 1964, just one week after the Fab Four landed in New York City.[39] Young audiences loved the song's in-your-face title, funny lyrics, and high-octane sound. The record begins with Carl Wilson playing lively Chuck Berry-style guitar licks. Mike Love's urgent lead vocal then kicks in, backed by Brian's remarkable falsetto and the group's signature harmonies. The teenage tale focuses on a beautiful young woman racing around town in her Daddy's Thunderbird when she's supposed to be in the library. When her father realizes what she's been up to, he takes back the car keys. But the pleasure-seeking girl won't be denied. She quickly accepts a boy's invitation to drive her around town so they can have "fun, fun, fun now that daddy took the T-bird away." The number 5 hit offered high schoolers everything they wanted: romance, fast cars, and guys coming to the rescue of pretty girls, enhanced by a victory over parents.[40]

The Beach Boys' familiar harmonies and quality records helped baby boomers cope in the months after Kennedy's death. "Don't Worry, Baby," a Top 30 hit in the spring of 1964, assured listeners that love could get them through difficult times and protect them from danger. The aching beauty of Brian's lead vocal was pure catharsis. It even affected the Beach Boys in the recording studio. "My high voice made them all cry," recalled Brian years later. "I was singin', sweetly and lovingly, a lyric that was about racing my car . . . I always overlooked the irony of it and got to the heart of it."[41]

The Beach Boys' creative mix of teen interests and sunny images of California led young people out of the darkness after JFK's death. As the first high school class of baby boomers was about to graduate in the spring of 1964, the

Beach Boys scored a number 1 hit with "I Get Around," an upbeat car song about teenagers looking for fun cruising up and down California streets. The group capped off 1964 with an album, *All Summer Long*, that included optimistic songs about surfing, cars, and romance. The last track on the album, "Don't Back Down," offered hope for the future. The song spotlights surfers riding huge waves. Suddenly, a twenty-foot wave appears and "slaps them upside the head [but] they're not afraid," sing the Beach Boys, "not my boys." The surfers just try harder. The optimistic message was clear to young listeners. When trouble appears out of nowhere—whether it's huge waves, broken hearts, or something worse—they can survive as long as they "don't back down."[42]

After 1964 the Beach Boys, like the heroic surfers they sang about, would ride perfect waves until they wiped out. But, they'd never back down. They scored two Top 10 hits in 1965: the bouncy "Help Me Ronda" reached number 1, while "California Girls," which picked up on the notion that perfection could be found out West, made it to number 3.

The Beach Boys' creativity peaked in 1966. Their *Pet Sounds* album debuted on the charts on May 28 and was the group's most sophisticated album to date. Most of the songs were written or cowritten by Brian, who arranged and produced the album. The music was unlike anything the Beach Boys had done before. Their garage band style gave way to more complicated orchestral arrangements, unusual chord sequences, and a variety of new instruments, including violins, flutes, harpsichords, and timpani. Other sounds such as sleigh bells, trains, and barking dogs were tossed into the mix. Gone were upbeat songs about surfing and cars. In their place were slower, more introspective songs. Although many fans were disappointed by the new direction, most music critics and musicians were impressed. "No one is educated musically 'til they've heard that album," insists Paul McCartney. He was particularly intrigued by Brian's melodic bass lines: "That I think was probably the big influence that set me thinking when we recorded [*Sgt.*] *Pepper.*"[43]

A few months after *Pet Sounds* was released the Beach Boys recorded what many consider to be their greatest song, "Good Vibrations" (1966). Just as Brian Wilson's early work reflected surfing, cars, romance, and other teenage interests of the early 60s, "Good Vibrations" mirrored the rise of the counterculture later in the decade. Tapping into psychedelic trends and more sophisticated rock sounds, the incredible song was unlike anything the Beach Boys or anyone else had ever done before. Each movement of the rock & roll mini symphony took listeners on a strange new musical experience, guided by the group's familiar voices set against innovative sounds. During the recording session, Brian incorporated a weird-sounding instrument that he recalled hearing as a kid. "One of my uncles had a Theremin," he explains, "the kind that you hold like a crystal ball. You move your hand up and down and it makes a sound: oOoOooOo."[44]

Mike Love initially didn't know how to write lyrics for Brian's avant-garde music. "Our fans are used to hearing 'Fun, Fun, Fun' . . . and 'Surfin' USA,'" he thought. "How are they going to take this sound?" Mike realized he had to connect "Good Vibrations" to something listeners could relate to, so he framed the lyrics around a romantic relationship. "It was 1966 and there was that whole hippie thing going on," explains Mike, "so I wrote the lyrics as a poem about a girl who's all into peace, love and flower power: 'I love the colorful clothes she wears and the way the sunlight plays upon her hair.'"[45]

The innovative record, which Brian Wilson calls "my single-song production masterpiece," rocketed up to number 1 and remained on the Top 40 charts for 14 weeks. Shortly after its run ended in early 1967, bad vibrations hit both the Beach Boys and America. Between 1967 and 1974 the nation came apart at the seams as the public became polarized over the Vietnam War, urban riots, the counterculture, campus protests, civil rights marches, assassinations, feminism, Watergate, and various culture wars. The Beach Boys were staggered by personal and professional problems. The constant touring and pressure that Brian felt to write brilliant new material led to an announcement in late 1964 that Bruce Johnston would replace Brian on tours. Bruce quickly became an integral part of the group not just on tours but also in the studio.

Brian ran into further problems when he, like many rock artists of the day, began experimenting with drugs and alcohol as a means to creativity. It did not end well. "I knew right from the start something was wrong," says Brian. "I'd taken some psychedelic drugs, and then about a week after that I started hearing voices, and they've never stopped." He struggled with the problem for years until he was finally diagnosed with schizoaffective disorder, a mental condition that includes hallucinations, paranoia, and other distortions of reality. Eventually, through therapy, Brian learned to live with the mental disorder, but the road back was not easy.[46]

With Brian reeling from personal problems and the nation caught up in political and social turmoil, the Beach Boys lost their way. Their optimistic music and connection to the innocence of Kennedy's America suddenly seemed terribly out of step with the troubled times. Between 1967 and 1974 the group managed only three Top 20 hits: "Heroes and Villains" (1967), "Darlin'" (1968), and "Do It Again" (1968). None cracked the Top 10, not even the nostalgic surf song "Do It Again."

Eventually, both the Beach Boys and America would bounce back when the horrors of the late 1960s and early 70s subsided. Interestingly, the group's comeback occurred in the summer of 1974 at approximately the same time that President Richard Nixon was brought down by the Watergate Scandal. By the time Nixon left the White House, most Americans felt disillusioned if not battered by all the political and cultural upheaval. Many baby boomers sought relief in *Endless Summer*, a double album of the Beach Boys' greatest hits from the early 1960s, which was released just a few weeks before the Watergate nightmare ended. The album skyrocketed to number 1 and remained on *Billboard*'s chart for an astounding 155 straight weeks. (To put this in perspective, the Beach Boys had not had a Top 10 album in eight years.)

The Beach Boys' triumphant return from the musical wilderness underscores their cultural significance. The hit album showcased ebullient teenage anthems from the early 1960s such as "Surfin' U.S.A.," "Fun, Fun, Fun," and others that offered escape from the troubles of the 1970s. The Beach Boys' familiar harmonies and rock & roll vision of the California Dream were a nostalgic balm for listeners who yearned for lost innocence and the promise of eternal happiness in the mythic West. Even the album title—*Endless Summer*—evoked the connection between the Beach Boys' California Dream and baby boomers' pursuit of happiness. The title recalled Bruce Brown's classic documentary, which followed two California surfers looking for the perfect wave. But, the Beach Boys' collection of early 60s hits led baby boomers on a much grander quest in search of an elusive utopia in the West of the American imagination.

The phenomenal success of *Endless Summer* guaranteed the Beach Boys' place in the rock & roll pantheon. Their California sound and songs about romance, surfing, cars, and early 60s youth culture became part of the rock music canon. Over the next several decades the Beach Boys would have problems both on and off stage. Brian experienced setbacks due to mental illness and drugs. Dennis suffered from substance abuse until his drowning in 1983. Carl, the youngest Wilson, held the group together until his death in 1998. But Mike Love, Al Jardine, Bruce Johnston, and eventually a reenergized Brian, kept the Beach Boys going through numerous recordings and live concerts. The Beach Boys retained their status as rock & roll icons not just for baby boomers, but for subsequent generations of young Americans who grew up listening to the group's cheerful oldies hits.

In 1988 the Beach Boys were inducted into the Rock & Roll Hall of Fame. In 2000 Brian entered the Songwriters Hall of Fame. And, in 2007 Brian Wilson was a recipient of the prestigious Kennedy Center Honor. "He is rock and roll's gentlest revolutionary," says the official statement. "There is real humanity in his body of work, vulnerable and sincere, authentic and unmistakably American."[47]

The Beach Boys came out of sunny California in the early 1960s and found everlasting fame with some of the most innovative songs in music history. But the Beach Boys' historical and cultural significance went beyond just hit records and albums. They became rock & roll troubadours for a new generation of teenagers who entered high school when John F. Kennedy became president. The group's songs and style captured the carefree spirit of the times and gave voice to the hopes and dreams of young listeners.

FUN IN THE WARM CALIFORNIA SUN

The coming of the Beach Boys in 1962 touched off surf music mania. Surf songs by other performers soon flooded onto the national and regional charts.[48] Liberty Records reissued the Mar-kets' regional hits from 1961, "Surfer's Stomp" and "Balboa Blue," and both made it onto the national pop charts in early 1962. Dick Dale and the Del-Tones followed up their path-breaking hit "Let's Go Trippin'" (1962), with a song destined to become one of surf music's all-time greatest instrumentals, "Miserlou." Although the song failed to chart nationally, it attracted considerable attention and raised the bar for surf music. In the early 60s it was covered by numerous bands, including the Beach Boys and Ventures.

"Miserlou" is "not a Greek folk song like everybody says. It's an Arabic song . . . an old Egyptian tune," explains Dick Dale. "As a child I used to listen to my uncle play it on a darbuka, an Arabic drum that you play with your hands." It was always played slowly so belly dancers could sway to it, he says. Dick's uncle "would have . . . little fingertip cymbals they'd play on the side, and you could hear them clicking." He'd then "play the oud, a stringed instrument plucked with a quill . . . and they'd go 'tickety tickety tang.'" That song, says Dale, "was the beginning of my lifestyle of picking that way [on a guitar]." But Dick made one important change—he speeded it up. "Originally, it was [very slow] and that was the belly-dancer rhythm," he explains. "Well, I took it and [said] 'I can't play that slow because it isn't . . . a fat, full sound.' So, I speeded it up and that made it real full."[49]

The surf music wave crested in 1963. The Beach Boys' spectacular success with "Surfin' U.S.A." and "Little Deuce Coupe" inspired other performers to record songs about surfing, cars, and California youth culture. Jan & Dean, two high school friends from southern California, were one of the most successful acts. Before Jan Berry teamed up with Dean Torrence, he and another high school buddy, Arnie Ginsberg, earned a Top 10 record with "Jennie Lee" (1958). When Jan & Arnie split up, Jan formed a duo with Dean. In 1959 Jan & Dean scored a Top 10 hit with the doo-wop influenced "Baby Talk." They followed up with other doo-wop records, including "Heart and Soul" (1961) and "Linda" (1963). "The doo-wop sound was huge in the '50s," explains Dean, "that was the music we were listening to as teenagers."[50]

Jan & Dean got involved with surf music because of the Beach Boys. "We were thrown together by buyers who were buying local acts to do hops and things like that," says Dean. "We saw what they were doing, and they were already aware of what we were doing, we just kind of enjoyed working with them." The two groups began hanging out and playing songs together on stage, which inspired Jan & Dean to try their hand at surf music. When Brian Wilson played them an early version of "Surfin' U.S.A.," the duo asked if they could record it. Brian refused, but offered them another surf song he was working on. "The basic structure was in place, maybe half the words," recalls Dean. "Brian [had] lost interest in it. He was concentrating on "Surfin' U.S.A.," which he wanted to finish for the Beach Boys. So he handed "Surf City" to us, and we recognized how good it was. We tweaked the words, then Jan went full bore on creating the best instrumental track he could. Brian liked Jan & Dean's approach and volun-

Jan & Dean (Courtesy of Dean Torrence)

teered to sing falsetto on the record. When Jan & Dean's "Surf City" was released in the early summer of 1963, it zoomed to number 1 on the charts.[51]

From that point on, Jan & Dean followed the Beach Boys' formula for success, singing about surfing, hot rods, and youth culture on the West Coast. Like the Beach Boys, the duo struck gold by tapping into the California Dream and eternal happiness in the mythic West. "Surf City" was followed by other surf hits like "Honolulu Lulu" (1963), "Ride the Wild Surf" (1964), and "Sidewalk Surfin'" (1964). Other records such as "Drag City" (1964), "Dead Man's Curve" (1964), and "The Little Old Lady (From Pasadena)" (1964) plugged into California car culture.

"Dead Man's Curve" became one of Jan & Dean's most important hits. The song about a drag race first appeared on their album *Drag City*, released in late 1963. A few months later the duo recorded a second version, which became a huge hit in early 1964. Produced and cowritten by Jan, the record opens ominously with horns, drums, and other instruments moving forward slowly like a funeral procession. Jan & Dean then relate a tragic tale about two guys who race down Sunset Boulevard toward a notorious bend in the road known as "Dead Man's Curve." Jan's character drives a superfast Sting Ray, while the guy who challenges him is in a hot Jaguar XKE. When the light at Sunset and Vine turns green the two cars take off. The Sting Ray grabs the lead. Faster and faster they go. As the screaming machines approach Doheny, the XKE begins to pass and the Sting Ray swerves. Just then, the two cars hit Dead Man's Curve. Listeners hear screeching tires and a crash. Suddenly, the song slows. The Sting Ray driver is in the hospital explaining what happened. When his fast car started to swerve, he saw his opponent slide into the curve: "I know I'll never forget that horrible sight," he tells the doctor. He learned the hard way that everyone was right— "won't come back from Dead Man's Curve." The song ends with Dean's piercing falsetto rising over the sound of screeching tires.[52]

Initially, Jan & Dean had reservations about "Dead Man's Curve." They and their record company feared that a song about a tragic drag race wouldn't appeal to a mass audience. So, they decided to showcase the song on the other side of the record, an upbeat tune about high school romance, which Jan had cowritten with Brian Wilson, Roger Christian, and Bob Norman. "'The New Girl in

School' was the intended A-side," explains Dean. "We figured if people thought 'Dead Man's Curve' was too morbid, we'd have something to fall back on." The duo was pleased when the record became a two-sided hit. "Dead Man's Curve" raced all the way up to number 8, while "New Girl" came in at number 37. Teenage listeners loved the up-tempo tale about a young guy who flips for a pretty girl who transfers into his high school. The catchy refrain features an exuberant falsetto soaring over irresistible doo-wop syllables: "papa-doo-ron-dey-ron-dey-ooh." "It was . . . the groove of the song," insists Dean. "To me that was your classic Brian Wilson-type song."[53]

After 1964 Jan & Dean managed only three more Top 30 hits: "You Really Know How to Hurt a Guy" (1965), "I Found a Girl" (1965), and "Popsicle" (1966). Then, tragedy struck. On April 12, 1966, Jan Berry was speeding down Sunset Boulevard in his Corvette Sting Ray just like the guy on Jan & Dean's morbid hit from two years earlier. Suddenly, Jan lost control and crashed into a parked truck, ironically just a few blocks away from the actual Dead Man's Curve. The 25-year-old singer never fully recovered from his extensive injuries, but he and Dean continued to perform until Jan's death in 2004.

Between 1959 and 1966 Jan & Dean were one of the most popular rock & roll acts around. They earned fourteen Top 40 hits, including one number 1 record, "Surf City." The duo's musical legacy was recognized in 2008 when "Dead Man's Curve" was inducted into the Grammy Hall of Fame. Despite the accomplishments, Jan was always underrated as a producer and arranger, says Dean, because most people only pay attention to a song's melody. "But the less obvious parts—that was Jan's genius." He adds, "Jan had a bunch of us working with him . . . myself, Lou Adler, Brian Wilson . . . But Jan was brilliant in taking . . . subtle things, recognizing how good they were, and putting them together to make a good record. We all worked as team, but Jan was the quarterback."[54]

Jan & Dean's hits about surfing, cars, teen lifestyles, and romance in sunny California struck a responsive chord with pleasure-seeking teenagers in Kennedy's America. After 1963 the duo was able to withstand the British Rock Invasion, partly because their fun-filled music—like the Beach Boys'—offered hope in the dark days after JFK's assassination. Young listeners could escape to "Surf City," "Drag City," and other rock & roll utopias in the mythic West. "It was all quite innocent," says Dean about the music he created with Jan. "We didn't mean to do it, but somehow it all worked."[55]

Two of the biggest surf hits of 1963 were instrumentals performed by teenage bands from southern California. The Chantays scored a number 4 hit with one of the top rock instrumentals of all time, "Pipeline." The story of how the five high school friends from Santa Ana, California, went from playing local teen dances to having a Top 10 hit just a few months later underscores the grassroots origins of surf music. The band was formed, says lead guitarist Bob Spickard, so he and his buddies could "make money and meet girls." Since they couldn't play instruments, they bought "how to" books and taught themselves the basics. One day, a friend from another band invited them to a scheduled gig in the San Bernardino Mountains. It'd be fun, he told them. They could even jam together. Most of the Chantays weren't old enough for a driver's license, so another friend drove them into the mountains. They got lost and wound up in a different town, where they stopped to talk to a young woman who was setting up a concession stand for a scheduled record hop. Bob Spickard and his bandmates volunteered to play music while everyone was arriving at the dance. She thought it was a great idea, since the local disc jockey still hadn't arrived. The Chantays quickly set up their instruments and started playing. By the time the deejay arrived, the hall was packed and everyone was enjoying the music. So he told the band to keep playing. "Before the evening ended, we wound up getting three different record offers," says Spickard. "We accepted one of them and recorded a demo." The guy who signed them sold the demo to Downey Records, a small Los Angeles label. Downey had them rerecord "Pipeline" in their studio and released it locally. "Before you knew it, phones were ringing off the hook," says Spickard, "and people were requesting the song."[56]

When Dot Records began distributing the record nationally in early 1963, it shot up to number 4 on the *Billboard* charts. The stunning instrumental begins with the cascading sound of an electric guitar, which captures the feel of a surfer shooting a curl. The fast-paced song powers forward with guitars, bass, electric piano, and drums taking listeners on a sonic journey riding huge waves off California's coast. Guitarists Bob Spickard and Brian Carman wrote the song when they were high school seniors. The title was inspired by a surf movie that Spickard and bass player Warren Waters saw at school. "We saw one of the Bruce Brown movies that showed the pipeline on the northern coast of Hawaii," explains Spickard, "and we thought 'Wow, that's a good name for our song.'"[57]

The Chantays made one important change when they rerecorded the song for Downey. "The original demo version . . . did not have the glissando, which is a characteristic part of the 'Pipeline' [hit version]," explains Spickard. "The glissando actually . . . was something we designed just prior to going into [the Downey studio]. They liked it, so we kept it. But, prior to that it had more of a Duane Eddy twang twang start, but not the glissando."[58]

Three months after the Chantays made their national debut, another teenage surf band from southern California hit the charts. The Surfaris scored a number 2 hit in the summer of 1963 with a wild instrumental called "Wipeout." The record opens with a crackling sound and weird voice saying "wipe out." Then comes a maniacal laugh followed by rolling drums. Electric guitars jump in, punctuated by pounding drums and crashing cymbals.

The fast-paced record was absolutely breathtaking. "'Wipe Out' was a concoction . . . it was just kind of thrown together," explains the band's saxophone player, Jim Pash. "Whenever we got lost for ideas, we just let [drummer] Ron Wilson play and let him carry the ball." Ron's inspiration for the song came from a drum cadence that he had recently composed for his high school marching band. "He simply speeded it up," says Pash. Even the bizarre voice that introduces the song was done on a whim. "The idea," says Pash, "was a surfer laughing at himself as he falls off his board wiping out." They created the memorable intro by having one of the band members break a piece of plywood over his knee close to the microphone. Their manager, Dale Smallin, then did what he called his "witch cackle." "Dale used to do it at parties and in elevators," explains Pash. "To hear a sound like that come out of this guy's body, it was . . . unnatural." Other bands have tried to imitate that laugh on their cover versions, he says, but "no one's been able to capture that crazy laugh."[59]

"Wipeout" turned out to be anything but for the Surfaris. Not only did the song become one of the most popular surf records of all time, but the flip side also became a hit in 1963. "Surfer Joe" developed a cult following thanks to the danceable beat and Ron Wilson's contagious lead vocal inspired by Buddy Holly's hiccupping style. The song revolves around a perfect California beach boy—a handsome guy with long blond hair, who rides a green surfboard and has a woody to match. This heroic surfer fits right in with other legends of the mythic West. Nobody can beat him when it comes to "hangin' five and walkin' the nose." Even a stint in the Marines can't stop him from shooting the curls. "Surfer Joe-o-oh," hiccups the lead vocalist in awe, "Go man go-o-oh."[60]

One 16-year-old never forgot the first time he heard "Surfer Joe." "A friend and I were hiking at night in New York's Allegheny State Park," he recalled. "Suddenly, we heard loud clomping—like a huge monster stomping through the woods. We realized the sound was coming from a nearby wooden pavilion. When we got closer we could hear music blasting out of speakers into the night. Turned out there was a dance going on inside, and kids were doing the surfer's stomp to a song called 'Surfer Joe,' which the deejay kept playing over and over and over again."[61] That teenager's experience shows that surf music and California beach culture had even penetrated the mountains of rural New York State by the summer of 1963.

Songs like "Surfer Joe" and "Wipeout" are evidence of the close ties between surf music and the era's youth culture. Surf music was the authentic sound of California beach culture, suggests the Surfaris' Jim Pash. "It's an indigenous southern California folk music that's a subset of instrumental rock & roll," he explains. "There's no question about it. When surf music tunes are played, it invokes southern California . . . at least the fantasy of what southern California looks like." Pash adds, "I didn't consider any of it rebellious."[62] Surf music was simply a new take on the California Dream and traditional images of the mythic West.

Although other California bands weren't as successful as the Surfaris and Chantays, their instrumental surf records also made the national pop charts in 1963. Jack Nitzsche, the arranger who helped create Phil Spector's Wall of Sound, earned a Top 40 hit with the majestic "The Lonely Surfer." It was joined on the charts by other topnotch surf instrumentals, including the Astronauts' "Baja" and the Rumblers' "Boss."[63]

* * *

One of the more striking things about early 60s surf music is that it was performed almost exclusively by white males. Exceptions were few and far between. Annette Funicello, who costarred with Frankie Avalon in beach party movies, found moderate success in 1963 with an album entitled *Annette's Beach Party*, which included songs like "Swingin' and Surfin'" and "Secret Surfin' Spot." The Allisons (a.k.a. Darlene Love and the Blossoms) earned a minor hit with "Surfer Street" (1963), which actually had nothing to do with surfing. Other minor hits included King Curtis's R&B rock instrumental "Beach Party," (1962) and Chubby Checker's "Surf Party" (1963). In the midst of those derivative surf songs, "there was exactly one black musician who made a mark in the swelling surf music scene. It was [Will] Glover," insists music writer Jim Washburn. Glover's band, the Pyramids, "was one of the prime movers in Southern California music. Their tough-sounding instrumental, 'Penetration,' reached No. 18 on the national charts in early 1964 despite having to compete against the first wave of the British Invasion."[64]

Surf music lacked diversity even though most other rock & roll styles of the early 1960s were offering increasing opportunities for women and people of color. The paucity of women surf artists was probably an offshoot of gender stereotypes in Kennedy's America. In the early 60s males were typically viewed as smarter, stronger, braver, and more athletic than females. Boys could surf with abandon while girls were expected to stay on the beach and look cute in bikinis as they cheered on boyfriends and protected their bouffant hairdos from ocean waves. Male surfers echoed the era's sexism. "Girls do fine when it comes to housework, raising children, doing office work, doing the Twist and even riding the ankle snappers at Malibu," said surf pioneer Buzzy Trent in a 1963 issue of *Surf Guide* magazine. But, girls lacked the ability to ride big waves. "You see, girls are much more emotional than men . . . and panic can be extremely dangerous in big surf . . . Girls are weaker than men and have a lesser chance for survival in giant wipeouts." He added, "Girls are intended to be feminine, and big-wave riding is definitely masculine."[65]

Trying to figure out why there were so few African Americans performing surf music is more problematic. Complex social, cultural, and economic factors undoubtedly came into play. For example, the Ku Klux Klan was popular in southern California in the 1920s and racist attitudes and de facto segregation were still common in the early 60s. In addition, racial tensions and prejudice in Kennedy's America probably made record companies reluctant to sign Black surf artists. Whatever the reason, the result was the same. Surf music was played almost entirely by white artists. "Surf music and the beach bands that played it, together with the California, surfing, and corporate promoters, enshrined the image that, in large measure, has defined Southern California in the popular imagination, a freewheeling paradise of young, golden-bronzed bodies with sun-bleached blonde manes, a place where whiteness was taken for granted," explains historian John J. Bukowczyk.[66]

Ironically, some Black surfers were integrating California beaches in the early 1960s. Tony Corley, who founded the Black Surfing Association, wrote a letter to *Surfer* magazine in 1974 stating: "Fear not, other surfing brothers, Mother Ocean knows no prejudices."[67] Even though there were more than a few Black surfers on California beaches, that reality never came through in surf music, movies, or other popular media.

The notion that surf music was the domain of white musicians aligned with images of the mythic West that celebrated heroic white males like Kit Carson, Wild Bill Hickok, and Buffalo Bill Cody. From early Western novels like Owen Wister's *The Virginian* (1902) to later movies such as *The Searchers* (1956) and *How the West Was Won* (1962), the hero was typically a brave white Anglo-Saxon cowboy, gunslinger, soldier, or scout. Arguably, the California "big beach blondie" on the Surfaris' "Surfer Joe" (1963) was cut from the same cloth as other legendary Western heroes. He is a bold man of action whose uncanny abilities and sheer determination enable him to triumph over rivals and nature. "Surfer Joe, go man go," sings the Surfaris' lead vocalist in awe.[68]

In the days after President Kennedy's assassination the upbeat sounds of surf music provided comfort and escape for many young listeners. As 1963 came to a close a garage band from Minnesota released what may be the weirdest surf record of all time. The Trashmen's "Surfin' Bird" peaked at number 4 on the charts in early 1964. The song featured a highly amplified staccato lead vocal, which managed to parody both the surfing craze and two minor R&B rock hits by the Rivingtons, "Papa-Oom-Mow-Mow" and "The Bird's the Word." One of the Trashmen, Tony Andreason, recalls the song's origin. The group was waiting backstage to play at a dance. Lead singer Steve Wahrer started fooling around singing "papa-oom-mow-mow" in a strange voice. "The more he did it, the more we laughed and the more we got into it," recalls Tony. The group decided to play the bizarre song on stage. The audience loved it, so the Trashmen kept playing it. Afterward, a deejay told them "You've got to record that. That is a hit. It's the weirdest thing I've ever heard." Soon after, they recorded it in the studio. The Trashmen were just starting to play surf music at the time, so they decided to call the record "Surfin' Bird."[69]

The success of the surreal "Surfin' Bird" demonstrates that surf music was still a draw in early 1964, but the parody foreshadowed the beginning of the end for the genre. By the time 1964 was over, surf music's popularity had faded. Other than "Surfin' Bird" (which actually didn't deal with surfing), only five songs about surfing made the Top 40 charts. Jan & Dean found success with "Sidewalk Surfin'" and "Ride the Wild Surf." In addition, there were three excellent surf instrumentals. The Marketts scored a Top 10 hit with "Out of Limits," based on the theme from Rod Serling's *The Twilight Zone*. The Ventures cracked the Top 10 with "Walk Don't Run '64," a surf music version of their 1960 hit. And, the Pyramids scored a Top 20 hit with "Penetration."

As surf music ebbed in 1964 the focus shifted to California's car culture. Along with the numerous hits by the Beach Boys and Jan &Dean, there were popular car songs such as Ronny & the Daytonas' "G.T.O." and the Rip Chords' "Hey Little Cobra," as well as one record about a "groovy little motor bike"—the Hondell's cover of the Beach Boys' "Little Honda."

Other records spotlighted California's legendary beach culture.[70] The Rivieras made it all the way to number 5 with their high-energy hit "California Sun" (1964). The song was originally recorded in 1961 by R&B rocker Joe Jones, but it stalled at number 89. Jones's subdued vocal backed by a plodding New Orleans horn section never gained traction on Top 40 radio. But "California Sun" became a rock & roll anthem when it was redone by the Rivieras, a garage band from South Bend, Indiana. They energized Jones's song by speeding up the pace and substituting electric guitars and a lively organ for the honking saxes on the original. Lead singer Marty Fortson's dynamic vocal added a sense of urgency to the quest for a teenage utopia in the mythic West. The Rivieras' upbeat version, released shortly after President Kennedy's assassination, offered escape and hope to baby boomers in desperate need of a new beginning. The record begins explosively with banging drums and the electrifying sounds of guitars and a spirited organ. Fortson then declares boldly that he's heading west where he belongs "where the days are short and the nights are long." A perfect life awaits in a legendary land where frisky girls and eager guys have never-ending fun doing the Twist, the shimmy, the fly, and other dances. As the song rushes to a climax, the lead singer captures the beach culture and youthful desire to find happiness in the mythic West: "Yeah, they're out there a-havin' fun in that warm California sun."[71]

After 1964 the initial surf music craze was all but over. Musical tastes changed rapidly after the Beatles and other British rock artists arrived on the scene. The Chantays, for example, had a rough time trying to follow up on their number 4 hit "Pipeline." "Our timing wasn't good," admits guitarist Bob Spickard. "After the Beatles hit, it was really hard to get work without doing just all English-type material. Surf music, unfortunately, did not have an opportunity to run its full cycle."[72]

The situation worsened as the 1960s spilled over into the 70s, and the nation was staggered by the Vietnam War, campus protests, urban riots, the counterculture, and more. The upbeat sounds of surf music were out of sync with the dark mood of a country wracked by chaos, violence, and despair. The changing times caused many surf bands to call it quits. The Trashmen, who gained notoriety with "Surfin' Bird," hung up their rock & roll shoes in 1967. "We saw the writing on the wall," explains guitarist Dal Winslow. "Vietnam was in full swing, rock music was going more psychedelic and getting more serious. It wasn't really our scene anymore."[73]

In 1965 only one song about surfing cracked the Top 40: the Tradewinds' depressing "New York's a Lonely Town." The record, which peaked at number 32, focused on a California surfer now living in New York City. He feels out of place walking down Broadway, complains that no one cares about surfing, and hates the sight of his woody covered with snow. "New York's a lonely town," he laments, "when you're the only surfer boy around."[74]

The Tradewinds' downbeat song is a good metaphor for surf music's decline after 1964. But if surf music was down, it was not out. Numerous surf bands continued to record and tour in the mid-1960s and beyond. The Beach Boys found success with nostalgic surf songs such as "Do It Again" (1968), as well as their greatest hits album *Endless Summer* (1974). Surf music was further energized in the late 1970s and 80s by the Ramones, Forgotten Rebels, and other bands that blended punk with surf rock. Surf music's popularity soared even higher when Quentin Tarantino showcased Dick Dale and the Del-Tones' "Miserlou" and other classic surf instrumentals in his 1994 film *Pulp Fiction*. The soundtrack sparked a surf music renaissance, resulting in a new wave of surf bands such as the Eliminators, Ghastly Ones, Surfrajettes, and Susan & the Surftones. The continuing popularity of surf music suggests that the elusive California Dream lives on.

SUMMER'S GONE

Surf music proved to be one of rock & roll's most innovative and enduring styles. It featured creative harmonies, solid rock & roll beats, and path-breaking sounds that made use of improved guitars, whammy bars, powerful amplifiers, and state-of-the-art recording technology. But surf music's importance isn't just about the quality of records. The music yields fresh evidence about life and thought in Kennedy's America.

The emergence of surf music in the early 1960s is linked to the rising importance of California and the West after World War II. In the post-war period, the West experienced cultural and economic boom times, which inspired millions of Americans to pack up their old lives, jump in cars, and head west on new interstate highways in search of the American Dream. In 1963 journalist Neil Morgan published *Westward Tilt: The American West Today*, which surveyed the West's past, present, and future. "The West," he said, "is the most dynamic region of America today." Surf music peaked in popularity the same year that *Westward Tilt* was published. Morgan's description of the West could just as easily be applied to the new rock & roll sound: "Young and eager, cocky and eternally hopeful, the West seethes with the spirit of why not?"[75]

The upbeat songs about surfing, cars, and youth culture reflect the optimistic mood of Kennedy's America. As the nation celebrated a charismatic, young president and anticipated an American Century that promised peace, prosperity, and the pursuit of happiness, many white, middle-class teenagers embraced surf music. The new California youth culture was a perfect fit for an era that prided itself on having fun, buying new improved products, and conquering new frontiers.

Surf music arrived on the scene just as the Cold War was heating up between the United States and the Soviet Union. The cheerful music was an excellent diversion from the Bay of Pigs Invasion, the Vienna Summit, and the Cuban Missile Crisis, but it also demonstrated that young Americans were eager participants in the era's Cold War culture. Surf music's enormous popularity suggests that many teenagers were in step with the nation's consensus behavior. Like their parents and other adults in Cold War America, these young people subscribed to the American Dream and the belief in life, liberty, and the pursuit of happiness—as much happiness as they could get. These neophyte capitalists were enthusiastic supporters of the era's consumer culture. They spent millions of dollars annually on cars, clothes, social activities, rock & roll, and all the latest fads, including surfing-related products such as hit records, movies, surf boards, clam diggers, board shirts, baggys, bikinis, and more.

Songs about surfing and California's car culture were predicated on the belief in American Exceptionalism. The superior technology that produced advances in surfing and fast cars exemplified American ingenuity, while the entire surf culture was built on the California Dream and other American myths. Whether new teen heroes were hot-shot surfers or hot rod enthusiasts, they personified the long-held belief in the superiority of the common man. They had the looks, brains, and talent to defeat all comers in surf contests, drag races, or "beach blanket bingo." Their adventures and accomplishments took place in a rock & roll utopia set in the mythic West—America's legendary land of opportunity. "[California] was the new American wonderland," explains Dick Clark. "[It was] the home of a free teen world with surfboards and woodies and those gorgeous California girls. Two girls, in fact, for every boy. It was the land where all the kids had cars and dates and friends and nobody was ever left out for long."[76]

Surf music's significance rests on its close connection to the era's youth culture. The interaction between artists and audiences gave the music a folk quality. "We were Americans growing up with everything that comes with that, and all of the experiences that you have along the way," explains Mike Love of the Beach Boys. "We completely identified with that, specifically with the beach life and surfing culture."[77] If songs by the Beach Boys and other surf artists reflected teenage interests, they also helped shape them. Young people from coast to coast bought surf records, danced the stomp, and practiced sidewalk surfing even in landlocked towns like Muncie, Indiana, and Bowling Green, Ohio. Surf music offers a revealing look at teenage life and thought in Kennedy's America. It suggests that young Americans shared the dominant culture's values. And, it provides valuable details about teenagers' daily activities involving not just surfing but also cars, music, dancing, school, consumer goods, and, of course, dating and romance.[78]

The Beach Boys epitomize the link between surf music and baby boom culture. In the early 1960s the group's numerous hit records about teenage interests resonated with young listeners. That strong connection never faded. The Beach Boys' electrifying harmonies are seared into the collective memory of baby boomers, as evidenced by the group's 2012 album, *That's Why God Made the Radio*. Released on the 50th anniversary of the Beach Boys' first hit, the album climbed to number 3 on the *Billboard* charts. The last track on the album—"Summer's Gone"—is an elegy to a time when the Beach Boys, baby boomers, and America were still young and innocent. Brian's haunting falsetto and the group's signature harmonies transport listeners back in time to when perfect waves were harbingers of new frontiers in the mythic West. Just as the 20-year-old Brian Wilson expressed the hopes and dreams of a new generation in 1962, the 70-year-old Brian gave voice to the bittersweet memories of aging baby boomers facing the setting sun in 2012. The character in the song realizes that summer's finally over as he sits and watches the waves. "We laugh, we cry," he sings. "We live then die . . . and dream about our yesterday."[79]

Part 2

OLD STYLES
ROCK ON

5

"On Broadway"

R&B Rock Takes Center Stage

The Drifters' "On Broadway" debuted on the pop charts on March 23, 1963. Produced by Jerry Leiber and Mike Stoller, the song begins ominously with a downtrodden Black man describing the difficulties of finding success in New York City. Everyone is awed by the bright lights and glitter of Broadway, he says, but none of that matters when you're hungry and going nowhere. Suddenly the dark clouds part and hope shines through. With violins and trumpets heralding change, the man sings confidently about the future. He dismisses the naysayers who think he can't succeed. "They're dead wrong, I know they are," he insists, "'cause I can play this here guitar and I won't quit 'til I'm a star on Broadway."[1]

The Drifters' Top 10 hit is just one example of the innovative sounds that could be found in early 60s R&B rock. The music offered pop instrumentation to rock & roll audiences accustomed to just electric guitars and drums. The song's message also differed from most other R&B rock hits. The pop-oriented lyrics evoked the American Dream, as well as the optimism of the era's civil rights movement.

Even the title of the Drifters' record underscored the song's connection to New York City's famous pop music district. By the 1960s the Brill Building at 1619 Broadway and other nearby buildings were the epicenter for pop music innovations that were reshaping not just R&B rock, but also country rock, pop rock, and other styles. Leiber and Stoller became role models for numerous independent producers and songwriters destined to become major forces in rock & roll, including Carole King, Gerry Goffin, Phil Spector, Barry Mann, Cynthia Weil, Doc Pomus, and Mort Shuman.

The polished pop found on records like the Drifters' hit would take R&B rock to new heights in the early 60s. But pop music was only one of the ingredients of the era's new R&B rock. The potent mix also included elements from gospel, rhythm and blues, country music, and old-time rock & roll.

The Drifters' "On Broadway" expressed the can-do spirit of early 1960s America. When the decade began, the American Dream seemed more real than ever. As America rocketed toward space, Kennedy's New Frontier promised equally exciting challenges at home. The civil rights movement was picking up momentum, and its success would spark movements for women's rights and the environment, as well as reforms that would transform American politics, society, and culture in myriad ways.

The changing times inspired veteran R&B rockers from the 1950s like Ray Charles, Sam Cooke, and the Coasters, as well as new arrivals such as Gary "U.S." Bonds, Doris Troy, and Jimmy Soul. Their innovative sounds moved R&B rock to center stage in Kennedy's America.

VETERAN SOLO ARTISTS

Many R&B rock singers from the 1950s found continued success in the early 60s. Leading the way was Ray Charles, who became a rock & roll superstar. He earned 17 Top 40 hits in the early 1960s, including three number 1 records, "Georgia on My Mind" (1960), "Hit the Road, Jack" (1961), and "I Can't Stop Loving You" (1962).

Although Charles made recording hits look easy, his rise to the top was anything but. Born Ray Charles Robinson in 1930 and blind from the age of six, Ray began his career in the late 1940s. Dropping his surname so as not to be confused with boxer Sugar Ray Robinson, he recorded a few R&B hits on indie labels. In 1952 he signed with Ahmet Ertegun's Atlantic Records. With the encouragement of Ertegun and producer Jerry Wexler, Ray began exploring the music he loved as a kid, including blues, gospel, R&B, jazz, country, and pop.

In December 1953 Charles, Wexler, and Ertegun traveled to New Orleans to record in Cosimo Matassa's studio, the home of Fats Domino's hits. "This was the landmark session," recalls Wexler, "because it had Ray Charles originals, Ray

Charles arrangements, [and] a Ray Charles band." The momentum continued into the next session in Atlanta. Ray recorded "This Little Girl of Mine" and "I Got a Woman," which became a number 1 hit on the R&B charts. Charles's bold mixture of gospel and R&B at those two sessions foreshadowed things to come. "What makes these sessions historically important is that this was the first time that someone had the audacity to mix sacred and secular black music," notes Ertegun. "Ray had taken the gospel hymn 'My Jesus Is All the World to Me' and rewritten it as 'I Got a Woman.' He had taken another gospel song made famous

Ray Charles (National Archives)

by Clara Ward, 'This Little Light of Mine,' and converted it into 'This Little Girl of Mine.'" Not everyone was pleased. "Ray Charles is mixin' the blues with spirituals," complained blues singer Big Bill Broonzy. "That's wrong."[2]

Over the next several years, Charles continued to perfect his gospel-tinged sound. After a few minor hits on the pop charts, Ray hit it big in 1959 with "What'd I Say (Part 1)." The high-energy song rocketed up to number 6, transforming Charles into a rock & roll star. The record featured a great dance beat, sexually suggestive lyrics, and the same call-and-response pattern found in gospel music. Audiences loved it and teenagers danced wildly to the beat, often shouting out improvised obscene lyrics. The timing of the hit couldn't have been better since Charles's Atlantic contract was expiring at the end of 1959. The newfound success landed Ray a better deal with ABC-Paramount Records, which offered him more money and greater control over his music.[3]

Ray Charles hit his commercial and artistic stride in the early 1960s, cranking out hit after hit for his new label. Each seemed more creative than its predecessor. Significantly, Ray was not locked into any one style. Rhythm and blues shaped hits such as "Hit the Road, Jack" (1961) and "Unchain My Heart" (1962). Traditional pop also contributed. "Georgia on My Mind," a number 1 record for Charles in 1960, was a Top 10 hit for Frankie Trumbauer in 1931. Before Ray made it to number 28 with "Ruby" in 1960, it was a Top 30 hit in 1953 for Vaughn Monroe. And Ray's "That Lucky Old Sun" (1963) was preceded by a hit version in 1949 by Frank Sinatra. Country and western music proved to be a gold mine for Charles, yielding five Top 10 hits: "I Can't Stop Loving You" (1962), "You Don't Know Me" (1962), "You Are My Sunshine" (1962), "Take These Chains from My Heart" (1963), and "Busted" (1963).

Charles's foray into country music was particularly impressive. When Ray first suggested an album of country songs, ABC-Paramount executives balked. It was a terrible idea, they said, and he'd wind up losing all his fans. But the singer was determined to move forward with the project. Ray's son later explained that his father didn't want to be pigeonholed. "He loved music, all genres of music, and he refused to be limited by other people's expectations," explains Ray Charles Robinson Jr. "What people failed to understand when he first turned to country music was that it was in his heart. He was a huge Hank Williams fan. He had grown up in the Deep South listening to country and western and gospel music."[4]

Ray's determination to follow his heart resulted in one of the greatest albums ever. *Modern Sounds in Country and Western Music* (1962) shot up to number 1 on the *Billboard* Top Pop Albums chart and produced two of the year's biggest hits. Ray's version of Don Gibson's "I Can't Stop Loving You" made it all the way to number 1, while his rendition of Eddie Arnold's "You Don't Know Me" came in at number 2. Charles's inventive takes on the country classics were anything but mere covers. His gospel-tinged R&B rock vocals were set against a musical backdrop that featured a full choir and lush orchestral arrangements. On both songs Ray followed the inverted call-and-response pattern associated with gospel music, where the choir sings first followed by the pastor or song leader. "He started using the technique when he recorded 'I Can't Stop Loving You' as a country song," explains his son. "The singers led with 'I Can't Stop Loving You,' and my dad came in with 'It's useless to say.'"[5]

Charles's innovative blend of R&B rock, gospel, pop, and country earned him four Grammy nominations. What Ray accomplished with his venture into country music mirrored what Elvis Presley had done with R&B a few years earlier. Where Elvis had produced a white, countrified version of rhythm & blues, Ray fashioned a Black, R&B version of country and western. The tremendous success of this musical integration of Black and white cultures reflected and possibly contributed to gains made by the civil rights movement in the early 1960s.[6]

Charles's critical and commercial success established him as one of the most significant artists of his time. His creative mix of R&B, gospel, country and western, pop, and jazz resulted in some of the finest hit records in rock & roll history and inspired later soul artists such as Aretha Franklin, Otis Redding, and James Brown. Ray's many contributions to popular music earned him numerous awards, including 17 Grammys, induction into the Rock & Roll Hall of Fame and Country Music Hall of Fame, and Kennedy Center Honors. In 1986 President Clinton awarded him the prestigious National Medal of the Arts. The title of his Top 20 album from 1960 best sums up the reason for his success—*The Genius of Ray Charles.*

* * *

Jackie Wilson was another R&B rock veteran who became a fixture on the early 60s pop charts. His powerful vocals, uninhibited performance style, and creative mix of rock & roll, pop, R&B, and gospel earned him numerous hits and throngs of dedicated fans. His first three hits were written or cowritten by Berry Gordy. In 1957 Jackie had a minor hit with "Reet Petite." His follow-up, "To Be Loved" (1958), became a Top 30 record. And in 1959, Jackie made it all the way to number 7 with "Lonely Teardrops," an up-tempo rocker that allowed him to dance wildly while shouting out a bluesy message about love gone wrong.

"Lonely Teardrops" was just the beginning. Wilson earned two more Top 20 hits in 1959 and then kicked off the 1960s with his biggest hit to date, "Night," which reached number 4 in 1960. The ballad, based on an aria from Camille Saint-Saëns's opera *Samson and Delilah*, gave Wilson a chance to showcase his powerful voice. His hot streak continued in 1960 and 1961 with ten additional Top 40 hits, including two that made the Top 10, "Alone at Last" (1960) and "My Empty Arms" (1961). After a dry spell in 1962 he bounced back the next year with two Top 40 records, "Baby Workout" (a number 5 hit) and "Shake Shake Shake."

Jackie Wilson's topnotch hits, operatic vocals, and dynamic performance style made him a rock & roll superstar. Berry Gordy recalls the first time he saw Jackie perform. "When he hit the stage . . . it was like a lightning bolt," insists Gordy. Wilson strutted around as he sang and danced with abandon, doing splits and twirls, jumping straight up and then suddenly he'd be down on his knees. "[Jackie] was sexy and knew it," said Gordy. "I had never seen women throw panties on stage before."[7]

Like most American rock & rollers, Wilson ran into hard times when the British Rock Invasion conquered the American pop charts in 1964. But, he staged a comeback with hits such as "Whispers (Getting Louder)" (1966) and "(Your Love Keeps Lifting Me) Higher and Higher" (1967). Jackie's final moment in the spotlight was a tragic one. He suffered a heart attack on stage in 1975 while singing and dancing to his signature hit "Lonely Teardrops." He never fully recovered and died in 1984.

In 1987 Jackie Wilson was inducted into the Rock & Roll Hall of Fame. When Dick Clark was asked which singer from the 1950s and early 60s impressed him most, he replied without missing a beat: "Oh yea . . . Jackie Wilson. He was called 'Mr. Excitement.' He was the consummate performer."[8]

Like Jackie Wilson, Sam Cooke became a rock & roll superstar by successfully combining gospel, rhythm & blues, and teen-oriented pop, but that's where the similarity ends. Where Jackie's approach was emotional and energetic, Sam's was smooth and laid back.

Raised in Chicago as the son of a preacher man, Cooke got his start with the Soul Stirrers gospel group. The success of Jackie Wilson, Ray Charles, and other gospel-influenced rock & rollers inspired Cooke to give pop music a try. Sam hit it big when his first major release, "You Send Me" (1957), became a number 1 hit. Female fans loved his smooth style and suave appearance. Industry insiders were impressed by his immense talent. Atlantic Records' Jerry Wexler declared him "the best singer who ever lived." Unlike most early rock stars, Sam Cooke was a successful composer. He wrote or cowrote several of his hits, including "You Send Me" (1957), "Chain Gang" (1960), "Cupid" (1961), and "Bring It On Home To Me" (1962).[9]

Cooke earned twenty-nine Top 40 hits, which weren't limited to just one style. "I have an intense desire to make all of my audiences happy," he said. Songs like "You Send Me" (1957) and "(I Love You) For Sentimental Reasons" (1958) targeted the pop audience, while "Wonderful World" (1960) and "Twistin' the Night Away" (1962) were aimed at baby boomers. "I like any song that has a good story," Cooke explained. "A repetitious phrase helps put the story across. A song should have a lilting melody."[10]

Sam also found success with songs like "Frankie and Johnny" (1963) and "Little Red Rooster" (1963), which were influenced by blues, gospel, and R&B. In addition, his live performances often included folk songs related to civil rights such as Peter, Paul, and Mary's "If I Had a Hammer" and Bob Dylan's "Blowin' in the Wind." Cooke was particularly impressed by Dylan's song. "[Sam] was so carried away with the message, and the fact that a white boy had written it," explains his biographer Peter Guralnick, that "he was almost ashamed not to have written something like that himself."[11]

Cooke eventually wrote and recorded his own civil rights masterpiece. Distressed by the racism he saw around him and inspired by Martin Luther King Jr.'s "I Have a Dream" speech in 1963, Cooke composed "A Change is Gonna Come." The dramatic gospel-influenced song probed the plight of African Americans and the demand for civil rights. In the last verse Cooke bares his soul, explaining there were times when he felt utterly hopeless, but now he feels hope. "It's been a long, a long time coming," he confesses, "but I know a change gonna come, oh yes it will." Cooke was startled by how quickly the complex song came to him, almost like a supernatural experience. "When he first played it for Bobby Womack, who was his protégé," explains Guralnick, "[Cooke] said, 'What's it sound like?' And Bobby said, 'It sounds like death.' Sam said, 'Man, that's kind of how it sounds like to me.'"[12]

Partly because of Cooke's hesitancy, the song wasn't released until January 1965. It appeared as the flip side of an upbeat dance song called "Shake." The A-side made it all the way to number 7 on the charts, while "A Change is Gonna Come" stalled at number 31. Significantly, the flip side became far more important in the long run. It became an unofficial anthem of the civil rights movement and was later covered by numerous African American artists, including Otis Redding and Aretha Franklin. Barack Obama even alluded to "A Change is Gonna Come" in his 2008 victory speech.

The diversity of Cooke's music leads to an obvious question: Who was the *real* Sam Cooke? Was he simply a talented pop singer who appealed to a wide range of listeners? Was Cooke a shrewd promoter who shifted like a musical weathervane toward whatever audience would buy his records? Or was he an authentic artist, who embarked on a journey of discovery which began with gospel music and led into rock & roll and pop en route to a unique sound that incorporated gospel, R&B, pop, folk, and soul music?

Sam Cooke was probably all of those things and more. Unfortunately, there's no way to know for certain what would have become of the talented singer, songwriter, and performer. Cooke's musical journey came to a sudden end on December 11, 1964, when he was shot and killed by a woman who managed a cheap motel in Los Angeles. Local law enforcement ruled the incident a justifiable homicide based on testimony that claimed the singer tried to rape one woman and assaulted another. But Cooke's friends, family, fans, and many others still vehemently dispute the findings. The controversy surrounding his death only added to his mystique.[13]

What the singer might have accomplished had he lived is pure conjecture. For certain, Cooke's music was evolving in the early 60s partly because of the social change swirling around him. At the same time that Sam was performing pop music to mostly white audiences at the Copacabana, he was becoming close friends with Muhammed Ali and Malcolm X. He also admired Martin Luther King Jr. and endorsed Black economic power. Cooke provided capital for family members to start businesses, and he became a successful entrepreneur with his own record label and music publishing business. He also wrote and produced songs that launched careers of Black artists such as Lou Rawls and Bobby Womack.

Sam Cooke supported racial equality long before it became fashionable. In 1958 he headlined the first integrated rock & roll show in Atlanta. Despite death threats from the Ku Klux Klan, Cooke performed anyway. In 1963 Sam stood up to a bigoted motel clerk in Louisiana who refused service to the singer, his wife, and band members. Cooke was jailed for disturbing the peace. A few months later he wrote "A Change is Gonna Come."[14]

Although Sam Cooke never got the chance to witness the change predicted in his seminal civil rights song, his innovative music lived on, touching the lives of millions of Americans of all colors. In 1986 he was inducted posthumously into the Rock & Roll Hall of Fame.

Fats Domino was another veteran R&B rocker on the pop charts in the early 1960s. The New Orleans singer, songwriter, and piano player extraordinaire started out as a rhythm and blues artist in the late 1940s before crossing over to the national pop charts with "Ain't That a Shame" (1955), "Blueberry Hill" (1956), and other rock & roll hits on Imperial Records. Cosimo Matassa, who engineered Domino's New Orleans recording sessions, attributed Fats's success to his inimitable style. "[Fats] could be singing the national anthem, you'd still know by the time he said two words, it was him," said Matassa. "Obviously, unmistakably, and pleasurably him."[15]

Although Fats Domino's record sales tailed off in the new decade, he still earned 16 Top 40 hits between 1960 and 1963. The most successful was "Walking to New Orleans" (1960). The Top 10 hit began with a guitar imitating the sound of someone walking. Fats then delivered an intimate vocal about a down-on-his-luck guy determined to make it back home. The simple melody was enhanced by violins, which provided a dramatic counterpoint to Domino's heart-breaking tale. Fats's longtime producer and arranger Dave Bartholomew initially didn't like the song. "This ain't nothin'. I gotta add something to this," Dave said. "[So], I put strings on it, and it did fine." Not only did "Walking to New Orleans" become Fats's biggest hit of the 1960s, but it was the most creative. That was the first Fats Domino record to feature a string arrangement, and it worked brilliantly. The use of violins to echo Domino's vocal offered an innovative twist on the call-and-response pattern commonly found in R&B and gospel music.[16]

Although other Domino hits, such as "My Girl Josephine" (1960) and "Let the Four Winds Blow" (1961), were less innovative, they still offered solid rock & roll that was perfect for dancing. Domino's star didn't fade until 1963 when he left Dave Bartholomew and Imperial and signed with ABC-Paramount. The new label recorded the quintessential New Orleans singer in Nashville and convinced him to tack toward a country music sound replete with pop-sounding backup singers. Fat's last Top 40 hit came in 1963 with the pop standard "Red Sails in the Sunset."

At his peak between 1955 and 1963, Fats Domino cranked out thirty-seven Top 40 hits, including eleven that made it into the Top 10. His music made listeners want to jump up and dance. Fats and Dave Bartholomew (who cowrote, arranged, and produced most of Domino's hits) offered a distinct New Orleans Sound, which mixed rhythm & blues, boogie-woogie, Dixieland jazz, country blues, and pop with the call-and-response pattern and rhythms associated with African music. "It wasn't actually the lyrics [to the songs]," explains Bartholomew, "but that big beat that we had, and everybody would just start movin' around."[17]

Domino's unique sound and style were largely responsible for his success, but the timing was also right. As the civil rights movement picked up momentum in the 1950s and early 60s, Fats demonstrated that an African American could succeed if he had skills and determination. His tremendous talent, warm smile, and gracious demeanor helped him connect with diverse audiences.

Fats Domino is now recognized as one of rock & roll's founding fathers. He and Dave Bartholomew were inducted individually into the Rock & Roll Hall of Fame and entered the Songwriters Hall of Fame as a team. And, in 1998 Fats Domino was awarded the National Medal of the Arts, the highest award given by the US government to artists. Perhaps the most telling accolade comes from Domino's longtime friend and bandmate, Billy Diamond, who witnessed the singer's ability to transcend race in an era of segregation. "The whites all through the country accepted Fats," explained Diamond. "Fats was the Martin Luther King of music."[18]

If Fats Domino represented the New Orleans tradition, other veteran R&B rock artists shared the same gospel heritage as Ray Charles and Sam Cooke, whose innovative sounds were transforming R&B rock. Albums such as Cooke's *Mr. Soul* (1963) even gave name to a new musical style. Hit singles by Roy Hamilton, Clyde McPhatter, and Jerry Butler offered additional prototypes for soul music.[19] Butler, for example, started out as a gospel singer and switched to rock & roll when he joined the Impressions. After the group scored a number 11 hit in 1958 with the gospel-influenced ballad "For Your Precious Love," Jerry embarked on a solo career and earned three hits in 1960: "He Will Break Your Heart," "Moon River," and "Make It Easy on Yourself." His soulful style, which mixed gospel, pop, and rock & roll, led to several later hits, including "Only the Strong Survive," which reached number 4 in 1969.

Traditional pop, blues, and R&B also influenced the music of veteran artists. Brook Benton found success blending pop music and R&B on songs like "The Ties that Bind" (1960) and "Hotel Happiness" (1963). His duets with Dinah Washington resulted in two Top 10 hits in 1960 influenced more by rhythm and blues: "Baby (You've Got What It Takes)" and "A Rockin' Good Way." R&B and blues influences were obvious on other records. James Brown scored his first Top 40 hit with his funk music prototype "Think" (1960). The following year, Slim Harpo made the Top 40 with "Rainin' in My Heart," a mournful blues song not to be confused with Buddy Holly's ballad of the same name. And in 1963 Rufus Thomas cracked the Top 10 with his R&B dance hit "Walkin' the Dog" (1963).[20]

Dee Clark earned three Top 30 hits in 1959 with songs that blended R&B with teen-oriented lyrics. "Nobody But You" and "Just Keep it Up" focused on young romance, while "Hey Little Girl" featured a Bo Diddley beat and suggestive lyrics about a sexy young woman in black silk stockings and skin-tight skirt. Dee's follow-up hits in 1960, "How About That" and "You're Looking Good," were even more explicit. The first one featured Clark singing about the "throbbing" in his brain and how he can't control himself when his girl "presses" her lips to his. "You're Looking Good" took it a step further. As the singer ogles a girl's beautiful body, he exclaims, "Look at those measurements, man alive—34-24-35!" The song excited teenage boys, but stalled at number 43 on the charts possibly because it was too risqué to get much airplay.[21]

Dee Clark bounced back in 1961 when he toned things down with "Raindrops," a soulful ballad that climbed to number 2. Written by Clark, the song featured an expressive vocal, memorable melody, and lyrics that reflected the era's gender stereotypes. The record begins with a crash of thunder. Dee then spins a sad tale about a broken-hearted guy who insists raindrops must be falling because a "man ain't supposed to cry."[22] Although Clark never had another hit, his creative blend of R&B, pop, and rock & roll made him one of the most successful singers of the early 60s.

VETERAN GROUPS

Numerous R&B rock groups that started out in the 1950s found continued success in the early 1960s. Several earned hits by blending R&B sounds with a pop music sensibility. The Platters, for example, landed four number 1 hits in the 1950s with pop ballads like "The Great Pretender" (1956), "My Prayer" (1956), "Twilight Time" (1958), and "Smoke Gets in Your Eyes" (1959). Their R&B-influenced pop sound led to additional hits in the next decade, including "Harbor Lights" and "To Each His Own" in 1960 and "If I Didn't Care" and "I'll Never Smile Again" in 1961. In recognition of their pioneering achievements, the Platters were inducted in 1990 into the Rock & Roll Hall of Fame.

If the Platters were always more pop than rock, the Coasters were just the opposite. With the help of two of the most talented songwriters and producers in the business, Jerry Leiber and Mike Stoller, the group developed an innovative rock & roll sound that was a seamless blend of R&B and pop. The successful collaboration between the Black singers and white producers is evidence of the era's increasing racial cooperation. The Coasters' Carl Gardner and Bobby Nunn met Leiber and Stoller in the early 1950s when they were all part of the Los Angeles rhythm and blues scene. Gardner and Nunn's first group, the Robins, scored a few regional hits with R&B songs written and produced by Leiber and Stoller. "The Robins were a perfect vehicle for [our] musical productions," explained Leiber. "Five voices to consider. Five voices to harmonize. Five voices, five characters, five actors, a veritable repertory company."[23]

When Leiber and Stoller accepted an offer in 1955 to become independent producers for Atlantic Records in New York City, they invited the Robins to come along. Only Gardner and Nunn accepted, so Leon Hughes and Billy Guy were recruited to form a new group named the Coasters (because they began on the West Coast). Over the years the group's roster changed, but the modus operandi stayed the same. The Coasters did the singing and comic routines, while Leiber and Stoller wrote and produced clever teen-oriented songs that combined humor and social commentary, including "Yakety Yak" (1958), "Charlie Brown" (1959), and "Poison Ivy" (1959).

Although the group's popularity waned in the early 60s, the Coasters charted a few more times. They had minor hits in 1960 with three satirical songs about poverty and inequality in America: "Run Red Run," "What About Us," and "Shopping for Clothes." The Coasters' last Top 30 hit was "Little Egypt" (1961). "This was the epitome of the comic playlets that we were writing for the Coasters," says Mike Stoller. The song describes a sexy hoochie-coochie dancer and pokes fun at sexual mores of the early 60s. Even though "Little Egypt" didn't sell as well as earlier hits like "Yakety Yak" and "Charlie Brown," Stoller always thought "it was more interesting in its construction."[24]

The Coasters and Leiber and Stoller loved working together. "We would be falling around on the floor laughing while we were rehearsing," recalls Stoller. "When we finished the record [the Coasters] would go out on the road . . . and when they came back in to learn new songs, they would . . . show us how they choreographed and performed these numbers, and it was a party, man, we always had a ball."[25] Ultimately, millions of listeners nationwide joined in the fun as they listened to Leiber and Stoller's songs and laughed at the Coasters' routines. In 1987 the Rock & Roll Hall of Fame inducted both the Coasters and Leiber and Stoller. The Coasters' entry said it all: "Witty. Engaging. Hilarious. Infectious. The Coasters are in a league of their own."[26]

The Drifters were another group that found success in early 60s rock & roll with the help of Leiber and Stoller. They began in 1953 as a rhythm and blues group on the Atlantic label. Led by Clyde McPhatter, they earned several hits on the R&B charts, including prototypical rock & roll songs such as "Money Honey" (1953). After McPhatter went solo in 1955, the Drifters underwent a drastic makeover. George Treadwell, who owned rights to the group's name, fired the remaining Drifters and hired Ben E. King and the Crowns as replacements. "Treadwell had us sign a contract whereby we received no royalties," explains King. "George just put us on a salary and everything else belonged to him." Atlantic Records' Jerry Wexler brought in Jerry Leiber and Mike Stoller to produce the new Drifters group. Wexler, according to Leiber, told the duo, "You've been doing so well with the Coasters that we're entrusting you with one of our most important acts . . . Just don't go over budget. Keep it simple."[27]

Leiber and Stoller disregarded Wexler's admonition almost before he left the room. "We did anything but keep it simple," admitted Stoller. "As the [Drifters] were rehearsing, I started playing a Borodin-like counterpoint on the piano. Jerry said, 'That sounds like strings.' I said, 'Why not?'" So the two producers brought in Stan Applebaum as orchestrator and added violins, a cello, timpani, and a Latin *baion* beat for good measure. When Wexler heard the tape of the new song, "There Goes My Baby," he spit his tuna fish sandwich against the studio wall. "I'd never release shit like this," Leiber recalls him saying. "You've wasted our money on an overpriced production that sounds like a radio caught between two stations." Leiber and Stoller convinced Ahmet Ertegun, who owned the company, to let them remix the song. Wexler eventually agreed to release the record. Leiber and Stoller felt vindicated when it shot up to number 1 and made the Drifters stars.[28]

"There Goes My Baby"—with its strings and things drenched in echo—revolutionized the sound of R&B rock. Earlier pop-influenced hits such as the Platters' "Twilight Time" (1958) and Jackie Wilson's "To Be Loved" (1958) used violins. But, Leiber and Stoller took it a step further, creating a seamless blend of rock & roll and pop that resulted in four more Top 20 hits for the Drifters: "Dance with Me" (1959), "This Magic Moment" (1960), "Save the Last Dance for Me" (1960), and "I Count the Tears" (1961). Lead singer Ben E. King felt a special connection to "Save the Last Dance for Me," which became a number 1 hit. The song, composed by Doc Pomus and Mort Shuman, was inspired by Pomus's experience of watching from his wheelchair while his beautiful wife danced with other men. That story motivated King in the recording studio. "[Pomus] gave me more than lyrics. He gave me a reason why the song was born," explained King. "I just closed my eyes in front of the microphone and I could see him watching his wife as she was dancing and I could sing the song because . . . the reason it was written was all in my head."[29]

In 1960 Ben E. King left the Drifters for a solo career. George Treadwell went back to the drawing board and brought in Rudy Lewis as the new lead vocalist from 1961 through 1963. Johnny Moore handled the job from 1964 until 1966. With Leiber and Stoller's continued guidance, the group earned ten more Top 40 hits, including three that made it into the Top 10: "Up on the Roof" and "On Broadway" in 1963, and "Under the Boardwalk" (1964).[30]

The collaboration between the Drifters and Leiber and Stoller resulted in innovative records that blended rock & roll, R&B, gospel, and pop. The hits featured outstanding vocals, excellent production values, and material written by some of the top composers of the day, including Leiber and Stoller, Pomus and Shuman, and King and Goffin. The best recordings combined unforgettable melodies with lyrics that explored urban culture, as well as larger themes involving African Americans, baby boomers, and the American Dream.

The Drifters' success paralleled the rise of the civil rights movement. And, their close ties to Leiber and Stoller are proof that racial cooperation was more than just talk in the early 1960s. Those two "were like brothers to us," explains the Drifters' Charlie Thomas. "There was real prejudice back then, but these guys didn't believe in it, and we didn't believe in it either."[31] The group's last Top 20 hit was "Saturday Night at the Movies" (1964), but their legacy lived on. In 1988 the Drifters were inducted into the Rock & Roll Hall of Fame.

While groups like the Drifters and Coasters were enjoying success with pop-influenced rock & roll hits, other veteran R&B rock groups made the charts by mixing rhythm and blues, gospel, and rock & roll.[32] The Impressions, who came out of Chicago's Cabrini-Green Homes public housing complex in the late 1950s, are a perfect example. The group's original lineup included Jerry Butler, Curtis Mayfield, Sam Gooden, and brothers Richard and Arthur Brooks. All five got their start singing with church choirs and gospel groups. After the Impressions' first big hit, "For Your Precious Love" (1958), Jerry Butler opted for a solo career and was replaced by Fred Cash. Shortly thereafter Curtis Mayfield emerged as the group's guiding force. His heartfelt vocals, unique guitar style, and expert songwriting and production skills soon made the Impressions the pacesetters of "Chicago Soul" music.

The Impressions' first big success in the post-Butler era was "Gypsy Woman" (1961). Written by Mayfield, the erotic ballad featured Curtis's expressive falsetto set to Latin rhythms and a hypnotic beat. Vivid lyrics described a seductive young woman with hair "as dark as night" and eyes like "a cat in the dark." The singer falls under her spell as she moves slowly through the gypsy caravan, flirting with all the men and dancing suggestively around the campfire. Mesmerized by her swaying hips and face "aglow" from the crackling flames, the singer wants her desperately.[33] The record's suggestive imagery and sensuous sounds helped make it a Top 20 hit.

When subsequent releases flopped the Brooks brothers returned home to Tennessee. Curtis Mayfield, Sam Gooden, and Fred Cash continued as a trio. The new lineup soon perfected a harmony sound that proved that less is more. "I think [the sound] was probably original for the Impressions in R&B and contemporary music, but there was nothing original about it if you ever sang gospel," explained Mayfield. "In gospel, you knew how to be a good singer, not only to sing lead but to be able to incorporate oneself into the blending of the group, too. And sometimes everyone comes out and sings in harmony a portion of the

Curtis Mayfield and the Impressions (Robert Pruter Collection)

lead part." That approach "made us a three-man group stronger than we were as a five-man group," said Mayfield.[34]

The novel sound was showcased on the Impressions' 1963 release "It's All Right." The record featured the trio trading lead vocals and gospel harmonies, while musical arranger Johnny Pate added depth with blaring horns that offered a counterpoint to guitar riffs and heavy percussion. Mayfield's lyrics underscored changes going on not just in the Impressions' music but also in African American culture. Ostensibly a romantic ballad, the song's subtle message assured listeners that Blacks would be all right because they had soul. The song points out that many Blacks wake up feeling sad, but there's a simple solution. "Hum a little soul, make life your goal," sing the Impressions, "and surely something's got to come to you."[35]

"It's All Right" became the group's biggest hit to date. The optimistic lyrics and innovative blend of gospel, soul, rock, and pop helped the record become a number 4 hit. No one was more impressed than Johnny Pate. "The group went into some high falsetto harmonic things that were really unheard of. Nobody had done it before," said the veteran musician.[36]

After 1963 the Impressions turned increasingly toward soul music and social commentary. "I'm So Proud" (1964) echoed the emerging notion of Black pride. "Keep On Pushing" (1964) encouraged African Americans to continue the struggle for equality. "Amen" (1964) reflected the prominent role of religion in the expanding civil rights movement. And, "People Get Ready" (1965)—written by Curtis just after he witnessed Martin Luther King Jr.'s "I Have a Dream" speech at the March on Washington in 1963—expressed optimism that the inexorable move toward freedom and equality was transforming America. "These songs were an example of what has laid in my subconscious for years . . . the issues of what concerned me as a young black man," explained Mayfield. "The musical strands and themes of gospel singers and preachers I'd heard as a child. It wasn't hard to take notice of segregation and the struggle for equality at this time."[37]

Songs by the Impressions became unofficial anthems of the civil rights movement and were sung at rallies and other gatherings. "We were young and didn't know these songs would have that effect," said Mayfield years later. "[Former civil rights leader] Andy Young . . . told me how they would sing 'Amen' and 'Keep on Pushing' during the freedom marches," explained Curtis. "It gave them inspiration to keep on doing what they were doing. It's great to know we had a role in that."[38]

Along with being the musical genius behind the Impressions' success, Curtis wrote and produced hits for Major Lance, Jan Bradley, and other African Americans in the early 1960s and beyond. He also owned and operated his own music publishing business as well as several record labels. In 1970 Mayfield went solo, and two years later he wrote and recorded the movie soundtrack for *Superfly*, which sold over five million copies.

Curtis Mayfield's career continued to soar until tragedy struck in 1990. At an outdoor concert in Brooklyn, a lighting scaffold collapsed, paralyzing the singer from the neck down. But Mayfield never quit. Following his own advice, he kept on pushing and wrote and recorded music until his death in 1999.

In 1991 the Impressions were inducted into the Rock & Roll Hall of Fame. Eight years later Curtis was voted into the Hall of Fame as a solo performer. "The Impressions traversed the sounds of the Fifties and Sixties as well as old and new social attitudes," notes the group's official biography at the Rock & Roll Hall of Fame. "Their music was the sound of the civil rights movement."[39]

Like the Impressions, the Isley Brothers—Ronald, Rudolph, and O'Kelly—got started in the late 1950s as gospel singers, picked up momentum as rock & rollers in the early 60s, and soared to even greater heights in the 1970s and beyond. Born and raised in Cincinnati, the Isleys sang in church choirs in the 1950s. "When we started singing, we sang gospel," explains O'Kelly. "It never got recorded. But when we did start to record as R&B artists, the feeling of gospel music was still there . . . We couldn't get rid of it if we tried."[40]

Determined to make it as singers, they moved to New York City in 1957 and recorded several doo-wop songs for small record labels. Although none charted, the records helped the trio land gigs at Harlem's Apollo Theater and Black clubs up and down the coast. They soon attracted a following, impressed by the group's gospel sound and dynamic performances. R&B great James Brown was amazed: "We saw the Isley Brothers coming from the back of the theater, swinging on ropes, like Tarzan, onto the stage . . . They hardly had to sing at all. They'd already killed 'em."[41]

The Isleys' frenetic style was inspired by Jackie Wilson. Their act even showcased a raucous version of "Lonely Teardrops." The song became "such a strong number for us that the promoters put us on last to close the shows," explains lead singer Ronald Isley. "Jackie's 'Lonely Teardrops' had this part at the end where he'd sing, 'Say you will,' and his backup singers would respond in kind. Then Jackie would ad-lib, 'Say it right now, baby, yeah, come on, come on.' That was straight out of gospel."[42]

One night in 1959 at the Uptown Theater in Philadelphia, the audience really got into the song, jumping up and down and screaming in delight. "The place was packed and the audience was yelling their approval, like at church," remembers Ron Isley. "The energy was so strong that I didn't want to end the song yet." So, he began ad-libbing just the way Wilson did. Ron screamed, "You know, you make me wanna shout!" The band jumped in as the audience went crazy. "I began to ad-lib more lines, like 'Kick my heels up' and 'Throw my hands up,'" says Isley. "I'd wait a second at the end of each line so my brothers and the audience had a chance to answer me with 'Shout.' That song just took over." Encouraged by the response, the group reprised the call-and-response pattern at every performance over the next ten days. When fans began showing up just to experience the hot closing number, Ron decided to kick things up a notch. He wrote a new introduction similar to the one on Ray Charles's 1954 R&B hit "I Got a Woman." "[Ray] had opened his song with a big drawn-out 'We—eee—ll,' and at the end he'd go into these gospel chord changes and a call-and-response thing with the band," explains Ron. "We went along with that on 'Shout,' with me singing 'Don't forget to say you will' and my brothers answering me with 'Say you will' and 'Say it.' Then I sang 'Come on, now' over and over. We really got everyone going."

By the time the brothers returned to New York, "Shout" had taken on a life of its own. Their producers, Hugo and Luigi, rushed them into the RCA studio to record a live-sounding version, which was released in August 1959. "As we performed 'Shout' at concerts to support the record, I came up with a dance, treating the audience like a congregation," says Ron Isley. "When I sang, 'Shout—a little bit softer now,' people would dance down low, rising slowly when I sang 'a little bit louder now.'"[43]

The high-energy song became the Isley Brothers' breakthrough hit in late 1959. Although the initial release peaked at only number 47, the record eventually became a cult classic. It picked up momentum when Joey Dee and the Starliters included it on their live album *Doin' the Twist at the Peppermint Lounge* (1961), and then released it as a single in 1962. The uninhibited song was a natural for the Twist craze sweeping the nation, sending the cover to number 6 on the charts. The Isleys' original was then rereleased and again charted. Over the next decade the song became a favorite of teenagers and garage bands everywhere. The Isleys' younger brother Ernie later explained why he thought "Shout" became the quintessential party song: "It contains everything rock 'n' roll is about—the energy, the freedom, the abandon."[44]

Following the success of "Shout," the Isleys signed with Wand Records. Their new producer, Bert Russell, encouraged them to record "Twist and Shout," a song he had cowritten the previous year for the Top Notes. The Isleys' slower version was dramatically different. It begins with an insistent beat. Ron Isley then jumps in, shouting "shake it up baby," as his brothers repeat the phrase. The call-and-response pattern continues throughout the song as Ron encourages his girl with lines like "work it out, baby" and "you got me goin' now." Horns establish a counterpoint to the beat, while the Isleys' suggestive "oohs" and trills add to the sexual tension. Finally, a crescendo of voices offers release, as the Isleys scream "Shake it up, baby, Twist and shout!" As the song comes to a climax, Ron Isley urges his girl onward, repeating "shake it, shake it, shake it, baby."[45]

The Isley Brothers' seminal hit added explicit sexuality to Chubby Checker's Twist craze. Teenagers loved the suggestive sounds and lyrics, and the Top 20 hit became a favorite at dances and parties across the country. Ironically, the success of "Twist and Shout" (1962) made it that much harder for the Isleys to sing anything else. Their initial follow-up was the contrived "Twistin' with Linda," which stalled at number 54. Things got even worse in 1963 when the group recorded "Surf and Shout," a lame attempt to cash in on the surf craze. Eventually, the brothers' sheer talent and determination helped them make it back onto the pop charts. In 1966 they earned their biggest hit to date with "This Old Heart of Mine." Soon afterward they formed their own label and expanded the group to include younger brothers Ernie and Marvin, and brother-in-law Chris Jasper. The reconstituted group hit its stride in the late 1960s and beyond with a string of critically acclaimed hits that ranged from funk and R&B to inspired covers of songs by Neil Young, Bob Dylan, and Carole King. In 1992 the entire group was inducted into the Rock & Roll Hall of Fame, and in 2014 they received a Grammy Award for Lifetime Achievement.

NEW WAVE OF SOLO ARTISTS

A new wave of R&B rock artists hit the pop charts in the early 1960s. The most intriguing new sound arrived in the autumn of 1960. The record begins with drums and handclaps pounding out a beat. An R&B-sounding voice then calls out, "I said a hey hey hey, hey, yea." Backup singers respond in kind. They repeat the call-and-response one more time. Then, the lead singer invites everybody to take a trip "down the Mississippi, down to New Orleans." The rock & roll journey then kicks into high gear, rocketing U.S. Bonds' "New Orleans" all the way up to number 6.

Listeners had never heard anything quite like the U.S. Bonds song. The uninhibited vocals, big beat, and blaring sax took Fats Domino's New Orleans Sound to a new level of partying. Audiences loved the music, but didn't know what to make of U.S. Bonds. Was this a group or one guy? The only thing for certain was the irresistible sound. There was urgency to the double-track vocals, insistent beat, and pulsating sax. The song's exotic southern imagery describing Mississippi queens, magnolia blossoms, and "honeysuckle hanging from a live-oak tree" added to the Gothic mood.[46]

The mysterious U.S. Bonds followed up with an even more sensational record that sounded like it was recorded at a raucous party. "Quarter to Three" begins with cheers and clapping. The lead vocalist then counts off to four. In the background, the crowd whistles and claps as backup singers launch a rock & roll riff of nonsensical doo-wop syllables. All the while, the lead singer talks excitedly to the crowd. Suddenly, there's an explosion of sound powered by a blasting sax and rhythmic drums. The lead singer then delivers a rowdy confession about dancing all over the room 'til a quarter to three. He praises the band that rocked all night long, Daddy G and the Church Street Five. "Everybody was as happy as they could be," he shouts, "because they were swingin' with Daddy G." To prove his point, he shouts "Blow Daddy!" When the sax man complies with a blast on his horn, the singer encourages him to add "just a little bit of soul now." All the while, the boisterous crowd shouts, shrieks, and dances up a storm.[47]

"Quarter to Three" became a rock & roll phenomenon. Teenagers listened intently as disc jockeys played the song repeatedly, and rumors soon spread that the lead singer had uttered some obscene words. Not surprisingly, even more kids began tuning in and turning on to the song, which pushed the record all the way to number 1. To this day, no one knows for sure what was said on that record. But, two things are certain: "Quarter to Three" is one of the greatest hits in rock & roll history, and fans still argue about whether the lyrics were obscene.[48]

The astonishing success of "Quarter to Three" forced the record's producer, Frank Guida, to clear up the confusion swirling around the singer and song. Guida was born in Sicily and raised in New York City. In the early 1950s he and his wife moved to Norfolk, Virginia, and bought a record store. Guida then launched the Legrand record label and scored a Top 40 hit when he cowrote and produced Tommy Facenda's "High School, U.S.A." (1959).

The next year Guida found even greater success producing and cowriting U.S. Bonds' "New Orleans." Guida was convinced the song would be a hit if he could come up with a gimmick to convince radio stations to play it. "After all," he reasoned, "who knows about Legrand Records in Norfolk?" Guida's plan was inspired. Instead of putting the unknown singer's real name, Gary Anderson, on the label, he chose something with instant name recognition: "I put on the label and marked the outside of the envelope 'By U.S. Bonds.'" Many deejays were intrigued by what sounded like a patriotic name or public service announcement. Others, including fans, just thought it was a cool name for a new band.[49]

When the record became a hit, Gary Anderson was upset because he wasn't credited on the label. But Guida didn't want to mess with success and refused to change the name. His instinct proved correct when the follow-up, "Quarter to Three," became a smash hit. Based on an earlier instrumental called "A Night with Daddy G," recorded by Legrand's studio band, the Church Street Five, U.S. Bonds' version added lyrics. The new record used the same double-tracked vocals and echo effects that had worked so well on "New Orleans," but Guida added something new. He brought teenagers into the studio and instructed them to talk, whistle, and shout like they were having fun. When he overdubbed the sounds, "Quarter to Three" sounded like a live recording.

U.S. Bonds' boisterous "Norfolk Sound" proved irresistible. But the song's remarkable success made it difficult for Guida to continue the ruse. To placate

Gary Anderson and to end the confusion of deejays, fans, and concert goers, Guida decided that all future records would identify the singer as Gary "U.S." Bonds. Although the name changed, the lively sound remained the same, producing subsequent hits such as "School is Out" (1961), "School is In" (1961), "Dear Lady Twist" (1962), and "Twist Twist Senora" (1962).

For a brief time, Gary "U.S." Bonds was one of the most influential R&B rockers around. One of his biggest baby boomer fans was young Bruce Springsteen. Years later, when Springsteen was putting together the E Street Band, he brought in sax man Clarence Clemons to achieve a similar "Daddy G" sound. Many concerts featured Bruce bringing down the house with a wild rendition of "Quarter to Three." In 1981 Bruce and his guitarist Steven Van Zandt wrote and produced songs for a new Gary "U.S." Bonds album. "[Bruce] had written a song called, 'Dedication,' that he said sounded so much like 'Quarter To Three' he wanted to record it with me," explained Gary. "But we were having so much fun doing it [that] . . . within two or three weeks . . . we had done a whole album." Although Bonds' comeback was short-lived, his initial hits are forever etched in the collective memory of baby boomers who came of age in the early 60s.[50]

Gary "U.S." Bonds' spectacular success convinced Frank Guida to roll the dice with another R&B rock artist. Once again, Guida came up with a gimmick to attract attention to an unknown but talented young singer. He convinced James McCleese to use a stage name, Jimmy Soul, which evoked the new musical style emerging in the early 60s. Next, Guida selected a song that blended a contemporary dance fad with his love of calypso music, which he discovered while stationed in Trinidad during World War II. The result was Jimmy Soul's Top 30 hit of 1962, "Twistin' Matilda," a reworking of Harry Belafonte's 1953 hit "Matilda."

Jimmy Soul hit the musical jackpot again the following year with "If You Wanna Be Happy," an upbeat record based on Roaring Lion's 1934 calypso song "Ugly Woman." Guida applied the same Norfolk Sound formula that had worked so well on the U.S. Bonds hits. The double-tracked vocals, hand claps, and crowd noise made it sound like it was recorded at a raucous party. "If you wanna be happy for the rest of your life, never make a pretty woman your wife," Jimmy sang cheerfully. Instead, a guy should marry an ugly woman who can cook and won't break his heart.[51] Today the lyrics are politically incorrect at best, but back in the early 60s the novelty song was totally in step with gender stereotypes. "If You Wanna Be Happy" became a number 1 hit in 1963, suggesting that young listeners loved Jimmy Soul's excellent vocal as well as the record's party atmosphere, gender jokes, and calypso sound.

Rhythm and blues influences powered other hit records. Fats Domino's New Orleans Sound helped three R&B rockers find success in 1961. Ernie K-Doe scored a number 1 hit with "Mother-In-Law," which featured Ernie's humorous tale about the "worst person I know" who was "sent from down below." Chris Kenner did almost as well with "I Like It Like That," a number 2 record that invited listeners to a mysterious club where they could "rock away" their blues. And, Lee Dorsey made it to number 7 with "Ya Ya," which showcased New Orleans-style horns, a barrelhouse piano, and bizarre lyrics about a guy "sittin' in Ya Ya waiting for my La La." Other singers were inspired by the R&B tradition that produced Jackie Wilson. In 1960 Jimmy Jones had two smash hits with "Handy Man" and "Good Timin'." The following year Bobby Lewis made it all the way to number 1 with a solid rocker called "Tossin' and Turnin'."[52]

Ben E. King had more enduring success. The former lead singer of the Drifters hit it big as a solo artist with his 1961 release "Spanish Harlem." Written by Jerry Leiber and Phil Spector and produced by Leiber and Stoller, the Top 10 hit featured King's expressive R&B vocal set against compelling Latin rhythms. The fresh sound and powerful lyrics about the beauty and determination of a young woman from a minority neighborhood resonated in an era when the notion of equal opportunity was gaining momentum. King's follow-up was an even bigger hit. "Stand By Me," which he wrote with his producers, Jerry Leiber and Mike Stoller, reached 4 in 1961. King's passionate vocal about love was powered forward by violins and a driving base line. Years later, Leiber was asked what made the record so popular. "The lyrics are good, King's vocal is great," he noted, "but, Mike's bass line pushed the song into the land of immortality." According to Leiber, that base line was "an insidious piece of work. It can put a hole through your head."[53]

Ben E. King earned three more Top 30 hits: "Amor" (1961), "Don't Play That Song (You Lied)" (1962), and "I (Who Have Nothing)" (1963). His career stalled when the Beatles and soul music arrived on the scene, but King wasn't done yet. In 1975 he made it to number 5 on the charts with "Supernatural Thing—Part 1," and in 1986 his original recording of "Stand By Me" became a Top 10 hit again when it was featured in Rob Reiner's movie of the same name.

Other new R&B rockers were influenced less by rhythm and blues and more by pop music. Gene McDaniels, who came out of a gospel and jazz background, scored Top 10 hits with "A Hundred Pounds of Clay" (1961), "Tower of Strength" (1961), and "Chip Chip" (1962). All three were produced by Snuff Garrett and featured pop-style musical arrangements and pop harmonies by the Johnny Mann Singers. Freddie Scott also found success with pop-influenced material. He hit it big in 1963 with "Hey Girl," written by Carole King and Gerry Goffin. Scott's emotional vocal powered the pop ballad all the way up to number 10.

The pioneering soul music of Sam Cooke and Ray Charles inspired even more R&B rock singers.[54] Arthur Alexander was one of the more intriguing new-comers. His soul sound—an earthy mix of traditional blues and country—was recorded in the same Muscle Shoals, Alabama, studio where later soul artists such as Percy Sledge, Aretha Franklin, and Wilson Pickett would record. Alexander managed only two minor hits in 1962, but both had ripple effects. "You Better Move On," a quirky blend of R&B, country, and jazz-influenced vocal inflections, peaked at number 24. It gained more popularity when it was covered in 1965 by the Rolling Stones. Alexander's other hit, the offbeat "Anna (Go to Him)," stalled at number 68, but became a rock & roll classic when the Beatles recorded it.

Major Lance played an even greater role in the rise of early 60s soul music. The talented R&B rocker earned three Top 20 hits in 1963 and early 64. All were written by Curtis Mayfield and featured soul-inspired vocals and funky R&B dance beats. "The Monkey Time," a number 8 hit in 1963, popularized a new dance. "Hey Little Girl," which peaked at number 13, relied on the same beat and referenced the Monkey. Lance's next hit turned out to be his biggest: "Um, Um, Um, Um, Um, Um" made it all the way to number 5 on the charts in early 1964.

One of the most significant developments in early 60s R&B rock was the spike in the number of women singers. The surging popularity of girl groups like the

Shirelles and Motown artists such as Mary Wells opened doors for female artists. Gains made by the civil rights movement and the nascent women's rights
movement also created a more receptive environment for Black women in the
music industry.

Several women found success with records that mixed R&B rock with pop.
Little Eva scored a number 1 hit in 1962 with "The Loco-Motion," written by
Carole King and Gerry Goffin. That same year Claudine Clark had a number 5
hit with "Party Lights," a bubbly song that showcased teenagers, parties, and
popular dance fads. Dee Dee Sharp earned several hits with songs that applied
R&B sounds to pop music dance fads, including "Mashed Potato Time" (1962)
and "Do the Bird" (1963). And, Barbara Lewis's smooth blend of R&B and pop
resulted in her breakthrough hit, "Hello Stranger" (1963). Her seductive vocal
combined with the Dells' doo-wop harmonies helped the ballad climb all the
way to number 3. Barbara returned to the Top 20 charts in 1965 with two more
pop-influenced songs, "Baby, I'm Yours" and "Make Me Your Baby."

While some female R&B rock vocalists tacked toward pop music, others
focused on gospel and soul. Maxine Brown earned two Top 30 hits in 1961, "All
in My Mind" and "Funny." That same year, the future Queen of Soul, Aretha
Franklin, scored her first Top 40 hit with a gospel-infused rendition of Al Jol-
son's 1918 chestnut "Rock-A-Bye Your Baby With a Dixie Melody." Darlene Love
was another gospel-influenced vocalist who arrived on the charts in the early
1960s. Along with singing on hits by the Crystals and other groups, the future
Rock and Roll Hall of Famer enjoyed success as a solo artist with "(Today I Met)
The Boy I'm Gonna Marry" (1963) and "Wait 'Til My Bobby Gets Home" (1963).

With civil rights demonstrations in the news, other African American
women singers marched confidently onto the national pop charts. Doris Troy, a
talented singer and songwriter, scored a Top 10 hit in 1963 with "Just One Look."
A creative mix of R&B, rock & roll, and pop, the song featured an irresistible
dance beat, lyrics about love at first sight, and a self-assured young woman who
promised never to give up. "I'm gonna keep on schemin'," she guarantees, "'til I
can make you . . . my own."[55]

If Troy's protagonist was determined to get her man, the young woman featured on Jan Bradley's Top 20 hit "Mama Didn't Lie" (1963) was equally determined

to avoid the wrong guy. Written by Curtis Mayfield, the upbeat song captured the essence of Chicago Soul and resonated with young women across the country. Bradley had grown up singing gospel music and knew instantly that she wanted to record Mayfield's song. "I loved his material," she explained, "it fit my voice, and lyrically it was saying what I wanted to say." Jan delivered the song's powerful message with passion. She warns teenage girls about male predators and says it won't happen to her because Mama explained their tricks. She'd never "get caught by the wink of an eye," she sings, "[because] Mama didn't lie." The hits by Jan Bradley, Doris Troy, and other R&B rock singers demonstrate that determined women were standing up for their beliefs long before the women's movement took hold in the late 1960s and 70s.[56]

NEW WAVE OF R&B ROCK GROUPS

The early 1960s witnessed a proliferation of new R&B rock groups. Along with all the girl groups and Motown groups discussed in earlier chapters, there were groups that found success by following the Platters' lead and mixing pop music and rhythm and blues. Ruby and the Romantics featured lead vocalist Ruby Nash with four male backup singers. They earned three hits in 1963, including the dreamy "Our Day Will Come," which made it to number 1. "When [that record] first came out, a lot of people thought I was a white girl," says Ruby, "until they saw us in person." At that point, the group's song—which climbed the charts as the civil rights movement was blossoming—took on new meaning for some listeners.[57]

The Essex (four Marines stationed at Camp LeJeune, North Carolina) were another pop-influenced R&B rock group that had a good year in 1963. Their first release, "Easier Said than Done," became a number 1 hit. Their follow-up, "A Walkin' Miracle," did almost as well, reaching number 12. Their record company promoted them with an album cover and publicity shots that portrayed the female lead singer and three male backup singers in military garb. The clean-cut, patriotic image of four African Americans in Marine uniforms played well with audiences at a time when the civil rights movement was gaining ground and America was on alert after the Cuban Missile Crisis of the previous year.[58]

Other new groups were inspired more by gospel or R&B.[59] Gladys Knight and the Pips, for example, earned their first hit on the pop charts with "Every Beat of My Heart." The bluesy ballad showcased Gladys's emotional, gospel-influenced lead vocal. It was followed by another heartfelt ballad, "Letter Full of Tears" (1963). After a dry spell, they came back strong in the late 1960s and beyond with numerous hits, including "I Heard It Through the Grapevine" (1967) and "Midnight Train to Georgia" (1973).

Rhythm and blues influences also shaped the sound of R&B rock duos, as evidenced by Don and Juan's "What's Your Name" (1962), Don Gardner and Dee Dee Ford's "I Need Your Loving" (1962), and Dean and Jean's "Tra La La La Suzy" (1963). The most popular of the three was "What's Your Name," which peaked at number 7. Listeners couldn't get enough of the ballad's climactic finish. Don and Juan pause for a split second . . . and then shout out in all their doo-wop glory "SHOOBY-DOOP-BOP-BWAH-DAH!"

R&B rock of the early 1960s showcased topnotch artists and innovative sounds that injected vitality into all of rock & roll. The dynamic music was the perfect soundtrack for the changing times. As the civil rights movement expanded and African Americans stepped into the national spotlight, more opportunities opened for Black artists and music. The resulting R&B rock didn't just mirror the times. It became a vehicle for racial integration.

6

"Let's Have a Party!"

Rockin' the Country

Wanda Jackson's "Let's Have a Party" was the wildest rockabilly hit of the early 1960s. The song was originally recorded by Elvis Presley for his 1957 movie *Loving You*, but it was Jackson's manic version—an explosive mix of rock and country music—that made the pop charts in 1960. Jackson's sexy appearance was as shocking as the song. Although she started out as a country and western singer, she never embraced traditional cowgirl outfits. Instead, she preferred skimpy camisoles that bared her shoulders, and tight-fitting, fringed dresses. Her seamstress mother made her first fringed shift. "All I had to do on that dress was tap my foot and everything moved," explained Wanda.[1]

Like many country artists, Jackson's career changed dramatically because of Elvis. Wanda met the rockabilly singer on a country music tour in 1955. Presley advised her to try her hand at rock & roll. "I'm just a country singer," she replied. Elvis insisted, "I am, too, basically. But, you can do this." Wanda agreed to give it a shot. Her first attempt, "I Gotta Know" (1956), alternated awkwardly between a country ballad and rock & roll. Jackson rocked a little more confidently on subsequent rockabilly releases, including the high-energy "Fujiyama Mama" (1957), an R&B song originally recorded by Annisteen Allen in 1955. However, nothing charted until "Let's Have a Party" cracked the Top 40 in 1960.[2]

"Let's Have a Party" turned out to be Wanda's first and last rock & roll hit. "In the '50s, when I had the nerve to jump out there and be the only girl recordin' this stuff, and singin' this wild stuff, and with my fringe flyin' and my guitar twangin', and breakin' strings, I didn't ever get any recognition," said Wanda. Music writer Rick Kienzle suggests, "America was barely used to the idea of hip-shaking male rockers, much less rockin' gals."[3]

In any case, Jackson shook up rock & roll. Her high-energy "Let's Have a Party" echoed the upbeat mood of early 60s America. It expressed the era's materialism and hedonistic culture, particularly teenagers' interests in parties, dancing, and sex. It also anticipated changing gender roles. "Wanda Jackson wasn't afraid to step outside the prim confines of a woman's place in pop—sonically, lyrically, and aesthetically," explains music writer Holly George-Warren. "With her unique bluesy yelps and raucous growls, sensual and energized stage presence, and catchy, rhythmic repertoire, Jackson helped change the face of popular music."[4]

After "Let's Have a Party," Wanda tacked back toward country music and earned Top 30 hits with two traditional country songs, "Right or Wrong" (1961) and "In the Middle of a Heartache" (1961). But her claim to fame remained "Let's Have a Party," which became a cult classic and achieved added popularity when it was featured in the 1989 film *Dead Poet's Society*.

Wanda Jackson was only one of many country singers who followed Elvis Presley down the rock & roll highway. Top 40 radio of the early 60s played a variety of country-influenced styles, including rockabilly and innovative blends of country, pop, and rock. Some of the artists like Elvis Presley, the Everly Brothers, Brenda Lee, Roy Orbison, and Wanda Jackson would eventually be enshrined in the Rock & Roll Hall of Fame. Others, such as Jack Scott, Sue Thompson, and the Fendermen would never become superstars, but they, too, would have glorious moments in the rock & roll spotlight.

ROCKABILLY

When the 1960s decade began, rock & roll's biggest draw was still Elvis Presley. After the rockabilly pioneer was discharged from the army in 1960, his first three releases—"Stuck on You," "It's Now or Never," and "Are You Lonesome Tonight"—became number 1 records. He followed up with two more number 1 hits: "Surrender" (1961) and "Good Luck Charm" (1962). Bass player Bob Moore recalls the sheer pandemonium at a 1961 Elvis concert in Hawaii. "There was a huge crush of people. Young women tearing at your clothes. A million flashbulbs. It was blinding," he says. "Our view from the stage was like looking into a sky of exploding stars."[5] Paradoxically, Elvis's superstar status led to his demise as a legitimate rock & roller. Ever since the 1950s he had dreamed of making it big as a movie star. After he got out of the army, Presley decided to roll the Hollywood dice. The rock & roll Elvis would soon give way to movie Elvis.

Hollywood salivated at the thought of the King of Rock & Roll on the silver screen. "A Presley picture is the only sure thing in Hollywood," said producer Hal Wallis. Not surprisingly, Wallis and other studio bigwigs collaborated with Presley's manager, Colonel Tom Parker, and together they rode the Elvis box office bandwagon. They cranked out nine movies in just four years, from *G.I. Blues* (1960) to *Fun in Acapulco* (1963). Presley's manager had no illusions his star was making artistic films. "All they're good for is to make money," admitted the Colonel.[6]

Presley enjoyed the big bucks and all the Hollywood glitz, but he also felt more than just a twinge of regret. This was not the kind of success Elvis had envisioned when he launched his film career with *Love Me Tender* (1956). He had ambitions of becoming a serious actor like Marlon Brando or James Dean. His first four films offered glimpses of his potential. "*King Creole* . . . is Elvis's best movie to date," wrote one critic in 1958. "It gives Presley his chance at a more substantial dramatic role . . . and he rises to the occasion."[7]

After Elvis was discharged from the army he still wanted to be a serious actor. Following *G.I. Blues,* a light-hearted musical comedy, Presley starred in a serious drama. *Flaming Star* (1960), a Western directed by Don Siegel, showcased Presley as a sensitive young man caught between the cultures of his white father and Indian mother. The storyline resonated at a time when the civil rights movement was picking up momentum, but it spooked Colonel Parker. Hoping to avoid racial controversy, the Colonel insisted that Siegel lighten the mood by having Elvis sing. Years later, the director noted that Parker's attempt to transform *Flaming Star* into a light musical was a bad omen for Elvis's career. "I found [Elvis] sensitive and very good," said Siegel, "[but] his advisors—namely the Colonel—were very much against doing this kind of role . . . Obviously they didn't want to get him off a winning horse."[8]

Evidently, Elvis fans agreed more with the Colonel than they did with Siegel. Both *Flaming Star* and Elvis's subsequent drama, *Wild in the Country,* barely broke even at the box office, suggesting that moviegoers preferred comedies that featured a singing Elvis to serious dramas with fewer songs. Colonel Parker, with Elvis in tow, was willing to give customers what they wanted for a price—a very big price. The cagey Colonel knew that Hollywood was eager to rent if not buy the King of Rock & Roll, no matter what the cost.

Economic reality soon overwhelmed Elvis's dream of becoming a serious actor. Presley's 1961 film *Blue Hawaii* was the tipping point. Prior to that musical comedy, movies like *King Creole* and *Flaming Star* had given Presley a chance to develop acting skills, but despite positive reviews the dramas did not do well at the box office. Then came the smash hit *Blue Hawaii*. Moviegoers were wowed by the glamorous stars, snappy pop songs, and spectacular scenery. Most didn't mind the mediocre acting or flimsy storyline. *Blue Hawaii* became a box office bonanza and platform to sell Elvis records and other products. The film grossed almost $10.5 million, ultimately becoming Presley's most commercially successful film. The soundtrack was also a huge success. The *Blue Hawaii* album spent 20 weeks at the number 1 spot on *Billboard*'s Top Album chart and went on to became Elvis's best-selling album of all time.

Like a tidal wave, *Blue Hawaii* swept away any plans Elvis might have had to star in dramas. Both Hollywood producers and Colonel Parker urged the singer to give audiences what they wanted—musical comedies. Sadly, he went along with it. Throughout the rest of the decade, Elvis movies (except for the Western *Charro*) followed the *Blue Hawaii* formula. The musical comedies were filmed in exotic locales and featured thin plots, silly dialogue, lots of glitz, a ton of ephemeral pop songs, and numerous opportunities for Elvis to dance and romance sexy starlets. The hero was invariably a rock & roll version of Horatio Alger. His wholesome values, determination, good looks, and abilities, not the least of which was singing, enabled him to succeed, get the girl, and live happily ever after. All in all, a perfect fit for the hedonism and values of Cold War America.

Elvis had reservations about the direction his movie career was headed. But, in the end, he sold his rock & roll soul for a Hollywood pot of gold. Maybe the fast-talking Colonel Parker simply bamboozled the former "Hillbilly Cat." Conceivably, Elvis wasn't able to stand up to sophisticated Hollywood moguls. Or, maybe he was just swallowed up and spit out by the same Hollywood star-making machinery that had destroyed the careers of other aspiring actors. In any case, Presley stayed on the Hollywood express bound for fame, fortune, and glory.

Every once in a while, Elvis expressed concern about the films he was cranking out. "The only thing that's worse than watching a bad movie is being in one," he told a reporter. The songs in the films were just as disappointing. Presley's initial movies featured some excellent rock & roll, including "Jailhouse Rock" (the title song of the 1957 film) and "Hard Headed Woman" (from *King Creole* in 1958). But the movie soundtracks got increasingly worse in the 1960s. Occasionally, a good song would pop up such as "Can't Help Falling in Love" in *Blue Hawaii*, but overall, the songs found in Elvis movies of the 1960s ranged from mediocre to outright horrible. Gordon Stoker, a member of the Jordanaires who sang on most of Elvis's hits and Hollywood soundtracks, witnessed Presley's frustration firsthand. "Sometimes [during a recording session] he'd walk over to us and say, 'Man, what do we do with a piece of shit like this?'"[9]

Despite the reservations, Elvis kept making musical comedies. Repeatedly, he promised himself that somewhere down the road he would try something more serious. But his addiction to Hollywood kept him hooked on cinematic fluff. Presley's insecurities, materialistic desires, and Colonel Parker's arguments allowed Elvis to rationalize the types of movies he was making. "Well, I would like to play a dramatic role, but I don't" he said. "I haven't had enough experience in acting. And, until I'm ready for it, it would be foolish to undertake something very dramatic."[10]

Whether Presley would have succeeded as a serious actor is debatable. All that's certain is that he starred in 31 profitable albeit mediocre movies between 1956 and 1969. In the process, Elvis was co-opted by Hollywood. If die-hard rock & rollers were put off by the tame version of Presley presented in these glitzy but vacuous films, most Elvis lovers were more than satisfied. Ticket sales suggest that fans enjoyed the entertainment and couldn't get enough of Hollywood's stylized images of the telegenic Elvis and his homogenized, pop-oriented music.

The contrived movies might have been bad for Presley as a singer and serious actor, but they helped him hit the jackpot in Hollywood and Las Vegas. The slick, non-threatening films offered a polished image of Elvis and rock & roll in

the years following the payola scandal. Even though Hollywood Elvis was no longer an authentic rock & roller, he was still a superstar.

If early Elvis represented wild rockabilly back in the 1950s, the Everly Brothers
embodied the music's softer side. Don and Phil had a country music pedigree.
Their parents, Margaret and Ike, loved country and western and performed at
barn dances, country jubilees, and on local radio. But the real talent in the family
belonged to the sons. By the mid-1950s the boys were singing alongside their
parents, wowing audiences with their pristine harmonies. In 1954 Ike landed an
audition for his boys with Chet Atkins, who headed RCA's Nashville branch. Impressed by the teenagers' singing and songwriting, Atkins placed two of Don's
compositions with country artists Kitty Wells and Anita Carter.[11]

When the Everly family moved to Nashville in 1955, Atkins introduced Don
and Phil to Wesley Rose, president of Acuff-Rose Music Publishing. Rose was
convinced the talented duo could help his company tap into the teenage market, so he signed them as songwriters and then helped them land a recording
contract with Archie Bleyer's Cadence label.[12]

In March 1957 the Everly Brothers went into a Nashville studio to record
"Bye Bye Love," composed by two of Acuff-Rose's most talented songwriters,
Boudleaux Bryant and his wife, Felice. The Everlys liked the country song, but
Don suggested a new Bo Diddley-type introduction to give it a more youthful
feel. After Bleyer heard Don play the riff, he agreed they should give it a try. One
of the musicians that day, guitarist Ray Edenton, explained, "Don came in with
that big Gibson jumbo guitar [which had] a booming bass sound [and] Don
just . . . banged out that intro. It was an incredibly innovative sound." Record buyers agreed, sending "Bye Bye Love" all the way to number 2. "Without that intro," said Phil Everly, "who knows what would have happened? Once Don came
up with that, we were off."[13]

The Everly Brothers became one of rock & roll's hottest new acts. Their
pitch-perfect harmonies and plaintive country vocals twanged at teenage heartstrings. If "Bye Bye Love" was country, it was also pure rock & roll. As acoustic
guitars slammed out power chords, the duo told a woeful tale about teenage
heartbreak. "I feel like I could die," they sang. "Bye bye, my love, goodbye."[14]

The Everly Brothers (Jim Pierson Collection)

Their next release, "Wake Up Little Susie," also written by the Bryants, became the Everlys' first number 1 record. Once again, Don and Phil made effective use of their extraordinary harmonies and precision guitar work, and once
again they sang lyrics aimed at teenagers. This time around the Everlys told an
amusing tale about a young couple who fell asleep during a boring film at a drive-
in. The duo followed up with additional hits that targeted young listeners. They
scored with romantic ballads written by Boudleaux and Felice Bryant, including
"All I Have to Do Is Dream" (1958) and "Devoted to You" (1958). They rocked on
upbeat hits such as "Claudette" (1958) and "('Til) I Kissed You" (1959). And,
they offered humorous takes on high school life on songs like "Bird Dog" (1958)
and "Problems" (1958).

In the early 1960s, the Everly Brothers made personal and professional de-
cisions that would rock their lives. Don and Phil began the decade by signing a
new record deal with Warner Brothers. The million-dollar contract was, at that
point, the largest ever given to a rock & roll act. The entertainment giant offered
better marketing potential and opportunities in movies and television. But there
was a downside. When the brothers moved their base of operations from Nash-

ville to Los Angeles, they left behind Music City's familiar RCA Recording Studio B, as well as the topnotch producers, engineers, and studio musicians who helped shape the Everlys' sound, including guitarists Chet Atkins and Ray Edenton, pianist Floyd Cramer, drummer Buddy Harman, and bassist Floyd Chance.

The new record deal caused Don and Phil to part ways with manager Wesley Rose. The brothers were angry that Rose had written himself into the Warner contract with veto power over new Everly releases. Rose denied he had a veto, explaining that he and the Everlys always had an understanding that singles would be written by Acuff-Rose songwriters. When the brothers insisted on releasing their version of Bing Crosby's 1934 hit "Temptation," Rose felt betrayed. He retaliated by cutting off the Everlys' access to material written by Acuff-Rose songwriters, including the Bryants. "Leaving Wesley was no problem for us, but missing the Bryant songs was a tremendous problem," said Phil. "It's like a Rolls-Royce compared to a Chevy. Now, you might have a great Chevy, but a Rolls-Royce is something else, and Boudleaux's songs will be mostly Rolls-Royce songs."[15]

The new decade introduced other problems. The move to Hollywood put additional strain on their lives and careers. Hoping to get into movies, the brothers took acting classes for six months with no satisfactory results. Meanwhile, Warner Brothers began pressuring them to move toward pop music to ensure a long-lasting music career. A more serious problem lurked in the shadows. The Everlys were exhausted from constant touring. In an effort to help out, their old boss at Cadence Records, Archie Bleyer, referred Don and Phil to one of the most respected physicians in New York City. Dr. Max Jacobson had a sterling reputation based on innovative approaches to nutrition and vitamin therapy. His patients included celebrated musicians, artists, writers, and politicians, including President John F. Kennedy. Many were later surprised to learn that the potent mix of vitamins and drugs that the doctor injected into their veins included amphetamines. *The New York Times* reported that many patients insisted that the shots gave them "boundless energy and more productive and pleasurable lives." But, more than a few, including Don Everly, complained that the mystery cocktails caused anxiety, sleeplessness, and depression, as well as addiction to speed.[16]

Despite the mounting personal and professional problems, the Everly Brothers' career showed no signs of slowing down, at least not at first. They earned six Top 20 hits in 1960, partly because two different record companies bombarded the pop charts with competing Everly releases. Cadence was miffed by the duo's defection. So, every time the brothers released a new song on Warner Brothers, Archie Bleyer countered by releasing an Everly recording from the Cadence sound archives. Cadence launched a preemptive strike several weeks before Warner was able to issue its first Everly record. In January 1960 Cadence hit the pop charts with the romantic "Let It Be Me," which climbed all the way up to number 7.

The Everly Brothers struck back hard in early April with their initial Warner Brothers release, "Cathy's Clown." Written by Don and Phil, the song rocketed up to number 1. As their stunning harmonies weave in and out, the brothers sing plaintively about an unfaithful girlfriend. In keeping with gender expectations, they try to stand tall, because a man can't crawl. But, they die each time they hear people say, "Here he comes, that's Cathy's clown." Don explained, "Part of the inspiration for 'Cathy's Clown' was . . . [Ferde Grofé's] 'Grand Canyon Suite': 'domp-de-domp-de-da-da-da, boom-chaka-boom.'" Plus, "I had this girlfriend called Catherine." The record connected with teenage listeners, who appreciated the anguished harmonies about heartbreak set against a pronounced rock & roll beat.[17]

Additional Everly hits in 1960 included "When Will I Be Loved" and "Like Strangers" on the Cadence label, as well as "So Sad (To Watch Good Love Go Bad)" and "Lucille" on Warner Brothers. Although Cadence won some victories in 1960, the Warner label eventually won the record war since Bleyer had no new material to release.

The Everly Brothers began 1961 with a two-sided smash hit. "Ebony Eyes" told a sad story about a young soldier waiting for his fiancé to arrive on an airplane only to learn that the plane has crashed. The tearjerker soared to number 8. The flipside, "Walk Right Back," was an even bigger hit, peaking at number 7. The song juxtaposed stunning harmonies and an upbeat guitar riff against desperate lyrics about a failed relationship. The result was an optimistic sound and message, which assured listeners there's always hope for a broken heart.

After the double-sided hit, the Everly Brothers' music went in a totally different direction. Warner executives convinced Don and Phil that the key to long-term success was to tack toward adult pop music just as Elvis had done. The Everlys' last two hits of 1961—covers of Bing Crosby's 1934 hit "Temptation," and jazz singer Ethel Waters's 1933 ballad "Don't Blame Me"—were steps in that direction. In August Warner Brothers released the Everly Brothers' new album, *Both Sides of an Evening*, which included pop standards like "Mention My Name in Sheboygan" and "My Gal Sal." The album flopped, suggesting that teenagers were put off by the rock & roll duo's renditions of old pop songs.

When 1962 began there was a hopeful sign that the dreadful pop experiments were over. In January the Everlys debuted the haunting "Crying in the Rain." Composed by Carole King and Howard Greenfield, the powerful pop rock ballad blended the duo's smooth harmonies with state-of-the-art Brill Building sounds, including strings and upscale production values. The record, which featured expressive vocals and sad lyrics about lost love, offered rock & roll catharsis to millions of listeners suffering from broken hearts. The song also reinforced gender stereotypes that maintained that real men did not cry or reveal hurt feelings in public. The song's proud protagonist vows to hide his sorrow and pain from his ex-girlfriend. "I'll do my cryin' in the rain," sing the Everlys.[18]

Just when it seemed like the Everly Brothers were back on track as rock & roll singers, they released the brassy "That's Old Fashioned (That's the Way Love Should Be)." The unabashed pop song featured a big band arrangement and trite lyrics about a couple strolling under the silvery moon, playing the nickelodeon, and discussing marriage. On the plus side, the song's nostalgic message and defense of traditional values resonated with many listeners in a Cold War era that glorified marriage. Evidently there were still enough Everly fans around, because the record became a Top 10 hit.

"That's Old Fashioned" turned out to be the brothers' last big hit. Their last three releases in 1962 failed to make the Top 40, and an album, *Instant Party*, did not chart at all. The disappointing album was a troubling sign that the legendary duo was abandoning rock & roll. Even faithful fans could not fathom why an Everly album would include pop chestnuts like "Bye Bye Blackbird" or schmaltzy show tunes such as "Oh! My Papa (O Mein Papa)."

Subsequently, the Everly Brothers' career imploded. Incredibly, not one of their records released in 1963 made *Billboard*'s Top 100 singles chart. In retrospect, the 1962 hit, "Crying in the Rain," offers a good metaphor for the Everlys' inability to cope with growing problems. Like the song's protagonist, Don and Phil appeared fine in public, but they were hurting inside. In the early 1960s both brothers had to cope with moving to a new record company, changing managers, relocating to new cities, constant touring, and worrying about careers, while also dealing with deteriorating personal relationships, health issues, and life's daily stresses. Then came news that Don and Phil were about to be drafted for a two-year stint in the army. They enlisted in the Marine Reserves in 1961 and served six months active duty instead. "What we needed was to take a long vacation, to get off the merry-go-round," noted Phil. "There were too many people making too much money off us, keeping us going." He added, "The tensions between Don and I . . . Everything that was happening then contributed to it."[19]

Growing dependence on prescription drugs accelerated the brothers' downward spiral. "The first signs of the Everlys' problems appeared on their first tour of the UK in 1960," explains music writer Ray Connolly. "Don . . . had a nervous breakdown, leaving Phil to carry on with the tour alone." The situation got worse in 1961. Don was addicted to the speed that he was unknowingly getting from Dr. Jacobson. The "vitamin" injections pumped Don up, causing insomnia, erratic behavior, drastic weight loss, and paranoia. His personal life fell apart. He divorced his first wife, and his relationship with his brother deteriorated.[20]

Don's prescription drug problem eased after he entered the Marine Reserves in November 1961. During the next six months of active duty, he went cold turkey and slowly recovered with the help of the military's rigorous basic training. Unfortunately, Don resumed Ritalin therapy shortly after he left active duty in the Marines. "People didn't understand drugs that well then," Don explained years later. "They didn't know what they were messing with. It wasn't against the law: I saw a picture of my doctor with the president, you know?" Don added, "Ritalin made you feel energized. You could stay up for days. It just got me strung out. I was so far out there I didn't know what I was doing. It got out of hand, and it was a real disaster."[21]

The reckoning came in October 1962, during an Everly Brothers tour in England. "Don was by then obsessed with Ritalin—and, in his growing paranoia, feeling smothered as an individual artist within that fading entity called the Everly Brothers," explains music writer Kurt Loder. "He attempted to kill himself by taking an overdose of barbiturates." He was rushed to a London hospital and had his stomach pumped. When Don got back to the hotel, he attempted suicide again. "This time," reports Loder, "his rescuers put him on a plane back to the States, where he was committed to the mental ward of a New York City hospital and given electroshock therapy." The solution was at least as bad as the initial problem. "They say shock therapy is good for some things, but it didn't do me any good," said Don. "It was a pretty primitive treatment at the time—once they gave it to you, you couldn't remember how long you'd been there. It knocked me back for a long time. I thought I'd never write again."[22]

In time, Don and Phil would bounce back from their struggles with personal and professional demons. But their valiant efforts did not come soon enough to prevent the duo's total collapse in 1963. Of all the unsuccessful records the Everly Brothers released that year, the most intriguing is "Nancy's Minuet." Composed by Don Everly, the song's foreboding sound and anguished lyrics captured the Everlys' dark mood: "I'm dancing round and round, acting just like a clown. I know I'll never be free."[23]

The Everly Brothers later made a brief comeback. They returned to the charts with "Gone, Gone, Gone" (1964) and "Bowling Green" (1967). They performed frequently in concerts and even landed their own TV show in 1970. Don and Phil split up in 1973 and then reunited in 1983. Their last hit record came a year later with "On the Wings of a Nightingale," written by Paul McCartney. When Phil died in 2014 from complications related to chronic obstructive pulmonary disease, Don said "I was listening to one of my favorite songs that Phil wrote and had an extreme emotional moment just before I got the news of his passing." He added, "I took that as a special spiritual message from Phil saying goodbye. Our love was and will always be deeper than any earthly differences we might have had."[24]

The Everly Brothers' musical legacy is vast. They recorded many of rock & roll's all-time greatest hits, and their pristine harmonies became the benchmark for later artists, including Simon & Garfunkel and the Beatles. The Everlys' innovative sound changed rock & roll, infusing it with country harmonies that softened the music's rough rhythm and blues edge. The Everlys put Nashville on the rock & roll map. "They were the first consistently successful rock & roll act to come from there," notes Colin Escott. "Their management and their songs came from Nashville, and they recorded there with local session men."[25]

Over the years, the Everly Brothers have received numerous awards and accolades. They were members of the first class inducted into the Rock & Roll Hall of Fame in 1984. They received a Grammy Lifetime Achievement Award in 1997. And, they entered the Country Music Hall of Fame in 2001. The brothers' harmonic blend of country music, rhythm and blues, and rock & roll produced an innovative country rock sound that had wide appeal in the 1950s and early 60s. "I didn't think Presley was as good as the Everly boys," said Chuck Berry. "And I didn't think the Beatles were as good as the Everly Brothers either."[26]

Like the Everly Brothers, Brenda Lee came out of Nashville in the 1950s and went on to become a rock & roll superstar. Her professional breakthrough came in 1956, when the 11-year-old Brenda sang "Jambalaya" at a Red Foley concert in Georgia. Impressed by the youngster's incredible voice, Foley invited her to appear on his *Ozark Jubilee* TV show. When fan mail came pouring in, he hired her as a regular. Foley's manager, Dub Allbritten, then landed a Decca recording contract for Brenda and arranged guest appearances on network TV, the Grand Ole Opry, and in Las Vegas and Europe.[27]

Decca producer Owen Bradley remembers Brenda's first recording session in Nashville on July 30, 1956. The 11-year-old cut two country songs, "Jambalaya" and "Bigelow 6-200": "The thing that struck me was how unconcerned she was to be such a small kid," said Bradley. When the tape began rolling, she suddenly yelled "Stop!" Little Brenda pointed calmly at one of the musicians and explained he had missed a note. "The bass player said yes, he had," recalled Bradley. "Nobody else had caught it."[28] With Presleymania going strong in 1957, Brenda took a few tentative steps toward rock & roll with teen-oriented songs such as "Rock the Bop" and "Dynamite."

Brenda hit her stride when she recorded "Sweet Nothin's." Written by rock-abilly artist Ronnie Self, the song became her first hit on the national pop charts. "Sweet Nothin's" made its debut just before Christmas 1959. By early April it was the number 4 hit in the country. The record begins with an intimate exchange between a young girl and her boyfriend. After he whispers something provocative in her ear, she responds, "Alright." The record then blasts off bound for uncharted territory in boy-girl relationships. Brenda's sassy and suggestive vocal details how her boyfriend says things she likes to hear. He tells her secrets, they walk hand in hand, and give each other special looks. They also make out on the porch until her Mama turns off the light and says, "Come in darlin', that's enough for tonight."[29]

Lee's smash hit stood out from most of the songs heard on Top 40 radio in 1960. Rock & roll fans loved the pounding beat, honking sax, and suggestive lyrics. Never before had they experienced a young girl singing so boldly about sex. Listeners were amazed to learn that Brenda was just 14 years old when she recorded "Sweet Nothin's." They were also surprised when they found out she was white, because the song sounded like R&B. "I was even played a lot on black radio stations," she noted.[30]

Lee's next release, "I'm Sorry" (1960), made it to number 1. The rockabilly ballad featured Brenda singing passionately about the anguish of young love. She apologizes repeatedly to her boyfriend for the hurt she's caused. Her heart-wrenching vocal is complemented by a slow, insistent rock beat and dramatic violins, which etched the haunting ballad into the minds of young listeners. "'I'm Sorry' was one of the first Nashville sessions to use strings," notes Owen Bradley. "We decided to let the fiddles answer—when Brenda sang, 'I'm sorry,' the fiddles would answer 'I'm sorry.'" Decca initially balked at having a teenage girl singing so intimately about an intense romantic relationship. Company executives had not liked "Sweet Nothin's" either, insisting that both Ronnie Self compositions were unsuitable for a young female singer. "I held those songs for a couple of years before I could get the record company to believe enough in them to record them," explains Brenda. "I always thought they were great songs, and fortunately the public proved me right."[31]

Decca was pleased when the flipside of "I'm Sorry"—an upbeat rockabilly song entitled "That's All You Gotta Do"—also went Top 10. The two-sided hit was evidence of Lee's versatility. The power and range of her expressive voice and unique blend of rock & roll, country, rhythm and blues, and pop would make her one of the most successful rock & roll artists of the early 1960s. "[Brenda] has a big voice, and she is able to get the rhythm and beat into her voice. Some people—even some people with great voices—can't do that," explains Bradley. "A good singer must get you involved with the song and Brenda does that . . . She can sing any type of song."[32]

Lee recorded some of the greatest ballads in rock & roll history. Most focused on heartbreak, including her two number 1 hits of 1960, "I'm Sorry" and "I Want to Be Wanted," and other Top 10 hits such as "Emotions," "You Can Depend on Me," and "Fool #1" in 1961; "Break It To Me Gently" and "All Alone Am I" in 1962; and "Losing You" in 1963. Lee's state-of-the-art country rock built on the sophisticated sounds that producers Leiber and Stoller pioneered with the Drifters. Her powerful ballads boasted wonderful melodies, irresistible hooks, and lush arrangements with strings, horns, and choral groups. Her number 4 hit from 1962, "Break It To Me Gently," is a perfect example. The record features teen-oriented lyrics and spotlights Brenda's dramatic vocal backed by the Anita Kerr Singers, Nashville studio musicians, and pop-influenced violins. "'Break It to Me Gently'" was one of my first forays . . . into the R&B field," explained Brenda. "It was just one of those great songs and there's just magic."[33]

Lee's hits transformed not just early 60s rock & roll but country music as well. They proved there was a huge mass audience for records that blended country music, rock & roll, and pop. "I feel that Brenda has done as much as any other artist to build and mold what became known as the Nashville Sound," insists Owen Bradley. "The more successful she became, the more that known and unknown artists came [to Nashville] to get the same sound . . . She proved that pop could be done in Nashville."[34]

Lee was as adept at singing up-tempo rock & roll as she was slow ballads, as evidenced by "That's All You Gotta Do" (1960) and "Dum Dum" (1961). The latter became a number 4 hit and checked all the boxes for many rock & roll fans. "Dum Dum" had a great vocal, catchy refrain, a blaring sax, and solid dance

Brenda Lee album cover, 1961 (Courtesy of the Rock & Roll Hall of Fame and Museum)

beat. The lyrics alluded to a subject of particular interest to teenagers—sex. In the first verse Brenda sounds like a young Mae West, as she sings suggestively, "Your Ma's in the kitchen, your Pa's next door, I wanna love you just a little bit more."[35]

Lee's albums also featured solid rock & roll. She covered rock classics such as Ray Charles's "What'd I Say," as well as more obscure songs like "Let's Jump the Broomstick." The original was recorded in 1959 by an R&B group, Alvin Gaines and the Themes. Lee's rockabilly version gained wide exposure in 1960 when it appeared on her best-selling album *Brenda Lee*. The fast-paced song showcased Brenda's rockabilly credentials. "Let's Jump the Broomstick" was outright subversive. Its close ties to African American culture provided a racial subtext. Here was a young white girl from the South singing a rhythm and blues song about "jumping the broom," an African American marriage tradition that dated back to the days of slavery. The song also undermines the era's traditional attitudes toward gender and family. When Brenda shouts out the rebellious lyrics, she demonstrates that a female can rock as well as Elvis or any other male. The song makes it clear that the young woman is in charge. The strong-willed teenager tells her boyfriend they're going to get married even though her entire family is against it. "Come a little baby, let's jump the broomstick," she insists. "Come and let's tie the knot."[36]

Brenda was equally at home with country music. As a child, she sang at local fairs and on country and western stations, and she never lost touch with her country roots. Brenda recorded country songs such as Hank Williams's "Jambalaya" and Kathryn Fulton's "Fool #1," and her country rock hits were recorded in Nashville accompanied by talented country musicians such as Boots Randolph on sax, Floyd Cramer on piano, Buddy Harman on drums, Bob Moore on bass, and Grady Martin, Ray Edenton, and Harold Bradley on guitars.[37]

Traditional pop music added another key ingredient to Brenda Lee's sound. She became rock & roll's equivalent of a torch singer as she recorded pop-influenced rock ballads, as well as her renditions of pop songs. "All Alone Am I," her number 3 hit from 1962, is a perfect example. "[That] was a Greek song," explains Brenda, "It was in the movie, *Never on Sunday*, and . . . written by Manos Hadjidakis. We got the song with just the melody and loved it. They translated it into English, we recorded it, and it became a hit record." Few, if any, rock & roll fans knew the pop music backstory. All they knew was that they could relate to Lee's emotional song about heartbreak. Brenda Lee even transformed a pop song written by a Tin Pan Alley composer into a rock & roll classic. "'Rockin' Around the Christmas Tree' was sent to me by Johnny Marks, who . . . wrote 'Rudolph the Red Nose Reindeer,'" says Brenda. "I thought it was a really good song . . . with timeless lyrics." The record was released in 1958 and went nowhere. When it was reissued after Brenda became a rock & roll star, it became a Top 20 hit in 1960 and has remained a holiday favorite ever since.[38]

From the very beginning, Brenda Lee was hard to label. Was she a rock & roll singer? A country artist who crossed over to the rock charts? A pop performer? "I don't think I really ever considered myself to be any kind of singer. I just consider myself a singer," she explains. "I have been lucky that I've been able to sing all types of music . . . and charted in several fields of music. So, I've tried not to label myself."[39]

Regardless of what she sang, Brenda's sound and style resonated with audiences. The first thing most people noticed was the sheer power and emotion of her voice. Brenda's dramatic vocals could make people laugh or cry, feel loved or unwanted, sad or hopeful—sometimes all within the space of one three-minute record. Making it even more phenomenal was the fact that the booming sound came from a young girl who was just 4 feet 9 inches tall. Her dynamic performance style was equally impressive and led to the nickname "Little Miss Dynamite." "That name was given to me in England when I went over there," explains Brenda. "I had a record out ["Dynamite"], people saw me work on the stage . . . just all over the place, jumping up and down, growling and singing."[40]

Nothing about Brenda was contrived. She chose her own material, selected her hairstyles and fashions, and acted the way she wanted on and off stage. The self-assured young woman determined what she would sing and how she would sing it. The final decision, says Brenda, came down to "if the lyrics were good, if the song said something, if it was honest, and if I could deliver it." Fortunately, she had a producer who agreed with her approach. "Owen and I worked together . . . but the end decision was mine," she explains. At the same time, she was always willing to listen to Bradley's opinion. "If he said, 'No, I really want you to do this song,' then I was more than willing to try it. And a lot of times things like that worked out to my benefit." Similarly, neither her producer nor record label tried to shape Brenda's image. "I just had to be who I was," she says, "and fortunately it worked."[41]

Brenda's comment that her approach "worked" is an understatement. The fact that she was just 15 years old when she made the pop charts provided an immediate connection to the young audience. Brenda wasn't surprised that girls could relate to the experiences she sang about. "A lot of my songs were . . . [about] unrequited teenage love, heartbreak, and whatever," she says. "I got a lot of mail where girls said they felt drawn to my songs because, like me, they didn't have a boyfriend, they liked somebody that didn't like them, or they were lonely or things like that." Brenda's songs and style empowered young women. "When she's singing sad songs, songs of loss, Brenda Lee is never weak. That's her message, underneath it all," insists country singer Alison Krauss. "You always know she's going to recover, and you never feel sorry for her."[42]

Lee's rock & roll career peaked during the Kennedy years, but her popularity plummeted when the times and tastes suddenly changed. The mood of the country became more serious after the young president's assassination. Public concern grew as the Vietnam War escalated, the civil rights movement descended into violence, and society started to unravel. As the nation became polarized over politics, war, race, gender, and culture wars of the late 1960s and 70s, baby boomers turned increasingly to the Beatles, Bob Dylan, and other politically and socially relevant artists. At that point, Brenda Lee, like many American rock & rollers from the more innocent days of the early 1960s, fell out of step with the young audience and changing times. Brenda's last big hit was a number 11 song in 1966 that belied its title—"Comin' on Strong." Even "Johnny One Time," the outstanding ballad that earned Lee a Grammy nomination in 1969 for Best Female Pop Vocal Performance, stalled on the pop charts.

In response, Brenda returned to what she knew best, country music. During the 1970s and beyond, she earned numerous hits on the country charts, including "Nobody Wins" (1973) and "Big Four Poster Bed" (1974). The transition was seamless. "I've never said to myself I'm a rock singer so I can't sing pop, or I'm a pop singer so I can't sing country," she explained. "I've always thought why can't you sing it all?" Living in Nashville enabled Brenda to fine-tune her career and life. "I've always loved my career. But after I married and had a family, that became very important to me, and I had some roads to choose and some priorities to set," she explained. "For the first several years of my career, I ate, breathed, and slept show business. Later, I chose not to do that." Instead, she opted "to have the best of both worlds and have my family life and career . . . That means I may not be as 'hot' as a lot of artists are, but I may be happier."[43]

Brenda Lee's fans never forgot her initial success as a rock & roll singer. Between 1960 and 1963 she earned twenty-three Top 40 hits, including two number 1 records and ten more that landed in the Top 10. Her hits not only provide evidence of the diverse sounds heard on rock & roll stations in the early 60s, but they reveal much about the times. They were intertwined with youth culture, gender attitudes, and traditional values in Kennedy's America. Her music is proof of the folk connection between early rock & roll and baby boom audiences.

Brenda would eventually sell over 100 million records worldwide with hits on the rock, pop, R&B, and country music charts. She would be inducted into the Rock & Roll Hall of Fame, the Country Music Hall of Fame, and Rockabilly Hall of Fame. She also would garner four Grammy nominations and receive a Lifetime Achievement Grammy. Brenda Lee's place in rock & roll history was summed up best by John Lennon: "She has the greatest rock and roll voice of them all."[44]

Brenda Lee wasn't the only great voice to emerge from country rock in the late 1950s and early 60s. Roy Orbison also found success with a string of rock & roll hits recorded in Nashville. But his route to the Music City was anything but direct. Born in 1936 in Vernon, Texas, Orbison grew up in Wink, a small, dusty West Texas town dominated by football and oil fields. As a youngster, Roy loved all types of music. "When I started playing for the public at age 8, I did everything from 'In the Mood' to country songs by Lefty Frizzell and Hank Williams," said Roy. "Plus there was an influence of Western swing, with Bob Wills and Mexican music from Texas. So that, mixed with rhythm and blues, is what I am."[45]

In 1949 Roy and four high school friends formed a country band, the Wink Westerners. When Presleymania hit the quintet changed their name to the Teen Kings and added rockabilly and R&B to their repertoire. Soon afterward, they drove to nearby Clovis, New Mexico, to record songs at Norman Petty's studio (where Buddy Holly and the Crickets got their start). One of the Teen Kings' recordings, "Ooby Dooby," was released on a small label in early 1956 and got airplay on nearby stations. Sam Phillips, who owned Sun Records in Memphis, liked what he heard and offered the Teen Kings a contract. The group was ecstatic because Sun was the legendary label that launched Elvis and other rockabilly greats.[46]

The West Texas band set off immediately for Memphis and pulled into town on March 26, 1956. The next morning Phillips rushed them into the studio to rerecord "Ooby Dooby." The record debuted on the national pop charts on June 16, 1956, eventually peaking at number 59. When subsequent releases failed to chart, most of the band returned to West Texas. But Roy stayed on at Sun as a singer, songwriter, and studio musician. None of Orbison's solo efforts charted in 1957, but some of his compositions were recorded by established stars like Johnny Cash and Buddy Holly and the Crickets.[47]

Orbison's big break came in 1958 when the Everly Brothers recorded "Claudette," a fast-paced rocker Roy had written about his wife. The brothers' version was released as the B-side of "All I Have to Do is Dream." Within weeks, the Everlys had a two-sided hit. "Dream" climbed all the way to number 1, while "Claudette" came in at number 30. The duo's manager, Wesley Rose, was elated and signed Roy as a songwriter for Acuff-Rose Music Publishing in Nashville. He also became Roy's manager and got him a recording contract with RCA-Nashville. Roy recorded seven songs for RCA in 1958 and early 1959, but none charted. When RCA released him, Roy was recruited by Monument Records, a fledgling label that Fred Foster started in Baltimore and then relocated to Nashville. "I was looking always for the unique artist, preferably one who wrote," said Foster. Orbison fit the bill and the two men clicked right from the start. Roy smiled in agreement when Foster said, "let's forget about gimmicks [like] 'Ooby Dooby.' We need to make music that will last, that we can be proud of."[48]

Orbison's first Monument recording session took place on June 3, 1959, but was uneventful. The second session on September 18 was more promising. Roy showed up with a new song that he had composed with fellow Texan Joe Melson. "Uptown" combined a rockabilly beat with lyrics that told a story about a young man determined to make it big. He works as a bellhop in a high rise and yearns for the beautiful woman in the penthouse who doesn't even know he exists. Someday he'll have money, he vows, and then she'll come around. "I'll have a big car, fine clothes, and then I'll be . . . uptown in penthouse number three," he sings. The upbeat song not only celebrated the era's consumer culture, but it plugged into the popular notion that America was a land of opportunity.[49]

Fred Foster was impressed with a rockabilly song that made a social statement, but he ran into problems in the recording studio. "[Roy] was so timid and his voice was so small and thin . . . I had strings and Boots Randolph on sax plus a big rhythm section and I really couldn't get [Roy] above the band," he recalled. Recording engineers only had two tracks to work with back then, and Foster knew it would sound horrible if he put Roy's voice on one track and everything else on the other. So, Foster and engineer Bill Porter jerry-rigged a solution: they put Orbison behind a coat rack and buffered him with coats and other stuff. Three days later, Foster got a phone call from *Billboard*'s publisher congratulating him on his accomplishment. Fred had no idea what the guy was talking about. The publisher explained, "You've invented the isolation booth . . . you know the coat rack." Years later, a bemused Foster told his granddaughter, "I don't know if I did or didn't, but I never had anyone correct me. So I got with Bill Porter and said I wanted walls I could roll around, let's . . . make a frame, stuff it with insulation, tack burlap over it and then we can roll them around and make a little room for Roy in the middle of the studio." The "Uptown" session allowed Foster and Orbison to experiment in other ways. Together they crafted a sound that would serve Roy well on subsequent records. "Uptown" was at once retro and innovative. It featured a basic rockabilly beat and 1950s doo-wop harmonies, but also sophisticated lyrics and modern pop sounds, including violins.[50]

Although "Uptown" was only a minor hit in 1960, it set the stage for Orbison's first million-seller later that year. Roy scored a number 2 hit with another Orbison-Melson composition, "Only the Lonely." The record built on "Uptown's" innovative approach. It begins with a chorus softly singing a doo-wop style refrain: "Dum-dum-dum-dumby-doo-wah, Ooh-yay-yay-yay-yah, Oh-oh-oh-oh-wah, Only the lonely." Roy then jumps in with a stunning vocal that sounds like Elvis in ballad mode. The melody is driven forward by Orbison's crystal-clear voice backed by Nashville's talented studio musicians, the Anita Kerr Singers, and violins, which drill the musical hook into listeners' brains.

Orbison's declaration—"Only the lonely know the way I feel tonight"—hit home with baby boomers who had just encountered their own romantic woes in their first year of high school. Although the plaintive ballad spotlighted teenage heartbreak, the last verse offered hope. "Maybe tomorrow, a new romance," sings Roy dramatically. "No more sorrow, but, that's the chance . . . you gotta take if your lonely heart breaks."[51] The uplifting ending was a perfect fit for the hopeful mood of teenagers on Kennedy's New Frontier.

"Only the Lonely" made Orbison a rock & roll star. His next two releases, "Blue Angel" (1960) and "I'm Hurtin'" (1961), followed the same formula, showcasing Roy's emotional voice backed by innovative arrangements. Despite their commercial success, the three hits only hinted at Orbison's enormous potential. Roy's next record would be the game changer.

The full "Orbison Sound" made its first appearance in 1961 on Roy's number 1 hit "Running Scared." The song's story line was intriguing. The singer wonders what his girlfriend would do if her old boyfriend returned. Which guy would she choose? The theoretical question becomes real when her old flame suddenly reappears. The rock & roll drama takes listeners on an exhilarating musical journey. The trip begins slowly. Backed only by an acoustic guitar, Roy sings plaintively, "Just runnin' scared each place we go, so afraid that he might show." The second time through the pace picks up. Electric guitars and drums join the mix. Like Ravel's *Bolero*, each successive verse adds to the rhythmic tension by introducing new instruments and fuller sounds. By the last verse Orbison is at full throttle—backed by loud guitars, pounding drums, soaring violins, blaring horns, and a spirited choir taking the song higher and higher. As the record builds to a climax, Roy sings, "My heart was breaking, which one would it be?" A split second later he unleashes the answer, hitting a powerful end note that launches listeners into the rock & roll stratosphere—"You turned around and walked AWAY WITH ME!"[52]

Listeners were stunned by the emotional power. Ironically, the inventive recording was almost scrapped because Orbison couldn't hit the climactic note. Producer Fred Foster explained that the singer's voice was overwhelmed by the lavish production, which included a backup band plus "11 strings, 6 background vocalists, [and] 8 rhythm players." The louder the sound got, the more Orbison's voice disappeared. Roy would hit a falsetto note, explained Foster, but it "just wasn't able to cut through all the muscle we had behind him." The producer told Roy that he had to hit that climactic note at full voice instead of a falsetto, otherwise they'd have to jettison the project. Orbison agreed to give it another shot. On the next take Foster held his breath as the song picked up momentum. "There's a certain feeling you get when the magic, when the stardust is falling . . . I could feel it." Then came the moment of truth when Roy hit that last note at full voice. "The musicians came up out of their seats," recalled Foster. "[One of them] looked at me with . . . pure astonishment like what in the world have we just heard?"[53]

Nobody was more surprised than Orbison. He later explained that the thought of abandoning the musical arrangement "embarrassed me into hitting [the last note] real hard." That was the moment when Roy discovered his incredible vocal range. "It was a whole new world," he says. "I sort of knew then that there were no limitations." Foster agrees: "After that, [Roy] never had any trouble hitting full-voice high notes at all." Orbison went on to write and record numerous "climax" hits that showcased his extraordinary talent, including "Crying" (1961), "The Crowd" (1962), and "It's Over" (1964). "When he'd write these songs with a big range, it was sort of operatic," notes Foster. "Nobody was doing that."[54]

"Running Scared" offered listeners a modern sound that demonstrated how much country rock had changed since the 1950s. Like earlier country rock hits, "Running Scared" used electric guitars and drums, but also featured innovations such as strings, horns, and better production values. Even the song's musical structure set it apart from earlier records. Most adhered to the basic formula of a verse followed by a catchy refrain, but "Running Scared" did not have a musical hook or chorus. The record "never repeats anything," explains Foster. "It starts and tells the story and then builds all the way to the climax and there it is. Nobody had done that before." Creative engineering by Bill Porter added to the unique sound. The song "started real soft, and built and built as the arrangement went on . . . from the very beginning of the song to the very end, there's a 25 dB [decibel] dynamic range," he explains. "In those days that was unheard of. If you had 3dB you were doing great."[55]

"Running Scared" was just one of many memorable Orbison songs recorded between 1960 and 1964. During that span he earned sixteen Top 30 hits, including two number 1 records, "Running Scared" (1961) and "Oh, Pretty Woman" (1964). Roy's best records were on the cutting edge of early 60s rock & roll. Each was a mini–rock opera that revolved around a dramatic teen-oriented plot, powered by his Caruso-like voice and creative orchestral arrangements. "It's music that will last forever," says Foster proudly.[56]

The quality of those records only partly explains their phenomenal success. One cannot exaggerate the importance of that *voice*. "My voice is a gift," said Orbison. With no formal musical training, he could only guess how many octaves he could span. "Better than three," he thought. Dion, who toured extensively with

Roy in the early 60s, experienced firsthand the impact of that voice. "I'd be two feet away and when [Orbison] hit those high notes, it was quiet and heartfelt," he recalled. "But the emotion would go through you like a power drill."[57]

Listeners recognized Roy's inimitable voice instantly. And, they were seldom disappointed by the musical magic carpet ride Orbison took them on. Young audiences were captivated by "Running Scared," a tension-filled tale of teenage angst. The fact that the girl gets to determine the boy's fate no doubt appealed to many young women at a time when gender equality was more hope than reality. Hits like "Candy Man" and "Oh, Pretty Woman" oozed sexuality, while "Workin' for the Man" spotlighted a young rebel's determination to triumph over the upper class. Roy's records mirrored America in other ways. Hopeful songs such as "Uptown" and "Blue Angel" suggested that teenagers shared the optimism of Kennedy's New Frontier. "Pretty Paper" offered a darker view. Released just before Christmas 1963, the Top 20 hit echoed Michael Harrington's best-seller from the previous year, *The Other America*, which examined how poverty was ignored in the world's richest country. Orbison's "Pretty Paper" described prosperous holiday shoppers rushing about to buy presents totally oblivious to a poor man on the sidewalk peddling gift wrap to passersby. "In the midst of the laughter he cries 'pretty paper, pretty ribbons of blue,'" sings Orbison.[58]

Orbison's ethereal voice transported listeners to gossamer worlds. Many of his biggest hits explored dreams, including "Dream Baby" (1962), "Leah" (1962), and "In Dreams" (1963). Other songs such as "Blue Bayou" (1963) and "Shahda-roba" (1963) found hope in nostalgic worlds or fantasy lands. Years later Orbison laughed as he explained, "Without the word *dream,* or the concept dream, and without the word *blue* and the emotions, I would have been really limited in the things I've written and performed."[59]

Orbison's iconic image—a pale-skinned troubadour with black hair, dark glasses, and black clothes—contributed to the mystique. Roy didn't look like that at the start of his career. In 1960 when he appeared on Dick Clark's Saturday night TV show, Roy seemed more like a meek, Walter Mitty-type character. Dressed in a conservative suit and tie, his hair was light brown and well-combed. Since Orbison wasn't wearing the thick glasses he needed to see clearly, he walked slowly and carefully to center stage while strumming his guitar and lip-synching to his first hit, "Uptown." His appearance soon changed. First, he dyed his hair jet black to look like a rock & roll star. Serendipity applied the finishing touches. During a 1962 tour he accidently left his regular glasses on the airplane. "I only had the sunshades," he explained, "and I was quite embarrassed to go onstage with them, but I did it." The next year Orbison found himself in the same predicament when he opened for the Beatles in England. "I walked onstage with my sunglasses on, and all over Europe we were an instant success." He added, "I probably wore something black that night, and that's how come the black outfits and dark sunglasses stuck."[60]

The new look was a perfect match for the Orbison Sound. Wearing dark glasses and dressed in black, Roy finally looked as "cool" as his music sounded. The mysterious image underscored the danger that lurked in the shadows of Orbison's transcendent music. The flip side of Roy's glorious promise of everlasting love in an exotic world was the utter despair and eternal suffering of love gone wrong, as evidenced by songs such as "Crying" (1961), "Love Hurts" (1962), and "It's Over" (1964). Roy's voice heightened the emotional impact. Bruce Springsteen later recalled listening late at night to Roy's "unearthly voice" on the stereo. "At the end of 'It's Over,' when [Orbison] hits that note where it sounds like the world's going to end, I'd be laying there promising myself that I was never going to go outside again and never going to talk to another woman," explained Springsteen.[61]

In early 1964 Roy Orbison earned a number 1 record with "Oh, Pretty Woman," his last big hit on the Monument label. Soon after, he signed a lucrative deal with MGM, but their promises of better marketing and movie stardom never panned out. Roy's star faded when musical tastes changed in the late 1960s. Personal tragedies, including the deaths of his wife, Claudette, in a motorcycle accident, and his two sons in a house fire, added to his problems.

Orbison later rebounded with more than a little help from his friends. In 1975 Springsteen revived interest in the all-but-forgotten star when he mentioned him in the epic lyrics to "Thunder Road." Other singers added to the momentum with hit versions of Orbison songs, including Linda Ronstadt's "Blue Bayou" (1977) and Van Halen's "Oh, Pretty Woman" (1982). In 1987 Roy was inducted into the Rock & Roll Hall of Fame. The following year, he and k.d.

lang won a Grammy for their stunning remake of Roy's classic, "Crying." After
a successful star-studded concert on cable TV, *Roy Orbison and Friends: A
Black and White Night*, Roy teamed up with George Harrison, Bob Dylan, Tom
Petty, and Jeff Lynne to record one of 1988's most successful albums, *The Traveling Wilburys, Volume 1*.

Tragedy then struck again. In the midst of his comeback, Orbison died suddenly on December 6, 1988. When his final album, *Mystery Girl*, was released
posthumously in 1989, it became a bestseller. The album included new songs
such as "You Got It" (which became a Top 10 hit) and "In the Real World," which
channeled the magic of Orbison's earlier hits. The latter song offers the best epi-
taph for Roy's legendary career and tragic life. "If only we could always live in
dreams," sang Orbison. "But in the real world, we must say real goodbyes."[62]

Although other country rock singers did not achieve the spectacular success
of Roy Orbison, they still left their mark. The Fendermen, a rockabilly duo
from Madison, Wisconsin, made their debut in 1960 with a supercharged version of Jimmie Rodgers's country classic, "Mule Skinner Blues." The record was
powered by relentless guitar riffs and a wild vocal that blended Buddy Holly's
rockabilly style with Jimmie Rodgers's country yodel. The explosive mix included weird lines like "Well hey, hey, little water boy . . . bring the buck buck
buckets down—quack quack. Ha Ha ha ha ha ha." Moments later, the record
ends inexplicably with the duo shouting, "cha, cha, cha."[63] Listeners weren't
sure what to make of the song, which seemed to poke fun at everything and
everybody. All they knew was "Mule Skinner Blues" had a fresh sound that was
funny and cool, which was more than enough to propel the record all the way
up to number 5.

Veteran country rock singers also found success.[64] Johnny Burnette started
as a rockabilly singer in the 1950s. He earned four Top 20 hits the next decade
with pop-influenced material aimed directly at teenagers: "Dreamin'" (1960),
"You're Sixteen" (1960), "Little Boy Sad" (1961), and "God, Country, and My
Baby" (1961). Jack Scott did even better, recording some of the finest rock & roll
hits of the 1950s and early 60s. Unlike most country rockers who came from
the South or West, Scott hailed from Windsor, Ontario, but he could rock with

the best of them. He debuted in 1958 with a two-sided hit, a lively rockabilly song called "Leroy," backed by a country rock ballad, "My True Love." He followed up with other memorable ballads, including "Goodbye Baby" (1959) and "What in the World's Come Over You" and "Burning Bridges" (both in 1960). The impressive ballads featured mournful vocals and dark chords that resonated with young listeners captivated by tragic love songs. Scott's career nosedived when musical tastes changed. "After the psychedelic trend came in," he said, "I just lost interest. Elvis was rock 'n' roll to me."[65]

Ironically, one of the most commercially successful country rockers in the early 1960s was Buddy Holly, who died in a plane crash in 1959. His music lived on through recordings he made between 1957 and 1959 and later hit records by Bobby Vee, Tommy Roe, and other artists influenced by Buddy's sound and style. The transformation of Buddy Holly the man into Buddy Holly the legend kept rockabilly music alive in the early 1960s and beyond.

Buddy Holly and the Crickets came out of Lubbock, Texas, with a unique "Tex Mex" rockabilly sound and scored a number 1 hit in 1957 with "That'll Be the Day." Jerry Allison, who cofounded the group with Buddy, marveled at Holly's dynamic stage presence. "He had the same type of charisma as Elvis," said Jerry. "He was passionate and danced around."[66] Buddy and his bandmates followed up with other hits such as "Oh Boy" (1958) and "Maybe Baby" (1958). Holly also earned hits as a solo artist, including "Peggy Sue" (1957) and "Rave On" (1958). In a weird coincidence, his final hit was "It Doesn't Matter Anymore," which peaked at unlucky number 13 a few weeks after his death.

Rock & roll fans would soon prove that Holly did matter. News of the plane crash that killed Holly, Ritchie Valens, and the Big Bopper (J. P. Richardson) touched off memorial concerts and record hops nationwide. A few weeks later, Tommy Dee earned a Top 20 hit with "Three Stars" (1959), a maudlin tribute record that suggested that three new stars were now in the night sky.

As "Three Stars" climbed the pop charts, Buddy's record label released *The Buddy Holly Story*, a greatest hits memorial album that became a bestseller in 1959. The liner notes detailed Holly's meteoric rise and tragic end. The well-received album led to a follow-up, *The Buddy Holly Story, Volume 2* (1960),

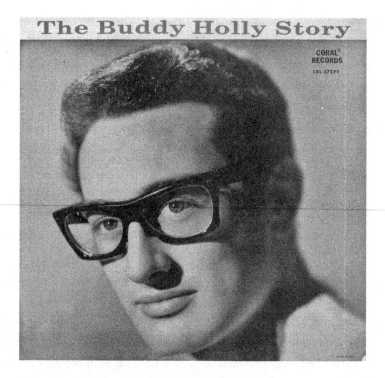

Album released shortly after Holly's death in 1959 that contributes to growing legend
(Richard Aquila Collection)

with liner notes written by his widow, Maria Elena Holly. The growing market
for "new" Holly recordings resulted in a third posthumous album, *Reminiscing*
(1963). Produced by Buddy's former manager, Norman Petty, it featured previously unreleased Holly recordings overdubbed by the Fireballs (known for their
1961 instrumental hit, "Quite a Party"). The heartfelt liner notes were written
by Buddy's parents.

Holly's rockabilly sound lived on through the music of other artists in the
early 1960s. His distinct vocal style inspired Bobby Vee's "Rubber Ball" (1961)
and "Walkin' with My Angel" (1962), Tommy Roe's "Sheila" (1962), and Jimmy
Gilmer and the Fireballs' "Sugar Shack" (1963). These new pop rockers introduced a new generation of teenagers to Holly. Once young listeners understood
the connection between current rock stars and Buddy, they often turned to Holly's
original recordings.

Holly's sound and style were also kept alive by the Crickets, who continued to record and perform. By 1961 the Crickets' lineup included original members Jerry Allison (drums) and Joe B. Mauldin (bass), as well as guitarist Sonny Curtis, keyboardist Glen D. Hardin, and lead vocalist Jerry Naylor. After Buddy's death the Crickets released three excellent albums: *In Style with the Crickets* (1960), *Bobby Vee Meets the Crickets* (1962), and *Something Old, Something New, Something Blue, Something Else* (1962). Allison and Curtis also found studio work backing up artists such as the Everly Brothers, Bobby Vee, and Johnny Burnette. In addition, Curtis became a successful songwriter, composing the Everly Brothers' "Walk Right Back" (1961), Bobby Vee's "More Than I Can Say" (1961), and the Bobby Fuller Four's "I Fought the Law" (1966). Years later Curtis would write and sing "Love is All Around," the theme song for *The Mary Tyler Moore Show.*

The British Rock Invasion in the mid-1960s added to the growing Holly legend. The Beatles, inspired by Buddy, recorded an almost identical cover of "Words of Love" (1965). Paul McCartney noted, "At least the first 40 songs we wrote were Buddy Holly-influenced."[67] Other British groups, including the Rolling Stones, Peter and Gordon, and the Hullaballoos, recorded Holly songs or paid tribute in other ways. The Hollies named themselves after Buddy. The lead singer of Freddie and the Dreamers even donned black horn-rimmed glasses in an effort to look like the American star.

The Buddy Holly legend continued to grow. In 1971 Don McLean released "American Pie" and an accompanying album dedicated to Holly. Both became number 1 sellers and etched into public memory the image of Buddy Holly as one of the most creative and important forces in rock & roll history. Subsequently, numerous artists including Linda Ronstadt, Waylon Jennings, Santana, Leo Sayer, John Lennon, and Paul McCartney recorded Holly songs. McCartney even purchased the entire Buddy Holly catalog in 1976.

The metamorphosis of Buddy Holly from Texas country rocker to American Legend was completed in 1978 with the release of a full-length motion picture, *The Buddy Holly Story.* The Oscar-winning film told a tragic tale based loosely on the rockabilly singer's life and music. The movie's success completed the circle. The legend began in 1959 with the first memorial album, *The*

Buddy Holly Story, and was completed twenty years later by a movie of the same name.

Several factors help explain the transformation of Buddy Holly into a mythic figure. Like the subject of A. E. Housman's poem "To an Athlete Dying Young," Buddy died at the peak of a promising career. His recordings suddenly took on a dramatic finality. No longer were they just the brilliant beginnings of a musical career. They now represented the totality of Holly's music. Many fans and critics praised the dead artist, recognizing his achievements and wondering what might have been. Buddy joined a select group whose art became even greater in death.

At his best, Buddy Holly was a talented and innovative singer, songwriter, and musician. His ability to write, sing, and play classic rock & roll like "That'll Be the Day" and "Peggy Sue" was the cornerstone of his career. But Holly also demonstrated potential for artistic growth, as evidenced by more sophisticated records such as "Words of Love" and "Listen to Me," which made use of double-tracked vocals and overdubbed electric guitars.

Buddy's distinct sound and appearance contributed to the myth. His vocal style, including the use of tone changes, voice inflection, and the carrying of a syllable over several beats to form a hiccuping effect, gave him a unique sound. Buddy's black horn-rimmed glasses helped him stand out from the crowd. But Holly was no teen idol. He didn't have the good looks of an Elvis or Ricky Nelson, or the powerful voice of a Roy Orbison. Instead, he seemed just like millions of other young males who wanted to be rock & roll stars. Buddy came across as an underdog in a country that always had a special place in its heart for underdogs.

The undying popularity of Buddy Holly in the early 1960s and beyond suggests that the American people value excellence and creativity. It also illustrates Americans' fascination with common-man heroes and tragic figures. In addition, the rise of the Holly legend offers glimpses of capitalism in action. Buddy's road to everlasting fame was paved by careful planners who kept his name and music alive through posthumous releases of records, tributes, Holly imitators, articles, books, and even a major motion picture. But none of them would have succeeded had there not been continued interest in the man and his music. Over the years many fans have noted the spooky coincidence that Holly's last hit record was "It Doesn't Matter Anymore." The title of one of his other songs is undoubtedly a more fitting tribute to Buddy Holly's lasting impact—"Not Fade Away."

OTHER COUNTRY-INFLUENCED HITS

Not all country-influenced music heard on rock & roll stations was rockabilly. Johnny Tillotson crafted an innovative sound that combined rock & roll with country and pop music. He began his career as a country singer, performing regularly on local radio and television shows in and around Jacksonville, Florida. In 1958 Johnny signed with Archie Bleyer's Cadence Records and scored minor hits the following year with two teen-oriented songs, "Dreamy Eyes" and "True True Happiness."

Tillotson's next release, "Why Do I Love You So" (1960), was written by Cliff Rhodes, a friend and fellow student at the University of Florida. "We used to go around together and sing in the evening outside of the girls' dorms, and [Cliff] would sing that high falsetto part," says Johnny. "All the ladies would come out, and we'd serenade them." He adds, "When I saw the reaction of the girls . . . I thought this would make a good record." Tillotson's hunch proved right when his version on Cadence Records became a hit. Teenagers loved the innovative mix of country, pop, and rock & roll, and identified with the emotional lyrics about young love.[68]

In the early 1960s the handsome Tillotson was one of the top teen idols in America. Although many critics blasted teen idols as fake rock & rollers, Johnny says that label never bothered him. "It was great to be [included] in a group with Ricky Nelson, Bobby Rydell, Bobby Vee, Fabian, and Frankie Avalon," he said. "I had no idea I would be perceived that way, so you can imagine what a nice compliment that was." He notes, "I don't sing for critics. I only sing and record for one group, and that's the audience."[69]

Tillotson was anything but a manufactured teen idol. Nobody told him how to sing, perform, dress, or style his hair. He also wrote many of his hits, including "It Keeps Right On A-Hurtin'" (1962). "This is a song that I wrote when I heard my Dad was quite ill," he explains. "Instead of tears, musical notes came to my head." Initially, Johnny didn't want to record his "emotionally motivated" song. He also worried that the song sounded "a little too country" for rock & roll fans. Archie Bleyer disagreed and convinced him to record it. The record became a number 3 hit and received a Grammy nomination for Best Country & Western Recording.[70]

In addition to his own compositions, Tillotson helped select other songs to record. Typically, he and Archie Bleyer would discuss possibilities. That's how his number 2 hit "Poetry in Motion" (1960) came about. When Archie brought him the song, Johnny immediately recognized its potential. He suggested that Boots Randolph be used as the sax player, because his sound was perfect for the record. "What I like [best] about 'Poetry in Motion' is that it's like holding up a mirror to a girl no matter what her age," said Johnny in an NPR interview in 1998. Tillotson rejects the notion that the song was sexist. He points out that over the decades women have always reacted positively to "Poetry in Motion" because it deals with "feminine grace and beauty." He adds, "I love singing it in live performances, because I can sing it right to the women in the audience, and it's really about them."[71]

Recording sessions were collaborative efforts involving Tillotson, Archie Bleyer, and talented Nashville musicians. Johnny's 1962 hit "Send Me the Pillow that You Dream On," is a good example. Tillotson had been singing that country song for years, but his approach changed dramatically when he cut the record in Nashville on May 20, 1962. As soon as he heard the arrangement with strings and different chord progressions, it took his vocal in a totally different direction. "The arrangement sounded so fresh, and I was with so many people that were inspirational in that session," he explained. "There was just a great feeling in the room . . . there was so much talent and energy there, it couldn't help but rub off on me, as well."[72]

Johnny Tillotson went on to become one of the most successful country rock stars of the early 1960s. He earned fourteen Top 40 hits, including four that made the Top 10: "Poetry in Motion" (1960), "Without You" (1961), "It Keeps Right On A-Hurtin'" (1962), and "Talk Back Trembling Lips" (1963). His songs connected with millions of fans and spanned several markets, including rock & roll, pop, and country music. In 2011 the Florida Artists Hall of Fame inducted

Johnny, noting: "Tillotson is widely regarded as one of the most important fore-runners in bringing country music to the pop music market." "I've been fortunate doing this all my life," says Johnny. "It's like a dream come true."[73]

John D. Loudermilk was another country-influenced singer who made it onto the pop charts with teen-oriented songs that blended rock & roll, pop, and country music. One of Nashville's top songwriters and singers, he earned Top 40 hits with "Sittin' in the Balcony" (1957) and "Language of Love" (1961). Loudermilk also wrote songs for other artists. George Hamilton IV scored Top 20 hits with "A Rose and a Baby Ruth" (1956) and "Abilene" (1963). Johnny Ferguson found success with "Angela Jones" (1960), which featured a doo-wop-influenced vocal, catchy pop melody, and lyrics about high school romance. And, Sue Thompson struck pop music gold with three Loudermilk compositions. "Sad Movies (Make Me Cry)," a number 5 hit in 1961, was a tearjerker about a young woman who goes to the movies alone and sees her boyfriend kissing her best friend in the dark theater. Sue's follow-up, "Norman," did even better. The bouncy song—with its irresistible catch phrase "Norman—oooh, oooh, oohh"—climbed all the way to number 3 in 1962. Later that year Thompson earned her last Top 20 hit with "James (Hold the Ladder Steady)," a song about a teenage couple determined to elope.

Skeeter Davis, who started her career in country music and returned to it after the British Rock Invasion of 1964, also found success on the pop charts. In 1963 she earned two Top 10 hits with teen-oriented songs: "The End of the World" and "I Can't Stay Mad at You." The attractive young singer's heartfelt vocal on "The End of the World" was particularly impressive. The heartbreaking ballad about love gone wrong resonated with the nation's fastest growing demographic—the millions of baby boomers who had just reached their teen-age years. Davis's success showed that women were making their mark in music as well as in society. In addition, the song's apocalyptic title and lyrics were sub-tle reminders of the Cold War's potential danger. "The End of the World" de-buted on the record charts just weeks after the Cuban Missile Crisis brought the United States and Russia to the brink of nuclear war.

Skeeter's number 2 hit is a perfect example of the innovative country rock that was popular in the early 60s. Produced in RCA-Nashville's Studio B by Chet

Atkins, it was a creative blend of country, pop, and rock & roll. It featured a double-tracked lead vocal and sophisticated use of horns and violins. The band included some of Nashville's finest musicians. They were part of a larger group nicknamed the A-Team, which included Floyd Cramer (piano), Boots Randolph (sax), Buddy Harman (drums), Bob Moore and Floyd Chance (bass), and Chet Atkins, Ray Edenton, Grady Martin, and Hank Garland (guitars). These studio musicians played the same role in Nashville that the Funk Brothers did at Motown. Various A-Team members played on most songs recorded in Nashville, including hits by Elvis Presley, the Everly Brothers, Brenda Lee, Roy Orbison, Johnny Tillotson, and more. The resulting Nashville Sound was as creative and successful as the better-known Motown Sound.

7

"A Teenager in Love"

Veteran Pop Rockers in the Early 60s

Dion and the Belmonts' 1959 hit "A Teenager in Love," epitomizes the polished pop rock that had emerged by 1960. Almost anybody watching the white doo-wop group from the Bronx lip-synching to their record on Dick Clark's *American Bandstand* on June 1, 1959, could not help but notice the contrast between their rough demeanor and the song's smooth sound and sensitive lyrics.

The four Italian American singers named their group after a street in their neighborhood. "We all went out and got jackets and . . . wrote out our names on [them] with paint," recalls Dion. "We put our names, Belmonts, on the back of the black jackets . . . and we thought we were hot stuff." When they performed on Clark's program that Monday afternoon, they looked just like the street toughs that they were. With their Brylcreemed hair combed straight back in DAs, they seemed like hoods straight out of *Blackboard Jungle*. Even though they were wearing matching suits and ties, it didn't cover up the obvious: these guys looked menacing and had an attitude to match. Dion notes that the Belmonts "hardly made records parents wanted to burn. But, there was something about the sight of those four Italians, decked out in city slicker clothes, snapping their fingers and acting like Negroes that must not have set too well with the folks in the Midwest." Dion adds, "We were kind of exotic, which, back then meant foreign, and that, in turn, meant dangerous."[1]

Ironically, "A Teenager in Love" became Dion and the Belmonts' signature song. The group members all had loose connections with New York street gangs, yet here they were singing an innocuous pop song written by Doc Pomus and Mort Shuman, two professional composers from the Brill Building in midtown

Manhattan. At first, Dion balked at making the record. He thought the song was maudlin and not the kind of macho Bronx blues that he and his group usually sang. But executives at Laurie Records insisted that the pop song would be a smash hit, so Dion and the Belmonts gave it a shot.[2]

"A Teenager in Love" zoomed up the charts. The romantic message struck a responsive chord with young listeners everywhere. The record begins with the Belmonts singing "Oooh, oooh, wah, oooh, oooh." Lead singer Dion then makes his entrance: "Each time we have a quarrel, it almost breaks my heart 'cause I am so afraid that we will have to part." He moves quickly to the moment of truth. As the Belmonts fall silent and the band stops playing, Dion pauses for dramatic effect. Then, his anguished voice cries out, "Why must I be a teenager in love?"[3] That musical question tugged at teenage heartstrings throughout the spring of 1959, helping the record climb all the way to number 5.

"A Teenager in Love" says a great deal about the era's pop rock. It suggests that the style was a mass-produced product aimed directly at teenagers. At the same time, the song had folk-quality lyrics that resonated with young audiences. The performance was also authentic. Dion and the Belmonts were anything but contrived. "The music we made together was the pure sound of the neighborhood," explains Dion. "One guy would start humming a melody, another would join in, and a song would take shape." Dion admits that "A Teenager in Love" was more formulaic than the rhythm and blues usually sung by the Belmonts.[4] But, their Bronx soul would not be denied. Dion's plaintive vocal backed by the Belmonts' pure doo-wop harmonies added an authentic feel to what otherwise might have been pure pop fluff.

Dion and the Belmonts' hit record reveals the tensions inherent in pop rock. The style was an amalgam of traditional pop and rock & roll with varying amounts of R&B, country, or other musical styles tossed in for good measure. The potent mix defied classification. Was it a new type of electrified folk music bubbling up from teenagers or was it just mass-produced pop being spooned out from above? Was it white music or Black? Authentic or artificial? The composers of "A Teenager in Love" didn't attempt to categorize their songs. Pomus and Shuman understood that it was almost impossible to place music in any kind of hierarchy. "That may get tricky," explains Mort Shuman. "There are all degrees and one person's frothiness is another person's deepness."[5]

Pop rock was indeed "tricky," to say the least. Some of it was excellent and as authentic as any rock & roll style around. Other pop rock was just a poor imitation of the real thing. Yet, all pop rock shared common elements. First and foremost, pop rock—like all rock & roll styles—targeted the baby boom audience. It featured rock & roll beats and lyrics geared to young listeners. Most records were performed by young white males, although the number of hits recorded by women and minorities rose throughout the early 1960s. And songs were either composed by professional writers or written by the artists themselves.

Many of the most popular pop rock singers of the early 60s began their careers in the 1950s, including groups like Dion and the Belmonts and the Fleetwoods, as well as solo artists such as Ricky Nelson, Connie Francis, Paul Anka, and Bobby Rydell. These veteran pop rockers helped shape early 60s rock & roll. Their hits not only provide glimpses of teenagers in love, but they reveal fresh details about baby boom culture and everyday life in Kennedy's America.

POP ROCK AND THE BRILL BUILDING SOUND

The Brill Building at 1619 Broadway was the epicenter for pop rock. Its Manhattan neighborhood housed songwriters, music publishers, recording studios, record labels, radio stations, accountants, even booking agents and promoters to plan concerts and tours. The original nickname for New York's music district, Tin Pan Alley, fell by the wayside after the arrival of rock & roll. By 1960 the Brill Building was synonymous with the teen-oriented pop rock that was being written, published, produced, and distributed in the city's music district. Significantly, the "Brill Building" designation encompassed not just music written in the actual building at 1619 Broadway, but also songs that came from nearby buildings, especially 1650, 1674, and 1697 Broadway.[6]

The songwriters, producers, and arrangers who worked in New York's music district injected new energy and innovations into rock & roll. They introduced sophisticated lyrics, inventive musical structures, and creative arrangements that featured Latin rhythms, choruses, horns, violins, cellos, and more. The resulting Brill Building Sound was noticeably different from Tin Pan Alley. Early 60s pop rock didn't sound like the traditional pop of Frank Sinatra or Perry Como. It was created by a new generation of composers who were consciously writing for the rock & roll audience. Leading the way were Jerry Leiber and Mike Stoller. The transplanted Californians established the model for independent songwriters and producers by skillfully mixing rhythm and blues, rock & roll, and pop to produce hit records for both Black and white artists, including the Coasters, Drifters, and Elvis Presley.

Other songwriters toiling in cubicles in the Brill Building or nearby offices also hit it big with pop rock. Examples include successful songwriting partners like Doc Pomus and Mort Shuman, Neil Sedaka and Howie Greenfield, Carole King and Gerry Goffin, Barry Mann and Cynthia Weil, Jeff Barry and Ellie Greenwich, and Burt Bacharach and Hal David. Working as established teams, as individuals, or as partners with other writers, these composers wrote hits for country rockers like Elvis Presley and the Everly Brothers, R&B rock groups such as the Drifters and Shirelles, and pop rock singers like Connie Francis and Bobby Darin.

These writers were usually about the same age as their audience, so they could relate to young listeners' hopes and fears. Carole King, for instance, was just 18 years old when she and her 21-year-old husband Gerry Goffin wrote "Will You Love Me Tomorrow" for the Shirelles. Not surprisingly, the song about premarital sex hit home with teenagers. Even older writers aimed their material directly at young people. Leiber and Stoller were both married and in their late twenties when they wrote or produced teen-oriented hits like the Coasters' "Charlie Brown" (1959) and Jay and the Americans' "She Cried" (1962). Carole King suggests that the best records of the Brill Building era qualify as art. "You can sell lots of records by making something that's commercial," she says, "[but] if there's no emotional connection in it, I don't think it's art."[7]

The fresh Brill Building Sound, with its close ties to youth culture, gave pop rock more credibility with young audiences than stale Tin Pan Alley pop. The new cohort of professional songwriters understood that cultural battle lines were being drawn with Elvis and Sinatra on opposite sides of the generational divide.

Just as New York City's garment district was the center of the nation's fashion industry and annually attracted thousands of buyers from across the country, the Brill Building district became the place to go for music. It offered one-stop shopping for all the latest fashions in pop music and rock & roll.

Significantly, the polished music that emanated from the Brill Building or nearby offices was not the only type of pop rock in the early 1960s. All across America, quality pop rock was written and performed by individuals with no direct ties to the Brill Building district. Yet, even they were influenced by the sounds that began in New York City and then rippled across America. The songwriters, arrangers, and producers from the Brill Building neighborhood raised the bar for rock & roll. Their innovations included sophisticated lyrics, double-tracked vocals, creative musical structures, and pop-style arrangements that incorporated strings and other instruments. This Brill Building Sound reverberated throughout early 60s rock, influencing girl groups, doo-wop, dance songs, country rock, R&B rock, even the Motown Sound. Of course, most rock & roll fans in the early 1960s were blissfully unaware of the connections between their favorite songs and the Brill Building. All that they knew was that these excellent hits offered the perfect rock & roll soundtrack for teenagers in Kennedy's America.

POP ROCK PROTOTYPE: PAT BOONE

Some of the most successful pop rock singers of the early 1960s got their start in the previous decade. Pat Boone was the prototype. The 21-year-old's first hit came in 1955 with a cover version of the Charms' R&B song "Two Hearts." He followed up with additional covers of R&B hits, including Fats Domino's "Ain't That a Shame" (1955) and Little Richard's "Tutti' Frutti" (1956). He then switched gears and reeled off hits with pop rock ballads like "April Love" (1957).

Pat attributes his success not only to the types of songs he was singing, but also to his ability to connect with young audiences. "Kids identified with me because I was like them," he explains. Even the clothes he wore on stage were not a gimmick. "I was just wearing what all the other high school and college kids were, virtually in [all] America."[8]

Boone was the ideal teen idol for the conservative Eisenhower years. He was polite, religious, patriotic, and a model husband and father. His traditional values and clean-cut appearance projected a comforting, positive image at a time when many Americans were anxious about organized crime, juvenile delinquency, communist subversion, and racial integration. "I made [rock & roll] music seem safer," suggests Boone. "I was a good role model, [whereas] Elvis they weren't too sure about."[9]

Boone's popularity continued in the next decade. He scored a number 1 hit in 1961 with "Moody River," which combined a bouncy melody with macabre lyrics about teen suicide. Pat explains, "[The song] is about a girl who jumps in the river and drowns and leaves a goodbye note of remorse . . . for her boyfriend who she feels she's been unfaithful to and can't live with it." Boone suspects that the "happy sound of the piano riff" offset the dark lyrics. "In Japan and other countries where they don't understand English that well, when I start singing 'Moody River' they start clapping their hands. They think, 'Oh, this is a happy song. This is great.'"[10]

Boone's last big hit was "Speedy Gonzales," which peaked at number 6 in 1962. Initially, his producer Randy Wood didn't think they should record the up-tempo song. "I was doing movie themes and love ballads," explained Boone. "[Randy] said, 'people don't want to hear rock & roll from you anymore.'" When Pat insisted, his producer relented "just to get me off his back." Jimmie Haskell was brought in to arrange the music and they went into the studio to cut the record. "We no sooner got into the song than Randy's radar picked up," said Pat. "Within six weeks after we recorded it, 'Speedy Gonzales' was number 1 around the world." Teenagers who had grown up watching the Warner Brothers' Speedy Gonzales cartoon character loved the song about a Mexican lothario with a funny voice. Mel Blanc, who provided the voice for the cartoons, also played the character on the record.

Some listeners today condemn "Speedy Gonzales" as an example of racism or cultural appropriation. But, back in 1962 most people felt the song was a harmless novelty hit that satirized a common ethnic stereotype. In an interview in 1998 Pat was asked if he ever got any complaints about the Speedy Gonzales character. He recalled one specific reviewer in the early 1990s who suggested he should remove the song from his repertoire "because of the social or political implications." But that's the only complaint he ever got. "When I sing in San Antonio, LA, or any part of the country where's there's a large Hispanic population, they clamor for 'Speedy Gonzales.' They love it," says Pat. "They know it's just fun . . . and they don't take any umbrage at all."[11]

Between 1955 and 1963 Pat Boone earned thirty-three Top 30 hits, including six number 1 records. He also became a movie and TV star, as well as a best-selling author. Pat was America's first pop rock teen idol. His records not only reflected the times, but they helped expand the market for rock & roll by offering listeners a less threatening sound. While many rock & roll fans dismissed Pat as just a pop singer, millions of others viewed him as an authentic rock & roller. Boone notes that radio stations in the 1950s held contests to determine the most popular rock & roll singer. "It usually boiled down to . . . Elvis and me," he recalls. "Elvis . . . won two out of the three contests, but I would win at least a third of them . . . So, yes, I was part of the [rock & roll] scene and a very influential part."[12]

RICKY NELSON

Ricky Nelson was another veteran pop rocker who enjoyed success in the early 1960s. Ricky got hooked on rock & roll in the 1950s listening to singers like Elvis Presley and Carl Perkins. His father was intrigued by the new music for different reasons. Ozzie Nelson was a former bandleader and the guiding force behind one of television's most popular shows, *The Adventures of Ozzie and Harriet*, which starred the couple and their sons David and Ricky. He had witnessed Elvis's meteoric rise and envied the ratings of TV shows that showcased the new sound. So, Ozzie repeatedly asked the 16-year-old Ricky if he'd like to sing rock & roll on the show. The shy youngster wasn't interested—until he realized that a girl he liked at school might be impressed if he made a record.

When Ricky volunteered to sing, his dad immediately contacted friends in the music business. A few weeks later Ricky went into an LA studio and recorded three songs, one of which was a lively version of Fats Domino's "I'm Walkin'." Ozzie then wrote a script that spotlighted Ricky singing the song at a school dance. On the April 10, 1957, episode of *Ozzie and Harriet*, Ricky lip-synched

"I'm Walkin'," while girls in the make-believe school gym swooned. The next day teenagers nationwide rushed out to buy the record. "I'm Walkin'" skyrocketed to number 4 on the charts, establishing Ricky as rock & roll's newest star.[13]

Despite the Hollywood connection, Ricky was like millions of other teenagers who turned to rock & roll because of Elvis Presley. His first record showed that pop rock could be just as authentic as rockabilly or R&B rock. The fact that young Ricky was backed by a topnotch band that included both R&B and country musicians demonstrates that pop rock, like other rock & roll styles, was a musical, racial, and cultural hybrid.

Ricky (or Rick as he was known after he turned 21) went on to become one of rock & roll's biggest stars. Between 1957 and 1963 he earned 32 Top 40 hits, including two number 1 records, "Poor Little Fool" (1958) and "Travelin' Man" (1961). Nelson could rock with the best of them, as evidenced by fast-paced hits like "Believe What You Say" (1958) and "Hello Mary Lou" (1961). He could then turn around and sing intimate ballads such as "Lonesome Town" (1958) and "I'm Not Afraid" (1960). The only time Nelson stumbled was when he recorded hackneyed pop songs like "Yes Sir, That's My Baby" (1960).

Nelson's pop rock style resonated with his teenage fan base. Songs like "Young Emotions" (1960) and "Young World" (1962) spotlighted young listeners. Other hits zeroed in on specific teen interests. "Be Bop Baby" (1957) glorified a girl who wore blue jeans and loved to dance, while "Waitin' in School" (1958) captured the rhythms of high school life. "Teenage Idol" (1962) offered inside information on what it was like to be a rock & roll star. "Down Home" (1963) anticipated the nostalgic feelings that the first wave of baby boomers would experience after high school graduation.

Many fans cheered Ricky as a teen idol similar to Pat Boone, but Nelson's music was always more rock than pop. His expert vocals were often backed by the Jordanaires (who sang on Elvis's hits), and his excellent rock & roll band featured lead guitarist James Burton (who later played with Presley and was inducted into the Rock & Roll Hall of Fame). Burton was impressed by the honesty in Nelson's music. "He had a great feel for the type of songs he sang and what he enjoyed singing, as well as a soft, smooth voice," said Burton. "We made some really nice music in our time," he said. "I think Rick's music is . . . just as good today as the day we recorded it."[14]

Burton is particularly fond of two Nelson songs from 1961, "Travelin' Man" and "Hello Mary Lou." "If you can believe it, those two songs were the 'A' and 'B' side of the same single," he points out. "Travelin' Man" became a number 1 hit. It showcased Nelson's self-assured vocal, backed by the Jordanaires and a topnotch rock & roll band led by Burton on lead guitar. The mid-tempo ballad featured a swaying melody, irresistible beat, and colorful lyrics that expressed male fantasies about freedom, world travel, and girlfriends in every port. His exotic conquests were about as racially and ethnically diverse as the times would allow. He brags about a "pretty senorita" in Mexico, a "cute little" Eskimo, a "sweet fräulein" in Berlin, and a "China doll" in Hong Kong.[15]

The flip side, "Hello Mary Lou," was also a Top 10 hit. Written by Gene Pitney, the innovative record opens with a cowbell. It then rushes full steam ahead, powered by Nelson's urgent rockabilly vocal and a blistering James Burton guitar solo. "'Hello Mary Lou' sounds so different because it was about 15 layers of overdubbing," explains producer Jimmie Haskell. "What we got when we were finished was a totally unique sounding record." Haskell adds proudly, "that's me playing the cowbell at the start."[16]

Unlike most teen idols, the young Nelson retained creative control in the studio. He would listen to suggestions from band members, his father, his producer, and others, but he always had the final say. James Burton helped him achieve the exact sound he wanted. "Rick and I pretty much worked the songs up, and we would put our ideas together. I would tell Rick what I liked and vice versa," explains James.[17]

Regardless of what type of song Nelson recorded, he followed his rock & roll heart. His unique sound—teenage rockabilly with a suburban Hollywood touch—proved that pop rockers could be authentic rock & rollers. Rick Nelson's rock & roll legacy was officially recognized in 1987 when he was inducted posthumously into the Rock & Roll Hall of Fame. Nelson's records, said John Fogerty, "were so valid and such high quality [that they] captured the heart and soul of rockabilly."[18]

NEW YORK POP ROCK

While Ricky Nelson was perfecting his pop rock sound in Hollywood, another young pop rocker destined for stardom was recording in New York City. Paul Anka, a 16-year-old singer-songwriter from Ottawa, Canada, scored his first hit in 1957 with "Diana." The number 1 record featured his urgent vocal about unrequited love set to a calypso beat punctuated by a blaring saxophone.

Paul's boyish good looks and talent helped him become one of the most successful artists of rock & roll's first decade. Between 1957 and 1963 he earned twenty Top 30 hits, including two number 1 records, "Diana" and "Lonely Boy." "I had this talent for [writing] stupid little teenage songs at a moment in time when teenagers wanted stupid little teenage songs," jokes Anka. "I was a lonely boy and I knew there were plenty of us out there . . . Put your head on my shoulder—that was your objective that weekend." He adds, "All that I understood only too literally by the mere fact that I *was* a teenager."[19] Anka's ability to relate to his young audience made him one of the top teen idols of the early 60s. He put together an impressive string of hits, including "Puppy Love" (1960), "Summer's Gone" (1960), "Dance On Little Girl" (1961), and "Love Me Warm and Tender" (1962). He also made frequent guest appearances on *American Bandstand* and toured with Buddy Holly and the Crickets, Fats Domino, Chuck Berry, and other rock & roll greats.

Anka never forgot his early days as a rock & roll star. "I have a strong feeling for those years, because we were really pioneers," he explains. "We had to fight for everything we could get. The attitude then was what we were doing wasn't going to last." That might explain why Paul and other rock & rollers donned tuxedos, played Las Vegas, and often recorded pop-sounding ballads. "Bobby Darin and I idolized Frank Sinatra and the Rat Pack," says Anka. "All we knew was to look up to them. There was nobody else to follow. Ultimately, [other rock & rollers] didn't penetrate the nightclub scene as Bobby and I did. That's where we got our (performing) chops." The Vegas connection proved invaluable when Paul's rock & roll career crashed after the Beatles arrived on the scene. "I wasn't afraid to say, 'this teenage thing has got to end,'" he explains.

He was confident he could still succeed in nightclubs. "We're not creating a cure for cancer here," he says. "This is show business."[20]

Anka's talent and determination helped him make the transition from teen idol to Las Vegas superstar. Arguably, Paul didn't have that far to go. Though his early fans regarded him as a rock & roll star, he was always closer in sound and style to traditional pop singers than he was to bona fide rockers. When Anka finally traded in his rock & roll shoes for pop music, his fans stuck by him. He went on to compose the theme song for Johnny Carson's *Tonight Show*, as well as pop hits such as Frank Sinatra's "My Way" (1969). He even made it back onto the pop charts with several Top 10 hits, including "(You're) Having My Baby," a number 1 hit in 1974.

During the 1950s and early 60s Paul Anka was one of rock & roll's most successful singer-songwriters. His hits resonated with young listeners, demonstrating that many rock & roll fans had values and tastes similar to adults. His innovative sound helped shape the direction of rock & roll. Anka's use of violins on records such as "You Are My Destiny" (1958) paved the way for other rock & rollers to use string arrangements, including Buddy Holly, Brenda Lee, the Shirelles, and Drifters. Holly was so impressed with "You Are My Destiny" that he asked Paul to write something similar for him. "That's how I came to write 'It Doesn't Matter Anymore,'" explains Anka. "The direction [Buddy] wanted to go in was to add string arrangements to his songs, develop a lusher, sweeter sound behind his vocals."[21]

Anka began his career as a rock & roll teen idol and later gained recognition as one of the most talented performers and songwriters of his generation. His long-term success came not only from obvious talent, but also from his ability to connect with audiences. "All of my songs back then [in the late 1950s and early 60s] were a composite of things I really felt myself . . . I was a teenager writing for other teenagers—and however simplistic that was, it was new, appealing, and kind of sexy in a teenage way," explained Paul Anka. "I may not have been the best at any one thing, but somehow the package came together: writer, performer, the right age, the look and that was it."[22]

* * *

Connie Francis is another early 60s pop rock star whose roots can be traced back to New York's Brill Building district in the 1950s. Connie, an Italian American whose real name was Concetta Franconero, got an early start in the music business. "At eleven-years-old I was doing songs . . . with my bobbie socks and my accordion, on the Ted Mack's Amateur Hour," she explains. In 1950 she brought down the house when she sang "Daddy's Little Girl" on *Arthur Godfrey's Talent Scouts*. Godfrey was impressed but couldn't pronounce her last name, so he advised her to change Franconero to something simpler like *Francis*.[23]

Connie's successful appearances led to work singing demos in the Brill Building district, which in turn helped her land an MGM recording contract. Francis hit it big when she recorded "Who's Sorry Now," an old pop standard from 1923. The record was her father's idea. The 18-year-old Connie hated the old-fashioned song, but agreed to give it a try. At first the record went nowhere, but then lightning struck. On January 1, 1958, she and her brother—like millions of other teenagers—were home watching *American Bandstand*. Suddenly, Dick Clark announced a song by a new girl singer and predicted it would be a hit. "I said to myself 'good luck to her,' sort of with sour grapes," Connie recalls. "Then [Dick] played 'Who's Sorry Now' and it was a big shock because it had been out three months." Sales spiked, sending the record all the way up to number 4. "If . . . Clark hadn't happened along," she later noted, "there simply would have been no career."[24]

Connie was initially promoted as a rock & roll singer. Up-tempo hits such as "Stupid Cupid" (1958) and "Lipstick on Your Collar" (1959) proved she knew how to rock. Even ballads like "Who's Sorry Now" (1958), "My Happiness" (1959), and "Frankie" (1959) made ample use of rock & roll beats and piano triplets. But Francis was always more than just a rock & roll singer. Starting with "Who's Sorry Now," she recorded numerous pop songs, including "Love Is a Many Splendored Thing" (1961) and "Al Di La" (1963).

Connie also performed country-influenced music. By the early 1960s, country artists like Marty Robbins were crossing onto the pop charts, and Ray Charles was wowing audiences with innovative blends of country and R&B. Connie had grown up listening to country and western, so she jumped on the country bandwagon. She scored three number 1 hits with country-style songs: "Every-

Connie Francis (Richard Aquila Collection)

body's Somebody's Fool" (1960), "My Heart Has a Mind of Its Own" (1960), and "Don't Break the Heart That Loves You" (1962). Her 1962 album *Country Music Connie Style* became a bestseller. In addition to country and pop music, Connie took a shot at the international market. She toured extensively overseas and recorded songs in a variety of languages, including Italian, Spanish, German, Greek, and French.

Connie Francis's diverse catalog mirrored life in Kennedy's America. Her records reinforced the traditional values of America's Cold War culture. Connie gave voice to the country's patriotism with songs like "God Bless America" (1959) and "In the Summer of His Years," a tribute to John F. Kennedy released just after his assassination. Other songs such as "Mama" (1960) and "When the Boy in Your Arms (Is the Boy in Your Heart)" (1961) idealized marriage and the family, supporting the notion that traditional institutions would shield Americans from communism. Even Connie's clean-cut image underscored mainstream values. A feature story in the October 1962, issue of *TV Radio Mirror* portrayed the young singer as the quintessential All-American girl. It noted that despite all the success, Connie still "secretly yearns for a home and children of her own."[25]

If Connie's image and hit records endorsed the era's consensus behavior, her success was a sign of the changing times. By the early 1960s women were breaking glass ceilings in various professions. Francis not only helped pave the way for female rock & roll singers but she also opened doors and minds for young women across America. Teenage girls could relate to her takes on young love and family. They cheered when a triumphant Connie sang to her ex-boyfriend "who's sorry now," and they applauded when Connie showed her unfaithful boyfriend the door on "Lipstick on Your Collar." Many fans saw her as a typical girl next door. She didn't have the extraordinary looks of Ann-Margret or perky personality of Shelley Fabares. Instead, she was just like millions of other young women across the country who dressed modestly, acted properly, went to church regularly, and loved their families. Other hits targeted the new youth culture that emerged in post–World War II America. Songs like "Where the Boys Are" (1961), "Vacation" (1962), and "Follow the Boys" (1963) focused on young love, while her 1962 album, *Do the Twist,* spotlighted the latest teenage dance craze.

If some of Connie's records were linked to youth culture, others reflected the growing diversity of American society. With white ethnic groups on the rise in post–World War II America, Connie found success with albums such as *Spanish and Latin American Favorites, Jewish Favorites, Irish Favorites*, and *Italian Favorites*. The liner notes to her 1961 album *More Italian Favorites* reveal Connie's pride in her ethnic background. "Recording my first Italian LP, and now this one, has made me realize how lucky I am to have been born of this heritage— with its passionate love of life, beauty and music."[26]

Between 1958 and 1964 Connie Francis earned thirty-two Top 40 hits. Several factors contributed to her success. Her powerful and expressive voice was enhanced by well-written songs and top-notch Brill Building arrangements and production work. Her friendship with Dick Clark undoubtedly helped. Connie's songs were played regularly on *Bandstand*, and she frequently performed on Clark's daytime show and Saturday night program. Connie Francis was in the right place at the right time. Her sound and style resonated with both young and old listeners, bridging the gap between Eisenhower's America and Kennedy's New Frontier.

In the late 1950s Connie Francis met Bobby Darin, a fellow singer hoping for a break in New York's Brill Building district. The two began dating long before either of them hit it big. They even talked about marriage, but Connie's strict father intervened. That ended the romance, although Connie and Bobby remained lifelong friends.[27]

Darin went on to become a pop rock legend. His initial hits included solid rockers like "Splish Splash" (1958) and "Dream Lover" (1959). Then he startled fans with an abrupt turn toward traditional pop. When Darin told his friend Dick Clark that he was going to record "Mack the Knife" from Kurt Weill's *The Threepenny Opera*, Dick told him he was crazy. Soon afterward, Darin debuted "Mack the Knife" on Clark's Saturday-night show. Clark was impressed by Bobby's dramatic entrance. He stepped out of the darkness into "a misty pool of light." Dick adds, "It was a total departure from the rollicking, bouncy hits he'd come to be associated with. But [Darin] was right and I was wrong. The song became his biggest seller, hitting the number-one spot on all the charts [in 1959]."[28]

Over the next couple of years Bobby recorded swinging renditions of pop standards, including "Beyond the Sea" (1960) and "You Must Have Been a Beautiful Baby" (1961). He also changed his image. Darin traded his sweaters and tight pants for a tux, and strutted into the spotlight at the Copacabana and dinner clubs across America. Audiences cheered wildly as the dynamic singer belted out his hits while snapping his fingers like a junior Sinatra.

By 1962, with Ray Charles's countrified R&B sound gaining popularity, Bobby got soul and recorded Ray's "What'd I Say." He also wrote and recorded three country-influenced songs that became Top 10 hits: "Things" (1962) blended pop rock and country music; "You're the Reason I'm Living" (1963) channeled Charles's "I Can't Stop Loving You;" and "Eighteen Yellow Roses" (1963) featured a gentle melody reminiscent of Marty Robbins's "El Paso." In the mid-1960s he tried his hand at Broadway material such as "Hello Dolly" and "Mame." Later, when folk rock became vogue, Darin switched to message songs like "If I Were a Carpenter" (1966).

Many rock & roll fans dismissed Darin as just a pop singer who was trying to cash in on the latest musical trend. Others were confused by his lack of direction. Legendary rock superstar Neil Young was more than puzzled. "I used to be pissed off at Bobby Darin because he changed styles so much," said Young in 1988. "Now I look at him and think he was a fucking genius." Young went through similar musical changes in his own career, so he thinks he understands what motivated Darin. Bobby had that "driving force that makes [people] wanna do whatever has to be done," explains Young. "Darin kept tryin' to do everything he wanted to do, whatever it was."[29]

En route to stardom, Bobby Darin often crossed paths with Neil Sedaka, another singer-songwriter looking for a break in the Brill Building district. Neil, a musical prodigy, took lessons at the Juilliard School of Music when he was in second grade, and by high school he loved not just classical music, but also pop music, show tunes, and rock & roll. Neil and his friend Howie Greenfield, who shared his eclectic tastes, soon began composing songs. Several were recorded by Atlantic Records artists, but none charted. The two teenagers kept knocking on doors in the Brill Building district and eventually landed an audition with Aldon Music Publishing. The owners, Don Kirshner and Al Nevins, were impressed and signed the duo as songwriters and Sedaka as a solo artist. Kirshner then helped Neil land an RCA recording contract.[30]

Sedaka's first Top 20 hit as a singer was "The Diary" (1959), a doo-wop style song that he cowrote with Greenfield. Over the next five years Sedaka earned eleven Top 30 hits, including Sedaka-Greenfield compositions such as "Oh! Carol" (1959), "Calendar Girl" (1961), and "Happy Birthday Sweet Sixteen," "Breaking Up Is Hard To Do," and "Next Door to an Angel" (all in 1962). His career nosedived when the British Invasion came in 1964. But, he made a comeback in the late-1970s with hits such "Laughter in the Rain" and a slowed-down remake of "Breaking Up Is Hard To Do."

Neil's hits are evidence of the innovative pop rock of the early 1960s. "There was a Neil Sedaka sound, certainly," says Sedaka. "My left hand [on the piano] was the bass lines . . . and my right hand was the sweeteners. The 'dooby-doos' and the 'tra-la-las' were a trademark. It was original. The multiple voices were original. The dance beat was very important. Tempo is very important to me, and not rushing the tempo. I wanted them to hear every word."[31]

Most rock & roll fans weren't consciously aware of Sedaka's innovations. All they heard was an appealing, bubbly brand of rock & roll. The double-tracked vocals were as sweet as sugar and were complemented by equally sweet backup harmonies with nonsensical syllables straight out of doo-wop. The confection was often topped off with the celestial sounds of chimes, xylophones, and glock-enspiels. Even when Sedaka sang about love gone wrong on hits such as "Break-ing Up Is Hard To Do," it came across as bouncy and upbeat. Yet, Sedaka's hits weren't just pop fluff. "We sold records because our songs were musically solid and had more than four chords," explains Sedaka. "The bridge of 'Breaking Up Is Hard To Do' [was] the first time in rock 'n' roll that a minor seventh chord was used."[32]

Sedaka's talent as a singer-songwriter helped make him one of the most suc-cessful pop rockers of the late 1950s and early 60s. His cheery, upbeat records reflected teen romance and interests as they captured the innocence of baby boomers during the Kennedy years.

PHILADELPHIA POP ROCK

Just as the Brill Building helped establish New York's reputation for pop rock, Dick Clark's *American Bandstand* served as a springboard for Philadelphia pop rockers. The City of Brotherly Love offered great opportunities for independent record companies that knew how to play the teen idol game. The biggest win-ners were Chancellor Records, Cameo-Parkway, and Swan.

Chancellor was founded in 1957 by Bob Marcucci and Peter DeAngelis. Re-alizing that the record business was tilting toward teen idols, Bob recruited Francis Avallone (a.k.a. Frankie Avalon), an Italian American from South Philly who played trumpet and occasionally sang for a local band, Rocco and the Saints. Marcucci recognized the 17-year-old's potential the moment he saw him on stage: "He just had something that was unbelievably charismatic." Although his first few records flopped, Marcucci remained confident. Frankie soon hit it big with "Dede Dinah," an upbeat rock & roll song composed by Marcucci and DeAngelis. On December 12, 1957, Frankie lip-synched to the song on *Bandstand*. By February "Dede Dinah" was the number 7 hit in the country.[33]

Over the next five years, Avalon cranked out eleven Top 30 hits. Girls couldn't get enough of the cute teen idol. His picture adorned covers of teen magazines, and Frankie became one of the most frequent and popular guests on *Bandstand*. By his third appearance, Avalon needed a police escort to protect him from screaming fans. "It was always so nuts inside that little studio, it all just blurs in my memory into total teenage madness."[34] What Avalon saw as "teenage madness," Marcucci viewed as dollar signs. He promoted his young star non-stop. By the early 1960s Avalon was one of America's most popular singers. He also appeared in films, such as *The Alamo* (1960) and *Voyage to the Bottom of the Sea* (1961), and costarred with Annette Funicello in several beach party movies.

Avalon's success convinced Marcucci to offer a recording contract to another Italian American teenager from South Philly. Fabian Forte looked like a teen idol from central casting. The tall, dark, and handsome 15-year-old was a cross between Elvis Presley and Ricky Nelson. There was one problem, though. The kid insisted he couldn't sing. Marcucci thought Fabian was just being modest . . . until he got him into the recording studio. But Chancellor Record's co-owner wasn't about to give up. Marcucci became a rock & roll version of Professor Henry Higgins as he taught Fabian how to dress, how to act, and how to perform. In addition, Marcucci and DeAngelis worked with the teenager on his singing, and they hired excellent studio musicians and Brill Building songwriters.[35]

Chancellor's marketing strategy was applied not just to Fabian, but to Avalon as well. Knowing teenage girls were turned on by teen idols, Marcucci made sure that record sleeves included photographs of the handsome young singers. He also outfitted Frankie and Fabian in beautiful sweaters or great suits with matching accessories. "These boys had the best of everything," he explained. "I bought nothing but the best clothes for them. Elegant." He wanted Frankie to have a cute, boy-next-door look, and Fabian a "sexier look. They were the two best-dressed kids in that era."[36]

Marcucci transformed Fabian into a teen idol with help from his friend, Dick Clark. The *Bandstand* host recognized Fabian's potential the moment he saw him on stage. "The little girls at the hop went wild," he said. "They started screaming and yelling for this guy who didn't do a thing but just stand there." Later on during the payola scandal, Clark refuted charges that Fabian and Avalon appeared frequently on *Bandstand* because he owned part of Chancellor Records. Clark testified he had no financial interest in Chancellor. "My deal with Bob and Pete was a simple gentleman's agreement," he explained. "I said to them 'If you find a star, allow me the pleasure of introducing him and then, on occasion, have him come back to visit *Bandstand* after he's big.'" Clark added, "I knew that if I could help build Frankie Avalon then along the way it would be helpful to me. The same with Fabian."[37]

In 1959 and 1960 Fabian seemed unstoppable. Fan clubs proliferated and teen magazines followed his every move. He appeared frequently on TV and in movies, and even had a fashion line of Fabian sweaters. His biggest hits—"Turn Me Loose," "Tiger," and "Hound Dog Man"—capitalized on his good looks and reflected the era's stereotype of the macho male. Fabian's rock & roll star soon burned out, though. He managed two final Top 40 hits in 1960, "String Along" and "About This Thing Called Love." Fabian attributes much of his success to *American Bandstand*. "I remember once they brought me and Frankie Avalon in at the height of our popularity," he recalled, "and the kids just went crazy . . . Frankie and I barely got to our cars in one piece."[38]

Critics did not share teenage girls' enthusiasm for Fabian, who became the poster child for manufactured teen idols who couldn't sing. *Time* called him the "Tuneless Tiger." Despite the naysayers, Fabian—like Frankie Avalon—attracted numerous fans who cheered him on as an authentic rock & roller. Over 50 years later those baby boomers still flocked to Fabian and Frankie Avalon concerts to enjoy the former teen idols' music and share memories of days gone by.

Cameo-Parkway Records, founded by Bernie Lowe for $2000 in 1956, was another major player on the Philadelphia music scene. Lowe, a longtime friend and business associate of Dick Clark, found success in the 1950s recording and producing hit records that got a lot of airplay on *American Bandstand*, including Charlie Gracie's "Butterfly" (1957), John Zacherle's "Dinner With Drac" (1958), and Dave Appell and the Appelljacks' "Mexican Hat Rock" (1958).

Two young pop rockers would become Cameo-Parkway's biggest stars in the early 1960s. Chubby Checker hit the charts first with "The Class," which debuted in May 1959. Over the next four years he earned nineteen Top 30 hits. Three became number 1 records, "The Twist" (1960 and again in 1962), and "Pony Time" in 1961 (see chapter1). Cameo's other new star arrived on the charts just one month after Checker. Robert Ridarelli was a good-looking Italian American from the same South Philly neighborhood as Frankie Avalon and Fabian. After his manager changed his name to the less-ethnic sounding Bobby Rydell, the 17-year-old became one of the era's top teen idols.

Bobby started performing as a child. His father brought the talented 5-year-old to various clubs, where he wowed audiences with his singing and impersonations. Decades later Bobby still vividly recalled one particular evening at the Earl Theater. "They used to bring in a lot of big bands like Dorsey and Benny Goodman," he explained, "and who's playing drums for Benny Goodman but Gene Krupa." The little boy was mesmerized and convinced his father to let him take drum lessons. By the time he was ten he was a regular on Paul Whiteman's local TV show. A few years later Bobby landed a temporary gig filling in for the drummer in a local band. Not long afterward, he sent audition tapes to record companies, hoping to make it as a singer or drummer. Bernie Lowe was impressed and signed the 17-year-old to a Cameo recording contract.[39]

Rydell earned his first hit in 1959 with "Kissin' Time," written by Bernie Lowe and his Cameo/Parkway partner Kal Mann. Teenagers loved the rollicking song, which proclaimed summer vacation "kissin' time USA." The number 11 record was just the beginning. Between 1959 and 1964 Bobby chalked up nineteen Top 30 hits and made numerous appearances on *American Bandstand*. He also got rave reviews for his role as Hugo Peabody in the movie *Bye-Bye Birdie*. Like other teen idols of the day, Bobby personified the clean-cut All-American boy. He was boyishly handsome, had a great smile, and an effervescent

Bobby Rydell (Courtesy of Bobby Rydell)

personality, as well as a magnificent pompadour and a seemingly never-ending supply of beautiful sweaters.

Rydell attributes much of his early success to Dick Clark. "I can't recall how many times I did . . . *Bandstand* because I lived in Philadelphia." Whenever a guest canceled at the last moment, Bobby would get a phone call asking him to rush down to the studio. "When [Clark] started playing a record, it immediately went cross country . . . [and kids] bought the record."[40]

Most of Rydell's hits were geared toward teenagers. "Wild One" (1959), "I've Got Bonnie" (1962), and "Forget Him" (1963) spotlighted young love. "Swingin' School" (1960) and "Wildwood Days" (1963) captured the rhythms of teen life. "The Fish" (1961) and "The Cha-Cha-Cha" (1962) showcased new dances.

"I'll Never Dance Again" (1962), which used dancing as a metaphor for teen romance, featured a powerful vocal and sound that resonated with young listeners. "That was one hell of a record," said Rydell. "Big orchestra. French horns. The whole nine yards."[41]

Despite all the teen-oriented hits, Bobby never thought of himself as a rock & roll singer. He saw himself as a pop singer and drummer. In his spare time he listened to jazz and pop artists like Frank Sinatra and Andy Williams. By the early 1960s he was headed more toward traditional pop, as evidenced by hits such as "Volare" (1960), "Sway" (1960), and "That Old Black Magic" (1961). "One of the biggest things that happened to me in my career was that first performance at the Copacabana . . . to not only do the hit records but to show the public that there was something more to Bobby Rydell than 'Kissin' Time' and 'Wild One,'" he explained. "The next day . . . the reviews came out—'POWER KEG OF TALENT'! That was kind of like the stepping-stone for me to do other things in my act rather than just all of the hits."[42] Rydell regrets that Cameo didn't do more to promote him as a pop singer. "I had really hoped that Bernie Lowe . . . would have started doing the big band things with me," he explains. "I really wanted to go into a studio and record what [Bobby] Darin did. Just go in there and swing doing Sinatra, Steve Lawrence, Andy Williams." He added, "That's where I really wanted to go, and they kind of missed out on that."[43]

Instead, Cameo promoted Rydell as a rock & roll singer. His numerous hits and TV appearances established him as one of the era's hottest teen idols. He was featured on covers of *Teen* and other fan magazines. And, teenage girls went crazy wherever he appeared. "It was exciting and scary," says Bobby. "Every girl out there thought she had a chance to marry you. They'd be screaming and hollering and crying."[44]

Unlike Paul Anka and Neil Sedaka, Bobby was not a songwriter. "I was so young," he points out, "whatever they put in front of me I recorded." But nobody ever told him how to sing. "I was a big Sinatra fan. I loved the way Frank phrased or got a lyric across to you. It wasn't just June, moon, spoon and all of that," says Bobby. "When Frank sang a lyric . . . it put you in a position where you understood, 'yea, I was there.'" Rydell adopted that approach. "Regardless of what song I did," he explains, "I always thought most about Frank's phrasing."

That approach, says Rydell, helped him connect with teenagers in the early 1960s, as well as older audiences later in his career.[45]

Bobby's appearance was as authentic as his vocal style. His hairstyle and preference for sweaters were the result of popular fashions of the day, not record company dictates. "I think all of us guys went through that," says Bobby. "I mean Frankie Avalon had that [look]. Fabian. Bobby Vee . . . A majority of the guys, you know 'teen age idols,' we were all into . . . some kind of sweater. It was the look back then. That's why kids could relate to us because that's what they wore."[46]

Rydell connected to listeners in other ways. "Let's face it," he says, "the fans back then . . . were all my age." As a result, they had similar interests, including dancing and romance. Rydell's audience aged with him. "Now they're in their 60s and 70s and have lived and been through life's ups and downs," says Bobby. "When they come to my shows, they still want to hear 'Wild One,' 'Volare,' and 'Forget Him.' But, when I interject other tunes like 'For Once in My Life' they can now relate to that too."[47]

Bobby's career made him an eyewitness to history in Kennedy's America. As the civil rights movement gained momentum, Bobby took part in integrated rock & roll tours like Dick Clark's *Caravan of Stars*. "I was the skinniest kid on the bus," he says. "I used to sleep in the luggage rack." Rydell never noticed any racial conflict between Black and white performers on the bus, but the travelers ran into problems with segregated restaurants and hotels in the Deep South. He remembers one occasion when he and the Black drummer for Joey Dee and the Starliters were walking out of a hotel. The two had become good friends and Rydell jokingly put his arm around the guy. "[Suddenly] he takes my arm and puts it down," says Bobby. "I said 'what's the matter,' and he said 'don't you know where you're at?'" Rydell notes, "at that point I had never thought of the Deep South as Black or white, purple, yellow, or whatever. We were all in show business together . . . and just hanging out. It never entered my mind where the hell we were at. He hipped me to it, which I thought was pretty cool." From that moment on, Bobby noticed racial divisions everywhere down South. "It was ugly. It was really kind of ugly," he explains. "We didn't care about color [on the bus]. We were friends, man. We were just trying to make music and make people happy."[48]

Rydell experienced another cultural shift when the British Rock Invasion took America by storm. "When the Beatles and the Rolling Stones all hit, disc jockeys never played American artists [anymore]," he explained. "We all said, 'what's this? We're the guys who made these [deejays] money and now all they're doing is playing British [songs].' And, of course, that hurt a lot of American artists, because we were no longer selling 45s . . . But, hey, we all survived."[49]

Rydell's last major hit was "Forget Him," which made it to number 4 in early 1964. Fortunately, his fans didn't take the title to heart. Bobby continued to perform on television and remained a popular concert performer both in the United States and abroad. In the mid-1980s he joined two other Philadelphia teen idols, Frankie Avalon and Fabian, and performed as *Bandstand's* "Golden Boys." Their never-ending tour was still going strong in the third decade of the twenty-first century. "I think [the music] has endured because it shows the innocence of a period in time that will never be again," explains Rydell. "People like to revisit an era when life was simple and roles in society were well defined. Not saying it was better or worse but everyone looks to their youth with nostalgia."[50]

With Bobby Rydell and Chubby Checker leading the way, Cameo-Parkway became a rock & roll powerhouse. Jon Cohen, the son of Cameo partner Kal Mann, attributed the success to the label's focus on teen interests. "The music industry was just starting to recognize teenagers as consumers," he explains. "This music . . . was designed for teenagers and the dances at high schools." Bernie Lowe even used his teenage daughters as a focus group. Several times a month, he'd bring dubs home for his two girls to hear. The songs they liked best often became Cameo's latest releases. Lowe hit the jackpot when he bet his company's future on the musical tastes and interests of baby boomers. The record label Bernie started for $2000 back in 1956 grossed over $9 million in 1962.[51]

Swan Records was a third independent record company in Philadelphia that became an important purveyor of pop rock. Dick Clark played a major role in Swan's success, just as he had with Cameo-Parkway and Chancellor. But unlike those two indies, Swan Records was owned by Clark in partnership with Bernie Binnick and Tony Mammarella.

Swan's initial success came with two hits that received considerable airplay on *Bandstand,* Billy and Lilly's "La Dee Dah" (1957) and Dickey Doo and the Don'ts' "Click Clack" (1958). But Swan's biggest star was Freddy Cannon, the label's entry in the teen idol sweepstakes. Like Bobby Rydell, Frankie Avalon, and Fabian, Freddy (a.k.a. Freddy Picariello) was a young, good-looking Italian American. Cannon didn't come from South Philly like those three. He hailed from Lynn, Massachusetts. Also, unlike the others, Freddy was a rock & roller at heart. As a teenager he put together a band, Freddy Karman and the Hurricanes, and recorded a demo of a song he had written, "Rock 'n' Roll Baby." Independent producer Frank Slay liked what he heard, and he and his songwriting partner, Bob Crewe, arranged to have Picariello record a revised version entitled "Tallahassee Lassie." Swan bought the master, changed Freddy's last name to Cannon, and released the record. On May 1, 1959, Freddy performed the song on *American Bandstand.* Ten days later "Tallahassee Lassie" debuted on the national charts and by June 29 it was the number 6 hit in the country.[52]

Dick Clark's association with Swan Records would soon end. During the payola scandal, ABC-TV gave Clark and his producer, Tony Mammarella, a choice: they had to divest themselves of their record label or they had to step down from *American Bandstand.* Clark chose the show; Mammarella opted for Swan. Afterward, says Clark, Tony and Bernie Binnick continued to drop by the *Bandstand* studio "to leave copies of their latest releases."[53]

Throughout the early 60s Freddy Cannon continued to be Swan's headliner, with teen-oriented hits such as "Transistor Sister" (1961) and "Palisades Park" (1962). Cannon's hits exemplify the formula pop rock manufactured by Philly labels in the late 1950s and early 60s. On his best records, such as "Tallahassee Lassie" and "Palisades Park," Freddy exhibited a high-energy approach that captured the spirit of rock & roll. But at his worst, on songs like "Chattanooga Shoe Shine Boy" and "Way Down Yonder in New Orleans," the sound was just formulaic pop music disguised as rock & roll.

Swan's success, like that of Cameo-Parkway and Chancellor, was closely tied to *American Bandstand.* Ironically, Swan's greatest opportunity to become a major player in the rock & roll world was frittered away because of *Bandstand.* In

1963 Swan got the American rights to release a record called "She Loves You" by an unknown British group called the Beatles. Bernie Binnick played the record for Dick Clark and explained that Swan had a four-month option on the group: "If we don't sell 50,000 copies EMI gets it back." Clark was not impressed when he heard the song, and was even less impressed when he saw the group's funny-looking haircuts. As a favor, Dick featured the record on *Bandstand's* "Rate-a-Record" segment. The teenage reviewers gave "She Loves You" a mediocre "73" rating. Binnick and Tony Mammarella concluded they were stuck with a "stiff." After the Beatles became a huge success on Capitol Records, Clark asked his former partners why they had not just bought the required number of records themselves. Had they done so, they would have retained the rights to the Beatles and become multimillionaires. Binnick just shook his head and said, "Why would we have done that? After all, both you and the kids on *Bandstand* agreed that the Beatles were going nowhere."[54]

THE POP ROCKING OF AMERICA

By the time the 1960s began, teen-oriented pop rock was being written and performed all across America. Paul Evans, born and raised in New York City, had hits with "Seven Little Girls Sitting in the Back Seat" (1959), "Midnite Special" (1960), and "Happy-Go-Lucky Me" (1960). Jimmie Rodgers, from Camas, Washington, found success with "Honeycomb" (1957), "Kisses Sweeter than Wine" (1957), "T.L.C. Tender, Love, and Care" (1960), and other records that mixed rock & roll with folk and pop music. Denver's Gary Stites earned hits with "Lonely for You" (1959) and "Lawdy Miss Clawdy" (1960). The 19-year-old Jimmy Clanton, from Baton Rouge, Louisiana, was even more successful. He scored a number 4 hit in 1958 with "Just a Dream," an anguished ballad he had written about young love. The song, combined with Jimmy's good looks, shy smile, and perfect pompadour, established Clanton as a top teen idol. Over the next few years he earned additional hits, including "Go Jimmy Go" (1960) and "Venus in Blue Jeans" (1962).

Several women pop rockers also made the *Billboard* charts. Following the lead of Connie Francis, they found success with songs aimed at young listeners. Former Mouseketeer Annette scored Top 20 hits with songs that featured demure young ladies hopelessly in love with guys: "Tall Paul" (1959) and "First Name Initial," "Oh Dio Mio," and "Pineapple Princess" (all in 1960). Dodie Stevens's number 3 hit, "Pink Shoe Laces" (1959) showcased a subordinate young woman who adored her boyfriend and his cool clothes. She followed up with several minor hits, including "No" (1960), which offered a troubling glimpse of the era's gender relationships. It featured a guy asking a girl for kisses and hugs. When she repeatedly says no, he threatens to telephone another girl. Dodie's character suddenly submits, saying "Must you go? Don't you know that a girl means yes, when she says no."[55]

VETERAN POP ROCK GROUPS

Several pop rock groups from the 1950s continued to chart in the early 60s.[56] Dion and the Belmonts were one of the most successful. Their Bronx doo-wop sound, a potent mix of R&B, pop, and rock & roll, earned them numerous hits. They began their run on the charts with "I Wonder Why" (1958), a high-energy rocker that climbed to number 22. What made the Belmonts a success, says Dion, "was the simple fact that we were out front doing the kind of music teenagers loved to hear. It was fast and sharp, as cool as the clothes we started to wear."[57]

Dion and the Belmonts followed up with other impressive hits aimed at young listeners, including "No One Knows" (1958), "Don't Pity Me" and "A Teenager in Love" (both in 1959), and "Where or When" and "When You Wish Upon a Star" (both in 1960). The group then split up. Dion went on to stardom as a solo artist (see chapter 8), while the Belmonts earned two Top 30 hits, "Tell Me Why" (1961) and "Come on Little Angel" (1962).

If Dion and the Belmonts emphasized the *rock* in pop rock, the Fleetwoods embraced the *pop*. The trio from Olympia, Washington—Gary Troxel, Gretchen Christopher, and Barbara Ellis—scored a number 1 hit in 1959 with "Come Softly to Me." Gary later recalled how the song came about. "The girls . . . had written their part of that song already," he explained. "But after they'd been singing it one day . . . Gretchen and I went walking . . . to the record store." Suddenly, Gary started singing some nonsense syllables: "dum, dum, dum do dum mm obby do." "Hey, slow that down a little bit," said Gretchen, "and see if it goes with what Barbara and I were singing." They were amazed when the two musical snippets fit together perfectly. "I don't know if it was really an accident or not," said Gary, "but it's really odd stuff."[58] Troxel's story demonstrates that not all pop rock was handed down from the top by professional writers from the Brill Building or elsewhere. "Come Softly To Me" is evidence that pop rock, like other types of rock & roll, sometimes had grassroots origins.

The Fleetwoods' unique harmonies earned them additional hits, including "Mr. Blue" (a number 1 hit in 1959), "Runaround" (1960), "Tragedy" (1961), "Lovers By Night, Strangers By Day" (1962), and "Goodnight, My Love" (1963). The trio offered a new take on the old doo-wop style. If their polished harmonies recalled traditional pop groups of the 1940s and early 50s, their teen-oriented lyrics and use of voices to mimic instruments placed them squarely in the doo-wop mode. Even the Fleetwoods' appearance offered something new. Standing on stage in the spotlight, they looked more like a suburban high school prom king and his court than doo-wop singers fresh off the city streets. The handsome Gary, wearing a suit and tie, was flanked by Gretchen and Barbara, two attractive young women in formal dresses and heels. Although the success of the two female singer-songwriters helped pave the way for other women pop rockers, there was nothing rebellious about the Fleetwoods' overall look or sound. Their soft harmonies, romantic lyrics, and pretty melodies appealed greatly to middle-of-the road teenagers. The group's positive image and homogenized sound made doo-wop more acceptable to mainstream America.

The veteran pop rock singers on the record charts in the early 1960s would soon be joined by a second wave of pop rockers. The influx of new talent would not only energize pop rock, but would offer innovative sounds and styles for all of rock & roll. This new cohort of pop rock singers would include far more women and be a perfect fit for the changes occurring on Kennedy's New Frontier.

8

"Take Good Care of My Baby"

Pop Rock's Second Wave

In 1961 Bobby Vee earned a number 1 hit with "Take Good Care of My Baby." The teenage tale about lost love grabs the listener's attention immediately. Accompanied only by a piano, Bobby confesses he is heartbroken because his girl left him for another guy. As the music kicks in, he asks the new boyfriend to take care of her and never make her blue. Bobby knows that had he been true his girl never would have left. Now all he can do is wish her well. But, he adds, "If you should discover that you don't really love her, just send my baby back home to me."[1] Vee's tearjerker taught young listeners important rock & roll lessons about love, dating, and the consequences of infidelity.

Bobby Vee and "Take Good Care of My Baby" are perfect examples of early 60s pop rock. Vee was the quintessential teen idol—an All-American Boy with good looks and a winning smile. Although his number 1 hit was recorded on the West Coast, it epitomized the era's pop-influenced rock sound that emanated from New York's Brill Building district. Written by Carole King and Gerry Goffin, the song featured a strong melody and marvelous musical hooks. It showcased pop rock innovations such as a double-tracked lead vocal and a sophisticated arrangement enhanced by pop-style harmonies and violins. At the same time, the song was still solid rock & roll. Vee's singing style was influenced by Buddy Holly, and the session players were topnotch rock & roll musicians. Bobby proudly describes his sound as "in-your-face pop and rock & roll."[2]

This chapter focuses on a new group of pop rock singers who arrived in the early 1960s. It explores the pop-influenced sounds associated with the Brill

Bobby Vee (Richard Aquila Collection)

Building, as well as the more basic rock & roll played by young singers and groups across the country. The hits of all these pop rockers offer insights about youth culture and life in Kennedy's America.

POP ROCK'S SECOND WAVE

When Bobby Vee arrived on the scene in the early 1960s, he was part of pop rock's second wave, made up mostly of young male and female singers more in tune with Kennedy's America than Eisenhower's. Their optimism, energy, and creativity were perfect fits for Kennedy's Camelot.

The emergence of these new pop rockers was linked to economics and demographic change. The birth of rock & roll in the mid-1950s created huge earnings for the music business. In 1950 record sales were around $189 million. By the decade's end they had skyrocketed to $603 million, partly because of the new teenage music. The payola scandal and an economic recession caused a dip in sales in 1960 and early 1961, but the record industry bounced back. By the end of 1963 record sales totaled $698 million, due mostly to an increased demand for rock & roll. During the early 1960s baby boomers flooded into high schools across the country, adding almost three-and-a-half million additional students to America's high school population. A large portion of them listened to Top 40 radio and bought rock & roll records.[3]

The proliferation of pop rock in the early 1960s led to exciting innovations and new energy for rock & roll. Dion rode the crest of pop rock's second wave. When the 60s decade began he was already famous as lead singer of Dion and the Belmonts. The group hit it big in the late 1950s with "I Wonder Why" and other doo-wop-influenced hits. Their success continued in 1960 with the number 3 hit "Where or When." Then, without warning, Laurie Records announced the group was splitting up. "I just had a different vision than they had," explains Dion. "[The Belmonts] kept trying to gear the whole career into kind of jazz mellow harmonies. And, I was just a rock & roll die-hard."[4]

Dion the solo artist was a different entity than Dion, lead singer of the Belmonts. His fresh rock & roll sound and energetic style matched the upbeat mood of the early 1960s. Even his image changed when Laurie Records marketed him as a teen idol rather than a member of a doo-wop group. His first solo release in 1960, "Lonely Teenager," took direct aim at the burgeoning baby boom market. His follow-up, "Runaround Sue," made it clear he wanted to rock. The song unleashed the rock & roll energy Dion had experienced growing up in the Bronx. "We made a lot of music just sitting on the stoops and making sounds," he explains. "If you go down to the Apollo Theater, they had a horn section. We didn't have a horn section up in the Bronx. Our group was like a poor man's horn section." He adds, "We would just take the sounds of the neighborhood and the attitude of the neighborhood and just roll it up in a song and express it."[5]

"Runaround Sue" was the ultimate expression of that neighborhood sound. The record starts slowly as an anguished Dion explains his sad story about a flirtatious girl he once knew. It then explodes into shouts and claps as Dion unleashes a classic rock & roll wail. This was in-your-face rock & roll, powered by Dion's urgent vocal, pounding drums, a blaring sax, and great doo-wop harmonies by the Del Satins. "Now listen people, what I'm telling you," warns Dion, "keep away from Runaround Sue." Teenagers loved it, and the record rocketed up to number 1. "That song was invented in the schoolyard," explains Dion. "It was spontaneous. It's the kind of mantra you could get into and sing for 45 minutes." Dion cowrote it with Ernie Maresca, a buddy from the Bronx. It was inspired by "a real girl we knew in the neighborhood."[6]

Dion followed up with another sensational hit, "The Wanderer" (1962). "That was born from Ernie's ideas," notes Dion. The song described "a guy in the neighborhood . . . and he had tattoos all over him, and he was bigger than life." Dion's emotional vocal, backed by a driving beat and wailing sax, helped the record climb to number 2. "I *swaggered* through the tune," he says, "putting a little growl into it, relishing Ernie's great macho lyrics."[7]

Dion's first hit album as a solo artist, 1961 (Richard Aquila Collection)

"Runaround Sue" and "The Wanderer" made Dion a rock & roll superstar. Before 1962 was over he signed a lucrative contract with Columbia Records. His first single, "Ruby Baby," debuted in January 1963. Written by Leiber and Stoller, the primitive rocker featured Dion's blues-influenced vocal accompanied by doo-wop harmonies, hand clapping, and basic rock instrumentation. When the record shot up to number 2, Columbia rushed out an album that revealed the company's plans for their new star. The record label—like his old company Laurie—was convinced that Dion's long-term success required a transition to adult pop music. "It was like they were forcing me back into a mold I'd wriggled out of back before my solo days," he said. The only song on the *Ruby Baby* album that truly rocked was the title song. Most of the other tracks were formulaic pop, including big band versions of pop standards like "My Mammy."[8]

Ironically, while some Columbia executives were pressuring Dion to move toward adult pop, John Hammond, Columbia's legendary A&R man, was encouraging him to explore authentic roots music. Hammond introduced Dion to the Delta blues of Robert Johnson, the gospel sounds of Aretha Franklin, and the authentic music of folksingers like Bob Dylan and Phil Ochs. The extraordinary sounds convinced Dion that music could convey the innermost thoughts of singers and songwriters.[9]

When Dion applied Hammond's lessons about authenticity to rock & roll, everything clicked. He still wanted hits, but was determined to express himself through music. In 1963 he recorded a country song that allowed him to make a personal statement about the changing times. Dion had always been a big Hank Williams's fan. "This guy means what he says, and says what he means," explains Dion. "That's what got me on the road of doing what I'm doing." Dion's rendition of Hank's "Be Careful of Stones That You Throw" sold fewer copies than his previous hits, but still managed to reach number 31. Significantly, it anticipated the direction that music was headed. Message songs would soon be taking center stage.[10]

Dion's last two releases in 1963 got him back into the Top 10. Realizing that his best songs told stories about real people, he teamed up again with Ernie Maresca to write "Donna the Prima Donna." The song was an inside joke about Dion's sister, who liked Zsa Zsa Gabor. "[Donna] always wears charms, diamonds, pearls galore," he sings. Then comes the punch line: "She buys them at the five and ten cents store." The infectious sound and thundering beat, which Dion describes as "full-on pop doo-wop," propelled the fast-paced rocker all the way up to number 6. His follow-up, "Drip Drop," also reached number 6. The Leiber and Stoller composition was the perfect vehicle for Dion's blues-influenced vocal about heartbreak. Dion was proud of his authentic rock sound. "In my own eyes, I had gone from being a 'performer' to being an 'artist,'" he explained. "But, I still knew how to crank up a hit." [11]

Just when Dion hit his creative stride, his career spiraled out of control. Like many American singers, he fell victim to the British Rock Invasion of 1964, because his early 60s sound and style were out of step with the changing times. Dion's problems were exacerbated by personal demons, which landed him in a drug rehabilitation program. In 1968 Dion made a comeback with "Abraham, Martin, and John," a folk-rock elegy that soared to number 4. The return of the "Wanderer"—a rock & roll hero from Kennedy's Camelot—gave college-age baby boomers hope after the assassinations of John F. Kennedy, Martin Luther King Jr., and Bobby Kennedy. "The song came out of just wanting to express some hope . . . in a bad situation," explains Dion. "It simply said, 'you can kill the dreamer, but you can never kill the dream' because it's the people like us who pick it up and carry it further." [12]

Although Dion never had another Top 10 hit, he continued to record and perform. Throughout the rest of the century and beyond, he explored many musical paths, including folk, blues, pop rock, Christian music, and classic rock & roll. Regardless of style, Dion remained true to his inner voice. His approach, he says, "is honest, it's simple. You have something to say, and you're going to say it." [13]

At the peak of his career in the early 1960s, Dion's authenticity and the quality of his music pumped new energy into rock & roll. He offered listeners an innovative musical mix that included ingredients from various styles. It was, he says only half-jokingly, "kind of like *doo-wop-country-blues rock 'n' roll.*" His crystal-clear, melodic voice added texture to the sound. But, for Dion it was never just about the music. "Rock-and-roll is an expression of the times," he insisted in 1963. "[It's] perhaps the strongest musical folk idiom of the Fifties and Sixties."[14] Dion's comment was right on the mark, as evidenced by his hits that expressed the highs and lows of youth culture. Dion sang about the joys of young love and despair of shattered dreams, as well as the colorful characters found in high schools and neighborhoods across the country.

Dion's career offers other insights about American life. When he became a solo artist, Laurie Records balked at using his full name, Dion DiMucci, in part because it sounded too ethnic. "In 1960, the folks in Fort Wayne, Indiana, were still getting used to the pronunciation of pizza and lasagna," says Dion. "DiMucci was just too much to add to their plate."[15] By 1963, though, Italian Americans and other ethnic groups were moving up the social and economic ladders. The GI Bill and labor unions helped them achieve higher status and better paying jobs after World War II, while the rise of an Irish American Catholic, John F. Kennedy, to the presidency lessened discrimination against Catholics and white ethnics.

Dion's new record label, Columbia, tried to capitalize on the growing awareness of ethnicity. Initially, the company billed the young singer simply as Dion just the way Laurie had, but by the end of 1963 Columbia printed his full name, Dion DiMucci, on record labels. The experiment did not last long, because the company soon realized that the name change was confusing fans. Columbia then tried another idea. They had Dion record Italian-language versions of "Donna the Prima Donna" and other songs to better market his music abroad if not to proud Italian Americans at home. "To me, it was richly ironic that some critics cited me as an example of an emerging movement they called 'ethnic rock,'" says Dion. "Whatever, if people wanted to buy my records just because I had Italian blood, that was fine by me."[16]

Dion's experiences on integrated rock & roll tours in the South reveal details about race relations in Kennedy's America. There were no problems on the tour buses, he points out, because "the music brought us together." But racial tensions were evident when they arrived at segregated hotels and restaurants. Dion never forgot how African American singer Sam Cooke was treated. "Sam was the headliner in our show, and people were driving hundreds of miles and paying good money just for the chance to hear him sing," explains Dion. "Yet he couldn't stay in the same hotel as his white road crew. He couldn't eat with any of us."

Dion knew prejudiced people back home in the Bronx. "But nothing in my upbringing had prepared me for my experience with Jim Crow."[17]

Over a half-century later, those haunting memories inspired Dion to write and record "Song for Sam Cooke (Here in America)" (2020). The tribute recalls the 1962 rock & roll tour in the Deep South, where Sam repeatedly displayed dignity and bravery in the face of segregated hotels, restaurants, and racists. "You were the star, standing in the light. That won you nothing on a city street at night . . . here in America," sings Dion poignantly.[18]

From 1960 until the end of 1963 Dion was one of rock & roll's biggest stars. He earned thirteen Top 40 hits. Eight made it into the Top 10, including "Runaround Sue," which became one of rock's all-time greatest hits. In the decades since, Dion has continued to rock whether he's singing folk music, gospel, blues, or rock & roll. "Songs are like a diary to me," he says. "As I move through life, my perspective and my thought can be communicated through my music." Dion was inducted into the Rock & Roll Hall of Fame in 1989. On stage that night, Lou Reed recalled the first time he heard Dion sing. "[His] voice was unlike any other I had heard before. Dion could do all the turns, stretch those syllables so effortlessly, soar so high he could reach the sky and dance there among the stars forever . . . a voice that stood on its own, remarkable and unmistakably from New York—*Bronx Soul*."[19]

Bobby Vee was another pop rocker who made it big in the early 1960s. He is often tossed into the teen idol category, but his career didn't begin that way. He started out as a singer and rhythm guitar player in a garage band. "I never thought of myself as a teenage idol," he notes. "We were a good little rock & roll band, but, it wasn't a screaming kind of thing." All that changed once Bobby scored some hits and appeared on *American Bandstand.* "It was like a whole different thing. I remember one girl grabbed the back of my sport jacket and tore it right up the back. I couldn't believe it."[20]

Bobby's musical roots run deep in rock & roll history. On February 3, 1959, 15-year-old Bobby Velline (a.k.a. Vee) was eating lunch at home in Fargo, North Dakota, planning to attend a Buddy Holly concert that night. When a plane crash killed Holly, Ritchie Valens, and the Big Bopper, a radio station sent out an urgent request asking local talent to take part in a memorial concert. Bobby, his older brother, and two high school friends had recently formed a band, so they volunteered. "It was such an emotionally packed evening," Bobby recalled. "If you had to pick a way to *not* enter show business, this would be it. I mean, who would want to go on stage on a night like that . . . It was like a rock & roll requiem."[21]

Bobby Vee and the Shadows' performance that night impressed not just concertgoers but also local promoter Bing Bengtsson, who handed them a business card. Bobby phoned the next day, and Bing booked them for an upcoming event on Valentine's Day. "We played this dance and made sixty bucks," said Bobby. "We thought we were on our way." When Bing suggested they make a record, the four high school kids drove to Kaybank Studio in Minneapolis to record "Suzie Baby," which Bobby had written in tenth-grade study hall. Released on the Soma label, the record featured Bobby's plaintive teen vocal and his brother's unique guitar style. "[Bill] plucked at the strings with his thumb and fingernails . . . much like Mark Knopfler would do years later."[22]

When "Suzie Baby" became a local hit, a regional promotion man sent a copy to Snuff Garrett, a Liberty Records producer in Los Angeles. Snuff was impressed with the rockabilly sound, particularly Vee's lead vocal, so he immediately phoned him. "That record sounds just like Buddy Holly and the Crickets," said Snuff. "Jerry Allison [the Crickets' drummer] is in my office right now and he's got a tear in his eye." Bobby later noted, "that got my attention because I was a big [Holly] fan." A deal was worked out to reissue "Suzie Baby" on the Liberty label. A few months later Garrett offered a recording contract, which led to Bobby's success as a solo artist.[23]

The Buddy Holly sound shaped many of Bobby's early Liberty recordings. "[Snuff] was a friend of Holly's, and he believed that Holly was turning the page on rock & roll," explains Vee. Just before his tragic death, Buddy "had entered a brand-new phase with 'It Doesn't Matter Anymore,' 'Raining in My Heart,' and all those other wonderful songs that he recorded in New York with an orchestra. That's what Snuffy thought was the direction of rock & roll." Garrett experimented with that approach on Vee's early records. In the summer of 1960 Vee made it all the way to number 6 with "Devil or Angel." The cover of the Clovers' 1955 R&B hit blended Bobby's rockabilly vocal with doo-wop sounds, violins, and a pop-sounding chorus. "Sixteen years old and singing with a full orchestra and doing these songs that I had been buying a few years earlier by other artists . . . was a great experience," says Bobby.[24]

Vee followed up with another Top 10 hit, "Rubber Ball" (1961), which reinforced the Holly connection. Bobby's vocal echoed Buddy's hiccuping style, while the studio musicians on the up-tempo song included Jerry Allison (the Crickets' drummer) and guitarist Tommy Allsup, a member of Holly's band on his final tour. "Bobby didn't sound like Buddy," explained Snuff, "but he had the intone of sounding like Buddy." The Holly influence would be evident throughout Vee's career. Most of his albums featured at least one Holly song. In 1962 he recorded a bestselling album with Buddy's group entitled *Bobby Vee Meets the Crickets*. And, the following year he released a tribute album, *I Remember Buddy Holly*, made up mostly of Holly songs.[25]

Vee's versions of Holly songs introduced a new generation of teenagers to Buddy's music. "I certainly did everything I could to keep Buddy Holly's memory alive," he says, "because it was, and is, important to me." At the same time, he never consciously copied Buddy's sound. "Holly was a major influence and inspiration," points out Bobby, "[but] short of the occasional hiccup, I . . . never tried to imitate him." If there was any similarity, it was their honest approach to music. That's part of that time period's charm, insists Bobby. "These were guys that just had little bands or were singing on street corners or in garages . . . They made their own music and marched to their own drummer. It was honest."[26]

Despite his close ties to 1950s rock & roll, Bobby Vee is best known for state-of-the art pop rock hits such as "Take Good Care of My Baby" (1961), "Run to Him" (1961), and "The Night Has A Thousand Eyes" (1963). He and Snuff worked as a team to craft an innovative sound that combined rock & roll with experimental double-tracked vocals, pop choruses, and arrangements that featured violins, kettle drums, and other sounds not typically found in rock & roll. Although Vee recorded in LA, most of his hits were written by Carole King, Gerry Goffin, and other writers from the Brill Building district. Garrett would make frequent trips to New York, says Vee, and "find various songs and bring them to me to see if I liked them."[27]

Once they got into the studio, Bobby and Snuff had distinct roles. "Make no mistake, Snuff was the producer," says Bobby. "He understood moods and tension and things that songs are made up of." But Snuff never told Vee how to perform vocals. "Snuffy gave me free rein," says Bobby. "I did my own harmony parts and I think that was one of the things that I brought to the table and that I enjoyed most."[28]

Some of the most talented studio musicians in Los Angeles took part in recording sessions. Many of them were later recognized as members of the Wrecking Crew (the unofficial name for LA's top studio musicians). "Here we were cutting all those pop records and the rhythm section was Little Richard's rhythm section," notes Bobby. "These were all guys who came out from New Orleans and moved to Los Angeles." He adds, "We had the best players and state-of-the-art equipment."[29]

Vee's importance in rock & roll history isn't based just on the quality or success of his records. The young singer's close connection to his fans gave his music a folk quality. The teenage Vee and 22-year-old producer Snuff Garrett instinctively made choices that showed they were on the same wavelength as listeners. "We just went and recorded a bunch of songs that we liked," says Bobby. "America's youth were able to relate to it." He adds, "When I look back at my songs, I notice that there are certain common themes that deal with teen lifestyles." Hits such as "Sharing You" (1962) and "The Night Has a Thousand Eyes" (1963) explored troubled relationships. "Stayin' In" (1961) plugged into high school life. Other records like "Walkin' With My Angel" (1962) and "Hark is that a Cannon I Hear" (1962) glorified young love.[30]

The songs rang true because the messenger was believable. Bobby's age, appearance, and demeanor gave him credibility with young fans. "I wore what I wanted," says Vee. "I performed in suits and ties like most performers. I also was a sweater guy. So, those are the clothes I wore on my record covers." When Vee sang about shyness on "Bashful Bob" (1961), listeners knew exactly what he meant. The song worked in part because it wasn't contrived. "It was written for me by Dick Glasser, who was a staff writer . . . at Liberty Records," explains Vee. "I wasn't outgoing and that was Glasser's image of me—'Bashful Bob.'"[31]

Vee's songs reinforced America's Cold War values. Religion provided the backdrop for "My Prayer" (1960) and "Angels in the Sky" (1961), while marriage was idealized on songs such as "A Forever Kind of Love" (1962). Gender stereotypes frame other hits, including "Devil or Angel" (1960) and "Walkin' With My Angel" (1962).

Vee's career offers insights into changing attitudes toward race. Even though Bobby was a white pop rock singer, his studio band included Blacks and he toured extensively with African American artists. He recalls the racial tensions that surrounded integrated tours in the Deep South. Although there were never any problems between Black and white performers on the bus, situations popped up when they had to deal with segregated restaurants and hotels. Initially, "nobody really complained about it. It was just kind of a cold reality," he says. But as the civil rights movement picked up momentum in the early 60s, everyone on these tours began saying, "Wait a minute, this *does* matter. Somebody finally was able to spit the truth out and say 'We can't be doing this.'"[32]

Like many of his contemporaries, Bobby Vee ran into hard times when the British Rock Invasion hit in 1964. He bounced back in 1967 with the Top 10 hit "Come Back When You Grow Up," but his return to the charts was short-lived. By the end of the decade America was staggered by the Vietnam War, urban riots, and campus protests. Bobby's innocent pop rock style was out of step with the times. Though his star faded, Vee's legacy remained. Between 1959 and 1970 he made the Top 100 charts thirty-eight times, including fourteen Top 40 hits and six gold records. His commercial success, the quality of his music, and his close connection to fans made Vee was one of the most important singers of the early 1960s.

Bobby Vee kept on performing, recording, and rockin' right up until his death in 2016. "I never would have imagined that I or anyone else would be enjoying [rock & roll] as much . . . 35 years later," he said in 1994. "You know, for me to go out on stage . . . then look in the audience and see a 55-year-old guy with tears in his eyes . . . I mean, this is wild to me." That lasting connection between the music and fans underscores rock & roll's significance. Back in the early 60s, "we took this [music] on in such a personal way. It had something to do with honesty and truthfulness," he explains. "That innocence [is] what we connect with. And, I've just never been willing to let that go."[33]

In January 1961 Bobby Vee was enjoying success with his Top 10 hit, "Rubber Ball." That same month the song's composer, Gene Pitney, made his singing debut on the charts with another song he wrote, "(I Wanna) Love My Life Away." Pitney grew up in Rockville, Connecticut, listening to rock & roll. In high school he discovered that "if you could play four chords, you could play the Top 20," so he began taking guitar lessons and formed a band. After graduation he studied electrical engineering at a nearby college but never abandoned music. He recorded a few songs on local labels, but nothing charted. Gene then turned to songwriting and began knocking on doors in the Brill Building district. Veteran composer and music publisher Aaron Schroeder was intrigued by the teenager's voice and original material, so he signed Pitney to a songwriting contract. Gene was soon living off royalties from songs he wrote or cowrote, including Vee's "Rubber Ball" (1961), Rick Nelson's "Hello Mary Lou" (1961), and the Crystals' "He's a Rebel" (1962).[34]

One demo of an early Pitney composition turned out so well that Schroeder released it as a single. Gene recorded "(I Wanna) Love My Life Away" when he was just 19 years old. He plunked down $30 for recording time in a small four-track studio in New York City. Using his knowledge of electronics and recording techniques, Gene produced an innovative multi-track recording that featured overdubs of him singing lead and backup vocals, as well as playing the piano, guitar, bass, and drums. Schroeder released the demo on his newly formed Musicor label, and it became a Top 40 hit in early 1961. "Suddenly I was doing every television show, radio show and record hop they could book me into," recalls Gene. "Once I started recording [and] traveling on trains and buses and planes, I found I could not write."[35]

Pitney had other reasons to put songwriting on hold. His reputation as an up-and-coming singer and Schroeder's Brill Building connections gave him access to material written by some of New York's best composers. The follow-up to Gene's first hit was "Every Breath I Take," a pop rock ballad written by Carole King and Gerry Goffin and produced by Phil Spector. His next release was "Town

Without Pity," the title song for Kirk Douglas's movie. The record became Pitney's first major hit, peaking at number 13 in 1962. Gene's emotional vocal was a perfect fit for the dramatic ballad, which blended social commentary about youth culture with a driving rock beat and lush pop arrangement. Teenagers loved the record, which was perfect for slow dancing and making out, or feeling depressed if they couldn't do either. Adults and music critics were equally impressed when the song was nominated for an Academy Award and won a Golden Globe.

Although "Town Without Pity" lost the Oscar that year to "Moon River," Gene's impressive live performance at the awards ceremony transformed him into a combination rock and pop star. Soon afterward he was offered the chance to sing the title song for John Wayne's upcoming film, *The Man Who Shot Liberty Valance*. "The song had been written by Burt Bacharach and Hal David, John Ford was directing, it starred Jimmy Stewart, John Wayne and Lee Marvin," notes Gene. "I mean, you couldn't turn it down, and we didn't, and am I glad." Unfortunately, Pitney's recording didn't make it into the film. "We were in the studio about to record the song," he explains, "and Bacharach informed us that the film just came out." Others have suggested that John Ford rejected the pop rock song, because he didn't think it was right for his Western. In any case, Ford's film was released on April 13, 1962, and Pitney's song debuted on the pop charts two weeks later. Both became major hits.[36]

Audiences loved Pitney's "Liberty Valance," which climbed all the way up to number 4. The record grabs the listener's attention immediately with an ominous-sounding violin. Guitars and drums then establish the tempo as Gene unleashes a classic Western tale about good versus evil. When the song's villain (paradoxically named "Liberty Valance") terrorizes a town, people run and hide until a good guy steps up to save the day. The solid rock beat and exciting love story appealed to baby boomers, while the colorful lyrics about the mythic West hit home with listeners of all ages in Cold War America. The record hit the pop charts in early 1962, sandwiched between the building of the Berlin Wall in the summer of 1961 and Cuban Missile Crisis in the fall of 1962. The pop rock morality tale was a timely reminder of America's courage and values.

Pitney's next release, "Only Love Can Break a Heart," was another Bacharach and David composition. His emotional vocal on the ballad about young love was enhanced by a full chorus and soaring violins, punctuated by Gene's lonely whistle as a mournful saxophone plays in the background. Within weeks of its release in 1962, "Only Love Can Break a Heart" became a number 2 hit. That was the closest he ever came to a number 1 record. Ironically, Pitney was kept out of the top spot by the Crystals' "He's a Rebel," which he wrote.

In 1963 Gene earned hits with two more Bacharach and David compositions: "True Love Never Runs Smooth" peaked at number 21, while "Twenty Four Hours from Tulsa" came in at number 17. The latter told a dramatic story about a young guy who succumbs to temptation when he stops for the night at a motel just one day away from his girlfriend back home. The song picks up momentum as he sings breathlessly about the alluring woman he met at the rest stop. One thing leads to another—dinner, dancing, kissing, caressing, and more. By the song's end the guy has fallen for her many charms. He writes to his girlfriend and apologizes because he has fallen in love with someone new. Now, he says emphatically, "I can never . . . never . . . never . . . go home again." That record "opened up a global market for me," says Pitney. "It was a very good song, with a good tune, a good title, and a good story line. In other words, it had all the ingredients."[37]

Bacharach and David weren't the only songwriters behind Pitney's hits. In 1962 he scored a number 12 hit with "Half Heaven-Half Heartache," composed by Aaron Schroeder and Wally Gold. The following year he earned another Top 20 hit with "Mecca." The unusual song, written by Neval Nader and John Gluck, anticipated the rise of multiculturalism. It alluded to Mecca and used Middle Eastern imagery and sounds to explore the perils of forbidden love.

Pitney's exceptional voice and excellent material by Brill Building writers helped him survive the British Rock Invasion. As the Beatles and other British acts were taking America by storm in 1964, Gene scored two of the biggest hits of his career. "It Hurts to Be in Love," written by Howard Greenfield and Helen Miller, became a number 7 hit. The equally sensational "I'm Gonna Be Strong," by Barry Mann and Cynthia Weil, also made the Top 10. Pitney followed up with additional hits: "I Must Be Seeing Things," "Last Chance to Turn Around," and "Looking Through the Eyes of Love" in 1965; "Backstage" in 1966; and his final Top 20 hit, "She's a Heartbreaker" in 1968.

In 2002 Gene Pitney was inducted into the Rock & Roll Hall of Fame in recognition of his achievements as a singer and songwriter. "The secret of my success was very simple," he said. "When I found a great song, I grabbed it." Gene's explanation leaves out what may be the most important reason of all—his remarkable voice. Like Roy Orbison, Pitney had an extraordinary vocal range capable of producing stunning rock & roll arias. He was particularly proud of his performance on "I'm Gonna Be Strong." "I have a three-octave range and I knew I had the ability to hit notes like that," he explains. "I heard the demo in a publisher's office and it was a very straightforward song with the ending just on one note, not going anywhere. I put on one voice and then another one and then another." The result—a powerful end note that lasts a full fourteen seconds—surprised even Pitney. "That last phrase in the song—'how I'll break down and CRY'—how the notes change within that last word," says Gene. "I still get goose bumps every time I sing that song."[38]

Pitney's readily identifiable voice and emotional style contributed greatly to his success. "If heartbreak had a voice, it would be Gene Pitney's," insists writer Bob Greene. "[His] anthems of pure pain and despair . . . found a ready audience—tens of millions of young hearts were breaking every week." Although Gene's initial fame came as a rock & roll singer, he also recorded pop standards, country music, folk songs, and material aimed at the international market. His dynamic concerts added to his popularity in the United States and abroad.[39]

Pitney's final curtain call came on April 4, 2006, at a concert in Cardiff, Wales. Just as he had done numerous other times during his 45-year career, he closed the concert with the dramatic ballad that made him famous—"Town Without Pity." As the song ended, people stood and cheered. "The audience [was] in raptures," reported a local music critic. The next morning, Pitney was found dead in his hotel room from a sudden heart attack. Ironically, "Town Without Pity" was his first major hit and the last song he ever sang.[40]

Two months after Gene Pitney made his debut, an unknown singer-songwriter from Michigan arrived on the rock & roll scene. Del Shannon hit the charts in March 1961 with an innovative song destined to become one of rock & roll's greatest hits. It begins with a guitar strumming, followed by a foreboding piano riff. Then comes Shannon's desperate vocal about a guy walking in the rain wondering what went wrong with the love he thought was strong. He cries out in a soaring falsetto, "I *wah-wah-wah-wah*-wonder. Why—*why, why, why, why, why* she ran away. And, I wonder where she will stay—my little runaway."[41] Just when listeners think they've reached the rock & roll summit, keyboard player Max Crook unleashes a space-age sound unlike anything ever heard before in music history.

"Runaway" rocketed up to number 1 and stayed there an entire month. Shannon later explained how the song came about. One night, he, Max Crook, and the rest of his band were playing at the Hi-Lo Club in Battle Creek, Michigan. Out of nowhere, Max hit an A-minor chord on his piano, followed by a G chord. The unusual sound caught Shannon's attention, and they started jamming to it. The next day Del wrote lyrics and phoned Max to tell him they were going to perform the song that night at the club. "When we're on stage and I point to you," said Del, "play an instrumental." When the moment arrived, Max "played an instrumental that he never changed a note of after that," recalls Del, "and that was how we wrote 'Runaway.'"[42]

Max Crook played the solo on a homemade device, which he dubbed the "Musitron." It was an early version of what would later be called a music synthesizer. "I was seeking new and different sounds," he explains. "There were no exotic keyboards around at that point . . . so I sought out something I could tweak." The customized instrument, says Max, was a "three-octive, monophonic . . . keyboard with a slide on it" that enabled him to play "at a range of two cycles-per-second up to beyond human hearing." Max adds proudly, "I built the Musitron out of a variety of things. A clavioline was part of it, but I also threw in some resisters . . . tubes from television sets, parts for appliances, and other such household items."[43]

"Runaway" became one of the bestselling records of 1961 and made Del Shannon rock & roll's newest teen idol. Literally overnight he went from being Chuck Westover, an unknown singer at a local club in Michigan, to rock star Del Shannon, appearing at the famed Brooklyn Paramount alongside major rock & rollers. Years later Bobby Vee vividly recalled that first night at the Paramount. "[Del] came in . . . with this green and black mohair suit and this guitar he had picked up for $5.00," says Bobby. "He wanted to take it on stage, but everybody tried to talk him out of it, because it looked so horrible." Del finally agreed not to use the guitar. But then he complained, "I don't know what to do with my hands." That was one of the things that Bobby liked about Del. "He told you exactly what he thought. You always knew what was going on with him."[44]

Shannon's honesty came through in his music. Teenagers could relate to the heartfelt vocal and anguished lyrics on "Runaway." They also loved the unique sound, which combined Del's exciting falsetto, an innovative musical arrangement, and unusual chord progressions. Similar features propelled later hits such as "Hats Off to Larry" (1961), "Hey! Little Girl" (1962), and "Little Town Flirt" (1963). The quality of Shannon's music helped him survive the British Rock Invasion. He became the first American artist to cover a Beatles song when his version of "From Me to You" became a minor hit in 1963. The following year he made it to number 22 on the charts with a dynamic cover of Jimmy Jones's "Handy Man." He did even better in 1965 with two of his own compositions— "Keep Searchin' (We'll Follow the Sun)" and "Stranger in Town."

Shannon's personal demons eventually overwhelmed him. His insecurities were evident from the start. He never felt like he belonged. Most teen idols were 17 or 18 when they scored their first hit. Del was 26 years old and married with two kids, so he allowed his record company to knock five years off his age and lie about his marital status. He worried constantly about his short height, his weight, even his talent. "I had a tough time handling the success," he admitted years later, "the fear was unbearable." Shannon turned to alcohol for comfort. "[He] came from a long line of alcoholics," says Shirley Westover, his former wife of 31 years. "He'd get so wired on stage he could never sleep. He'd go down in the hotel bar or, if he wanted to get away from the fans, he'd drink in his room."[45]

Ultimately, Shannon lost his battle with depression. On February 8, 1990, he died from an apparent suicide. He gave his last performance just a week before at a Buddy Holly memorial concert alongside his close friend, Bobby Vee. "Del and I were together on his last show, up in Fargo, my home town," says Vee. "I was with him for two days during that depression he was going through." When Bobby asked him if he wanted to talk about it, Del assured him he was okay. After Del was done singing at the Fargo concert, he thanked everyone for their support. He then turned toward Bobby Vee, who was watching in the wings, and said, "I love you, Bob." Vee never forgot that moment.[46]

In retrospect, hints about Shannon's depression and fears can be found in his songs about sad, tormented characters. At the time, listeners had no way of knowing that Del's art imitated his life. In the early 1960s rock & roll audiences related to his dramatic tales of teenage heartbreak, loved his expressive vocals, and cheered his dynamic performances. They loved his sound, which he called "sort of 'pop' rock & roll." Fellow singers also appreciated his talent. "There's nobody probably on the face of the earth that I identified more with musically," says Dion. "We used to sit and sing George Jones and Hank Williams tunes . . . It thrilled me to hear him sing anything up-close with a guitar. It was just mesmerizing."[47]

Later rock stars also took notice. Paul McCartney recalls that he and John Lennon "took the lovely A-minor chord we heard in 'Runaway' and inserted it in 'From Me To You.' It was just funny when Del recorded the song, because part of the influence came from him."[48] Tom Petty was 10 years old when he first heard "Runaway." Decades later Petty and the Heartbreakers referenced Del and "Runaway" on their 1989 hit, "Runnin' Down a Dream." Tom also produced Shannon's comeback album, *Drop Down and Get Me* (1982). The close ties between Petty and Shannon touched off rumors that Del was going to replace the late Roy Orbison in the Traveling Wilburys, the super-group formed by Petty, George Harrison, Bob Dylan, Jeff Lynne, and Orbison. Although Shannon's death ended that possibility, the Wilburys later paid tribute to Del with an outstanding cover of "Runaway."

In recognition of his accomplishments as a singer-songwriter, Del Shannon was inducted posthumously into the Rock & Roll Hall of Fame in 1999. Three years later the phenomenal "Runaway" entered the Grammy Hall of Fame.

Approximately 100 additional male pop rockers arrived on the charts in the early 1960s. Johnny Preston earned a number 1 hit with "Running Bear" (1960), written by J. P. Richardson (a.k.a. the Big Bopper). The bouncy pop rock song told a tale about a young couple, Running Bear and Little White Dove, who were members of enemy tribes that lived across the river from each other. The desperate young lovers jump into the swirling water and swim toward each other. As they embrace and kiss, the deadly current pulls them down. "Now they'll always be together in that happy hunting ground," sings Preston. The song featured an infectious melody, an irresistible tom-tom beat, and melodramatic American Indian chants courtesy of the Big Bopper and country singer George Jones. Evidently, most people in Kennedy's America had no problem with the Native American stereotypes. "People laughed and weren't offended," insists Johnny Preston. "Even Indians loved it, and they always sang along when I performed it in concerts."[49]

Not long after the demise of Running Bear and Little White Dove, the Grim Reaper struck again on Mark Dinning's "Teen Angel" (1960). The young couple in the song got into trouble when their car stalled on railroad tracks. They saw a train coming and jumped out. Suddenly the girl went running back. Only after they pulled her body from the twisted wreck did her boyfriend realize what had happened; in her fingers, she was clutching his high school ring. "I'll never kiss your lips again," he sings to his 16-year-old girlfriend, "they buried you today."[50] In lieu of flowers, empathetic teenagers rushed out to buy Dinning's record, sending "Teen Angel" all the way up to number 1—rock & roll's equivalent of heaven.

By the 4th of July, rock & roll fans had gotten over "Teen Angel" and were ready to have fun. On that date in 1960 16-year-old Brian Hyland made his debut with "Itsy Bitsy Teenie Weenie Yellow Polka Dot Bikini." The novelty song reached number 1, thanks to millions of teenagers interested in romance, summer fun, and the sexy new fashion in swimwear. In 1962 three more new pop rock singers scored number 1 hits. Bruce Channel found success with the bluesy "Hey! Baby." Tommy Roe's "Sheila" featured a Buddy Holly-like vocal and the same tom-tom beat found on Holly's "Peggy Sue." And Bobby Vinton hit the charts at graduation time with "Roses Are Red (My Love)," a nostalgic tearjerker about high school love. Vinton followed up with two more romantic ballads in 1963: "Blue on Blue" peaked at number 3, while "Blue Velvet" made it all the way to number 1.[51]

Other pop rockers never had a number 1 hit, but they still managed moments in the rock & roll spotlight.[52] Ray Peterson earned a Top 10 hit in 1960 with "Tell Laura I Love Her," a heart-wrenching ballad about a star-crossed couple. Tommy and Laura were lovers. He wanted to buy her flowers, presents, and a wedding ring. Problem was, the kid had no money. So, he drove his hot rod to the racetrack, convinced he would win the $1000 prize. Faster and faster he raced until suddenly his car swerved and crashed in flames. As Tommy took his last breath he pledged his undying love for Laura. At the end of the song, Laura is sitting by herself as an organ plays funeral music. Alone in the chapel, she hears Tommy's haunting last words: "Tell Laura not to cry, my love for her will never die."[53]

Like Ray Peterson, Dickey Lee never made it to number 1, but he, too, found eternal rock & roll fame with a song about teenage death. In 1962 he made it to number 6 with "Patches," a chilling ballad about a double teen suicide. The boy in the song comes from an upper-class family and is in love with Patches, a poor girl who lives by the river in Old Shanty town. They want to marry, but his parents forbid it. When he learns that Patches has drowned herself in the river, the forlorn boy knows what he must do. "It may not be right, but I'll join you tonight," he sings mournfully, "Patches, I'm coming to you." Not only did the tearjerker appeal to young listeners' fascination with lurid tales about teen romance, but the song was a ready reminder that parents should not interfere in kids' lives. Less obvious was the song's subtext, which hinted at class divisions in Kennedy's America.[54]

Pop rocker Lou Christie also arrived on the charts in the early 60s. His soaring falsetto earned him hits in 1963 with two doo-wop-influenced songs that he cowrote with Twyla Herbert, "The Gypsy Cried" and "Two Faces Have I." "There was something about our chord patterns," explains Christie. "They were more classical or more international, [which] made the music more interesting instead of the standard 4 chord progressions, the usual *wha wha wha*." After 1963 Christie's career went into a tailspin, because like many American pop rockers, he could not keep pace with the Beatles and other British artists. But he eventually made a comeback in 1966 with two songs that appealed to young listeners. "Lightnin' Strikes" became a number 1 hit, thanks to Christie's emotional vocal, a catchy melody, and sexually suggestive lyrics. Christie followed up with the equally suggestive "Rhapsody in the Rain." His final Top 10 hit came in 1969 with "I'm Gonna Make You Mine."[55]

SECOND WAVE POP ROCK GROUPS

Solo artists weren't the only ones who found success with pop rock. New male groups chimed in with some of the most original sounds in rock & roll history. Two groups, in particular, were at the forefront of pop rock's second wave. The Beach Boys, led by singer-songwriter Brian Wilson, came out of California with innovative songs about surfing, cars, and teenage culture (see chapter 4). On the East Coast, the 4 Seasons rocketed to the top of the charts, powered by Frankie Valli's falsetto and excellent material written by keyboard player Bob Gaudio. "We didn't harmonize like the normal blending vocal group" explains Gaudio.

The 4 Seasons (Courtesy of Vee Jay Records)

"We were four distinctly different voices, unlike the Beach Boys, who had this brotherly [sound]."[56]

The 4 Seasons scored number 1 hits with their first three releases—"Sherry" (1962), "Big Girls Don't Cry" (1962), and "Walk Like a Man" (1963). But, the group was anything but an overnight success. By the time "Sherry" hit the charts, all four guys had been kicking around for years. Tommy DeVito and Nick Massi were in their mid-30s and Frankie Valli was 28. Back in 1956 Valli and DeVito were part of a group called the Four Lovers, who had a minor hit with "You're the Apple of My Eye." The youngest member of the 4 Seasons, 19-year-old Bob Gaudio, was actually the most successful. His first group, the Royal Teens, charted with two songs he cowrote: the number 3 hit "Short Shorts" (1958) and "Believe Me" (1959), which peaked at number 26.

The catalyst who brought the 4 Seasons together was Joe Pesci (later an Oscar-winning actor). After the Royal Teens split up, Gaudio joined Pesci in a jazz quartet. Joe was impressed with Bob's songwriting and had a hunch he'd hit it off with his friend who was a talented singer. Joe took Gaudio to a local club where Frankie Valli and the Four Lovers were performing. Gaudio was amazed when he heard Valli sing an old jazz song, "Moody's Mood for Love." "Frankie sang both parts—for the woman's part, he'd put a kerchief on his head. The range was pretty astounding," recalls Gaudio, "and that was when the lights and bells went off for me. I found the Holy Grail here." Valli was equally sold on Gaudio's potential. "I was very impressed by Bob's writing," he says. "When he played some songs for me, I was quite sure that he was the guy I wanted to hook up with."[57]

The Four Lovers needed a keyboard player and offered Gaudio the job. The group, which now consisted of lead singer Frankie Valli, bass player Nick Massi, guitarist Tommy DeVito, and keyboardist Gaudio, began playing clubs in and around Newark. One venue, the 4 Seasons Lounge in a bowling alley in Union, New Jersey, inspired a name change for the group. Shortly thereafter, the newly dubbed 4 Seasons met independent record producer Bob Crewe, who hired them to play and sing backup in recording sessions. Gaudio and Valli eventually convinced Crewe to give them a shot as recording artists. Crewe never regretted the decision, because the 4 Seasons' first record, "Sherry," became a number 1 hit.[58]

"Sherry," written by Gaudio, produced by Crewe, and released on the small Vee Jay label, introduced rock & roll fans to the group's innovative sound built around Frankie's voice. "He had over a three-octave range," explains Gaudio. "And I tried to capitalize on it. 'Sherry' came pretty much from that—that amazing falsetto." Given the enormous popularity of neo-doo-wop in the early 60s, many listeners assumed the 4 Seasons were the latest doo-wop group. But, despite Valli's prominent falsetto and Massi's rollicking bass voice, the 4 Seasons were not doo-wop singers. "We were in another place. We were in between [pop groups like] the Four Freshmen and doo-wop groups, but I wouldn't call it street doo-wop," says Gaudio. "There's a difference to me. I don't think we did the typical chord progressions that are synonymous with doo-wop. We really created songs to fit around our sound. The harmonies were more blocked out and not so many moving parts. It was more of a wall of vocal sound."[59]

"Sherry" catapulted the 4 Seasons to stardom. Young listeners loved the unique falsetto, fresh harmonies, and prominent dance beat, as well as the clever lyrics, which featured a guy asking a girl to come out and dance the night away. His ulterior motive becomes clearer when he asks her to wear her red dress, which looks so fine and makes him lose his mind. The phenomenal success of "Sherry" was exhilarating yet terrifying. One minute the 4 Seasons were playing bowling alleys and bars in Newark and recording demos for Bob Crewe at $15 a pop. The next minute, they had the number 1 record in America and were lip-synching on *American Bandstand*.

Songwriter Bob Gaudio felt the most pressure. "We were getting ready to try to find a follow-up to 'Sherry,' which was a little scary," he admits. When Crewe suggested the song could be called "Big Girls Don't Cry" (a line he remembered from an old movie), Gaudio jumped at it. "It was easier for me to start with a title than just go in the dark," he explains. Gaudio and Crewe co-wrote the song pretty quickly. "We blocked it out," says Gaudio, "and hopefully it was a little bit different than 'Sherry,' but not so far away that it changed the sound of the group completely."[60]

"Big Girls Don't Cry" was released in the fall of 1962 and shot up to number 1. Teenagers loved the tale about a young couple trying to outdo each other in the game of love. Initially, the girl outsmarts him. When he tells her they had to break up, she shrugs it off, saying "big girls don't cry." Only after he apologizes does he learn from her mother that the girl was up all night crying in bed. "You told a lie," he tells his girlfriend, "big girls do cry." Teenage boys and girls were intrigued by the musical mystery tale, which explored gender stereotypes of the early 1960s.[61]

The 4 Seasons' winning streak continued with "Walk Like a Man," their third straight number 1 record. Gaudio says the song, which he cowrote with Crewe, was "a definitive try at toughening up the lyrics and even the music was a bit funkier." "Walk Like a Man," like "Big Girls Don't Cry," focused on gender stereotypes and the battle of the sexes. Once again, the male triumphs. The teenage boy in the song tells his father that his girlfriend was lying to their friends to make him look bad. His Dad's response echoed the era's gender attitudes. "No woman's worth crawlin' on the earth," he advises, "so walk like a man, my son."[62]

With three number 1 hits in a row, the 4 Seasons thought they could do no wrong. "We were pretty cocky, I guess. Me in particular," admits Gaudio. The extraordinary success landed them a lucrative recording contract with Phillips Records. Their first release was "Dawn (Go Away)." The up-tempo melody was paired with downbeat lyrics about a boy from the wrong side of the tracks telling the upper-class girl he loves to go back to where she belongs. Cowritten by Gaudio and Sandy Linzer, the song offers a revealing glimpse of class tensions in Kennedy's America. The boy suggests that her family would never accept him, and he urges her to "think what the future would be with a poor boy like me."[63]

"Dawn" was an apropos title for the 4 Seasons' new beginning on the Phillips label. By the time the record was made, Nick Massi had left the group and the remaining members were experimenting in the studio. "We started using a few more musicians and added to the sound with more sophisticated arrangements," explains Gaudio. "Dawn" was the first song the 4 Seasons made using eight tracks. The recording process "was astounding," recalls Gaudio. "We didn't know what to do. It took three people to mix the darn thing. That's how we got the drums panning and the stereo effect."[64]

Unfortunately, "Dawn" was released just as the Beatles were taking America by storm. "Well, I'll tell you what happened," Gaudio says laughing. "We had 'Dawn' out. The Beatles were at number 1, 'Dawn' was stuck at number 2, and the Beatles had numbers 3, 4, and 5. We couldn't go anywhere." To this day, Gaudio doesn't know why the 4 Seasons were one of the few American acts to survive the British Rock Invasion. "It's just one of those things," he says. "I guess had we been putting out bad records, we wouldn't have survived. But the magic was still happening." That comment is an understatement. "Dawn" ushered in a new era for the 4 Seasons. From that point on, says Gaudio, "we started to get into [the process of] making records and what we could do with them." They followed up "Dawn" with several hits in 1964, including "Ronnie," "Save It For Me," and "Rag Doll," which became their fourth number 1 hit.[65]

Gaudio recalls how "Rag Doll" came about. "I was sitting in my car at 11th avenue in New York . . . it had the longest [stop] light in the world." Suddenly, this "tiny little urchin" came rushing out to wash his windshield. She had just gotten started when the light changed. Gaudio reached into his pocket looking for a few dollars to tip her, but the smallest bill he had was a twenty. So, he gave it to her and pulled away. He couldn't believe what he saw in the rearview mirror. "I saw this little girl standing there in the middle of the street with horns beeping because she just kept looking at the twenty-dollar bill," said Gaudio. "I just saw the look on her face as I was pulling away. And that was the inspiration for 'Rag Doll.'"[66]

The 4 Seasons continued to rack up hits throughout the mid-1960s. In 1965 they found success with "Bye, Bye, Baby (Baby Goodbye)" and "Let's Hang On." The next year they scored with "Working My Way Back to You," "Opus 17 (Don't You Worry 'Bout Me)," and a spectacular rendition of Cole Porter's classic, "I've Got You Under My Skin." The string of Top 20 hits continued in 1967 with "Tell It to the Rain," "Beggin'," and "C'mon Marianne." Gaudio and Bob Crewe also cowrote Frankie Valli's solo effort, "Can't Take My Eyes Off You," a number 2 hit.

The 4 Seasons' magic suddenly disappeared in 1968. With the country reeling from political assassinations, Vietnam War protests, urban riots, and campus unrest, the group's distinct sound, which echoed the innocence of early 60s America, was clearly out of sync with the dark times. Trying to keep pace with the counterculture and innovative concept albums such as the Beatles' *Sgt. Pepper's Lonely Hearts Club Band* (1967), Bob Gaudio cowrote and produced the 4 Seasons' *The Genuine Imitation Life Gazette* (1969). When the psychedelic album flopped, the 4 Seasons changed. Gaudio and Valli assumed Tommy DeVito's huge gambling debts in exchange for his resignation. The last two original members of the group continued recording and touring with a new 4 Seasons lineup. But Gaudio soon tired of the constant travel, so he quit the group. Afterward, he concentrated on songwriting and producing records for Frankie Valli, a revamped 4 Seasons, and other acts.

In the mid-1970s the 4 Seasons made a comeback with two songs written by Gaudio and Judy Parker, his girlfriend and soon-to-be wife. The latest iteration of the group earned a number 3 hit in 1975 with "Who Loves You," followed by the nostalgic "December, 1963 (Oh, What a Night)," a number 1 record in 1976. Frankie Valli also found success as a solo artist with three hits in 1975: "My Eyes Adored You," "Swearin' to God," and "Our Day Will Come." In 1978 he scored a number 1 hit with "Grease."

The original members of the 4 Seasons were inducted into the Rock & Roll Hall of Fame in 1990. But that wasn't the end of their rock & roll journey. In 2005 a musical, *Jersey Boys*, opened on Broadway and became a smash hit. Based on the 4 Seasons' lives and music, the show ran for 11 years and won 4 Tony Awards, including Best Musical. The original cast recording, produced by Bob Gaudio, won a Grammy in 2006. Both the Broadway show and a 2014 movie version directed by Clint Eastwood offered audiences a quintessential rags-to-riches tale. "I think it's a human story about guys that grew up in a relatively poor environment and made something of themselves," says Frankie Valli. The fact that the productions featured the 4 Seasons' hits added nostalgic appeal. The most colorful explanation for *Jersey Boys'* success came from one of its main characters, Tommy DeVito: "Is this like being in a fuckin' time machine, or what?"[67]

During the 1960s and early 1970s, the 4 Seasons earned twenty-seven Top 30 hits, including five number 1 records. The cornerstone for the phenomenal success was Frankie Valli. "His voice is amazing," says Gaudio. "[Frankie] has an incredible range . . . that's equally potent in any octave." Gaudio adds, "It wasn't just that [Frankie] could sing in falsetto, because . . . many of the early doo-wop groups did that style of singing." The difference is that Valli sang with "no break between his full voice and his falsetto . . . He could jump back and forth, and I had no boundaries to write." Valli's unique falsetto gave the 4 Seasons an instantly recognizable sound. "We decided that instead of the falsetto being the background, it would be the lead, singing the melody," explains Frankie. "The difference between what we did as far as the sound of the falsetto and the Beach Boys, they did it soft, we did it full."[68]

The group's musical and vocal arrangements contributed to the distinct sound. When Gaudio wrote "Sherry" he was thinking specifically about how the 4 Seasons' individual voices could enhance the sound. "When I heard the first note [in 'Sherry'] . . . and it started moving in falsetto, I envisioned—it needed support. You know, it needed a block harmony to surround it and support it." Massi helped shape the group's vocal identity. "Nicky was brilliant," says Gaudio. "He was kind of a savant." Initially, the 4 Seasons "sang as much four-part harmony on those street corners as we did doo-wop because Nicky was really good at pulling four-part out of the air."[69]

The 4 Seasons benefited from excellent material written by Gaudio and Bob Crewe. "[We] tried to keep the same basic structure harmonically," says Gaudio, but the writing process was never contrived. "I've always written for myself," he notes. "Sometimes you write for yourself and it works for the rest of the world, and sometimes it doesn't."[70]

Crewe's excellent production work added to the quality of the records. Crewe's early successes as a songwriter and arranger came with Top 10 hits like the Rays' "Silhouettes" (1957) and Freddy Cannon's "Tallahassee Lassie" (1959). He brought those skills into the studio with the 4 Seasons. The creative process from song selection to recording was a team effort that involved Crewe and the entire group. In any given situation, says Gaudio, "one person or another might have contributed more. But overall, it was a collaboration. It was just a magical time." That's not to say they always got along. "We had characters in the group . . . and we clashed," admits Gaudio. "That's part of what made the records what they were. They were edgy, they had some anger in them, they had some passion in them and it made us different than anything else on the radio."[71]

The 4 Seasons offered a fresh sound for a new generation of teenagers in an era that celebrated new, improved products, new ideas, new politicians, and new frontiers. The 4 Seasons—like President Kennedy—were young and brash, and sounded optimistic about the future. These four Italian Americans from

New Jersey embodied the American Dream. Frankie Valli, Bob Gaudio, Nick Massi, and Tommy DeVito started with nothing, but made it big through sheer talent and determination. They reached for the stars and wound up among the brightest in the rock & roll universe. But in the end they remained typical Jersey boys. Perhaps Frankie Valli's character in the Broadway musical, which the real Frankie insisted was 95 percent accurate, best summed up the 4 Seasons' legacy. People want to know, says Frankie's character, what was the high point for the group? "The Hall of Fame? Selling all those records? Pulling 'Sherry' out of the hat? It was all great," he admits. "But, four guys under a streetlamp, when it was all still ahead of us . . . the first time we made that sound—our sound—when everything dropped away and all there was, was the music—*that was* the best."[72]

While the 4 Seasons and Beach Boys were the most successful pop rock groups in the early 60s, numerous others made their mark. The Lettermen and the Kingsmen were on opposite ends of the pop rock spectrum. The Lettermen—Tony Butala, Jim Pike, and Bob Engemann—hit *Billboard*'s charts first. The three singers were in their early 20s when they scored a number 13 hit in 1961 with a pop rock version of Fred Astaire's classic from 1936, "The Way You Look Tonight." The romantic ballad featured the group's distinctive harmonies backed by a lush orchestral sound that enhanced a soft rock piano riff and beat, which made the record perfect for slow dancing at record hops.

The Lettermen's follow-up, "When I Fall in Love" (1962), was even more successful. The number 7 hit became a virtual anthem for teenagers with raging hormones. Many young couples across the country viewed it as "our song." They danced to it, romanced to it, even got their first kiss or more to it. The group continued their winning streak when "Come Back Silly Girl" made it to number 17 on the charts in 1962. The tearjerker about teen romance featured a young guy trying to win back his ex-girlfriend. "Don't know how long I can go on this way," he sings desperately, "I think of you most every day."[73]

The Lettermen's distinct sound and style resonated with young audiences. Performing in varsity letter sweaters, the handsome singers sang beautiful love songs that tugged at baby boom heartstrings. Their hit singles and bestselling albums such as *A Song for Young Love* (1962) established the group's reputation

as one of rock & roll's premier purveyors of songs that were perfect for slow dancing and making out. That reputation—like rock & roll itself—would never die.
Over the next several years, the Lettermen earned several more hits, including
"Going Out of My Head/Can't Take My Eyes Off You" (1968) and "Hurt So Bad"
(1969). In subsequent decades they would place over thirty albums on the bestsellers chart. They would also tour constantly, performing at high schools,
colleges, Chautauqua, and anywhere else baby boomers could be found.

The Lettermen's initial success in the early 1960s won them a loyal fan base
that never forgot their songs for young love. "I think we have been involved in
more romance than flowers and moonlight," says Tony Butala. "I'm very proud
that people still come up to me [decades later]. They may have gray hair or not,
but they'll say they fell in love to one of our songs. Being part of Americana is
not a bad thing."[74]

The Kingsmen's gritty garage-band sound was light years away from the Lettermen's soft pop rock. Ironically, both groups developed a huge following because
of the sexual nature of their hits. While the Lettermen's songs danced around
the subject, the Kingsmen's music did something about it. The Kingsmen exploded onto the pop charts in 1963 with their sensational version of Richard
Berry's R&B classic, "Louie Louie."

At a time when many hit records featured violins and sophisticated musical arrangements, "Louie Louie" boasted a primitive sound that recalled the early
days of rock & roll. The record begins with a keyboard playing a simple three-
chord progression, destined to become one of the most famous in rock & roll
history. In an instant, drums and electric guitars jump in. Then the real fun begins. The lead vocalist unleashes a passionate R&B-style vocal about . . . *who
knows what*? Young listeners couldn't figure out the garbled lyrics heard on car
radios or record players. The fact that nobody knew who the Kingsmen were,
where they came from, or whether they were Black or white added to the mystery. All teenagers knew was that they loved the fresh sound and big beat.[75]

"Louie Louie" debuted on the *Billboard* charts on November 9, 1963, just
two weeks before John F. Kennedy was assassinated. In the days leading up to
JFK's death and the weeks that followed, the cryptic song made its way up the

charts thanks to ubiquitous airplay on radio stations across the country. By the time "Louie Louie" peaked at number 2 on December 14, Americans young and old were in shock over the young president's death. As everyone searched for answers to explain the assassination, rumors and whispers of conspiracies spread from sea to shining sea.

In the dark days after Kennedy's death, anxious Americans looked suspiciously at anybody or anything that threatened the American way of life. "Louie Louie" became an obvious target. Just as concerned citizens during the 1950s Red Scare attacked rock & roll as a threat to American values, anxious adults in 1963 homed in on the Kingsmen's provocative record. They insisted the mysterious lyrics masked obscenities that would undermine the morals of American youth. On January 30, 1964, a concerned parent wrote to Attorney General Robert F. Kennedy, whose brother had been murdered just two months earlier. "I would like to see these people . . . prosecuted to the full extent of the law," said the irate parent. "When they start sneaking in this [explicit] material in the guise of the latest 'teen age rock & roll hit record' these morons have gone too far."[76]

By the time Bobby read the letter, government officials in Indiana were already on the case. Two high school students from Frankfort, a small town north of Indianapolis, got the ball rolling. After listening repeatedly to the record's slurred lyrics, they concluded "Louie Louie" was obscene and sent a letter of complaint to Governor Matthew E. Welsh. After he heard the record, the governor was convinced the teenagers were right. On February 1, 1964, Welsh encouraged Indiana radio stations to stop playing the "pornographic" song. He also asked the National Association of Broadcasters, the US Department of Justice, the Federal Communications Commission, and the Post Office to investigate possible crimes involving pornography, profanity, indecency, and interstate trafficking of obscene materials.[77]

The Kingsmen denied any wrongdoing. The five young white guys, barely out of high school, insisted they were just a local garage band from Portland, Oregon. "Louie Louie" was one of their favorite songs, so they decided to record it. The band members chipped in to pay $50 to rent a local studio and recorded "Louie Louie" in one take. When the lyrics controversy erupted, the group's drummer and cofounder, Lynn Easton, insisted, "We took the words from the original [Berry] version and recorded them faithfully. There was no clowning around." The 19-year-old lead singer Jack Ely explained he was slurring words that day because he had just gotten his braces off, plus he was having problems singing into the one microphone dangling overhead in the cramped studio.[78]

The Kingsmen were relieved when all the government investigations came up empty handed. On February 12, 1964, the UPI news service reported that the Federal Communications Commission, the Post Office, and Justice Department had looked into all the charges that "the record . . . had off-color lyrics which could be detected when the 45 rpm platter was played at 33-1/3 rpm." The inquiries were dropped because the examiners "were unable to determine what the lyrics of the song were even after listening to the records at speeds ranging from 16 rpm to 78 rpm."[79]

The inconclusive findings only added to growing public concerns. The "Louie Louie" Scare spread nationwide as handwritten versions of filthy lyrics began popping up in middle schools, high schools, and colleges everywhere. The FBI received information that "an unidentified college student . . . made up a series of obscene verses for 'Louie Louie' and then sold them to fellow students." Although nobody knew for certain where the bootleg lyrics originated, concerned citizens were more determined than ever to protect American youth from wicked rock & roll.[80]

During the spring of 1964, formal complaints were filed with FBI officials in Florida, Michigan, California, New York, Indiana, and Louisiana. In each instance, local officials forwarded to the FBI lab in Washington DC the complaint plus supporting documents, which included a copy of the Kingsmen's record and two sets of lyrics—Richard Berry's original words and the alleged "dirty" lyrics. Discerning listeners soon realized that if they played the record while reading the obscene lyrics, the song sounded outright filthy. But if they listened as they read Berry's official lyrics, it appeared to be an innocent tale about a guy sailing his boat to Jamaica to see his girl. The FBI—the nation's top law enforcement agency that had triumphed over communist spies, organized crime, and hardened criminals—couldn't crack the case involving a young garage band from Oregon. Every FBI lab test reached the same conclusion: the record was unintelligible at any speed. They found no conclusive evidence of criminal wrongdoing.[81]

Despite the findings, vigilant Americans remained on red alert. The "Louie Louie" Scare continued throughout the rest of 1964 and into the next year. Additional FBI lab tests occurred, but they always ended the same way. Because the record's lyrics were garbled, said the FBI, "it was not possible to determine whether this recording . . . is obscene."[82] By the end of 1965, "Louie Louie" was old news. Teenagers had moved on to new songs by the Beatles and other rock groups, while the stress levels of Americans had gone down. Two years had passed since Kennedy's assassination, and President Lyndon Johnson, who promised a continuation of JFK's policies, had won a landslide victory over Barry Goldwater. Hardly anyone even noticed when the Kingsmen's "Louie Louie" was rereleased in early 1966 and stalled at number 97 on the charts. Clearly, the "Louie Louie" Scare was over.

When all was said and done, the only thing that "Louie Louie" protests accomplished was that all the attention guaranteed the record's success. For a brief time the Kingsmen were the hottest garage band in the country, enjoying additional hits like "Money" (1964) and "The Jolly Green Giant" (1965). "Louie Louie" went on to become one of rock & roll's greatest party anthems. It was covered by numerous artists and performed by thousands of bands across the country. The Kingsmen's seminal hit eventually would be featured in the soundtracks of countless movies and TV shows. *Rolling Stone* ranked "Louie Louie" number 54 on its list of the 500 greatest songs in rock & roll history. In 2018 "Louie Louie" was one of only six songs inducted into the Rock & Roll Hall of Fame's new "Singles" category, which recognizes "the excellence of the singles that shaped rock 'n' roll."[83]

Most of the male pop rock groups that arrived on the charts in the early 1960s fell somewhere in between the pop rock polarities represented by the Kingsmen's raucous garage-band sound and the Lettermen's soft, pop-influenced harmonies. Several groups scored number 1 hits, including: the Hollywood Argyles, "Alley-Oop" (1960); the Tokens, "The Lion Sleeps Tonight" (1961); Marcels, "Blue Moon" (1961); Joey Dee and the Starliters, "Peppermint Twist—Part 1" (1962); Jimmy Gilmer & the Fireballs, "Sugar Shack" (1963). Others also cracked the Top 5, such as: the Safaris, "Image of a Girl" (1960); Dovells, "Bristol Stomp"

(1961); Capris, "There's a Moon Out Tonight" (1961); Jay and the Americans, "She Cried" (1962); Cascades, "Rhythm of the Rain" (1963).

Of all those groups, Jay and the Americans were the most consistent hit makers. Between 1962 and 1970 they earned ten Top 30 hits, including three Top 5 records—"She Cried" (1962), "Come a Little Bit Closer" (1964), and "Cara Mia" (1965). Their debut on the charts came in 1962 with "She Cried," produced by Leiber and Stoller. Although the doo-wop ballad had an innovative sound that featured kettle drums and violins, the lyrics were quite traditional. As the title suggests, the song reinforced the era's gender expectations. Jay and the Americans' bouncy follow-up, "Only in America" (1963), resonated with listeners for different reasons. Not only did the song echo the Latin rhythms popularized by the hit Broadway musical, *West Side Story*, but it plugged into the patriotic mood of Kennedy's America following the Cuban Missile Crisis. Kenny Vance, one of the founders of the group, notes that the record started out as a regional hit in Florida before it climbed to number 25 on the national charts. "There's a friend of mine . . . and he told me that when they were kids that had come from Cuba in 1963, 'Only in America' was an anthem for them," explains Vance. "They couldn't speak English, but phonetically they could all sing 'Only in America.'"[84]

The Lafayettes did not have the sustained success of Jay and the Americans, but they did have one magnificent moment in the rock & roll spotlight. In 1962 they scored a minor hit with "Life's Too Short," one of the greatest—yet somehow overlooked—records in rock & roll history. Powered by a foreboding bass line and frenzied drumbeat, the record features a stunning lead vocal by Frank Bonarrigo. "We gotta up and get married before my hair turns gray," he sings urgently to his girl, "I need you for real, baby, I've had my time to play." The tension created by the desperate vocal and primitive garage-band sound was at once the record's greatest strength and weakness. Although the dark sound made "Life's Too Short" a cult classic, it was a bad fit for the optimistic mood of the country in 1962. The record stalled at number 87 on the charts, and the Lafayettes faded from view. But neither rock & roll fans nor the group's members (most of whom were in high school at the time) ever forgot the Lafayettes' moment of glory. "It was a pretty wild time," says bass player Lee Bonner, who cowrote "Life's Too Short" with his friend Phil Huth. "To do that, as a teenager, was amazing, a fabulous experience. It's like we were stars, with people dancing to our music and applauding."[85]

"YOU DON'T OWN ME"

Males weren't the only ones succeeding as pop rock singers in the early 60s. Numerous women took the stage, inspired by pioneers such as Connie Francis, Brenda Lee, and the Shirelles. The decade witnessed not only the rise of successful girl groups such as the Paris Sisters and Angels, but also a new wave of women pop rockers that included solo artists and members of groups made up of females and males.

The growing number of young, female singers paralleled the rise of women in Kennedy's America. An increasing number were working outside the home, attending college, and entering graduate schools, law schools, and medical schools. Intelligent and competent women also gained high profiles in popular culture through TV programs such as *The Dick Van Dyke Show* and successful movies like *The Miracle Worker*.

The time was right for women rock & roll singers. The number of girls in high school spiked in the early 60s as the first cohort of baby boomers hit their teenage years. Record companies targeted these new consumers with pretty female pop rockers mostly in their late teens and early twenties. Their youthful voices, clean-cut images, and teen-oriented songs made them role models for girls and heartthrobs for boys.

Groups and duos that featured women were at the vanguard of pop rock's second wave of female singers. Women vocalists with male backup groups earned major hits. Kathy Young and the Innocents made it all the way to number 3 with "A Thousand Stars" (1960). The record's intimate vocal and seductive beat made it a perfect introduction to young love for baby boomers who had just started high school. The following year, Rosie and the Originals scored a number 5 hit with "Angel Baby," which revealed insights about passion and true love courtesy of Rosie's ethereal voice.

Pop rock duos that gave equal billing to women also made it big. In the summer of 1961 Dick and Deedee climbed to number 2 with "The Mountain's High." The dynamic ballad featured a solid rock & roll beat, stunning vocals, and lyrics that hinted at sex and rebellion. The young couple in the song is separated by adults in the middle of the night. Afterward, the boy and girl are determined to overcome tall mountains or any other obstacles in the way of true love. "If fate has its way," they sing, "we'll meet again some other day."[86] Dick and Deedee followed up with additional hits, including "Tell Me" (1962), "Young and In Love" (1963), "Turn Around" (1964), and "Thou Shalt Not Steal" (1965).

Dick and Deedee's success paved the way for other duos. Paul and Paula scored a number 1 hit in 1963 with "Hey Paula," which showcased a young couple rhapsodizing about marriage. Paul says he's been waiting for school to be through so he can marry her. She replies that she wants to marry him, too. With church music playing in the background, the two sing about marital bliss when "wishes we made will come true."[87] Their follow-up hits in 1963, "Young Lovers" and "First Quarrel," also glorified romantic relationships where boys and girls were equal partners. Dale and Grace offered a similar approach on their number 1 hit, "I'm Leaving It Up to You" (1963). These hits by pop rock duos offer interesting glimpses of gender, youth, and traditional values in Kennedy's America.

Women solo artists found even greater success. In 1961 16-year-old Linda Scott scored a number 3 hit with "I've Told Every Little Star," a bouncy pop rock version of a 1932 pop song composed by Oscar Hammerstein and Jerome Kern. Her follow-up, "Don't Bet Money, Honey," did almost as well, peaking at number 9. Written by Scott, the song offered a fresh female perspective on relationships. At a time when most young women were expected to be forgiving if guys lied or cheated, Linda takes a more aggressive approach. She makes it clear to her unfaithful boyfriend that she's had enough. You can almost hear teenage girls cheering as Linda delivers the knockout punch, telling him not to bet money their love will last.

Linda Scott was soon joined by other young women singers. Janie Grant earned a Top 30 hit with her composition "Triangle" (1961), which assured teenage girls it was okay to cry when love went wrong. Two hits by Timi Yuro offered options for dealing with heartbreak. In 1961 she scored a number 4 hit with "Hurt," which explained that she'd never hurt her ex-boyfriend the way he hurt her. She was far less gracious on her next Top 20 hit, "What's a Matter Baby

(Is It Hurting You)" (1962), one of the greatest revenge songs in rock & roll history. Her glee cannot be contained when she learns that the guy who jilted her has been dumped by his new girlfriend. "Now my hurting is just about over," she sings, "but baby it's just starting for you."[88]

The year 1962 witnessed the arrival of other women singers who found success with teen-oriented pop rock. The 16-year-old Shelley Fabares, who played the sweet daughter on TV's *The Donna Reed Show*, made it all the way to number 1 with "Johnny Angel." The song featured a girl hopelessly in love with her dream boy, who doesn't even know she exists. "I pray that someday he'll love me," she sings, "and together we will see how lovely heaven will be."[89] Teenage girls, hoping to meet their own Johnny Angel someday, identified with the song about unrequited love. Boys were equally impressed, albeit for different reasons. They fell in love with the pretty vocalist who seemed as sweet and innocent as her TV character. Reality and fantasy became one when Shelley Fabares was transformed into the hottest new singer in the country.

Just two months after "Johnny Angel" hit the charts, Joanie Sommers earned a number 7 record with another song about a guy named Johnny. Written by Brill Building veterans Hal David and Sherman Edwards, "Johnny Get Angry" begins with somber chords and a plunking piano. Then, Sommer's bouncy voice takes charge, singing an up-tempo trickster tale about a frustrated girl with a meek boyfriend. "I want a brave man, I want a cave man," she demands. "Johnny, show me that you care, really care for me."[90]

The mischievous lyrics turned gender stereotypes upside down. In the early 1960s the boy was supposed to lead, while the girl followed. "Johnny Get Angry" exposed the reality. Even as the girl longed to conform to the stereotype, her actions revealed that some young women were more aggressive, dominant, and thoughtful than their boyfriends. But young listeners were willing to overlook the obvious contradiction, since the clever song had a good beat they could dance to, a catchy refrain, and an awesome sound that included a kazoo playing the instrumental bridge. Although Sommers would never have another major hit, "Johnny Get Angry" earned her a special place in rock & roll history. The record's exploration of gender attitudes demonstrates that even contrived pop songs could offer revealing glimpses of everyday life.

The year 1962 also welcomed the arrival of Carole King—as a singer. She and her husband, Gerry Goffin, were already recognized as a top songwriting team. Carole stepped into the spotlight as a singer with her Top 30 hit "It Might as Well Rain Until September." Young listeners loved the imaginative musical arrangement, which featured violins mimicking rain drops. They also identified with Goffin's sad lyrics about a couple separated by summer vacation. "Gerry had a gift for tapping into what teenage listeners were thinking," says Carole. His knack for writing lyrics that expressed young concerns was evident on King's next release. The folk-influenced "He's a Bad Boy" (1963) explored tensions with parents, social expectations, and the pain of young love. The record stalled at number 94 on the charts, possibly because radio stations were reluctant to play a song about a juvenile delinquent who treats his girlfriend "cruel." After "Bad Boy," King put her singing career on hold so she could concentrate on songwriting and her two young kids. In 1971 she would make a triumphant return to the pop charts with "It's Too Late," the number 1 hit that established her as a singer-songwriter extraordinaire.[91]

In 1963 two more women singers, Little Peggy March and Lesley Gore, hit the charts. Both earned number 1 records with songs destined to become rock & roll classics. Peggy was barely 15 years old when "I Will Follow Him" debuted. The record begins with pounding drums and guitars. A male chorus chants emphatic doo-wop syllables, setting the stage for Little Peggy's dramatic entrance. She shouts out "I love him," three times, insisting she will follow him wherever he goes. In an era where a woman was expected to follow the man's lead, teenage girls found it easy to relate to this pop rock proclamation of true love. Little Peggy—diminutive even in name—made it clear that she was willing to follow her guy anywhere, even over deep oceans and high mountains. "I must follow him," she explains. "He is my destiny."[92]

Although most fans in 1963 assumed "I Will Follow Him" was a song about young love, more than a few reached a different conclusion. The record became a number 1 hit at a time when religion was prominent in Cold War America. Many members of the audience thought the "Him" in the song referred to God. Some fans, says Peggy, even wrote letters "saying 'it was because of your song that I decided to go into the convent.'"[93]

Lesley Gore also earned a number 1 hit with her first release. She turned 17 on May 2, 1963, and nine days later she cracked the pop charts. The instant listeners heard her record they were hooked. As horns blare, Gore shouts out a line that became one of the most famous in rock & roll history: "It's my party and I'll cry if I want to!"[94]

"It's My Party" told the story of a brokenhearted girl whose boyfriend cheats on her during her own birthday party. The record shot up to number 1 thanks to Lesley's convincing vocal, excellent production work by Quincy Jones, and an in-your-face musical arrangement by Claus Ogerman. Gore's next release offered fans an exciting and satisfying sequel. "Judy's Turn to Cry," a Top 5 hit in 1963, updates the original story. Gender stereotypes abound as Gore explains what happened. When she saw Johnny kissing Judy at the party, she kissed another guy to get even.

Lesley Gore's first hit album, 1963 (Courtesy of Jack Natoli,
Lesley Gore International Fan Club)

The jealous Johnny then jumped up and punched him. "So now it's Judy's turn to cry," sings Lesley triumphantly, "'cause Johnny's come back to me."[95]

Gore followed up with other songs about the perils of young love, including "She's a Fool" in 1963 and "You Don't Own Me," "That's the Way Boys Are," and "Maybe I Know" in 1964. "Gore embodied a new type of feminine . . . that is strong, outspoken and liberated," suggests music writer Margaret Farrell. "Her music gave authority to teenagers . . . In Gore's songs, she is the only one that is in control, whether that means crying until her eyes run dry or getting lost in old memories."[96]

Paradoxically, Lesley Gore's success caused her downfall. Her readily identifiable voice and polished pop rock sound seemed old-fashioned once the Beatles and other British rockers hit the American charts. After 1964 she managed only two more Top 20 hits, "Sunshine, Lollipops, and Rainbows" (1965) and "California Nights" (1967). Soon afterward she and her record label parted company. "Mercury released me . . . and I had no recording contract," she explains. "They didn't even give a reason . . . The records weren't selling. They didn't need a reason. British Invasion . . . we're finished with you . . . bye bye."[97]

If new trends in the music business ended her run on the pop charts, social change guaranteed her long-term success. Her seminal hit, "You Don't Own Me," was recorded in 1963—the same year as the publication of Betty Friedan's *The Feminine Mystique*. Both contributed to the rise of feminism. While Friedan was encouraging women to rethink their gender identities and prescribed roles as housewives and mothers, Gore was introducing teenage girls to similar thoughts through rock & roll. The assertive young woman on Gore's number 2 hit, which peaked in early 1964, makes it clear that she's going to live life on her terms. She points out to her boyfriend that she's young and free, and can say and do whatever she wants. She's not his plaything and doesn't want to be put on display. "You don't own me," she declares. "Don't tie me down 'cause I'd never stay."[98]

Ironically, "You Don't Own Me" was written by two men, John Madara and Dave White. (The two cowrote numerous songs, including "At the Hop," which became a number 1 hit in 1958 for White's group, Danny and the Juniors.) The moment they auditioned the song for Gore, she knew she had to record it. "I liked the strength in the lyric. But for me it was not a song about being a woman.

It was a song about being a person and what was involved with that," explains Gore. "Of course, it got picked up as an anthem for women, which makes me very proud."[99]

The powerful feminist message of "You Don't Own Me" took root in popular culture. The iconic song was used as the triumphant ending of the 1996 film *The First Wives' Club*. The connection to women's rights was underscored when Jessica Chastain and the female cast of *Saturday Night Live* sang the song on the night of the 2018 Women's March. After Lesley Gore came out as a lesbian in 2005, "You Don't Own Me" became a staple at gay pride celebrations. "The beauty of that song," notes Gore, "is that the verses start in a minor key, and then, when you go into the chorus, it goes into the major, and there's such a sense of lift and exhilaration."[100]

After the hit records stopped in 1967, Gore continued performing and recording. In 1983 she received an Oscar nomination for cowriting "Out Here On My Own" (from *Fame*). In addition, she got involved in various causes, including LGBT issues. At the time of her death in 2015 Gore was working on two new projects—a memoir and a Broadway show based on her life.

Lesley Gore is remembered best for iconic hits like "It's My Party" and "You Don't Own Me." Her songs expressed teenagers' emotions, hopes, and dreams, and are good examples of the tensions in early 60s pop rock. If some listeners dismissed the records as just pop fluff with contrived lyrics about young love, others celebrated Gore's hits as authentic rock & roll. Millions of teenage girls could relate to the heartbreak that Lesley sang about on her initial hit, "It's My Party." They thought her reaction was totally honest, because they knew they'd cry, too, if it happened to them.

Even though most women pop rockers did not achieve sustained success in the early 1960s, many left their mark with records that helped girls navigate the sea of love. Ann-Margret's bluesy "I Just Don't Understand" (1961) featured a young woman trying to cope with her boyfriend's behavior. Robin Ward's "Wonderful Summer" (1963) explored the pros and cons of summer romance. And, Ginny Arnell's "I Wish I Knew What Dress to Wear" (1964) showed how fashions could be weaponized in boy-girl relationships.

Hits by women pop rockers suggest that teenage girls subscribed to the traditional values of Cold War America. Jamie Horton's "My Little Marine" (1960) and Diane Renay's "Blue Navy Blue" (1964) featured patriotic girls supporting boyfriends in the military. Other songs such as Paul and Paula's "Hey Paula" (1963) and Little Peggy March's "I Wish I Were a Princess" (1963) spotlighted marriage and the family, which were viewed as cornerstones of the American way of life.

Most of the songs heard on Top 40 radio echoed mainstream gender attitudes. The women portrayed on hit records usually followed the lead of men. Marcie Blane's "Bobby's Girl" (1962) is a perfect example. The number 3 hit offers a revealing look at expectations for young women in Kennedy's America. It begins with Marcie explaining that people constantly ask her what she wants to be now that she's no longer a kid. She knows exactly what to say. She doesn't dream about becoming a doctor, lawyer, or teacher. There's only one goal in her life. "I wanna be Bobby's Girl," she proclaims. "That's the most important thing to me."[101]

Marcie Blane's song was not unusual. Most pop rock records, including Cathy Jean and the Roommates' "Please Love Me Forever" (1961), Shelley Fabares's "Johnny Angel" (1962), and Little Peggy March's "I Will Follow Him" (1963) endorsed traditional gender roles. But change was in the wind. Women took charge on Hayley Mills's "Let's Get Together" (1961), Timi Yuro's "What's a Matter Baby" (1962), and Lesley Gore's "You Don't Own Me" (1963).

Although women made gains in early 60s rock & roll, they still had a long way to go. "The girl groups and female solo artists were given equal time on the stage," says Bobby Vee, who toured with female artists. But many issues remained. "These were some pretty strong women," explains Vee. "They might look like fragile little dolls up there singing . . . in their sparkling dresses, but it was tough being out there on the road . . . and for a woman, it was ten times tougher." As the decade progressed, Vee noticed fewer gender problems. "By the late 60s, women came into the music business with a different feminist attitude . . . you know, 'I have every right, this is my time, and don't try to push me around.'"[102] Put another way, Lesley Gore's pop rock vision for gender equality in 1963— "You Don't Own Me"—became a reality for many women by the 1970s.

POP ROCK IN A YOUNG WORLD

Pop rock's talented new artists and fresh sounds energized rock & roll in the early 1960s. Pop rock's innovative use of multi-tracked vocals, choruses, and instruments like violins, cellos, timpani, and horns reverberated throughout the music industry, influencing country rock, folk music, pop, R&B rock, even the new Motown Sound.

Pop rock resonated in Kennedy's America. The music's connection to young listeners was obvious on songs about romance and other teenage interests, including dancing, dating, surfing, cars, and fashions. But pop rock hits also explored other subjects that expressed the era's optimism, materialism, and attitudes toward the Cold War, race, and gender. For millions of teenagers, pop rock was pure rock & roll—just as vibrant and authentic as R&B rock, rockabilly, or any other rock style.

In 1962, 13-year-old John Beland was a big fan of pop rock songs like Rick Nelson's "Young World" (1962). He grew up to be an accomplished songwriter and guitarist for the Flying Burrito Brothers and numerous other artists, but he never forgot the music of his youth. Songs like "Young World," he says, "still can take me back to that era when pop music was innocent and simple, before the anger and cynicism of the mid-to-late 60s would come along and change everything." He adds, "It was the era of Kennedy, Andy and Barney, Disney, Mickey Mantle, young love, surfing, cars—the American dream. 'Young World' takes me back to all that, when singers . . . sang songs that truly were aimed at the heart of a young teenager."[103]

9

"Wild Weekend"

Top Tunes, News, and Weather

In 1963 an obscure garage band named the Rebels scored a Top 10 hit with "Wild Weekend," a mesmerizing rock & roll instrumental. The band (later renamed the Buffalo Rebels or Rockin' Rebels to avoid confusion with Duane Eddy's group) were four high school students from Lackawanna, a steel town just outside Buffalo, New York. Their record debuted on *Billboard*'s Top 100 on December 29, 1962. By early spring it was the number 8 hit in the country. From the moment teenagers heard it, they were hooked. The fresh sound was pure unadulterated rock & roll, powered by a twangy electric guitar, insistent bass, pounding drums, and blaring sax.

The story behind the Top 10 record demonstrates the important connections between rock & roll, Top 40 radio, and young audiences. "Wild Weekend" started out as the theme song for Tommy Shannon's weekend radio show on Buffalo's WKBW, a powerful 50,000-watt station that broadcast up and down the Eastern Seaboard. "KB was just a monster," says Shannon. "It went into New York City, Baltimore, and Philadelphia at night, so a lot of people in the music business knew KB." He got fan mail from "places as far away as Goosebay, Labrador."[1]

WKBW became an instant success on July 4, 1958, when it launched the Top 40 format pioneered by Todd Storz, Gordon McLendon, and other station owners and operators in the mid-1950s. The formula was simple: play the Top 40 hit records over and over again regardless of style or quality. It didn't matter if it was rock & roll, traditional pop, R&B, country, folk, or anything else. If listeners liked it, Top 40 played it. For added excitement and variety, stations tossed in news, weather, and sports on the hour, as well as jingles, contests, and other gimmicks.[2]

WKBW dubbed its Top 40 sound "Future Sonic Radio." To promote the format, KB hired outstanding personality disc jockeys like Dick Biondi and funny man Perry Allen, who became radio ringmasters for the circus-like atmosphere at 1520 on the dial. Tommy Shannon was just a teenager when he landed a part-time job at the station as the host of a weekend show. "I was the kid on the staff," he explains. "KB played that up. I was . . . 18 or 19 and a hometown guy." Teenage listeners related to the handsome, young deejay, making him a local celebrity before he was 21.[3]

In 1960 Shannon and his friend Phil Todaro, decided to write a new jingle for the program. "We ended up with a melody that was very simple, only about four or five chord changes," recalls Shannon. "The lyrics were simple, too: 'top tunes, news, and weather, so glad we can get together on the Tommy Shannon show . . . KB radio.'" Unlike the station's other deejay themes, which sounded like 1950s pop, the Shannon-Todaro ditty had a rock & roll edge. Listeners were soon calling in or writing to request the jingle. "I thought 'I've got a winner here,'" says Shannon, "but I didn't know what to do with it."[4]

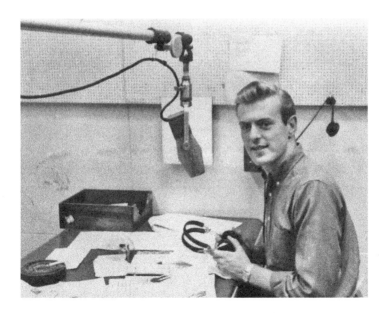

Tom Shannon in WKBW studio (Buffalo Stories Archive / The Steve Cichon Collection)

Fate intervened when Shannon hosted a record hop at a local high school. Four teenagers who had recently formed a band, approached the deejay and volunteered to play an instrumental version of his theme song during the dance. Tom told them to have a go at it. "They did such a great job that Phil and I decided to get them into a studio to record them." A few weeks later the record was released on a local label. The title, "Wild Weekend," was the tagline for Shannon's show. The record became a hit in Buffalo in 1960 and a Top 10 hit in 1963 when it was reissued nationally on the Swan label.[5]

The record's backstory and the garage band's fairy-tale success demonstrate the folk nature of early rock & roll. "Wild Weekend" was not written by Brill Building professionals in New York City to target youth culture. It was composed on the spot by a young deejay in Buffalo and then recorded by local high school students: Jim Kipler (guitar), Mickey Kipler (sax), Paul Balon (bass), Tommy Gorman (drums). Lightning struck when the record resonated with young listeners across America. This was rock & roll from the bottom up.[6]

The Rebels' "Wild Weekend" is just one of thousands of songs that became hits because of Top 40 radio. This chapter explores several of the diverse styles heard on Top 40 stations in the early 1960s. It covers rock instrumentals (except for surf instrumentals found in chapter 4), traditional pop, novelty records, country songs, and folk music. Not only did these disparate sounds contribute to a "Wild Weekend" of "top tunes, news, and weather" for radio audiences, but they echoed the rhythms of life in Kennedy's America.

THE "TWANGS" THE "THANG"

Instrumentals had been a pop music staple since the late 1800s. They appealed to rock & roll fans for the same reasons they had to earlier audiences: they had great melodies and were perfect for dancing, romancing, or just having fun. The first big rock & roll instrumental hit was Bill Doggett's "Honky Tonk" (1956). Other instrumentals soon followed, including Bill Justis's "Raunchy" in 1957; the Champs' "Tequila" and Duane Eddy and the Rebels' "Rebel Rouser" in 1958; and Johnny and the Hurricanes' "Crossfire" and Santo and Johnny's "Sleepwalk" in 1959.

Of all these pioneer groups, Duane Eddy and the Rebels were the most successful. Duane began his career playing with country bands around Phoenix,

Arizona. "I had a friend who was a deejay that became a record producer named Lee Hazlewood," says Eddy. "He decided to do an instrumental . . . with me. It was called 'Moovin' N' Groovin.'"[7] Released on Jamie Records, it became a minor hit in 1958.

The band's follow-up, "Rebel Rouser" (1958), reached number 6. The upbeat record featured Duane's unique twangy guitar, a wailing sax, and big beat perfect for fast dancing. He later recalled how the hit came about. "We went in the studio one morning, and we had no idea what we were going to do. I just started noodling around with a melody idea I had," explains Eddy. "I had the drummer play a backbeat, and with the melody that was developing we thought we'd have a sax answer it. We didn't have a [rock & roll] sax in Phoenix in those days . . . so we cut the track there that morning and later Lee took it to LA and overdubbed Gil Bernal on sax and a [R&B rock] group called the Sharps, who did the 'oohs' and 'ahs' and handclaps and yells."[8]

"Rebel Rouser" established Duane Eddy's famous "twang" sound. "That was something that somebody just said in the studio one day, that it sounded sort of 'twangy,' and we all laughed," says Eddy. "We then decided to call the first album *Have Twangy Guitar Will Travel* . . . and, it stuck through the years." He adds, "I've heard [the sound] described as everything from oversized telephone wires strung across the Grand Canyon to rattlesnake juice and cactus juice . . . We had an interesting echo chamber that we jerry-rigged from an old 2000 gallon water tank with a speaker on one end and a mike on the other . . . and then we overdubbed it and mixed it at Gold Star Studios in LA and added a little bit more of their echo on it. It gave it just a huge, big sound."[9]

Eddy's unique guitar sound, teen-oriented records, and teen-idol good looks made him a star. "Because They're Young," from Dick Clark's movie of the same name, became his most popular hit, climbing all the way to number 4 in 1960. The innovative rock instrumental featured Duane's twangy guitar backed by lush violins. Thinking the song would only be used in the movie, Duane wasn't thrilled when the record company released it as a single. "I thought, I can't play this on the road live because I don't carry a string orchestra with me," he explains. "But it became . . . the biggest hit I ever had."[10]

Eddy's musical style connected with listeners. All too often, musicians weren't "playing for the people that much," he says. "They don't play something that folks who don't play the instrument can understand. That's something our records did in those days." Duane's emphasis on melody provided excellent material for garage bands. "If young groups . . . couldn't sing," he explains, "they could learn to play 'Rebel Rouser,' and they could go play for a dance and they would have a hit record to play." Eddy proved that a guitarist's "speed and complexity did not necessarily equal skill and technique," says music writer Dan Forte. "There were also qualities such as tone, timing, dynamics, and, most of all, feel and expression. And those qualities seemed to be the ones synonymous with making hits."[11]

Teenagers loved Eddy's records. "The audiences thought we were cool because we were reflecting how they saw themselves," suggests Duane. "Rebel Rouser" mirrored teenagers' self-image. "First Love, First Tears" (1959) spotlighted young romance. "Shazam!" (1960) tapped into kids' love of comic book heroes. "(Dance with the) Guitar Man" (1962) capitalized on dance fads like the Twist. Popular culture influenced other hits. Duane recorded themes from TV shows and movies, including *Peter Gunn* and *Pepe*. The popularity of Westerns set the stage for "Ramrod" and "The Ballad of Paladin." Even the records' sound evoked the West: "I was a big fan of Roy Rogers and Gene Autry when I was a kid," explains Eddy, "and the Southwest [where Duane lived] has a wide-open feel to it. I guess the music kind of reflected that."[12]

Duane Eddy's sound and style suggest that rock & roll was not as rebellious as common wisdom has it. Early rock & roll "was very rebellious from the Tin Pan Alley type of music that was prevalent in those days from the ballad singers like Sinatra, Bing Crosby, and Patti Page," says Duane. "But socially it wasn't rebellious." Even rock & roll's close connection to Black music was in step with the era's growing demands for racial equality. Eddy was shocked by the segregation he witnessed firsthand when he and African American artists toured the South. "The first time I went out on a bus tour the only person I knew . . . was [African American singer] Thurston Harris. I sat down next to him. We left New York City about 8 o'clock in the morning . . . about ten or twelve acts."[13] When the bus arrived in Maryland it stopped at a Greyhound bus station. Since Eddy had spent the entire trip sitting next to Harris, he assumed they would also eat together. As they climbed off the bus, Thurston looked at Duane and said, "Well you go in that door and I'll go in this door." Thinking Harris was joking and the two doors led to the same eating area, Duane cracked, "No, you go in that door, and I'll go in this one." "No, I'm serious," replied Thurston. Duane never forgot the exchange that followed: "I said, 'What do you mean?' He said, 'Look.' I looked up and saw signs over the door. One said 'Colored.' One said 'White' . . . I turned red as a beet and . . . stumbled back to the bus and refused to eat." Duane added, "I got an education that day."[14]

Like many rock & roll artists, Duane Eddy helped undermine racism. "I think rock & roll played a big part in those days because white kids and Black kids before that stayed pretty much to themselves. There was a lot of segregation," explains Eddy. "But, we used to do these big bus tours, and there'd be . . . a mixture of Black acts and white acts." Teenagers would go to these shows, says Eddy, "and there would be [white] kids seeing this for the first time who had not seen Black acts before . . . and they were loving it." The same was true for African American teenagers. "A lot of Black kids came to our shows," says Eddy, "and they probably had not done that before. I think that was a first when they mixed together at shows."[15]

Eddy's records were also small victories for integration. His hits appeared on *Billboard*'s pop charts and R&B charts. Most of his recording sessions included both Black and white musicians, as well as African American singers. The Sharps provided backup singing, handclaps, and rebel yells on "Rebel Rouser" and other hits, while the Blossoms (a Los Angeles girl group that included Darlene Love) were billed as the Rebelettes when they sang on records such as "(Dance with the) Guitar Man."

In 1994 Duane Eddy was inducted into the Rock & Roll Hall of Fame in recognition of his innovative guitar style and numerous hit singles and albums. The best explanation for his success is summed up by the title of his 1960 album: *The "Twangs" the "Thang"*.

Duane Eddy and the Rebels weren't the only musicians from the 1950s to find success in the early 1960s. For example, veteran Nashville studio musician Floyd Cramer scored three Top 10 hits: "Last Date" (1960), "On the Rebound" (1961), and "San Antonio Rose" (1961). Sandy Nelson connected even more with young listeners. Just twenty years old when he hit the charts with "Teen Beat" (1959), the young drummer found continued success in the new decade with upbeat rockers like "Let There Be Drums" (1961). The Fireballs' success also spanned two decades. Their first Top 40 hit was "Torquay" (1959), followed by "Bulldog" (1960) and "Quite a Party" (1961). After adding Jimmy Gilmer as a vocalist, they earned additional hits, including "Sugar Shack" (a number 1 record in 1963), "Daisy Petal Pickin'" (1964), and "Bottle of Wine" (1968).[16]

NEW WAVE OF INSTRUMENTAL ROCK & ROLL

A second wave of instrumental groups hit the charts in the early 60s. The Ventures led the way, scoring a number 2 hit with their first release, "Walk—Don't Run" (1960). Formed in the Tacoma/Seattle area by Bob Bogle and Don Wilson, the group developed a unique sound using two electric guitars, an electric bass, and drums. Original members included Bogle (who played lead guitar and later bass), Wilson (rhythm guitar), and Nokie Edwards (bass and lead guitar, later replaced by Gerry McGee). Skip Moore played the drums on "Walk—Don't Run," but was then replaced by Howie Johnson, who in turn was replaced by Mel Taylor.

"Walk—Don't Run" was written and recorded by jazz guitarist Johnny Smith in 1954. Three years later, Nashville guitarist Chet Atkins did a country version. Wilson and Bogle loved Atkins' record, but couldn't duplicate the sound. "Chet's version was a complicated semi-jazz thing that he played finger-style," explains Don. "We tried playing along with it, but we couldn't even come close. It was far too advanced for us . . . In about three months, we had it completely rearranged into a rock style that we were satisfied with."[17]

The Ventures' backstory illustrates how rock & roll often began at the grass-roots level. Don Wilson and Bob Bogle were construction workers by day and played rock & roll in bars at night. No record company wanted to sign them, so the two paid a fee to record "Walk—Don't Run" in a local studio. Afterward, they released the record on their own label. Wilson's mother threw copies in her car and made the rounds to various radio stations. When Seattle's top rock & roll station, KJR, started playing "Walk—Don't Run," Dolton Records signed the group and reissued the song on their label. The record debuted on the pop charts on July 18, 1960. Five weeks later it peaked at number 2. The record earned the group two *Billboard* awards for "Favorite Instrumental Single of the Year" and "Most Promising Instrumental Group."[18]

No one was more surprised than the Ventures. "Our main intent," says Bogle, "was to become known locally, make more money in clubs and possibly make a living."[19] Instead, they struck rock & roll gold. Before 1960 was out the Ventures were the hottest instrumental band around. "Walk—Don't Run" struck a responsive chord with young listeners and garage bands everywhere. It had a fresh guitar sound, unforgettable melody, and great beat that was perfect for dancing. Even the title resonated with kids accustomed to having teachers, parents, and other adults ordering them to slow down. The lesson to be learned from the Ventures' instant stardom was not lost on music business insiders: If you want a hit record, target the huge baby boom audience.

The Ventures were inspired by earlier bands. "Duane Eddy was my biggest influence ever," says Don Wilson. "I still try to play [his songs] . . . on stage. It's a compliment to him." But the Ventures soon developed a unique sound that was the product of necessity. "I played very percussion-type, rhythm guitar because [initially] we had no drum and we had no bass player, just two guitars," explains Wilson. "Bob tried to fill out what an organ or a piano or whatever might do, by playing a melody and then coming to a certain note, maybe the endnote and he would play a chord for that note." People were amazed by the unusual sound, but Don points out that the innovation was a natural development. "Once we did pick up a bass player and a drummer, that was our style," he says. "We didn't know anything else."[20]

After "Walk—Don't Run," the Ventures released other teen-oriented records that were perfect for dancing. "Perfidia," a rock & roll version of a pop instrumental from 1941, made it to number 15 on the charts in 1960. "Ram-Bunk-Shush," a cover of Bill Doggett's 1957 hit, peaked at number 29 in 1961. Three years later the Ventures made it back into the Top 10 with "Walk, Don't Run '64," a surf version of their debut hit. And, in 1969 they earned a number 4 hit with "Hawaii Five-O" (from the TV series).

Unlike most rock & roll acts, the Ventures had more success with albums than singles. Once again, necessity was the mother of invention. When their singles stalled on the charts, the group turned to albums. "We had to come up with ideas for survival," says Don Wilson. "What we started doing was to take Top 40 hits . . . and Venturize them . . . by playing them with our sound."[21]

The band's distinct sound was powered by the creative interplay of guitars enhanced by reverb. "Any guitar player would tell you, Bob [Bogle] is the most unique-sounding guitar player ever," insists Wilson. "The way he used to do the whammy bar—that vibrato bar. He kept his little finger on it while he played it all the time. He'd make it sound, like at the end of a chord, *Wow-wow*. We were the first ones to ever get recognized for doing anything like that." Wilson's guitar style was equally recognizable. "I'm a little different than the ordinary rhythm guitar player who's got to just sit back there and strum," explains Don. "I have a few things of my own, like the rundowns on 'Pipeline' and 'Walk, Don't Run '64', so I get a little glory." The Ventures' records also featured a distinct echo sound. "The engineer that we had at the time on our first three albums . . . recorded on two track," explains Wilson. "He had this echo chamber which was a microphone hanging from the shower. We used that. That might have been a little bit different."[22]

In an era when most albums were just collections of unrelated songs or greatest hits, the Ventures' albums featured original songs and covers of hits organized around particular themes. *Twist with the Ventures* (1962), for example, included songs about the dance fad sparked by Chubby Checker, while *Surfing* (1963) showcased songs about the surf craze. The Ventures' ample use of vibrato and glissandos made them both popularizers and pioneers of surf music's "wet sound." "They have labeled us a surf group," says Don Wilson. "We're much more than surf, and I'm not putting surf down . . . It just so happens that we put out a surfing album and it's one of the biggest albums that has ever sold. So, people identify us with that."[23]

The Ventures' signature guitar sound and wide-ranging repertoire earned them a huge fan base in the United States and abroad, particularly Japan where they became more popular than the Beatles. In the six plus decades after their debut in 1960, the Ventures sold over 100 million records and landed numerous hit singles and albums on the *Billboard* charts. When the group was inducted into the Rock & Roll Hall of Fame in 2008, John Fogerty stated matter-of-factly, "The Ventures are the most popular instrumental rock & roll band of all time."[24]

* * *

Other new rock instrumental groups joined the Ventures on the pop charts. In 1960 the Viscounts earned a hit with the eerie "Harlem Nocturne." The record begins with an ominous bass line followed by the reverb of an electric guitar and the shimmering sound of cymbals. A throbbing sax then takes charge, unleashing a sexy if not outright wicked solo. The following year the Mar-Keys had an even bigger hit with an even sexier song. "Last Night" sounded like the type of bump-and-grind music one might hear in a strip joint. The record featured a sax riff that oozed sexuality, occasionally interrupted by a lusty voice groaning "ah, last night."[25]

New bands celebrated other teenage interests. Dancing set the stage for the Phil Upchurch Combo's "You Can't Sit Down, Part 2" (1961), fast cars powered the Duals' "Stick Shift" (1961), and a familiar cheer heard at high school sporting events inspired the Routers' "Let's Go" (1962). Instrumentals with novel approaches also appealed to young listeners. Billy Joe and the Checkmates cracked the Top 10 in 1962 with "Percolator (Twist)," which combined a new dance craze with a popular Maxwell House coffee commercial. And, saxophonist Boots Randolph earned a Top 40 hit with the ebullient "Yakety Sax" (1963), which evoked the comedic feel of the Coasters' 1958 rock & roll classic "Yakety Yak."[26]

Rock instrumentals mirrored other aspects of Kennedy's America. Gains made by the civil rights movement opened doors for integrated groups like Booker T. and the MG's, who scored their first hit in 1962 with "Green Onions." The era's growing multiculturalism and diversity produced popular songs such as Mongo Santamaria's "Watermelon Man" and Ray Barretto's "El Watusi" (both in 1963). The race to space launched the Tornadoes' "Telstar" all the way up to number 1 in 1962. And as the Cold War heated up between the United States and Soviet Union, the notion of American Exceptionalism and its connection to the American West spilled over into rock & roll. As adults watched a flood of Western movies and TV shows, teenagers celebrated the West with hits like Johnny and the Hurricanes' "Red River Rock" (1959), Jorgen Ingmann's "Apache" (1961), and the Ramrods' "(Ghost) Riders in the Sky" (1961).

Rock & roll instrumentals appealed to young listeners partly because they offered unforgettable melodies and sounds. "The record business like many other things is a band wagon business," explains Duane Eddy. "If something is happening then everybody is open to it." Garage bands and Top 40 radio jumped on the instrumental band wagon. "Radio loved instrumentals . . . which gave them a great intro to the news," suggests Eddy. "They wouldn't have to interrupt a song with lyrics. Deejays would just put on an instrumental and fade it out when the second hand came along to the hour, and they would start reading the news."[27]

Rock instrumentals became less popular after 1963. Although they didn't disappear completely, the changing times made it harder for them to compete. The rise of folk music placed greater emphasis on lyrics, while the British Rock Invasion accelerated changing musical tastes. "That's when I faded away," says Duane Eddy. "When the Beatles came, the whole music situation changed."[28]

WONDERLAND BY NIGHT

Rock instrumentals were just one part of the eclectic mix featured on Top 40 radio. Audiences could hear an incredible variety of songs played one after another—rock & roll, traditional pop, jazz, novelty records, R&B, country, and folk. "You could go from 'Because They're Young' and 'Theme from a Summer Place' to Little Richard and 'Tutti Frutti,'" says Duane Eddy. "There just wasn't anything that couldn't happen.[29]

Although performers came from vastly different musical backgrounds, they all hoped to score a major hit by tapping into the teenage market, which was growing rapidly in the early 60s due to the millions of baby boomers entering high school. In 1961 a 37-year-old German orchestra leader named Bert Kaempfert accomplished that goal with his million-seller, "Wonderland by Night."[30]

Kaempfert's record debuted on America's pop charts on November 14, 1960, less than one week after John F. Kennedy was elected president. By the time JFK was inaugurated on January 20, 1961, the pop instrumental was the number 1 record in the country. The coincidence is striking. Just as a fairytale-like mood would surround Kennedy's Camelot, a similar dreamlike quality enveloped Kaempfert's achingly beautiful record. The song more than lived up to its evocative title as teenagers slow-danced to it or fell asleep listening to it at night.

The success of "Wonderland by Night" demonstrates that many rock & roll fans weren't locked into one musical style. They were willing to listen to and buy any record on Top 40 radio that appealed to them. Number 1 hits such as "Wonderland by Night," Percy Faith's "Theme from a Summer Place" (1960), and Lawrence Welk's "Calcutta" (1961) demonstrated that record companies could make a ton of money selling pop instrumentals to baby boomers. Other teen-oriented pop instrumentals soon followed. Henry Mancini's "Song for Young Lovers" (1960) and Bill Pourcel's "Our Winter Love" (1963) showcased romance. David Rose's "The Stripper" (1962) spotlighted sex. And, at the end of the 1960/61 school year, Adrian Kimberly (actually Don Everly with studio musicians) scored a Top 40 hit with a bouncy big-band version of the graduation march, based on Elgar's *Pomp and Circumstance March No.1*, replete with a girls' choir shouting "no more pencils, no more books, no more teachers' dirty looks."[31]

Throughout the early 60s numerous pop instrumentals influenced by classical music and jazz made the *Billboard* charts. This new development coincided with the arrival of a new First Family that promoted the arts in the White House. "From 1961 to 1963 . . . the Kennedys hosted numerous concerts and performances and infused the Executive Mansion and the country with the same vitality, youth, and idealism that followed them on their journey to the White House," notes the White House Historical Association.[32] Young Americans who admired the president and First Lady couldn't help but notice White House galas featuring cellist Pablo Cassals, the Greater Boston Youth Symphony, or jazz artists such as the Paul Winter Sextet.

The high profile of jazz and classical music spilled over to Top 40 radio. Kokomo (a.k.a. pianist Jimmy Wisner) made it to number 8 on the charts with "Asia Minor," a pop version of Grieg's Piano Concerto in A Minor. B. Bumble and the Stingers earned two Top 30 hits by rocking the classics: "Bumble Boogie" (1961) was based on Rimsky-Korsakov's "Flight of the Bumble Bee," while "Nut Rocker" (1962) was adapted from Tchaikovsky's *The Nutcracker*.

Jazz musicians also attracted young audiences. In 1961 the Dave Brubeck Quartet's "Take Five" came in at number 25, while the Don Shirley Trio's "Water Boy" peaked at number 40. In 1962 Mr. Acker Bilk—an English clarinetist with a teacher-sounding moniker—scored a number 1 hit with "Stranger on the Shore." That same year, Kenny Ball and His Jazzmen reached number 2 with "Midnight in Moscow," which hit the charts as relations worsened between the

United States and Russia. The Village Stompers also earned a number 2 hit with "Washington Square" (1963), which benefited from Greenwich Village's reputation as the place to be for jazz artists, folksingers, beatniks, and bohemians.[33]

Pop instrumentals mirrored other aspects of daily life in Kennedy's America. TV shows inspired Henry Mancini's "Mr. Lucky" (1960), Lawrence Welk's "My Three Sons" (1961), and Nelson Riddle's "Route 66 Theme" (1962). Songs from movies also became hits, including: Don Costa, "Never on Sunday" (1960); Ferrante & Teicher, "Exodus" (1961); and Henry Mancini, "Moon River" (1961).

Veteran pop vocalists scored numerous hits with songs that appealed to baby boomers. Frank Sinatra earned a Top 30 hit with a suggestive version of "Ole McDonald" (1960). Tony Bennett made it to number 19 with one of the top romantic ballads of 1962, "I Left My Heart in San Francisco." The following year two pop singers cracked the Top 10. Al Martino's "I Love You Because" was perfect for slow dancing at record hops, while Nat "King" Cole's "Those Lazy-Hazy-Crazy Days of Summer" prepared young listeners for summer fun.

Hits by younger pop singers had even more appeal in the teenage market. Connie Stevens, who played Cricket Blake on TV's *Hawaiian Eye*, scored a hit in 1959 singing a duet with Edd "Kookie" Byrnes (the cool car hop on *77 Sunset Strip*). "Kookie, Kookie (Lend Me Your Comb)" spotlighted the jive-talking Kookie and his exasperated girlfriend, who wants him to stop combing his hair and kiss her. Teenagers loved the hip slang and romantic banter, sending the record all the way to number 4.[34]

Other young pop artists found success with songs by Brill Building composers who knew how to reach teenage listeners. Steve Lawrence recorded several hits about young love, including "Go Away Little Girl," a King and Goffin composition that became a number 1 hit in 1963. That same year, Lawrence's wife, Eydie Gorme, scored a Top 10 hit with Barry Mann and Cynthia Weil's "Blame It On the Bossa Nova," while Andy Williams made it to number 2 with "Can't Get Used to Losing You," written by Doc Pomus and Mort Shuman. Dionne Warwick's career took off when she teamed up with pop composers Burt Bacharach and Hal David to record romantic ballads that resonated with young audiences. Her first big hit came in 1962 with "Don't Make Me Over," followed by Top 10 records such as "Anyone Who Had a Heart" (1963) and "Walk on By" (1964).

Teenagers' growing awareness of international perspectives might help explain Top 40 hits that pop singers recorded partly or entirely in foreign languages, for example: Lolita, "Sailor" (1960); Joe Dowell, "Wooden Heart" (1961); Emilio Pericoli, "Al Di La" (1962); Kyu Sakomoto, "Sukiyaki" (1963); Wayne Newton, "Danke Schoen" (1963). Significantly, Newton's record debuted on the pop charts just three weeks after President Kennedy gave his famous "Ich bin ein Berliner" speech.

Other hits by pop artists suggest that young Americans subscribed to the traditional values of the era's Cold War culture. Religion informed Vic Dana's "Little Altar Boy" (1962) and Stan Kenton's "Mama Sang a Song" (1962). Marriage and family values were idealized on Patti Page's "Mom and Dad's Waltz" (1961) and Bob Braun's "Till Death Do Us Part" (1962). Mainstream attitudes toward gender came through loud and clear on hits such as Connie Stevens's "Sixteen Reasons" (1960), which featured an adoring young woman explaining why she loves her boyfriend.

Occasionally, a pop song served notice that the times were beginning to change. "I'm a Woman" (1963), sung by Peggy Lee and written by Leiber and Stoller, was virtually a feminist declaration of independence. The super woman on the record transcends the ultimate wife and mother of the 1950s. Although she still is the perfect mom, housewife, and lover, she now exhibits a new confidence and defiant attitude. "I can make a dress out of a feed bag," she insists, "and I can make a man out of you." Lee's bold pronouncement debuted on the charts eleven months before Lesley Gore's "You Don't Own Me." Both were early signs that feminism was gaining ground in Kennedy's America. Listeners got the message when Peggy Lee sang, "I'm a woman! W-O-M-A-N . . . and that's all."[35]

Many rock & roll fans loved traditional pop music. Johnny Mathis records became a staple for a young generation that enjoyed the Twist, but also loved slow dancing to romantic ballads. Mathis established himself in the 1950s as a younger version of crooners like Frank Sinatra and Nat "King" Cole. By the end of the decade he was the rock & roll generation's chief supplier of intimate mood music thanks to hits like "Chances Are" (1957) and "The Twelfth of Never" (1957). Mathis grew even more popular in the early 60s when baby boomers—rock & roll's second generation of teenagers—arrived on the scene. No high school record hop or party was complete without Johnny Mathis records. When lights dimmed, lovers of rock & roll turned appreciatively to Mathis's romantic ballads, including new hits like "Maria" (1960), "Gina" (1962), and "What Will Mary Say" (1963). In Kennedy's America, making out to the music of Johnny Mathis became a teenage rite of passage.

Pop singer Trini Lopez also became a favorite of young listeners. Born in a Dallas barrio to Mexican parents, Lopez started singing and playing the guitar as a kid. His dynamic performance style later caught the attention of fellow Texan Buddy Holly, who introduced him to producer Norman Petty. Lopez recorded a few songs at Petty's studio in Clovis, New Mexico. When the records flopped, Lopez moved to Los Angeles. Soon afterward, Frank Sinatra caught Trini's sensational act in a popular Hollywood club and signed him to his new Reprise Label. Trini's first album, *Trini Lopez Live at P.J.'s*, came out in 1963 and made him a star.

Lopez became one of the most popular and innovative singers on Top 40 radio in the early 60s. At a time when most hits were recorded in the studio and featured lush arrangements, Trini found success with songs recorded live with a small backup band. His repertoire included rock & roll, folk, traditional pop, even songs from Broadway musicals. Lopez was one of the first artists to combine folk music with a rock & roll beat, as evidenced by his hit version of Peter, Paul, and Mary's "If I Had a Hammer" (1963). And his Hispanic appearance and unabashed singing style helped bring ethnicity to the fore in early 60s rock & roll.

Trini's success personified the American Dream. He started his career singing on the streets of a poor Mexican neighborhood in Dallas and wound up performing on network TV and in glitzy nightclubs across the country. He even became pals with Frank Sinatra. "He was like my father," says Lopez. "I traveled with him and the Rat Pack in his Lear jet."[36] Ironically, the very things that helped Trini Lopez become a star—a lively nightclub act, varied musical repertoire, and wide-ranging appeal—made him a contrived pop star rather than an authentic rock singer in the eyes of many rock & roll fans.

DOES YOUR CHEWING GUM LOSE ITS FLAVOR?

Rock & roll audiences loved pop novelty songs. One of the most popular novelty hits of the early 60s was performed by British pop singer Lonnie Donegan. He scored a Top 5 hit on the American charts in 1961 with a record aimed directly at teenagers. The title boiled all the important questions in life down to one question: "Does Your Chewing Gum Lose Its Flavor (On the Bedpost Overnight)?" Donegan's answer suggests that many adolescents prided themselves on not taking their elders or life too seriously. "If your mother says don't chew it do you swallow it in spite?" he asks. "Can you catch it on your tonsils, can you heave it left & right?" He then mimics a choking sound: "eh, eh."[37]

Donegan's hit and similar novelty songs were part of a Tin Pan Alley tradition that dated back to the nineteenth century. They typically attracted attention with gimmicks or by poking fun at people, places, politics, and popular culture. One of the first novelty hits was Russell Hunting's "Michael Casey Taking the Census" (1892). The early twentieth century welcomed additional comedy songs, including Arthur Collins and Byron Harlan's "The Right Church, but the Wrong Pew" (1909), Billy Jones's "Yes! We Have No Bananas" (1923), and Spike Jones's "Der Fuehrer's Face" (1942).

Teenagers and the rise of rock & roll provided new comedy material. In 1956 Nervous Norvus (a.k.a. Jimmy Drake) earned a Top 10 hit with "Transfusion," which appealed to teenage interests in fast cars, slang words, and sick jokes. That same year Buchanan and Goodman hit it big with "The Flying Saucer (Parts 1 & 2)," a number 3 hit that poked fun at rock & roll, newscasts, and recent UFO sightings. Three teen-oriented novelty records became number 1 hits in 1958: David Seville's "Witch Doctor," David Seville and the Chipmunks' "The Chipmunk Song," and Sheb Wooley's "Purple People Eater." The following year, Spencer & Spencer (i.e., deejay Mickey Shore and Dickie Goodman of "Flying Saucer" fame) found success with "Russian Band Stand." The parody of Dick Clark's TV show echoed Cold War stereotypes that portrayed communists as blood-thirsty villains.[38]

Comedy records remained extremely popular in the early 1960s. Along with all the novelty hits earned by rock & roll singers (e.g., Brian Hyland's "Itsy Bitsy

Teenie Weenie Yellow Polka Dot Bikini" and the Trashmen's "Surfin' Bird"), there were comedy records by pop artists.[39] Ray Stevens earned his first Top 40 hit in 1961 with a novelty song that assured listeners they could cure all their ills by taking the new wonder drug described by the record's very long title: "Jeremiah Peabody's Poly Unsaturated Quick Dissolving Fast Acting Pleasant Tasting Green and Purple Pills."

Stevens followed up with other songs aimed at the teen market. "Santa Claus is Watching You" (1962) offered a darker and funnier version of old St. Nick. "He's everywhere, he's everywhere," warns Ray. Mr. Claus turns out to be the covert head of the CIA, and he's keeping his lascivious eyes on a young woman to make sure she's giving her boyfriend "good lovin'" every night. Stevens scored an even bigger hit in 1963 with "Harry the Hairy Ape," a rollicking tale about an animal that escapes from the zoo, terrorizes the city, and winds up becoming a rock & roll star.

Novelty records also took aim at American politics. During the 1960 presidential campaign between John F. Kennedy and Richard Nixon, the Chipmunks chimed in with "Alvin for President." Kennedy's victory inspired comedian Vaughn Meader to record a comedy album, *The First Family*, on which Meader and an ensemble cast impersonated the young president, his family, and various government officials. They poked gentle fun at Kennedy policies, practices, and family members. Although presidential parodies are now common, few comedians in the early 60s were bold enough to mock a sitting president. Not knowing how patriotic Americans of the Cold War era would react, the liner notes on Meader's album offered a disclaimer: "This album is for fun! Things are being suggested and said here about some of the great people of our time, and perhaps the very fact that they are able to laugh with us and enjoy this album is in part what makes them the great people that they are."[40]

Some listeners were not convinced. James Hagerty, press secretary for former president Eisenhower, insisted Meader's album disrespected the presidency and that "every Communist country in the world would love this record." But Kennedy had a more positive reaction, at least publicly. When a reporter asked whether he was entertained or annoyed by the album, the president smiled and said, "I listened to Mr. Meader's record, but I thought it sounded more like Teddy than it did me. So, *he's* annoyed."[41]

Kennedy's good-natured response cleared the way for Meader's success. Album tracks were played repeatedly on rock & roll stations across America. The album debuted on *Billboard* just before Christmas 1962, and zoomed to the top of the charts. *The First Family* eventually sold over 7.5 million copies and won a Grammy for Best Album of the Year. The fact that teenagers loved it as much as their parents suggests that the two generations had similar interests and values.

At a time when white, Anglo-Saxon Protestants dominated American society and culture, novelty hits offered musical equivalents of racial and ethnic jokes. For example, Larry Verne's number 1 hit from 1960, "Mr. Custer," recycled numerous American Indian stereotypes, including jokes about scalping, Kemo Sabe, and "running around like a bunch of wild Indians."[42]

Even when novelty records appeared to be harmless fun, they could still have a negative impact. "The Astronaut," a 1961 comedy hit by Jose Jimenez (a.k.a. Bill Dana), is a perfect example. The record debuted in July, 1961, just two months after President Kennedy announced the expansion of the US space program. The comedy routine was recorded live and starred Dana as a Mexican American who has become NASA's top astronaut. The record begins with an interviewer asking the astronaut to introduce himself. "My name . . . Jose Jimenez," says Dana's character as the live audience erupts in laughter at his thick accent. The rest of the record features the bumbling Jose struggling to answer questions about the space program. Many listeners loved the character and began doing their own impressions in broken English. "The Astronaut" became a huge hit on Top 40 radio, while the accompanying album rocketed all the way up to number 5 on *Billboard's* Top 200 albums chart. Jose Jimenez became one of the most popular figures on television. Dana starred in his own sitcom and performed his character on variety shows and at the White House. Astronaut Alan Shepard even adopted "Jose" as his code name. Many of Jose's biggest fans came from the Latino community, including celebrities like Ricardo Montalban and Vikki Carr. "They loved Jose," said Dana, "and identified it as a unique character and not as a . . . negative thing." If some listeners found innocent humor in the caricature, others were offended or emboldened by the racial stereotype. By 1970 Dana realized it was time to retire the Jose character. "It was [intolerant] people I met in this country who would tell me 'Boy, shore love it when you play the dumb Mexican' that made me want to drop the character." Dana later regretted the decision. He explained in 2011: "In retrospect [Jose Jimenez] was a perfect example of a person that wanted to be assimilated into American culture, learn the language, always looked spiffy . . . not a bit of the racist stereotype about the unkempt Mexican."[43]

A 1963 hit by Lou Monte, an Italian American pop singer from Lyndhurst, New Jersey, also sent mixed messages about ethnicity. "Pepino the Italian Mouse," performed partly in Italian, featured a feisty mouse who sounded like Alvin the Chipmunk. The number 5 hit celebrated Italian American culture as much as it ridiculed it, which might explain why many proud Italian Americans loved the record. At the same time, Pepino may have reinforced the stereotype that ethnic groups like Italian Americans(who originally hailed from southern Italy) were inferior to Americans who were native English speakers or whose ancestors came from northern Europe. Some white, Anglo-Saxon Protestant Americans probably shook their heads in dismay when they heard Monte's crude threat to throw the mouse into the "bagno" (toilet).

In 1962 Ray Stevens scored a number 5 hit with another novelty record that played off ethnic stereotypes. "Ahab, the Arab" told a funny story about a dashing sheik who wore a turban and had a scimitar by his side. Every evening around midnight, he jumped on his camel Clyde and galloped off to the Sultan's tent for a rendezvous with the most beautiful woman in the Sultan's harem. Fatima of the Seven Veils had "rings on her fingers, bells on her toes, and a bone in her nose, ho ho." The bouncy song was a non-stop barrage of jokes about Arabian nights, sheiks, sand, and camels, punctuated by wise cracks about recent hits like "The Twist" and "Does Your Chewing Gum Lose Its Flavor." Stevens even managed to throw in imitations of Fatima, the Arabic language, and Clyde the camel. In a 1999 interview for NPR's *Rock & Roll America*, Ray explained how he wrote the song. "I don't know where the idea came from, but I wrote it the night before a [recording] session," he said. "In the dead of the night out of desperation,

I reached out into the ether and pulled this one out of a hat, and sure enough it became a big hit." Even his Clyde imitation wasn't planned in advance. "I just made that up during the recording session . . . I had no idea what a camel sounded like, but I guess I came pretty close," he joked.[44]

Few listeners in the early 60s complained about the song's stereotypes, but the situation eventually changed. "I remember 'Ahab, the Arab,' and I played the song when it was a big hit [in 1962] and it didn't bother me as an Arab American at the time," said disc jockey Casey Kasem in a 1996 NPR interview. "Then I became politically conscious and recognized that anything that defames any ethnic group has a political effect on the people from that country." Ray Stevens offered a different perspective. "Back during the time ['Ahab, the Arab'] was written, it was not intended as a slur on any ethnic group. It was just a fun song," said Ray in 1999. "[It] has no political overtones whatsoever intended. If they're read into it, I'm sorry for that but it wasn't even considered back in 1962."[45]

Novelty records such as "Ahab, the Arab," "Pepino the Italian Mouse," and "The Astronaut" were at best benign attempts at racial and ethnic humor, which were often applauded by minorities who appreciated becoming part of the American story. Arguably, these songs reinforced national identity in Cold War America. Just as Americans defined themselves in contrast to Russian communists, hit records that poked fun at racial, ethnic, or religious minorities marked the boundary between *Americans* and *others*. At worst, these songs reveal the prejudices and anxieties of Americans in the early 1960s—a Cold War era when many Americans felt the United States was the leader of the Free World and American culture based on white, Anglo-Saxon Protestant traditions trumped everything else.

COUNTRY MUSIC CROSSES OVER

Top 40 radio's eclectic playlists offered opportunities for traditional country music to reach rock & roll audiences. Not surprisingly, country songs about romance had great appeal. In 1960 the Little Dippers (a.k.a. the Anita Kerr Singers) made it to number 9 with "Forever," which captured the innocence of young love. Don Gibson earned two Top 30 hits singing about tragic love affairs: "Just One Time" (1960) and "Sea of Heartbreak" (1961). Claude King made it into the Top 10 with "Wolverton Mountain" (1962), a humorous tale about the perils of courtship. "They say don't go on Wolverton Mountain if you're looking for a wife," he warns. The reason is simple. The notorious Clifton Clowers lived up there and had a pretty daughter, but an even sharper knife.[46]

Rock & roll fans paid close attention to country songs about infidelity. Two hits in 1960 viewed the problem from different perspectives. Both blended traditional country music with suggestive lyrics that any listener past puberty could relate to. Hank Locklin scored a Top 10 hit with "Please Help Me, I'm Falling," a mournful ballad about a married man attracted to another woman. He begs her to "close the door to temptation, don't let me walk in." Skeeter Davis made the Top 40 with an answer song. In keeping with the era's mores, Skeeter tells the guy they could never be happy living in sin. But the song's title anticipates gender equality: "(I Can't Help You) I'm Falling Too."[47]

Some country artists found success in the Cold War era with songs that celebrated America's past. Marty Robbins earned a number 1 hit with "El Paso" (1960), an epic ballad about gunfights, posses, and romance set in the mythic West. Johnny Horton hit it big with songs about US history: his number 1 record "The Battle of New Orleans" (1959) highlighted Andrew Jackson's stunning victory against the British during the War of 1812, while "North to Alaska" (1960) followed heroic Americans seeking gold on the northern frontier.

Jimmy Dean also scored hits with patriotic records. He made it to number 1 in 1961 with "Big Bad John," a proud tale about a fictional American who represented the superiority of the common man. Dean returned in 1962 with three additional hits that underscored America's greatness. "Dear Ivan" suggested that ordinary Americans could prevent war with Russia more effectively than politicians. "P.T. 109" recalled John F. Kennedy's heroism during World War II. And "Steel Men" praised blue collar workers who built America, sometimes at the cost of their lives.

Country songs about religion also charted in an era when America was locked in a Cold War struggle against atheistic communists. The Browns earned a number 5 hit with "The Old Lamplighter" (1960), a nostalgic ballad with religious overtones that recalled simpler times. Religion also gave flight to Ferlin Husky's "Wings of a Dove" (1961), which soared all the way up to number 12.

The inspirational song assured listeners that God would always protect them, sending "down His love on the wings of a dove."[48]

In addition, country music that addressed social and political issues attracted many young listeners. Bob Luman's "Let's Think About Livin'" (1960) encouraged people to look past daily headlines about crime and violence. Instead, he advises, "Let's think about livin', let's think about life." As the civil rights movement picked up momentum, Rex Allen made the Top 20 with "Don't Go Near the Indians" (1963), a commentary about racial prejudice, while Johnny Cash found success with his insightful album *Bitter Tears (Ballads of the American Indian)* (1964). In 1963 Bobby Bare earned hits with "Detroit City" and "500 Miles Away from Home," two songs that showed not everyone shared the optimism of Kennedy's New Frontier. Both records featured despondent protagonists who, despite hard work, fail to achieve the American Dream.[49]

IF I HAD A HAMMER

Top 40 radio's varied playlists showcased folk music in the early 1960s. "If I Had a Hammer," written by folksingers Pete Seeger and Lee Hays in 1949, became a Top 10 record for Peter, Paul, and Mary in 1962. The hit helped transform folk music into one of pop music's most commercially successful styles. Although American folk music had been around for centuries, it didn't become a major commercial success until the 1950s and early 60s when it received wide exposure through radio, television, print media, and concerts on college campuses. The growing number of college students in post–World War II America offered a new market for folk, which seemed more authentic and socially relevant than most styles heard on Top 40 radio.

Folk music's rise actually occurred in two waves—one in the 1930s and 40s, the other in the 1950s and early 60s. In each case, the music emphasized its populist roots and progressive politics. Music scholars Ron Eyerman and Scott Barretta explain, "Folk music, played with unamplified, 'traditional' instruments such as the guitar and banjo, and expressing themes taken from real-life experience, was seen as authentic popular music, and opposed to the 'unauthentic' popular music produced by Tin Pan Alley and other dispensers of mass culture."[50]

Ironically, one of folk's best-known groups played a major role in the commercialization of the music. The Weavers—Pete Seeger, Lee Hays, Ronnie Gilbert, and Fred Hellerman—earned a number 1 hit in 1950 with their pop-influenced rendition of Leadbelly's folk classic "Goodnight, Irene." Their approach, which blended traditional folk with lush pop orchestration, resulted in additional pop hits such as "On Top of Old Smokey" (1951) and "Wimoweh" (1952). The group was surprised by the sudden success. "I guess we just stepped into a vacuum," explained Seeger. "The old pop music had exposed its vacuity, and the pop music business was trying desperately to find something that sells, and along came the group called the Weavers. And they zoomed to the top of the charts."[51]

The Weavers' success on the pop charts touched off a folk music craze. They became one of the hottest acts around, selling millions of records, appearing on radio and television, and playing to sell-out crowds across the country. Suddenly, everything changed. When Senator Joseph McCarthy and others fanned the flames of anti-communism in the early 1950s, a political witch hunt resulted. Thousands of careers were ruined and lives destroyed by mere allegations that individuals were communists or associates of communists. The House Un-American Activities Committee (HUAC) subpoenaed Seeger and Lee Hays to question them about alleged ties to the Soviet Union. Hays pleaded the Fifth, but Seeger took a more defiant stance, asserting First Amendment rights. "I am not going to answer any questions as to my association, my philosophical or religious beliefs or my political beliefs," Pete boldly told HUAC. "I think these are very improper questions for any American to be asked, especially under such compulsion as this."[52] Committee members were not pleased and held the singer in contempt of Congress. "I was sentenced to a year in jail because I wouldn't cooperate with that silly committee," said Seeger. "But I only spent about four hours in jail because my lawyer got me out on bail." Eventually an appeals court acquitted him of all charges. Decades later, all Seeger could do was shake his head in disbelief at the injustice and time spent on the legal process. "It was very hard on my wife and family," he noted. "My wife later joked 'next time no appeal. Let him go to jail.'"[53]

Although Pete Seeger avoided jail, irreparable damage was done. Decca terminated the Weavers' recording contract, and the four folksingers were blacklisted on TV and radio. Even after McCarthyism subsided the entertainment industry avoided the Weavers. Although record deals and offers for TV appearances no longer came their way, the folksingers continued to play concerts at college campuses and other venues. They even made a triumphant return to Carnegie Hall in 1955, which sparked renewed interest in folk music.

As McCarthyism became a distant memory, folk music made a comeback. New groups, which Seeger proudly described as "children of the Weavers," were soon popping up on college campuses and in coffee houses across America. The Kingston Trio, in particular, stood out. Bob Shane, Nick Reynolds, and Dave Guard, three college students from the San Francisco area, hit it big with a pop-influenced folk sound inspired by the Weavers. Seeger remembers his first contact with them. "[Dave Guard] got started because he sent me $1.59 for my little mimeographed book, *How to Play the Five-String Banjo*," explains Pete. "About a year later, he wrote me another letter. He said, 'we put that book to good use. I and two others now have a group called the Kingston Trio.'"[54]

The three young folk singers avoided political problems by crafting a sound and style that was more collegiate than beatnik. They had short hair, were clean-shaven, and wore matching striped shirts or other preppy attire. Rather than political or protest songs, they stuck mostly to standard folk ballads. The Kingston Trio scored a number 1 hit on the pop charts in 1958 with "Tom Dooley," a traditional ballad about a guy sentenced to death for killing a man. By the end of the decade the trio was one of the most popular groups on Top 40 radio. Their records were a smooth blend of folk and pop, often delivered with a humorous touch, as evidenced by hits such as "The Tijuana Jail" (1959) and "M.T.A." (1959).

The Kingston Trio's success continued into the 1960s with a string of hit singles and albums. Most of the releases were folk songs like "El Matador" (1960), "Bad Man Blunder" (1960), and "Reverend Mr. Black" (1963) that reinforced traditional values, but the trio occasionally recorded material with a harder edge. Young audiences loved the moody "Scotch and Soda" (1962), which dealt with getting high on lovin' and alcohol. "Greenback Dollar" (1963) questioned Americans' love of money and blipped out a swear word to ensure airplay on Top 40 radio, thereby adding a dash of rebelliousness to the group's image.

"Where Have All the Flowers Gone" (1962) was arguably the Kingston Trio's most political song. The anti-war record debuted on the charts in January 1962, just after the Berlin Crisis had brought the United States and Soviet Union to the brink of war. The song's depressing message would become even more relevant by October when the Cuban Missile Crisis threatened to end in nuclear holocaust. The hit record told a chilling tale about young girls picking flowers. They marry guys who go off to war. The soldiers die and are buried. Flowers spring up in graveyards. And, a new generation of little girls picks them. As the song ends, the Kingston Trio ask solemnly, "When will they ever learn?"[55]

The record label listed Pete Seeger as the composer. But the backstory reveals how difficult it is to trace origins of some folk songs. "The idea came from an old Russian song about soldiers galloping off to join the czar's army a hundred years ago," explains Pete. But then Seeger added phrases like "long time passing" and "when will they ever learn?" When a camp counselor heard Seeger's record, he began singing it to kids at a summer camp outside of New York City. To keep their interest, he added two more verses, "Where have all the soldiers gone? Gone to graveyards. Where have all the graveyards gone? Covered with flowers," explains Seeger. "The kids [at camp] liked the song turning on itself." Pete adds, "The kids went back [home] to New York City . . . and somehow Peter, Paul, and Mary heard it and started singing it. Then, the Kingston Trio heard it and made a record." When the Kingston Trio learned about Seeger's connection to the song, they listed him as the composer. Pete then assigned 20 percent of the royalties to the camp counselor who added the last two verses. Seeger laughed as he recalled one final complicating factor. "I thought I wrote the tune until years later a friend of mine . . . reminded me about an old Irish lumberjack song I used to perform years earlier . . . I just slowed it down."[56]

The Kingston Trio's commercial success coupled with the changing times sparked a folk music boom in the early 1960s. Americans of all ages were inspired by President John F. Kennedy's inaugural address, which included the memorable line "Ask not what your country can do for you—ask what you can do for your country." JFK's New Frontier promised a progressive agenda that would address civil rights, education, poverty, space, and more. The blossoming civil rights movement underscored the notion that change was in the wind.

Folk music, with its pedigree of activism, offered the perfect soundtrack for the nation's progressive mood. In late 1962 the Kingston Trio released an album entitled *New Frontier*, which captured the era's Zeitgeist. The liner notes were written by the group's newest member, John Stewart, who replaced Dave Guard in 1961. Stewart suggests that Kennedy's New Frontier is a call to action: "It seems . . . to be the watchword of the new generation." The album's title song spoke directly to young listeners as it echoed Kennedy's inaugural address about a new generation born to face the challenges at hand. "Let every man sing out freedom's song," proclaim the Kingston Trio. "This is the new frontier."[57]

Folk music's call to action resonated with young listeners. For many college students and baby boomers about to enter college, folk music suddenly seemed far more relevant and exciting than rock & roll songs about high school romance, the Twist, and cars. Hootenannies—practically New Frontier rallies—became the rage at high schools and college campuses across the country as folk music won over millions of new fans.

The number of folk songs on the pop charts grew rapidly. The Brothers Four earned a number 2 hit with "Greenfields" (1960). The following year the Highwaymen made it to number 1 with "Michael (Row the Boat Ashore)." Additional folk tunes hit the charts in 1962, including Peter, Paul, and Mary's "If I Had a Hammer," the Chad Mitchell Trio's "Lizzie Borden," and the New Christy Minstrels' "This Land is Your Land." Folk's popularity soared even higher in 1963 when Kennedy's presidency was at its zenith. Along with numerous hits by the Kingston Trio and Peter, Paul, and Mary, there were popular folk songs such as the Rooftop Singers' "Walk Right In," the New Christy Minstrels' "Green, Green," and Joan Baez's "We Shall Overcome," which she sang at the March on Washington in 1963.

Pete Seeger recalls how "We Shall Overcome" became a civil rights anthem. "Experts don't agree on the origin of the song," says Pete. By the early twentieth century, several religious songs had lyrics that suggested "I'll be alright someday" or "I'll overcome someday." An important change occurred in 1946 when workers in South Carolina, most of whom were Black women, went on strike against the American Tobacco Company. They sang numerous gospel songs on the picket lines, says Seeger, and one of the workers, Lucille Simmons, began singing an old gospel song about overcoming very slowly, almost like a funeral dirge. She made one important change. "Lucille changed the 'I' to 'We,' singing 'We will overcome,'" explains Seeger. "A white woman [Zilphia Horton] heard this song sung by the union folks." She loved it and began singing it for people at the Highlander Folk School in Tennessee, which "had long advocated races getting together and putting an end to Jim Crow and segregation."[58]

Seeger learned the song from Horton, and then added a few verses and printed it in his *People's Songs* newsletter in 1948. Shortly thereafter, Pete and fellow folksinger Frank Hamilton visited Los Angeles and heard a gospel choir perform "We Shall Overcome." "We were mightily impressed by that 'soul beat' they added," explained Pete. "Instead of dividing the beat into four little beats, [they] divided it into three little beats." Hamilton played that version for his friend, Guy Carawan, who worked at Highlander. "Guy taught the song to a bunch of young people at a workshop in 1960, and they loved it, especially with that soul beat," notes Seeger. "About a month or two later, Guy's at the founding convention of the Student Nonviolent Coordinating Committee, and they said 'Oh Guy, you'll have to teach us that song.'" Pete described what happened next. "When Guy stood up, everyone else stood and they crossed hands and swayed as they sang 'We Shall Overcome.' They didn't want him to stop." Within weeks the song spread throughout the South. "We Shall Overcome" was not just one of the songs associated with the civil rights movement, says Seeger, "It was *the* song." Pete suggests that one of the most extraordinary things about the song is that it offered a sense of hope that inspired people to action. "It's a contradiction right in the middle of existence," he explains. "You pray to God 'please improve things.' But then any sensible person realized they have a duty and you get out and try to do something yourself."[59]

The song's call to action inspired not just civil rights demonstrators but also folk singers and their audiences. Along with the folk singers on the pop charts, there were numerous others like Bob Dylan, Joan Baez, Phil Ochs, Odetta, Eric Andersen, and Tom Paxton, who began attracting audiences with albums that featured folk songs about social and political issues. But none of these artists would have greater commercial success in the early 1960s than a trio that arrived on the pop charts in 1962—Peter, Paul, and Mary.

* * *

By the end of 1962, Peter, Paul, and Mary had their first Top 10 hit, "If I Had a Hammer (The Hammer Song)," as well as the number 1 album in the country. Titled simply *Peter, Paul, and Mary*, the cover featured a photo of the young folksingers looking directly at the camera and smiling. Seated on a stool in the center was Mary Travers with long blonde hair. Standing to her right was Peter Yarrow. He had dark hair and a goatee, and held the top of his upright guitar. On the other side of Mary was the tall Paul Stookey. He, too, had dark hair and a goatee, and his guitar stood at his feet pointing upward. The brick wall behind them suggested they were in a coffee house, but these grinning folksingers were clearly not beatniks. The guys wore coats and ties, while the young woman wore a collegiate sweater and held a bouquet of yellow flowers. The back cover described "the folk singers three" as "rousing . . . and real." The dynamic songs on the album backed up the claim. Peter, Paul, and Mary wrapped their superb harmonies around classic folk songs such as "If I Had a Hammer," "Cruel War," "500 Miles," and "Where Have All the Flowers Gone." The liner notes made it clear that this group offered a fresh and new musical approach that required the listener's undivided attention. "No dancing, please," the liner notes declared boldly in a year when the Twist was still the rage.[60]

The trio's meteoric rise to the top of the pop charts reveals much about youth culture, the pop music scene, and the changing times. In 1961 Peter Yarrow's manager, Albert Grossman, asked him to consider forming a folk group. On Albert's recommendation, Yarrow went to a Greenwich Village coffee house to check out a possible member. "I saw Noel Stookey at the Gaslight," Peter recalled. "He was a comedian and also sang and played guitar. He was incredible." But Stookey was not a folksinger. "His background had nothing to do with it," explained Yarrow. "He had a rock & roll group, but he was really something."[61]

Not long afterward, Yarrow and Grossman were at the Folklore Center in Greenwich Village. "It was information central where all the folksingers would gather," says Yarrow. They noticed a picture on the wall of a young singer named Mary Travers. Intrigued, Grossman set up a meeting with Yarrow, Stookey, and Travers to discuss the possibility of forming a trio. "Noel Stookey . . . didn't know folk songs," recalls Peter, "so . . . we sang 'Mary Had a Little Lamb.'" The

Peter, Paul, and Mary's first album, 1962 (Richard Aquila Collection)

three singers and Grossman couldn't believe their ears. The harmonies were perfect, says Yarrow, "and, no matter who sang the lead, it was *incredible*." When Grossman suggested that they could call themselves "Peter, Paul, and Mary" to emphasize their individuality, Noel agreed to use "Paul Stookey" as a stage name.[62]

Grossman spent the following months rehearsing the trio. Their voices blended perfectly, and each person seemed to know intuitively how to contribute to the overall sound. Their intricate three-part harmonies weaved in and out effortlessly, adding fresh touches to traditional folk ballads, gospel tunes, and topical songs about politics, war, and daily life. After countless hours of rehearsing, Peter, Paul, and Mary were ready for their debut at the Bitter End, the premier coffee house in Greenwich Village. "The first night we sang the audience went bananas," Yarrow later recalled. "The next night you couldn't get in. And, that was the case for the rest of . . . the five or six weeks we were there."[63]

Grossman landed them a recording deal with Warner Brothers, and they got right to work on their first album. Released in March 1962, it shot up to number 1. The first single off the album was "Lemon Tree," written by Will Holt. That song "opened the door," explained Mary Travers in a 1998 NPR interview. "'Lemon Tree' wasn't really a folk song. It was a song written in the folk song genre. But it was wonderful because it introduced many listeners to folk music."[64]

Peter, Paul, and Mary followed up with a more traditional folk song that would become an even bigger hit—"If I Had a Hammer (The Hammer Song)," composed by Pete Seeger and Lee Hays. "We learned that song from the Weavers," said Mary. "What an incredible influence they were. If anyone were our mentors, they were." In retrospect, it was a bold move for the trio to record the song, because the composers were still blacklisted. Right wingers during the McCarthy era believed the song's "hammer" alluded to the Soviet Union's iconic hammer and sickle. Some insisted that the lyrics about spreading justice, freedom, and love "between my brothers and my sisters all over this land" were leftist propaganda.[65]

Peter, Paul, and Mary's success with "If I Had a Hammer" suggests that America's political mood had changed considerably since McCarthy's heyday. But, the trio still received some pushback. "Yea, we had a strange moment with that song," recalls Mary. The popular TV show *Hootenanny* (broadcast on ABC in 1963–64) offered the group $10,000 to perform their hit on an upcoming show. "That was a lot of money back then," she says. "We told them rather innocently 'we'd love to do the program but we've got to do it with Pete Seeger.'" After a long pause, the show's representative said, "uh, we don't think he has college appeal." Peter, Paul, and Mary couldn't help but laugh, given Seeger's reputation for staging enthusiastic hootenannies on college campuses. "We'll do your program for nothing if you let us use Pete Seeger," they countered. Mary never forgot the answer. "They said 'we don't like to have our policy dictated by the artist.'" She adds, "It was some cockamamie crap, if you'll excuse my language. The bottom line was Pete was still blacklisted, and we didn't do *Hootenanny.*"[66]

After Peter, Paul, and Mary scored a Top 10 hit with "If I Had a Hammer," there was no stopping them. Their fresh sound and distinct look made them one of the hottest acts on Top 40 radio. Their performance on Dick Clark's *American*

Bandstand on May 2, 1963, was a veritable rock & roll imprimatur for the folk music boom. During performances, the dark-haired Peter and Paul stood like goateed bookends on either side of Mary Travers. Her striking appearance—tall and thin with long, straight blonde hair—coupled with her impressive voice and the equal turns she took singing lead transformed her into a proto-feminist icon. Young women at high schools and colleges across the country were soon copying the Mary Travers look by ironing their long hair. Decades later, Mary was still puzzled by the response. "Yea, my hair did become a role model for girls," she joked. "But, I always had a lot of trouble with fame. How can you deal with that and be sane?"[67]

Mary Travers is proud, though, that the quality of her voice and equal partnership with the two males in the group may have pointed the way for other young women in the early 1960s. She makes it clear that she was not the only prominent female folksinger around. "In the folk world, there were several like Joan Baez, Judy Collins, and Odetta, who were forces to be reckoned with." Back then, she notes, it was easier for women to succeed in folk music than in pop or rock & roll. "Folk music has always celebrated women who are strong, who have lost husbands in mining accidents, or major figures in the labor movement like Mother Jones," she explains. "There are lots of women heroes in folk music."[68]

In 1963 Peter, Paul, and Mary earned several hit singles, including three Top 10 hits: "Puff the Magic Dragon" was a bittersweet song about growing up, "Blowin' In the Wind" offered a powerful civil rights message, and "Don't Think Twice, It's All Right" featured provocative lyrics about love gone wrong. Although "Stewball" stalled at number 35, it was always one of Mary's favorites. "I love Stewball," she says. "It's really a song about believing in yourself. Basically, if the guy would have bet on Stewball, he would've won . . . Audiences love to sing along to that one."[69] Peter, Paul, and Mary also earned two best-selling albums in 1963: *(Moving)* reached number 2 on *Billboard*'s Top 200 album charts, while *In the Wind* made it all the way to number 1. Not only did the trio become one of the most popular acts around, but they introduced America to a new artist destined to become the most successful folk singer of all time—Bob Dylan.

Peter, Paul, and Mary scored a number 2 hit in 1963 with Dylan's "Blowin' in the Wind." Their follow-up was another Dylan composition, "Don't Think

Twice, It's All Right." The group's popular album *In the Wind* included the two hits along with one more Dylan song, "Quit Your Low Down Ways." It also featured liner notes written by the up-and-coming folk singer. Dylan's moment in Peter, Paul, and Mary's spotlight convinced fans to buy his debut album, sending *The Free Wheelin' Bob Dylan* (1963) all the way to number 22 on the charts.

Mary Travers explained how her group met Bob Dylan. "[He] worked in Greenwich Village . . . when we were all starving to death together," she explained. "Then our manager [Albert Grossman] became his manager and we heard Dylan's songs." The moment they heard "Blowin' in the Wind," they knew they had to record it. The civil rights message was stunning. "That's how artists select songs," notes Mary. "They recognize something in a song that they want to talk about."[70]

Peter, Paul, and Mary transformed Dylan's previously unknown song into a civil rights anthem. Mary never forgot the thrill of singing "Blowin' in the Wind" to an audience of over 250,000 people at the March on Washington in 1963. "That was a watershed moment for all of us. It was an incredible experience," she said. "Standing at the foot of the Lincoln Monument staring out at the Washington Monument and a sea of Black and white Americans, young and old and determined to help America's promise of equality become a reality was a revelation to me." She adds, "I really could believe at that moment and all the rest of my life that human beings acting in concert for the greater good of other human beings was possible."[71]

Peter, Paul, and Mary went on to record numerous hit singles and albums in a career that lasted until Mary's death in 2009. Later hits included "I Dig Rock and Roll Music" (1967), "Day is Done" (1969), and "Leaving On a Jet Plane" (a number 1 hit in 1969). Between 1962 and 1970, they earned eleven Top 20 albums, including two number 1 albums. In addition, they toured endlessly, bringing their music of hope to countless numbers of people, young and old.

Peter, Paul, and Mary never gave up on the dream of changing the world through music. "What we believed—and I think this is from the Weavers—was that artists have a responsibility to their community," explained Mary Travers in 1998. "It wasn't just sing a pretty song, take the money, and go home. Fame has a responsibility. Certainly every public person . . . has a responsibility . . . to weigh in on something they think is really important." Peter, Paul, and Mary always lived up to that goal. The same energy and optimism that can be found on the trio's recordings from the early 1960s powered their music for the rest of their career. "I look at this as a work in progress," explained Mary. "But, the goal is a reasonable goal. If we can imagine peace, we will someday achieve it."[72]

The popularity of Peter, Paul, and Mary, the Kingston Trio, and other folk artists of the early 60s was a sign of the changing times. The folk music revival was evidence that McCarthyism was in the past and that most Americans were now receptive to change. A quest for a national purpose captured public attention when Sputnik shocked America out of its 1950s complacency in 1957. Kennedy's election in 1960 demonstrated that most voters agreed with the optimistic goals he outlined after he won the Democratic nomination. JFK promised to "get the country moving again." Americans, he said, were "on the edge of a New Frontier . . . a frontier of unknown opportunities and perils—a frontier of unfilled hopes and threats."[73]

Teenagers' social and political awareness expanded after Kennedy took office. When baby boomers entered high school in the early 1960s and began thinking about college, they became more attuned to important issues of the day. Many paid close attention to growing Cold War concerns. They viewed civil rights protests on the nightly news, and listened intently to President Kennedy's optimistic comments about new frontiers. In such an atmosphere, many members of the rock & roll generation turned eagerly to folk songs that tapped into the era's rising idealism and activism. Folk music left an indelible mark not just on baby boomers, but also rock & roll. Its emphasis on meaningful lyrics and topical material influenced music of the early 60s and later led to the rise of folk-rock.

In the early 1960s Top 40 radio offered playlists that were as diverse as listeners' interests. Alongside rock & roll were other sounds, including traditional pop, jazz, R&B, country, and folk music. All these hits connected with audiences. "You don't have to be a musicologist, psychologist, or social scientist to know that music has always played a very important part in the human psyche and culture," explains Mary Travers. "Music reflects the times, but sometimes it shapes behavior as well. There's a synergy between what's happening in society and the music's articulation of what's happening."[74]

For many young people, the early 60s was a time of hope and discovery. That brief moment of great expectations was captured in Bob Dylan's liner notes to Peter, Paul, and Mary's 1963 album, *In the Wind*. He describes hanging out with the trio and other folksingers at the Gaslight coffee house in Greenwich Village. "We was lookin at each other . . . an findin out about ourselves," recalls Dylan in a writing style influenced by Woody Guthrie. "It is 'f these times that I remember most sadly—For they're gone—And they'll not never come again."[75]

Part 3

ROCKIN'
on the NEW
FRONTIER

10

"God, Country and My Baby"

Rock & Roll and the Culture of the Cold War

Johnny Burnette's "God, Country and My Baby" (1961) debuted on the pop charts as Cold War tensions heated up between the United States and Soviet Union. When President Kennedy returned from a tense Vienna summit with Russia's Nikita Khrushchev, the superpowers were on the verge of war. Kennedy and the Soviet leader tangled over a variety of issues, particularly the future of Germany, which was partitioned after World War II. Over the next few months JFK took specific steps to demonstrate America's resolve to stand up to the Soviet Union and defend its West German ally. The president dispatched additional troops to Europe. He increased the size of the military, called up the reserves, and ordered more ICBMs. Kennedy also encouraged Americans to build fallout shelters—just in case.

With war clouds on the horizon, Johnny Burnette's song hit the airwaves. Produced by Snuff Garrett, the record begins dramatically with drums rolling, cymbals crashing, and violins tossed in for good measure. "They say we sail tonight and we may have to fight, I want with all my might to stay," sings Burnette, "but, I'll go ... for God, country ... and my baby." Years later, Garrett recalled how the song came about. The USA was "fixin' to go to war [over] the Berlin Crisis," he explained. "That was the corniest song ... It had a heavenly chorus ... It did everything but do a symphonic reading on Iwo Jima. We really waved the flag on that boy ... That war never got off the ground and neither did the record." Actually, the sales figures weren't that bad. The patriotic ditty resonated with young listeners, sending it all the way up to number 18 on *Billboard*'s Top 100 pop singles.[1]

The Top 20 hit was just one of hundreds of teen-oriented songs that were intertwined with early 60s' politics and culture. The rock & roll evidence presented throughout this book reveals the important connections between the music and the times. This chapter pulls it all together, providing an overview that spotlights the music's historical and cultural significance. Rock & roll—like a vast oral history project—offers new details and fresh insights about politics, youth, gender, race, ethnicity, and daily life in Kennedy's America. The overwhelming majority of songs heard on *American Bandstand* and Top 40 radio suggest that most teenagers were anything but rebellious. Instead, they conformed to the politics and traditional values of America's Cold War culture just like the hero of Johnny Burnette's "God, Country and My Baby."

ROCK & ROLL AND THE CULTURE OF THE COLD WAR

Rock & roll was born and raised during the Cold War. Like the rest of 1950s America, the music got caught up in Cold War politics. Popular singers like Connie Francis, Pat Boone, and Johnny Cash recorded civil defense radio spots. Some records tried to defuse nuclear fears through humor: Bill Haley and His Comets' "Thirteen Women (And Only One Man in Town)" (1954) found bizarre comfort in a post–World War III world, the Cuff Links' "Guided Missiles (Aimed at My Heart)" (1956) placed ICBMs in the context of teenage romance, and Bobby Marchan and the Clowns' "Rockin' Behind the Iron Curtain" (1959) suggested rock & roll could help defeat the communists by getting them to dance.

Significantly, the influence of the Cold War extended beyond foreign policy. A Cold War culture took root in America after World War II and blossomed in the 1950s and early 60s. It touched almost every aspect of life and thought, including youth culture, gender, race, and institutions involving religion, marriage, and the family. Anxious Americans promoted traditional values—or at least what passed as traditional values—to protect themselves against communists. Having survived McCarthyism and other attacks, rock & roll was ready, willing, even eager to endorse America's ubiquitous Cold War culture.[2]

Patriotism was one of the hallmarks of the culture of the Cold War. Historian Stephen Whitfield explains, "The search to define and affirm a way of life, the need to express and celebrate the meaning of Americanism, was the flip side of stigmatizing Communism." Rock & roll exhibited its own celebrations of Americanism. Prior to the Beatles hitting it big in 1964, singers from outside the USA had a difficult time getting airplay on American radio stations. Their records were usually dismissed as poor imitations of authentic American rock & roll.[3]

American rock & roll artists often exhibited patriotism. After Elvis Presley was drafted in 1958, he told fans he was honored to serve his country and was repeatedly photographed in uniform. Other singers followed Elvis's lead, including the Everly Brothers who wore their Marine uniforms when they performed on Ed Sullivan's TV show. Patriotic songs bombarded the airwaves. Connie Francis earned a Top 40 hit in 1959 with a stirring rendition of "God Bless America." When Cold War tensions increased after the U-2 incident, Red River Dave found success with "There's a Star Spangled Banner Waving Somewhere, Number 2 (The Ballad of Gary Powers)" (1960). Other popular songs such as Johnny Horton's "Battle of New Orleans" (1959) and Bud and Travis' "Ballad of the Alamo" (1960) recalled celebrated moments in American history.[4]

Hit records spotlighted traditional myths. The legendary American West was celebrated on songs such as Gene Pitney's "The Man Who Shot Liberty Valance" (1962) and Bo Diddley's "Gunslinger" (1963). The superiority of the common man powered Jimmy Dean's "Big Bad John" (1961) and Jay and the Americans' "Only in America" (1963). The notion that anyone could make it in America transcended racial barriers, as evidenced by the success of numerous Black rock & rollers, as well as hits like Fats Domino's "I'm Gonna Be a Wheel Someday" (1959), Gene Chandler's "Duke of Earl" (1962), and the Drifters' "On Broadway" (1963).

The coming of John F. Kennedy gave young Americans and rock & roll even more reason to rally around the flag. Young people were attracted to the charismatic young president, who symbolized youth, vitality, and hope for a better future. "Most Inaugural speeches have been forgettable cheerleading exercises," notes presidential historian Robert Dallek. But JFK's stood out. "Kennedy's address was not only beautifully written but contained language that people quote to this day: 'Ask not what your country can do for you—ask what you can do for your country.'" Dallek adds, "The speech and Kennedy's eloquent delivery set a tone of hope for Americans—hope that the United States would once more rise to the international and domestic challenges threatening to undermine its future as a great nation."[5]

American youth identified with Kennedy, the youngest elected president in American history, far more than they did with his predecessor, the grandfatherly Dwight D. Eisenhower. JFK was handsome, rich, wore cool clothes, and didn't wear hats because it would mess up his hair. Nicknamed Jack, he had a beautiful young wife and two cute little kids. Kennedy lived a glamorous lifestyle, played touch football with his brothers, loved to sail, and was always ready with a quip. Just after he was elected president, Kennedy attended his last meeting as a member of the Harvard Board of Overseers. Students cheered the moment he walked into University Hall. The president-elect smiled warmly and then assured the friendly crowd, "I am here to go over your grades with [Harvard's president] Dr. Pusey, and I'll protect your interests."[6]

Kennedy inspired young people to believe in themselves and America. He insisted they could make a difference through the Peace Corps and public service. He also challenged them to help the country stay strong by becoming more active physically. Toward that end, he launched a presidential physical fitness program that was implemented by schools across the country. To promote the mission to make the nation stronger, the president even worked with DC comics to develop a special Superman comic book entitled "Superman's Mission for President Kennedy." "Comic books were the social media of its time," explains Tom Putnam, director of the John F. Kennedy Presidential Library and Museum, "It was one of the best ways to reach this age group back then."[7]

The young president became a pop culture hero, celebrated in print, on TV, in films like *PT 109*, and on hit records played on rock & roll stations coast to coast. Jimmy Dean scored a number 8 hit with "P.T. 109" (1962), a patriotic ballad about Kennedy's heroism in World War II. A few months later, 7-year-old Little Jo Ann charted with "My Daddy is President," which reinforced popular images of the president playing with his kids in the White House. Impressionist Vaughn Meader found even greater success with *The First Family* (1962), a best-selling comedy album that poked loving fun at JFK and his family. People listening to Top 40 radio couldn't help but hear these glowing tributes. The wealthy Ivy Leaguer came across as a regular guy who loved his family and believed in freedom and justice for all. He was smart, funny, yet tough when necessary. Who better to lead America in the Cold War against the communists?

When Cold War tensions pushed the United States and Soviet Union to the brink of war, rock & roll remained a staunch Kennedy ally. The Berlin Crisis produced two hits. Johnny Burnette's "God, Country and My Baby" (1961) demonstrated American males' willingness to fight, while Miss Toni Fisher's "West of the Wall" (1962) condemned the Berlin Wall for separating her from her lover and taking away everyone's freedom. Pro-military songs also hit the charts. Titus Turner found success with "Sound Off" (1961), a rock & roll version of a military marching song. The following year, Bo Diddley released "Mr. Khrushchev," a patriotic call to arms. "JFK can't do it by his self," sings Bo, "c'mon fellas, let's give him a little help." Other records, including the Shirelles' "Soldier Boy" (1962) and Diane Renay's "Navy Blue" (1964), suggested teenage girls could do their part by supporting boyfriends in the military.[8]

There were signs, however, that some young Americans were worried that the Cold War might erupt into a hot one. Jimmy Dean's Top 30 hit "Dear Ivan" (1962) was an open letter to a Russian citizen, which suggested that people on both sides of the Cold War shared the same basic needs and didn't want political differences to cause World War III. Other records revealed growing dissatisfaction with Cold War policies. The Kingston Trio's "Where Have All the Flowers Gone" (1962) condemned the futility of war, while Bob Dylan's "Hard Rain's A-Gonna Fall" (1963) warned of nuclear holocaust.

Despite occasional songs of social protest, Kennedy and his New Frontier programs and policies remained popular with young people. One of JFK's boldest moves was the space program. In May 1961 the president told a joint session of Congress that America had to win the race for space "if we are to win the battle that is now going on around the world between freedom and tyranny." He added, "I believe that this nation should commit itself to achieving the goal, before this decade is out, of landing a man on the Moon and returning him safely to the Earth. No single space project . . . will be more exciting, or more impressive to mankind, or more important." Following Kennedy's speech, NASA consolidated various projects into the Apollo Program, which aimed at a lunar landing. Kennedy's new space program resonated with proud Americans, who cheered on pioneering astronauts like Alan Shepard and John Glenn.[9]

Records heard on Top 40 radio echoed the public's fascination with space. Just weeks after the president's address, Jose Jimenez (a.k.a. Bill Dana) found success with "The Astronaut" (1961), a comedy record about the first Hispanic astronaut headed toward space. The following year the Tornadoes scored a number 1 hit with "Telstar," an instrumental named after the famous US communications satellite that relayed the first transatlantic TV signals from America to Europe. The year 1963 welcomed additional songs inspired by the race to space. Joe Harnell and His Orchestra made it to number 14 with a jazzy instrumental, "Fly Me to the Moon—Bossa Nova," which combined public interest in Project Apollo with the latest dance craze. The Ran-Dells did almost as well, reaching number 16 with their bizarre novelty hit "The Martian Hop." The upbeat song featured weird space creatures, unearthly sound effects, and lyrics about teen dances, all set to a great dance beat. Even a surf band rode the wave of the space program's popularity. The Astronauts—a group from Boulder, Colorado—found success with a high energy surf instrumental, "Baja."[10]

The optimism associated with Kennedy's New Frontier fueled the popularity of folk music in the early 60s. Along with established folk singers like the Kingston Trio, came new artists such as Peter, Paul, and Mary, the Highwaymen, Brothers Four, Joan Baez, and Bob Dylan. Hootenannies—which picked up on the social and political activism associated with the civil rights movement and the promise of Kennedy's New Frontier—were held at high schools and universities across the country. These sing-alongs were spotlighted on popular records such as "Hootenanny Saturday Night" by the Brothers Four and "Hootenanny" by the Glencoves' (both in 1963). The connection between folk music and Kennedy was underscored by the Kingston Trio's 1962 recording, "The New Frontier," which echoed JFK's inaugural address.

* * *

The music heard on Top 40 radio reinforced America's Cold War culture in other ways. "Communists were our mortal enemies and they were atheists. Religion, therefore, came to seem essential to the fight against Communism," write historians Douglas T. Miller and Marion Nowak. "It is not surprising that the religiosity of the era became entwined with super patriotism."[11] The boom in organized religion spilled onto the pop charts. The 1950s welcomed numerous songs that alluded to God and religion, including number 1 records like the Platters' "My Prayer" (1956) and Laurie London's "He's Got the Whole World in His Hands" (1958). The trend continued throughout the early 60s with hits such as Annette's "Oh Dio Mio" (1960), Dorsey Burnette's "Tall Oak Tree" (1960), and the Singing Nun's uplifting "Dominique" (1963), which soared to number 1 in the weeks after President Kennedy's assassination.

Many Americans believed that traditional family values provided additional protection against communism. Historian Elaine Tyler May writes, "In the early years of the Cold War, amid a world of uncertainties brought about by World War II and its aftermath, the home seemed to offer a secure private nest removed from the dangers of the outside world."[12] Numerous rock & roll songs underscored the importance of the family and marriage. Parents were praised on hits such as the Shirelles' "Mama Said" (1961) and Paul Petersen's "My Dad" (1963). Other songs glorified marriage, including Ronnie and the Hi-Lites' "I Wish That We Were Married" (1962) and the Dixie Cups' "Chapel of Love" (1964). And "going steady"—the teenage version of monogamy—was promoted on Elvis Presley's "Wear My Ring Around Your Neck" (1958), Bobby Vee's cover of Buddy Holly's "Well . . . All Right" (1962), and Neil Sedaka's "Let's Go Steady Again" (1963).

Rock & roll endorsed other traditional values. Elvis Presley's "(You're So Square) Baby I Don't Care" (1957) and the Crickets' "Please Don't Ever Change" (1962) were odes to "good girls," while the Everly Brothers' "That's Old Fashioned (That's the Way Love Should Be)" (1962) idealized holding hands, sitting next to each other in booths at the soda shop, and other familiar dating rituals. Early 60s rock & roll projected an All-American image. Record companies frequently promoted clean-cut teen idols such as Frankie Avalon, Connie Francis, Chubby Checker, and Bobby Rydell. If singers or songs strayed too far from the norm, they were quickly brought into line, as evidenced by the numerous investigations into the Kingsmen and their controversial "Louie Louie" (1963).

Rock & roll was also a strong supporter of American capitalism. Stars like Elvis Presley, Ray Charles, Mary Wells, and the 4 Seasons personified the American success story, while the highly profitable and competitive music business exemplified capitalism at work. Large and small record companies mass produced records aimed at the burgeoning teenage market. Radio stations profited by promoting the latest hits. The rock & roll craze was tailor-made for America's consumer culture, which emphasized conspicuous consumption and planned obsolescence. No sooner did records climb to the top of the charts than they began to fall, only to be replaced by more recent releases. The hits just kept on coming. And, teenagers kept on buying to keep pace with latest fads and products. Rock & roll contributed to the rise of a national teenage culture. Young people danced to the same beat literally and figuratively. Like the older generation, baby boomers bought into the consumerism, conformity, and consensus behavior of Cold War America.

Rock & roll offered young consumers a cornucopia of products, fashions, and fads. Car songs helped popularize little deuce coupes, GTOs, and Sting Rays, while hits like Jimmy Clanton's "Venus in Blue Jeans" (1962) and the Dovells' "Betty in Bermudas" (1963) promoted fashions. Rock & roll also marketed fads from surfing to new dances like the Twist and Monkey. Barrett Strong's "Money (That's What I Want)" (1960) didn't even try to hide its crass, materialistic message. Rock & roll might have sounded different to adults, but the music's capitalistic message should have been familiar to everyone in Cold War America.

In an era when concerns about atomic bombs sent Americans scurrying for fallout shelters, rock & roll offered ways to cope with Cold War anxieties. Some records explored teenage fears about nuclear destruction. Sammy Salvo's "A Mushroom Cloud" (1961)—composed by Boudeleaux Bryant, who wrote numerous hits for the Everly Brothers—focused on a young couple who lived in fear of nuclear holocaust. "I cling to my baby and she clings to me," sings Salvo. "We talk of the future, but what do we see? There's a mushroom cloud that hangs in the way."[13] Skeeter Davis's number 2 hit from early 1963, "The End of the World," offered teenagers a more subtle and commercially successful critique of

America's Cold War culture. Its somber sound and nihilistic lyrics about love gone wrong were a perfect fit for the anxious mood of young audiences in the months after the Cuban Missile Crisis.

Other songs used humor to defuse atomic bomb fears. Dore Alpert's "Fallout Shelter" (1962) featured a guy who locked himself in a fallout shelter to get away from his horrible girlfriend. Sonny Russell got some airplay in 1963 with "Fifty Megatons," a high energy rockabilly song that told a weird but funny story about an H-Bomb explosion, a UFO, and space alligators. That same year Mike Russo's "Agnes (The Teenage Russian Spy)" joked about Cold War espionage.

Two novelty records suggested that even nuclear clouds had silver linings. Wanda Jackson's "Fujiyama Mama" (1957) compared the power of an atomic blast to her explosive sexuality. The record fizzled in the US possibly because of the suggestive lyrics and the fact that it hit the airwaves just twelve years after the bombing of Hiroshima and Nagasaki. (Ironically, the song was a smash hit in Japan.) Ann-Margret's "Thirteen Men" (1962) found sexual satisfaction in the aftermath of nuclear holocaust. Her cover of Bill Haley and the Comets' original recording, "Thirteen Women (And Only One Man in Town)" (1954), made one important change that reflected evolving attitudes toward gender in Kennedy's America. This time around, the singer is the last surviving woman, and she's being pleasured by thirteen guys. "Boy, they sure were a lively pack," she sings suggestively.[14]

Cold War anxieties might also help explain the popularity of the "death rock" phenomenon. In 1960 teenagers experienced the ultimate escape on three dark hits: Mark Dinning's "Teen Angel," Ray Peterson's "Tell Laura I Love Her," and Johnny Preston's "Running Bear" (see chapter 8). Mortality rates continued to rise over the next few years, as evidenced by the Everly Brothers' "Ebony Eyes" (1961), Pat Boone's "Moody River" (1961), and Dickey Lee's "Patches" (1962). Boone suggests a possible connection between death rock and the troubled times. "I guess we go through certain phases where morbid themes strike some kind of responsive chord," he notes. During the early 60s "there was a cloud of war [with Russia]. There was unrest . . . It was during that period that young people across America were beginning to feel a sense of futility and great concern creeping in. They didn't know what to make of it."[15]

Following John F. Kennedy's assassination, death rock spiked in 1964 with the Shangri-Las' number 1 record "Leader of the Pack" and J. Frank Wilson and the Cavaliers' number 2 hit "Last Kiss." The death rock genre then tailed off. Jimmy Cross's "I Want My Baby Back" (1965) was the low point (or apex depending on one's perspective). It parodied the genre with a macabre tale about a young guy who wants his dead girlfriend back. In the last verse he digs her up, climbs into the coffin with her, closes the lid, and sings triumphantly in a muffled voice "I got my baby back."[16]

ROCK & ROLL AND THE CHANGING TIMES

Early 60s rock & roll also offered glimpses of social change. One of the biggest changes involved the baby boom generation. Born between 1946 and 1964, these 76½ million kids comprised approximately one-third of America's population by the mid-1960s. The first wave of baby boomers to reach high school were the 3½ million teenagers who arrived in the 1960–61 academic year just as John F. Kennedy was elected and sworn in as the nation's 35th president. Every subsequent year of JFK's presidency witnessed almost four million additional baby boomers entering high school nationwide.[17] Not surprisingly, rock & roll and other musical styles heard on Top 40 radio took direct aim at this huge market.

Rock & roll's close ties to youth culture gave it credibility. This was their music—a teenage folk sound powered by relevant lyrics, electric guitars, and a big beat. Most of the singers and songwriters were about the same age as their audiences and shared similar interests, which underscored the music's authenticity. Brenda Lee was just 15 years old in 1959 when she recorded her first big hit, "Sweet Nothin's." The subjects she sang about on subsequent hits—romance, dating, loneliness, and alienation—resonated with both male and female listeners. Her records showed teenagers they were part of a larger peer group experiencing similar problems. Young women, in particular, could relate to the teenage singer. "I was interested in going to school, cheerleading, and being with my friends," explained Brenda. "I was kind of like the girl next door, kind of your best friend, that kind of image, which I liked because it was true."[18]

Bobby Vee, who was 17 when he earned his first Top 10 hit, "Devil or Angel" (1960), had a similar connection to fans. When a reporter asked him in 1961 what he liked best about his new career, Bobby replied, "The chance to meet thousands of boys and girls of my own age group throughout the United States and to talk to them about the subjects in which we are most interested."[19]

Throughout the early 1960s, the records heard nationwide on Top 40 radio promoted youth culture. Hits such as Johnny Burnette's "You're Sixteen" (1960), Neil Sedaka's "Happy Birthday, Sweet Sixteen" (1961), and the Crystals' "What a Nice Way to Turn Seventeen" (1963) glorified the teen years. Other songs focused on teenage interests, including romance, sex, dancing, parties, cars, fashions, and fads. The Cascades' number 3 hit "Rhythm of the Rain" (1963), for instance, featured excellent harmonies, a catchy melody, and a creative arrangement that used sounds of thunder and rain to convey the anguish of teenage heartbreak.

The vast majority of records suggest that young Americans supported the era's Cold War culture and consensus behavior as much as the older generation. For example, Johnny Horton's "Johnny Freedom" (1960) and Jimmy Dean's "P.T. 109" (1962) celebrated American heroes. The Castells' "Sacred" (1961) placed young love in the context of religion. And the Dreamlovers' "When We Get Married" (1961) and Paul and Paula's "Hey Paula" (1963) underscored the importance of marriage.[20]

The Beach Boys' "Be True to Your School" (1963) was less obvious but equally revealing. The number 6 hit spotlights an enthusiastic teenager proud of his school. The young guy wears a letterman sweater he got for playing football and track, and he cruises around town in a car with a high school decal on the back windshield. He can't wait for the upcoming football game and promises his school will crush their rival. "Be true to your school now," he urges his classmates, "just like you would to your girl or guy."[21]

The song captures the rhythms and feel of high school in the early 60s. But, it also echoes the optimism and patriotism of Kennedy's America. Although Brian Wilson and Mike Love set out to write a song about high school life, they wound up with a record that is a microcosm of America in 1963. Their song about school spirit is a rock & roll equivalent of the nationalistic spirit of Cold War America. The Beach Boys sing proudly about being number 1, and they are ready to smash their archenemy. In keeping with the era's gender attitudes, the guy in the song is eager to fight on Friday night's battlefield, while his girlfriend offers auxiliary support. The Beach Boys might as well have been singing, "Be true to your school, just like you would to your [*country*] . . . Let your colors fly." Regardless of intent, the Beach Boys' hit demonstrates the connections between rock & roll, baby boomers, and daily life in Cold War America.

Rock & roll became a cultural binding force for the baby boom generation. Record sales and the extraordinary popularity of *American Bandstand* and Top 40 radio suggest that most teenagers enjoyed the music and were familiar with the popular artists and hits that became part of their generation's collective memory. Even baby boomers who weren't rock & roll fans found it hard to avoid the ubiquitous sounds that blasted from car radios, sound systems at high school dances, or record players at parties.

Early 60s rock & roll provided most members of the baby boom generation with similar perspectives and experiences. Regardless of race, religion, ethnicity, gender, class, or neighborhood, they absorbed rock & roll images and messages that were in line with the era's consensus behavior and politics.

Rock & roll performers offer new details about race relations in Kennedy's America. Many African American singers born and raised in the North were shocked by the racism they encountered on tours south of the Mason-Dixon Line. "We couldn't do the shows in the main theaters," notes the Chantels' Lois Harris. "We had to be split into the white audience and the Black audience. And in many cases, the show was in the basement of the theater for the black audience and then, for the white audience it was in the main theater. Or, it was a theater where the Black people had a separate entrance, and were way up in the top of the theater where they could hardly see anything," she explains. "We were . . . from New York and discrimination was a lot more subtle . . . but when we got down South it was really in our faces."[22]

Smokey Robinson of the Miracles was equally appalled. "We had to go to the Black side of town to stay in rooming-houses and places like that to have a place to spend the night." Even the restrooms were demeaning. "They had three toilets—one said 'men,' one said 'women,' and around the back somewhere, if it wasn't an outhouse, it said 'colored,'" recalls Robinson. "So that meant, if you were colored, you weren't a man or a woman. You were just *colored* and you could go in there."[23]

Robinson's colleague on the Motown label, Martha Reeves, remembers one particular incident when three African American men on their tour bus tried to use a restroom at a gas station down South. They asked the station attendant, "Hey, man, where's the bathroom?" Reeves explains, "That's not protocol. The rule in the South . . . was you say 'yassir' and 'no suh.'" The attendant at "this little gas station . . . got very upset and came [back] to the room with the shotgun. He said, 'Y'all n—, go back on the bus.'"[24]

White performers who traveled alongside Black artists on Southern bus tours were surprised by the blatant racism. Decades later, Duane Eddy still had vivid recollections of his first tour in the segregated South. "We had a Black road manager . . . and he explained to me how things were . . . I had no experience with it," says Eddy. "We had no apparent racism out in Arizona where I grew up, and I went to school with Black kids and was friends with them, and with Indians, Mexicans, too. We just didn't have that problem, at least that I was aware of." One particular incident demonstrated that segregated facilities were separate but definitely not equal. "The sheriff got on the [tour] bus and said the white [performers] could go into the dressing room, but the Black ones would have to use the shed down there," recalls Eddy. "That really ticked me off."[25]

Some white artists refused to go along with racist rules. African American singer Sonny Turner of the Platters remembers an incident that occurred when the group was touring down South with Dick Clark's Caravan of Stars. The integrated bus would pull into a town and drop Black singers off at a cheap hotel and then take white singers to a better place on the other side of town. "A lot of the white performers wouldn't do it," explains Turner. One white singer told him, "I'm not going over there. To hell with them people. Sonny, what room are you in? Give me a room next to yours." Turner adds, "They resented that crap. We're on the road together, we sing together, we perform together, we eat together. A lot of white guys are like, 'Shit, this is America, isn't it?'"[26]

Rock & roll was not immune to race issues. Bo Diddley insisted that he and other African American artists were cheated out of royalties and never got the recognition they deserved because of race. "[It was] bad news, baby. Bad news.

It was a hurtin' thing. I never knew what all that crap was about," he said. "This is America, and this is music . . . That type of hatred causes the downfall of everybody not just one person. It's a bad disease, you know?"[27]

African American singer Jan Bradley also experienced racial discrimination. One year before she earned a major hit with "Mama Didn't Lie" (1963), she was rejected by a major record label because of the color of her skin. Years later Bradley could still recall the conversation between her manager and United Artists' Art Talmadge. From the waiting room, Jan overheard Talmadge explain that his label wasn't interested in her because she was Black. Bradley had the last laugh. When "Mama Didn't Lie" rose up the charts just as African Americans were getting lots of media coverage because of civil rights, Talmadge called back to offer Jan a contract. Since she had already signed with Chess Records, she happily rejected his pitch.[28]

Dion, a white pop rocker, witnessed other examples of racial discrimination. "Most of the guys who were playing on my records . . . were Black," he explains. But record companies and industry insiders weren't about to advertise that in an era of segregation. "When we made a movie . . . you couldn't have Black musicians playing behind you because the movie wouldn't play in certain parts of the country," he explains. "They had to put some white musicians behind me just lip-synching the parts and stuff."[29]

Ironically, even though rock & roll was more diverse and multicultural than most of America, numerous hit records spotlighted racial and ethnic stereotypes. The Clovers' "Love Potion Number Nine" (1959) and the Coasters' "Little Egypt" (1961) featured comedic caricatures of African Americans. Little Anthony and the Imperials' "Shimmy Shimmy Ko-Ko-Bop" (1960) showcased the alleged sexual prowess of African natives. And, Mongo Santamaria's "Watermelon Man" (1963) picked up on another well-known stereotype. American Indians were treated like cartoon characters on Larry Verne's "Mr. Custer" (1960) and Johnny Preston's "Running Bear" (1960). Hispanic stereotypes set the stage for "The Astronaut" (1961) by Jose Jimenez (a.k.a. Bill Dana), Pat Boone's "Speedy Gonzales" (1962), and the Righteous Brothers' "Little Latin Lupe Lu" (1963). Additional stereotypes powered Lou Monte's "Pepino the Italian Mouse" (1963), Ray Stevens' "Ahab, the Arab" (1962), and Bobby Goldsboro's "Me Japanese Boy" (1964).

The fact that rock & roll made use of the same stereotypes that permeated the era's Cold War culture reinforced the narrow notion of what it meant to be an "American" in the Eisenhower/Kennedy years. Significantly, even racial and ethnic minorities sometimes sang and cheered these stereotypical novelty hits, possibly because the songs offered them at least a moment in the pop culture spotlight and acknowledged they were part of America's melting pot.

Despite continuing discrimination toward African Americans and other groups, rock & roll evidence suggests that America was becoming more racially and culturally diverse in the early 1960s. Hit records on *Billboard*'s pop charts demonstrate that more opportunities in the music business were opening up for Black performers. Between 1960 and 1964 African Americans made up about 10.6 percent of the US population, yet approximately 30 percent of all the records that made the Top 40 charts in 1960 were performed by Black artists. By the end of 1963 African American performers accounted for 36 percent of all the Top 40 records.[30]

The desegregation of the pop charts meant that African American artists like Ray Charles, Mary Wells, Sam Cooke, and the Shirelles were being cheered by millions of white listeners. If hit records made Black performers more acceptable to white audiences, they also promoted white singers with Black audiences. By the early 1960s Brenda Lee, Rick Nelson, and the Beach Boys were scoring hits on *Billboard*'s rhythm & blues chart. The fact that Blacks and whites frequently enjoyed the same songs by the same artists may have contributed to similar perspectives among listeners regardless of skin color.

Although most African American performers weren't consciously trying to undermine segregation, they often wound up doing just that. Beverly Lee of the Shirelles recalls the time her group played a segregated college in the South. "We were the first black female group to do that. And we were called that famous 'n' word," she says. "They did later send us a letter of apology. But after that, they started sending other black artists down to the colleges." She adds proudly that many whites down South loved the Shirelles' music. "So there was a demand for us to come there. And we opened the doors." Martha Reeves, who toured the South with other Motown artists, suggests their concerts helped bring racially mixed audiences together. "When you say, clap your hands, everybody clapped their hands," she explains. "When we say, get up and dance, everybody got up and danced. And the prejudice and the hatred was forgotten, at least during show time."[31]

Rock & roll offers other evidence that integration was on the rise in Kennedy's America. Most listeners were not aware of it at the time, but integrated bands and production teams were responsible for many hits on Top 40 radio. Black groups like the Shirelles and Chiffons worked closely with white songwriters, musicians, and producers, while white artists benefited from interaction with talented African American production people, studio musicians, and songwriters. For instance, Lesley Gore's producer was the legendary Quincy Jones, while Bobby Vee's studio band included top African American musicians such as bandleader-arranger Ernie Freeman, bass player Red Callender, and drummer Earl Palmer.

Rock & roll promoted racial equality in additional ways. African American artists like Sam Cooke and Curtis Mayfield were vocal supporters of the civil rights movement. In 1963 the Shirelles, Ray Charles, and Clyde McPhatter joined Martin Luther King Jr. on stage for a special concert in Alabama to raise money so civil rights activists could attend the upcoming March on Washington. And it's hard to exaggerate the impact that Berry Gordy Jr. and Motown Records had on racial attitudes. The phenomenal success of Motown, which promoted Black performers, musicians, songwriters, and producers, was living proof that Martin Luther King Jr.'s calls for racial equality and integration were taking hold in early 60s America.

The integrated rock & roll bus tours that crisscrossed the country offer fresh perspectives on segregation in Kennedy's America. "You didn't have to really go that far south," insists Eddie LeVert of the O'Jays, a popular R&B rock group. "All you had to do was drive down to Cincinnati and Louisville and you'd be in that place where 'OK, Blacks must go through the back, you've got to go upstairs at the movie theatre, you can't drink at this fountain, you can stay over there but you can't eat here.'" R&B rock singer William Bell adds, "The segregated era crept into your psyche. It made you examine everything around you and question a lot of things."[32]

Despite all the racial problems, or possibly because of them, racial camaraderie emerged on integrated tour buses. Close friendships developed, and Black and white performers helped each other in difficult situations. African American singer Dee Dee Sharp experienced a particularly scary incident in the early 60s. "I will never go back to Jackson, Mississippi, ever again," she said years later. "[Whites] actually stoned the bus. Stoned it. *Stoned it.* The Dovells [a white group on the tour] covered my mother and I to keep the stones from coming into the bus." African American performers likewise helped out white friends. Dion recalls the threatening situation he found himself in when he and Sam Cooke were on tour and went to see James Brown perform in an all-Black neighborhood in Memphis. "We were traveling in the South and it was kind of the opposite way around. He stood up for me in those situations where people had attitudes in a community that wasn't mine." Sam would tell troublemakers, "Hey, the boy's with me."[33]

Not only did integrated bus tours promote friendship between Black and white performers, but they also had a positive impact on audiences. These one-night stands were examples of integration in action. Rock & roll fans of different races came together under the same roof to enjoy the music of Black and white performers. Dick Clark's Caravan of Stars literally set the stage for racial harmony. Clarence Collins, a member of the R&B rock group Little Anthony and the Imperials, notes Clark "got [Blacks and whites] in there together . . . and eventually in the South they forgot all about what color you were."[34]

Motown tours had similar experiences down South. When Smokey Robinson and the Miracles first performed there, audiences were separated by race. "It was ropes down the center. There were barriers down the center. There were Black people upstairs and white people downstairs or vice versa," explains Smokey. "Sometimes the stage was in the center of a big arena and Black people would be on one side and white people would be on the other side. It was ridiculous." But the ropes and other barriers soon came down. "We cured all that with the music, man," says Smokey proudly. That type of segregation "pretty much disappeared. I noticed the crowds [integrating] before I noticed the hotels."[35]

The music heard on Top 40 radio did even more to advance racial equality. Peter, Paul, and Mary's "Blowin' in the Wind" (1963) and Joan Baez's "We Shall Overcome" (1963) became anthems for the civil rights movement. The prominence of Ray Charles, Sam Cooke, and other African American artists on the early 60s pop charts was proof that Blacks could succeed in America. Several of their hits addressed social and economic concerns. The Coasters charted with trickster tales that undermined racism, including "What About Us?" (1960) and "Shoppin' for Clothes" (1960). Sam Cooke's "Chain Gang" (1960) focused on the incarceration of Black men. The Crystals' "Uptown" (1962) exposed racial divisions in urban America. And Ray Charles's "Born to Lose" (1962) and "Busted" (1963) expressed anguish over broken dreams and poverty. Two other songs helped energize the civil rights movement: Sam Cooke's "A Change is Gonna Come" and Curtis Mayfield and the Impressions' "Keep on Pushing" hit the airwaves in 1964 as the nation was considering passage of the Civil Rights Act of 1964 and the Voting Rights Act of 1965. The songs' powerful messages, which echoed Martin Luther King Jr.'s recent "I Have a Dream" speech, inspired countless numbers of Americans to demand equality and justice for all.

"If it hadn't been for music," noted Congressman John Lewis, a prominent civil rights activist, "the Movement would have been like a bird without wings."[36]

Rock & roll provides valuable information about gender attitudes in Kennedy's America. Following World War II, the common wisdom was a woman's place was in the home as a wife and mother, which dovetailed with the emphasis on the family in Cold War America. Most teenage girls accepted the notion that they would get married, have babies, be loving and nurturing, and follow a man's lead in all matters. Even First Lady Jackie Kennedy maintained that wives should defer to and support their husbands. "I think women should never be in politics," she said in a taped interview conducted shortly after she left the White House. "We're just not suited for it." A wife's role, she said, was to "create a climate of affection" and provide her husband with "children in good moods" in order to relieve the tensions related to his job.[37]

Rock & roll generally shared the dominant culture's attitudes toward gender. Hits such as Sue Thompson's "(James) Hold the Ladder Steady" (1962) and Paul and Paula's "Hey Paula" (1963) featured women eager to marry. The notion that women should be faithful auxiliaries to men appeared in numerous songs, including two hits in 1962 by the Shirelles—"Soldier Boy" and "Welcome Home, Baby."

Although rock & roll might have been revolutionary in some ways, it was often outright conservative when it came to women. Put another way, rock & roll was every bit as sexist as the rest of America in the early 1960s. The music viewed males as aggressive and dominant and females as passive and subordinate. Teenage girls could take the lead only on special occasions. They could invite boys to Sadie Hawkins dances, for example, or could ask boys to dance at record hops if the deejay announced "this next song is a 'lady's choice.'" In most other situations, boys were in charge.

Numerous hits showcased boys who asked girls for dates, maneuvered for a first kiss, and popped the question to go steady or get married. The high school boy on Johnny Ferguson's "Angela Jones" (1960) met Angela at her locker, offered to carry her books, and promised to marry her. The boy on the Crystals' "Then He Kissed Me" (1963) was even more assertive. He walked up to her at a record hop and asked her to dance, held her tight, walked her home . . . and then he kissed her. In comparison, the girls on Linda Scott's "I've Told Every Little Star" (1961) and the Essex's "Easier Said than Done" (1963) were reluctant to make the first move.

Most songs reinforced the belief that girls should be passive, follow the boys' lead, and hope for the best, as evidenced by Marcie Blane's "Bobby's Girl" (number 3 in 1962) and Little Peggy March's number 1 hit "I Will Follow Him" (1963). Other records such as Darlene Love's "Wait Til' My Bobby Gets Home" (1963) and the Angels' "My Boyfriend's Back" (1963) suggested that young women had to depend on guys for love and protection.

Sometimes female dependency went too far. Three hits from 1962 featured young women desperate for attention. The woman on the Shirelles' "Baby, It's You" was so dependent on her man that she was willing to take anything he dished out. Joanie Sommers's "Johnny Get Angry" featured a teenage girl pleading with her meek boyfriend to act like a caveman and take charge. Similarly, the desperate young woman on the Crystals' "Please Hurt Me" told the guy she loved that she wouldn't cry if he cheated on her. She was even willing to have her heart broken if it meant having him for a while.

Even the way teenage boys and girls handled rejection reflected gender stereotypes. Teenage boys had to be tough, as evidenced by songs such as the 4

Seasons' "Walk Like a Man" (1963) and Gene Pitney's "I'm Gonna Be Strong" (1964). On the other hand, teenage girls were seen as the weaker sex, so they could let their heartbreak show. Tears flowed on hits such as Janie Grant's "Triangle" (1961), the Caravelles' "You Don't Have to Be a Baby to Cry" (1963), and Lesley Gore's epic weeper, "It's My Party (and I'll Cry If I Want To)" (1963).

Like the dominant society in Cold War America, rock & roll objectified women. Women were placed on pedestals on Johnny Tillotson's "Poetry in Motion" (1960), Jimmy Clanton's "Venus in Blue Jeans" (1962), and the Beach Boys' "Surfer Girl" (1963). Other records treated women as sex objects. Dee Clark's "You're Looking Good" (1960) praised a young woman with "34-24-35" measurements. Ricky Nelson kept score of his conquests on "Travelin' Man" (1961). Jan and Dean bragged about having "two girls for every boy" in "Surf City" (1963). And Jimmy Gilmer and the Fireballs' "Sugar Shack" (1963) focused on a cute waitress with "a black leotard and her feet are bare."

If teenage girls didn't conform to expected behavior, they were quickly put down by guys. Hit records like Dion's "Donna the Prima Donna" (1963) and Del Shannon's "Little Town Flirt" (1963) warned guys about young Jezebels. Other songs, including Joe Jones's "You Talk Too Much" (1960) and the Halos' "Nag" (1961), condemned young women who voiced opinions. One of the most insulting putdowns can be found on Jimmy Soul's number 1 hit from 1963, "If You Wanna Be Happy," which advised guys to marry ugly women who can cook rather than pretty girls who can't be trusted. But by far the most disturbing song was the Crystals' 1962 recording, "He Hit Me (and It Felt Like a Kiss)," which featured a young woman beaten by a guy because she was unfaithful.

If most rock & roll girls were passive and dependent, rock & roll boys were typically aggressive and dominant. Testosterone almost dripped from the grooves of Fabian's Top 10 record, "Turn Me Loose" (1959). Bobby Rydell boasted on "Wild One" (1960) that he was going to "tame" a girl who fooled around with other guys. And Bo Diddley's "You Can't Judge a Book by the Cover" (1962) featured a macho guy telling a woman that she's misjudging him. "I look like a farmer," he growls, "but I'm a lover."[38]

Back-to-back hits by Dion—"Runaround Sue" (1961) and "The Wanderer" (1962)—offer a fascinating glimpse of gender stereotypes in Kennedy's America.

During a 1995 NPR interview Dion was asked about the obvious double standard in the songs. "Runaround Sue" features a young woman who is vilified because she played around with every guy in town, while "The Wanderer" glorifies a young man who kept score of his conquests with tattoos on his arms and chest. In retrospect, Dion acknowledges that the two hits treated males and females differently. "I'm not saying it was right," he explains. "It was really expressing the times, and the way we were [back then]." He adds, "I mean, you start singing 'The Wanderer' now, it makes people an instant jerk, including myself."[39]

While most songs heard on Top 40 radio supported the era's double standard, rock & roll evidence suggests that gender roles were evolving in the early 60s. The sheer number of women singers shows that female voices and perspectives were becoming more prominent in Kennedy's America. Women singers—either solo artists or members of groups—accounted for 16 percent of the Top 40 hits on the national pop charts in 1960. By 1963 they were responsible for 34 percent of all Top 40 hits. To put those figures in perspective, in 1973 when the Women's Liberation Movement was celebrating *Roe v. Wade,* women singers appeared on only 21 percent of the Top 40 hits on the *Billboard* charts.[40]

Women who voiced strong opinions were fixtures on the early 60s record charts, as evidenced by the success of Connie Francis, Brenda Lee, Lesley Gore, Mary Travers, and Mary Wells, as well as the Shirelles, Ronettes, and other girl groups. Numerous songs featured independent, young women. The obvious example is Lesley Gore's "You Don't Own Me," which debuted on the charts on December 28, 1963, and by February 1 was the number 2 hit in the country, topped only by the Beatles' phenomenal "I Want to Hold Your Hand."

Some songs, including the Shirelles' "Tonight's the Night" (1960) and Anita Bryant's "Wonderland by Night" (1961), made it clear that teenage boys weren't the only ones interested in sex. Bryant's vocal rendition of Bert Kaempfert's instrumental is particularly interesting. Although it lacked the lush instrumentation of Kaempfert's number 1 record, it still became a Top 20 hit, possibly because of the suggestive lyrics written by African American songwriter Lincoln Chase (best known for composing LaVern Baker's 1957 R&B rock hit "Jim Dandy"). Surprisingly, Bryant's record avoided censorship, maybe because the extremely religious Bryant had a squeaky-clean image and was second runner-up in the 1959 Miss America pageant. Ironically, her "good girl" image made the lyrics she sang even more striking. The first verse describes a young couple sitting under a moonlit sky with stars twinkling overhead. When they kiss, they realize they might be heading for trouble. One thing leads to another until heaven welcomes the couple to "paradise, blessing our love." When the sun rises, the young woman is still in rapture as she recalls the night before when "love decided to unite you and I." The last line of the song features Bryant singing joyfully about "our wonderland by night" as a sexy-sounding trumpet brings the song to a climax.[41] Bryant's record might have been more pop than rock, but the suggestive lyrics were as hot as any rock & roll song on the radio.

Hits on the *Billboard* charts often showcased determined women who did not suffer male fools lightly. Mary Wells's "You Beat Me to the Punch" (1962) featured a young woman who overcomes the accepted norms for gender relationships when she takes charge and dumps her unfaithful boyfriend. Sometimes just the sound of a record suggested that women were gaining ground in the battle of the sexes. Jackie DeShannon's "Needles and Pins" (1963) offered an aggressive vocal and hard rock sound that stood out from the polished pop rock hits of most female singers. Powered by electric guitars, banging drums, foreboding horns, and in-your-face lyrics, it builds to a powerful conclusion as the young woman in the song eagerly anticipates revenge against her ex-boyfriend. She knows she should forgive him, but she wants him to feel the identical pain he caused her—those same "needles and pins a-hurtin' him."[42]

Rock & roll evidence proves that gender expectations were also changing for guys. Macho men were starting to give way to more sensitive ones. Young males revealed their loneliness on Dion's "Lonely Teenager" (1960) and the Videls' "Mr. Lonely" (1960). They confessed to shyness on Bobby Vee's "Bashful Bob" (1961). And, they opted to be kind, gentle, and respectful toward young women on hits like James Darren's "Conscience" (1962).

Young men on other records admitted to shedding tears (although gender etiquette, not to mention male egos, demanded they cry where nobody could see them). They cried tears on their pillows or stepped outside on starry nights. The guy on Harold Dorman's 1960 hit "Mountain of Love" got creative and

climbed up a mountain after his girl left him for another guy. "Teardrops fallin'
down a mountainside," he sings, "many times I've been here, many times I've
cried."[43] The crying technique-of-choice on most hits was for guys to simply hide
their tears by going outside in a rainstorm, for example in Dee Clark's "Raindrops" (1961), Del Shannon's "Runaway" (1961), and the Everly Brothers' "Crying in the Rain" (1962).

A few guys openly confessed to crying on songs like Roy Orbison's "Crying"
(1961), Bobby Vee's "Please Don't Ask About Barbara" (1962), and the Crickets' "Teardrops Fall Like Rain" (1963). Orbison's song about love gone wrong
was particularly impressive. The last 50 seconds of the tragic ballad are pure
rock & roll opera. As Roy's voice climbs higher and higher, intense backup
singers, driving guitars, pounding drums, and soaring violins add to the drama.
The powerful climax features the emotional Orbison singing, "Yes, now you're
gone. And from this moment on, I'll be crying . . . Yeah, cry-ing. Cry-ing . . . Oh-
oh-oh-ver YOU!"[44] Listeners were left in awe if not on the verge of tears. Teenage girls—as well as teenage boys—came away knowing that if Roy Orbison
could cry over love gone wrong, so could they.

Rock & roll and other songs heard on *American Bandstand* and Top 40 radio
reflected and helped shape youth culture of the early 1960s. The music created
shared memories for millions of teenagers in high school in the early 1960s. Hits
from that era—"Quarter to Three," "Runaround Sue," "Hit the Road Jack," "Surfin'
U.S.A.," "Soldier Boy," "It's My Party," even "Teen Angel"—aren't just "oldies" or
ephemeral bits of nostalgia. They are important musical markers in the history of
a generation. They have talismanic power to recall specific events, people, places,
and days gone by.

Although a half century has passed, many charter members of the baby
boom generation can still remember the music's quality, vitality and power.
"Fifty-nine, '60, '61, '62, '63," wrote Bruce Springsteen in his autobiography, "the
beautiful sounds of American popular music. The calm before the storm of Kennedy's assassination, a quiet America of lost lovers' laments wafting along the
airwaves."[45]

11

"This Magic Moment"

Rock & Roll in Kennedy's America

In 1960 John F. Kennedy defeated Richard Nixon to become the youngest elected president in American history. That same year an R&B rock group named the Drifters scored a Top 20 hit with "This Magic Moment." Produced by Jerry Leiber and Mike Stoller, the record begins with the ethereal sound of violins. Suddenly, the Drifters jump in, describing a special moment that started with a kiss. It was "so different and so new," sings the Drifters' Ben E. King. "I knew that you felt it too, by the look in your eyes."

Although the song dealt with young love, it could just as easily serve as a metaphor for a time when teenagers, rock & roll, and America were still innocent and confident about the future. The early 60s witnessed Kennedy's "brief shining moment," as well as a "magic moment" for the baby boom generation and rock & roll. The first wave of baby boomers entered high school in 1960, and for most of the next four years they shared good times and high hopes set to a rock & roll soundtrack that featured some of the music's greatest songs and singers. Until November 22, 1963, optimistic teenagers had every reason to believe the Drifters when they sang, "This magic moment will last forever 'til the end of time."[1]

Ironically, early 60s rock & roll was soon forgotten by most fans and music experts. Common wisdom now maintains that rock & roll was moribund after Buddy Holly's death on February 3, 1959—"the day the music died"—and wasn't resuscitated until the Beatles came along in 1964.

This book rejects the myth of rock & roll's demise and restores early 60s rock & roll to its rightful place in the spotlight. It shows that the early 60s comprise a unique and important chapter in rock & roll history. Not only was the music excellent and innovative, but early 60s rock & roll was in tune with the times. It reflected and shaped baby boomers' actions and attitudes, as well as America's Cold War culture. Of course, that leads to an obvious question: *If early 60s rock & roll was really that good then why was it so quickly discredited and discarded?* The answer lies in all the tumult and change that transformed America between the mid-1960s and the early 1970s.

THE MYTH OF ROCK & ROLL'S DEMISE

A Bob Dylan song from 1964 captured the uneasy mood of a nation on the threshold of major social, cultural, and political change. "There's a battle outside and it is ragin'," he sang. "It'll soon shake your windows and rattle your walls for the times they are a-changin.'"[2] The inexorable forces described in Dylan's seminal recording erupted in the turbulent era commonly known as "the sixties."

Early 60s rock & roll was one of the first victims of the anti-establishment mood that gained momentum in the mid- to late 1960s. The music's reputation came crashing down as a tsunami of social change swept over America. The first wave hit on November 22, 1963. All that came before President Kennedy's assassination suddenly seemed distant and no longer relevant. Post-assassination America quickly moved in new directions to distance itself from the shock of November 22. JFK's successor, Lyndon Johnson, announced an ambitious political agenda involving civil rights and a War on Poverty, which he insisted would be a fitting tribute to the fallen president.

Baby boomers seeking shelter from the horror of November 22 got help from an unexpected source. The Beatles debuted on the American pop charts on January 18, 1964 (although bootlegs of "I Want to Hold Your Hand" and other Beatles' songs were played on several US stations just three weeks after Kennedy's murder). The British group offered American teenagers a fresh sound, different style, and new identity just when they needed it most. In the youth culture's darkest hour, the Beatles lit the way, providing comfort, escape, and hope for the future.

Significantly, the Beatles were more than just talented rock stars. They were "cultural revitalization figures" who helped rescue America's dispirited youth culture. Anthropologist Anthony F.C. Wallace defined cultural revitalization figures as leaders of a "deliberate, organized, conscious effort ... to construct a more satisfying culture." Throughout history, these figures were usually religious or political leaders. For example, John Wesley (early Methodism), Wovoka (the Ghost Dance), and Lenin (the Russian Revolution) appeared in times of need to revive a deteriorating culture. The Beatles extend Wallace's theory to pop culture. They arrived in America when many young people were suffering from high stress and cultural disillusionment. The British band offered hope and revitalized the youth culture through new sounds and styles. Beatles fan Dan Sawers never forgot the group's impact on his life. "John Lennon meant more to me than John or Bobby Kennedy," he said. "He influenced my hair style, thoughts, values, musical tastes, and molded my adolescent years. Because of him, I even learned how to play the guitar."[3]

The coming of the Beatles changed American music forevermore. Prior to late 1963, almost every artist on the *Billboard* charts was American, one more sign of US hegemony after World War II. The notion that foreigners could credibly perform American rock & roll was inconceivable. But then came JFK's death. Afterward, American teenagers were desperate for distractions and new approaches.

The Beatles and other British rock & rollers with their different look, distinct style, innovative sound, and upbeat harmonies offered a new way forward for troubled American youths. Within weeks, many rock & roll stars who had been fixtures on the record charts prior to Kennedy's death were swept away by the British Rock Invasion. Established American artists with their pop-influenced songs backed by orchestral arrangements suddenly seemed less authentic than the Merseybeat of the Beatles, Rolling Stones, Dave Clark Five, Kinks, and other self-contained bands powered by electric guitars and drums. Even the clean-cut good looks, neatly combed hairdos, and preppie sweaters favored by Frankie Avalon, Bobby Rydell, and most American rock & rollers gave way to the mop top haircuts and Mod look of British rockers.

Unable to keep pace with the rapid musical and cultural changes swirling around after JFK's assassination, many American rock & rollers were cast off as remnants of the "old" youth culture and replaced by the Beatles and other British artists who offered fresh sounds and images to a "new" American youth culture desperate for a new beginning. The shift in musical tastes was often abrupt. Many top American rock & roll stars saw their careers implode after the British Rock Invasion hit in 1964. For example:

Fats Domino: Top 30 hits (1955–63): 29
                Top 30 hits (after 1963): 0
Duane Eddy: Top 30 hits (1958–63): 12
                Top 30 hits (after 1963): 0
Brenda Lee: Top 30 hits (1960–63): 19
                Top 30 hits (after 1963): 4
Bobby Rydell: Top 30 hits (1959–63): 19
                Top 30 hits (after 1963): 0

The death of Kennedy and birth of the Beatles were not the only things that undermined early 60s rock & roll. After 1963 the pace of social change increased exponentially as wave after wave of political and cultural upheaval swept across the land. When the optimism of Kennedy's America gave way to increasing violence, social unrest, and polarization over civil rights, Vietnam, the counterculture, and myriad culture wars, the early 60s became just a quaint memory. Kennedy's Camelot was clearly a thing of the past, and early 60s rock & roll with its innocence, hope, and support for the New Frontier seemed just as dated. In the midst of protests over war, human rights, and other serious concerns, rock & roll of the early 60s appeared naive and out of step with the darker times.

As the first cohort of baby boomers entered college in the fall of 1964, the songs they had listened to in high school seemed terribly out of place in post-JFK America. The times were a-changin', and so was the youth culture. Upbeat songs about the Twist, hot rods, teen romance, and youthful fads gave way to more "relevant" music. After 1964, songs by the Beatles, Rolling Stones, and other British bands were a better fit for America's evolving youth culture. Other styles also seemed more current. Motown and soul music echoed changes in the civil rights movement. Folk-rock offered sophisticated lyrics about war, society, and culture. And the psychedelic music of the counterculture promoted peace and universal brotherhood, as well as changing attitudes toward sex, drugs, and rock & roll. Not surprisingly, college-age baby boomers discarded the teenage sounds and styles of early 60s rock & roll as readily as they had gotten rid of high school rings, letter sweaters, and yearbooks.

Even the aesthetics of youth-oriented music changed rapidly in the mid- to late 1960s, resulting in more refined sounds that made early rock & roll seem less significant by comparison. In 1969 art historian Carl Belz published *The Story of Rock*. The pioneering study suggested that between 1964 and 1968 *rock & roll* evolved into *rock music*, a higher art form. "The music has revealed a growing sophistication," wrote Belz. "[It] has been manifested in the broadened range in the subject matter of rock lyrics and in the increasing concern with rock's own artistic tradition." Belz added, "Rock's growing awareness of art means it has begun to elicit comparisons with the contemporary fine arts, not only music, but poetry, painting, and theater."[4] As rock's artistic reputation soared, the reputation of early 60s rock & roll plummeted. By the decade's end many rock critics and fans were dismissing early 60s rock & roll as inconsequential pop music.

Making matters worse, the counterculture of the late 1960s and early 70s condemned early 60s rock & roll as contrived and part of the Establishment. Pat Boone noticed a discernible change in attitudes as the Vietnam War, campus protests, and civil unrest picked up momentum. "It was a really turbulent time," he explains. "Kids were just becoming more and more independent and that turned to outright rebellion and rejection of all the guidelines from the past." As a result, established rock & roll figures like Pat and Dick Clark came under fire because they were seen as part of the Establishment. "Dick and I were still living [and looking] like we [always] had," he explains. "We were subtly out of fashion."[5]

The tumultuous events of the mid- to late 1960s and the hurricane-force winds of change that were sweeping across America combined to discredit early 60s rock & roll. America's youth culture had traveled light years since the death of JFK. As baby boomers entered a new decade in the 1970s, the music and culture of the early 60s seemed long ago and far away. The notion that rock & roll was moribund prior to the coming of the Beatles took root. A number 1 record that became a cultural phenomenon in 1971–72 helped transform the growing myth of rock & roll's death into common wisdom.

BAD NEWS ON THE DOORSTEP

On a cold February morning in 1959, a young boy was delivering newspapers on his route in New Rochelle, New York. Suddenly, a headline about a plane crash caught his eye and stopped him in his tracks. Twelve years later, his haunting recollection of that startling news would provide the backdrop for a number 1 hit that became a pop culture phenomenon.

In 1971 the former paperboy, Don McLean, was a promising 26-year-old folk singer. An avid music lover interested in the world around him, he hit on the idea of writing a song that could connect the dots between baby boomers, rock & roll, and the changing times. "American Pie" was released as a single on October 24, 1971. Within weeks, it became the top selling record in the country and a major hit around the world.[6]

Unlike most hits, which were shorter than 3 minutes, "American Pie" came in at an epic 8 minutes and 36 seconds. The ambitious tale was a musical tapestry of rock & roll allusions, baby boom benchmarks, and cultural history. Audiences listened intently as the modern-day troubadour took them on a magical, folk-rock mystery tour that recreated the baby boom experience of growing up in 1950s and 60s America. Deciphering McLean's lyrics became the latest craze as fans argued endlessly about the song's hidden meanings and fascinating cast of characters. Did they recall the Book of Love? Who were the King and Queen? The Jester? And, the Father, Son, and Holy Ghost? Or, could they identify the quartet practicing in the park? Audiences might not be able to figure out all the details, but the big picture was clear. "American Pie" described the coming of age of a young generation, as well as the end of innocence for both rock & roll and baby boomers.

McLean's musical puzzle became a baby boom anthem. It begins with the singer-songwriter remembering how he felt when he learned about Buddy Holly's death back in 1959. He was 13 years old and delivering newspapers. As he tossed one onto a doorstep, a headline about the plane crash caught his eye. "I can't remember if I cried when I read about his widowed bride," he explains in the song, "but something touched me deep inside the day the music died." Following the poignant first verse, the singer takes listeners on a whirlwind musical journey through baby boom history with nostalgic references to rock & roll stars, legendary hits, high school record hops, junior proms, favorite TV shows, late 60s protests, the counterculture, and more.[7]

"American Pie" became an instant cultural phenomenon. The reaction "was electric. Just electric," explains McLean. "It was some kind of weird energy around the song the minute it came out." Both the single and the accompanying album (which was dedicated to Buddy Holly) shot up to number 1 on the *Billboard* charts in 1972. The single remained on the charts for nineteen weeks, while the album was a fixture for almost a year. The song's intriguing lyrics and memorable refrain, "Bye-bye, Miss American Pie," struck a responsive chord among baby boomers who shared McLean's generational memories. Like the singer, these listeners felt "out of luck" on "the day the music died." The song "is clearly an elegy for something that once was and it speaks to the spirit of a people who are changing, people who see a shifting of the cultural landscape," explains English professor Robert McPartland. "A hopeful world is vanishing, a dream has come undone."[8]

"American Pie" became one of the most celebrated songs of all time. In a survey of the top songs of the twentieth century cosponsored in 2001 by the National Endowment for the Arts and the Recording Industry Association of America, "American Pie" came in at number 5 (topped only by "Over the Rainbow," "White Christmas," "This Land Is Your Land," and "Respect"). The iconic song was inducted into the Grammy Hall of Fame in 2002. And, in 2016 "American Pie" was added to the Library of Congress's National Recording Registry, which includes "culturally, historically, or aesthetically significant" recordings.

En route to its extraordinary commercial and artistic success, "American Pie" etched into the public imagination a specific connection between the death of Buddy Holly and the end of early rock & roll. McLean's memorable line—"the day the music died"—became shorthand for the theory that authentic rock & roll no longer existed in the early 1960s.

FROM MYTH TO COMMON WISDOM

Critics, scholars, and fans hammered the final nails into the music's coffin. "Many followers of rock 'n' roll history believe that the true spirit of the music died in the late fifties," explains writer Alan Betrock, "and that the first few years of the sixties were filled with mechanized and bleached pap heralded by the arrival of the so-called 'teen idols.'" Music scholar Reebee Garafalo took it a step further, dismissing the music of the late 1950s and early 60s as "schlock rock." "In a few short years," he says, "rock 'n' roll had degenerated from Sam Phillips's dream of a white man who could sing black to a white high-school kid who couldn't sing at all."[9]

Larry Lehmer makes a similar argument in his book *The Day the Music Died* (even the title accepts the myth of rock & roll's demise): "The plane crash that killed Buddy Holly, Ritchie Valens, and J. P. Richardson was one of a series of events that saw rock 'n' roll turn away from its roots toward a more slickly packaged product." Historian Glenn Altschuler agrees. "Between 1958 and 1963, rock 'n' roll faltered," explains Altschuler. The music industry in those years "created a commercially viable ersatz rock 'n' roll."[10]

The twin pillars of the rock & roll establishment—*Rolling Stone* and the Rock & Roll Hall of Fame—added to the myth that rock & roll died in 1959 and would not be resuscitated until after the Beatles arrived on the scene. "There are few dates that can be clearly pinpointed as turning points in rock & roll," writes Greg Shaw in the *Rolling Stone Illustrated History of Rock & Roll.* "One would be February 3, 1959, when Buddy Holly died, and with him, at least symbolically, rock & roll's first rush of breathless innocence."[11]

The Hall of Fame's actions spoke louder than critics' words. In comparison to other eras in rock & roll history, few artists from the early 60s have been enshrined in the Hall. Indeed, the absence of many important and highly successful singers from those years is nothing short of staggering. Among the overlooked are Pat Boone, Paul Anka, Connie Francis, Neil Sedaka, Chubby Checker, Lesley Gore, Gary "U.S." Bonds, Bobby Rydell, Frankie Avalon, Tommy Roe, Johnny Tillotson, the Chiffons, Fleetwoods, Crystals, and Bobby Vee, to name just a few. They all had numerous hit records and were viewed by fans as rock & roll singers.

Yet, they have been dismissed as lesser talents or mere "pop singers" by many critics and the Hall of Fame.

By the twenty-first century, the myth of early rock & roll's passing was firmly in place. In 2009 CNN commemorated the fiftieth anniversary of the tragic plane crash that took the lives of Buddy Holly, Ritchie Valens, and the Big Bopper with this report: "The event has echoed through rock 'n' roll history for 50 years, representing, if not the end of rock 'n' roll itself, the close of an era, the end of the first bloom of rock anarchy and innovation. 'It was like a curtain coming down,' said Terry Stewart, president of the Rock and Roll Hall of Fame and Museum."[12]

ROCK & ROLL LIVES!

The myth of rock & roll's demise recalls Mark Twain's response to a popular rumor about his alleged passing in 1897. Uncertain if he was more amused or annoyed, the writer supposedly quipped, "The reports of my death are greatly exaggerated."[13] The same can be said of early 60s rock & roll. Contrary to popular belief, rock & roll was very much alive after 1959. The music was vibrant and closely linked to the needs and interests of baby boomers.

The early 60s—as many devoted fans and music scholars know—witnessed some of the top artists and greatest hits in rock & roll history. Even just a quick glance at the record charts and radio playlists of that era underscores the quality and diversity of the music. The rock & roll songs featured on Top 40 radio included traditional doo-wop, rockabilly, instrumentals, and ballads, as well as innovative sounds and styles like surf music, Motown, Brill Building-influenced pop rock, soul music, dance fads, and Phil Spector's Wall of Sound. In addition, Top 40 radio exposed teenagers to other types of music, including pop, jazz, country, and folk music.

The importance of early 60s rock & roll, however, goes beyond just the quality of the music. As a nontraditional source of history, the music reveals important evidence about Kennedy's America that scholars might otherwise miss. Songs capture the rhythms of everyday life, including details about politics, work, school, fashions, fads, products, cars, movies, TV, and other aspects of American life and thought.

Rock & roll offers fresh perspectives about social change in post–World War II America. Hit records, concerts, and other aspects of the music business add to our understanding of race and ethnicity in the 1950s and early 60s. Rock & roll demonstrates that minorities had taken significant steps toward equality and integration years before most of the seminal events typically described in US history books occurred. The music also provides insights about gender attitudes during the Kennedy years. Hit songs reveal that many young women were dissatisfied with the era's cult of domesticity. With the help of rock & roll, they were having "click moments" long before Betty Friedan published *The Feminine Mystique*, the book often viewed as launching the modern women's movement.

In addition, rock & roll offers fresh evidence and insights about youth culture in Kennedy's America. Hit records detail young listeners' hopes, dreams, and fears. They offer compelling evidence that teenagers and rock & roll were not as rebellious as common wisdom has it. "I was there [in the 1950s and early 60s]," says country rocker Brenda Lee. "It was just kids coming to shows identifying with a person that was finally their own age who was singing music that they liked and was exciting and fun." These kids weren't rebellious, she insists, "They were just having fun."[14]

Early rock & roll reflected the era's conformity and consensus behavior at least as much as conflict or rebellion. For many baby boomers, rock & roll was neither a revolutionary force nor the means to express generational conflict. It was simply their popular music, more a sign of consensus between the generations than conflict. Rock & roll demonstrates that America's Cold War culture was more broadly based than previously thought and that baby boomers shared the dominant culture's attitudes toward politics, consumerism, religion, race, ethnicity, gender, and class. Although seeds of change and generational conflict were being planted in the early 60s, the notorious Generation Gap would not open until later in the decade.

Rock & Roll in Kennedy's America recalls an exciting and important time for the music and the nation. In the early 60s the United States enjoyed unprecedented prosperity, power, and prestige and was on track to fulfill its destiny in what was being called "the American Century." Most baby boomers and rock & roll shared the era's optimism.

Early 60s rock & roll doesn't fade from view until Kennedy's America does. The turning point came on November 22, 1963. The bullets that took John F. Kennedy's life also shattered America's innocence. The nation, baby boomers, and rock & roll would never be the same. After 1963 America seemed to change overnight as it plunged into a national nightmare fraught with violence over Vietnam, the counterculture, race, gender, ethnicity, class, and numerous culture wars.

But, for "one brief shining moment" in the early 60s, both President Kennedy and American youth were riding high. No wonder many people who lived through that era still smile knowingly whenever they hear the Drifters sing "This Magic Moment."

Acknowledgments

The research for this book began years ago when I was a history professor at Ball State University and wrote and hosted NPR's *Rock & Roll America*. That weekly program would not have happened without the help and support of University Provost Warren Vander Hill and a talented production team at Ball State's public radio station that included executive producer Stewart Vanderwilt, producer/engineer Stan Sollars, and assistant producer Brian Eckstein. The show began on Indiana Public Radio and later ran for two seasons on NPR and NPR Worldwide. Not in our wildest dreams back then could we have predicted that one day the entire series would be archived in the Rock & Roll Hall of Fame and Museum (see https://library.rockhall.com/ld.php?content_id=55828914).

Rock & Roll America provided me with the resources and opportunities to interview approximately 60 key players from rock & roll's first decade, including singers, musicians, songwriters, producers, and disc jockeys. Portions of many of those exclusive interviews along with others I have conducted are being published for the first time in this book. I am extremely grateful to all the interviewees noted at the end of the book and in the notes. Their valuable insights and new details about the music and the times add considerably to our knowledge of early 1960s rock & roll.

I'd also like to thank everyone at Johns Hopkins University Press for their many contributions during the publication process, particularly history acquisitions editor Laura Davulis and assistant acquisitions editor Ezra Rodriguez. Special thanks go to my literary agent, Christopher Rogers, who provided excellent advice and helped my idea for a book become a reality.

Over the decades, friends have added to my understanding of the power and significance of rock & roll. Ken and Trudy Feltges often served as sounding boards for my ideas about history, popular culture, and rock & roll. Jim Meighan helped broaden my musical tastes. And Dan Sawers has been on a rock & roll journey with me through parts of two centuries. Both of us have come a long way since the days of "Hark, Is That a Cannon I Hear?"

My family has made this book possible and worthwhile. My brother Phil was there from the very beginning and never let me forget what real rock & roll was. On the other side of the generational divide, my son Stephen and his wife, Meredith, and my daughter Valerie and her husband, Jeff, are constant reminders about the most important things in life. And, my grandchildren—Katherine and Esther—offer joyful opportunities for me to introduce the next generation to that old-time rock & roll. My deepest gratitude goes to my wife, Marie. Her constant support, faith in this project, and superb editing contributed greatly to the book. For all of that and more, *Rock & Roll in Kennedy's America* is dedicated to her.

Interviews

AUTHOR INTERVIEWS CONDUCTED *for*
NATIONAL PUBLIC RADIO'S *ROCK & ROLL AMERICA*

Jerry Allison (Crickets) (January 5, 1999)

Dave Bartholomew (Fats Domino's producer and co-writer) (July 2, 1998)

Pat Boone (June 12 and 25, 1998)

Tony Butala (Lettermen) (February 17, 1998)

Dick Clark (August 4, 1998)

Dick Dale (July 2, 1998)

Bo Diddley (January 21, 1998)

Dion (October 19, 1995)

Duane Eddy (August 12, 1998)

Snuff Garrett (Producer) (March 13, 1998)

Bob Gaudio (October 1999)

Casey Kasem (November 25, 1996)

Brenda Lee (October 17, 1995)

Peggy March (March, 1998)

Don McLean (January 18, 1999)

Jim Pash (Surfaris) (July 27, 1998)

Johnny Preston (January 1998)

Martha Reeves (March 8, 1998)

Pete Seeger (May 13, 1994)

Tom Shannon (Deejay) (June 17, 1998)

Bob Spickard (Chantays) (August 12, 1998)

Ray Stevens (February 5, 1999)

Johnny Tillotson (January 21, 1998)

Mary Travers (October 8 and 9, 1998)

Bobby Vee (February 14, 1995)

ADDITIONAL AUTHOR INTERVIEWS

Artie Butler (Producer) (June 12, 2017)

Bobby Rydell (August 6, 2013)

Jay Siegel (Tokens) (May 2, 2018)

Bobby Vee (October 17, 1990 and July 25, 2006)

Notes

INTRODUCTION

1. Jay and the Americans, "Only in America" (United Artists, 1964). Composers: Leiber and Stoller.

2. Jerry Leiber and Mike Stoller with David Ritz, *Hound Dog: The Leiber and Stoller Autobiography* (New York: Simon & Schuster, 2009), 175, 176.

3. Richard Aquila, interview with Bobby Vee (October 17, 1990).

4. Numbers are based on data from the National Center for Health Statistics, https://www.cdc.gov/nchs/data/statab/natfinal2003.annvol1_01.pdf (accessed June 27, 2021).

5. Landon Y. Jones, *Great Expectations: America and the Baby Boom Generation* (New York: Ballantine Books, 1981), 2, 3, and chapters 1 and 2; Frank Friedel and Alan Brinkley, *America in the Twentieth Century* (New York: Knopf, 1982), 388; Douglas T. Miller and Marion Nowak, *The Fifties: The Way We Really Were* (New York: Doubleday, 1975), 270.

6. Richard Mabey quoted in R. Serge Denisoff, *Solid Gold: The Popular Record Industry* (New Brunswick, NJ: Transaction Books, 1975), 30.

7. Richard Aquila, interview with Dion for NPR's *Rock & Roll America* (October 19, 1995).

8. Dick Hebdige, *Subculture: The Meaning of Style* (New York: Methuen Books, 1979); Dick Clark and Richard Robinson, *Rock, Roll, and Remember* (New York: Popular Library, 1978), 191.

9. Jones, *Great Expectations*, 72.

CHAPTER 1. "IT'S NOW OR NEVER"

1. *Elvis: Commemorative Edition* (Lincolnwood, IL: Publications International, 2002), 134, 135; Jerry Hopkins, *Elvis: A Biography* (New York: Warner, 1971), 253–57; Ernst Jorgensen, *Elvis Presley: A Life in Music—The Complete Recording Sessions* (New York: St. Martin's Press, 1998), 119.

2. Peter Guralnick, *Careless Love: The Unmaking of Elvis Presley* (Boston: Back Bay Books, 1999), 59–63; Jorgensen, *Elvis Presley*, 121–23.

3. Jorgensen, *Elvis Presley*, 126.

4. Elizabeth McKeon and Linda Everett, *Elvis Speaks: Thoughts on Fame, Family, Music, and More in His Own Words* (Nashville: Cumberland House, 1997), 93.

5. *Elvis: Commemorative Edition*, 138–41

6. Jerry Osborne, *Elvis: Word for Word* (New York: Gramercy Books, 1999), 156–57; *Elvis: Commemorative Edition*, 137.

7. *Elvis: Commemorative Edition*, 145.

8. Ibid., 138.

9. See Kerry Segrave, *Payola in the Music Industry: A History, 1880–1991* (Jefferson, NC: McFarland, 1994).

10. Richard Allen Schwartz, *Cold War Culture: Media and the Arts, 1945–1990* (New York: Facts on File, 1997), 338, 322, 323.

11. John A. Jackson, *Big Beat Heat: Alan Freed and the Early Years of Rock & Roll* (New York: Schirmer, 1991), 243; Marc Fisher, *Something in the Air: Radio, Rock, and the Revolution That Shaped a Generation* (New York: Random House, 2007), 82.

12. Fisher, *Something in the Air*, 82; David Szatmary, *A Time to Rock: A Social History of Rock 'N' Roll* (New York: Schirmer, 1996), 67, 68; Jackson, *Big Beat Heat*, 244.

13. *Variety* quoted in Glenn C. Altschuler, *All Shook Up: How Rock 'N' Roll Changed America* (New York: Oxford University Press, 2003), 146.

14. Altschuler, *All Shook Up*, 144–49; Jackson, *Big Beat Heat*, 252.

15. Jackson, *Big Beat Heat*, 246–50, 253–60, 280; Fisher, *Something in the Air*, 86–91.

16. Fisher, *Something in the Air*, 89.

17. Fisher, *Something in the Air*, 82, 83; Dick Clark and Richard Robinson, *Rock, Roll, & Remember* (New York: Popular Library, 1976), 254, 255; Jackson, *Big Beat Heat*, 285.

18. John A. Jackson, *American Bandstand: Dick Clark and the Making of a Rock 'N' Roll Empire* (New York: Oxford University Press, 1997), 168–90; Clark, *Rock, Roll, & Remember*, 271–92; Altschuler, *All Shook Up*, 153, 154.

19. Altschuler, *All Shook Up*, 147–49; Jackson, *Big Beat Heat*, 256, 263, 264, 265, 271, 274, 275.

20. Fisher, *Something in the Air*, 91; Jackson, *Big Beat Heat*, 256, 263, 264, 315; Altschuler, *All Shook Up*, 149–51.

21. Altschuler, *All Shook Up*, 149.

22. Fisher, *Something in the Air*, 91; Jackson, *Big Beat Heat*, 293, 294, 297–99, 301, 302, 308, 312, 315.

23. See Altschuler, *All Shook Up*, 161; Fisher, *Something in the Air*, 91–93; Alan Betrock in Paul Friedlander, *Rock and Roll: A Social History* (Boulder, CO: Westview Press, 1996), 70, 71; Robert Christgau in John A. Jackson, *Big Beat Heat*, 333.

24. Clark, *Rock, Roll, & Remember*, 140.

25. Michael Uslan and Bruce Solomon, *Dick Clark's The First 25 Years of Rock & Roll* (New York: Greenwich House, 1981), 89–92; Clark, *Rock, Roll, & Remember*, 137–38.

26. Jeff Tamarkin, "The Cameo Parkway Story," included with CD box set, *Cameo Parkway, 1957–1967* (ABKCO Industries, 2005), 7; Clark, *Rock, Roll & Remember*, 138–40.

27. Jackson, *American Bandstand*, 216; Joe Smith, *Off the Record: An Oral History of Popular Music* (New York: Warner Books, 1988), 107.

28. Clark, *Rock, Roll, & Remember*, 140; Jackson, *American Bandstand*, 207.

29. Bob Shannon and John Javna, *Behind the Hits: Inside Stories of Classic Pop and Rock and Roll* (New York: Warner Books, 1986), 98; Linda Martin and Kerry Segrave, *Anti-Rock: The Opposition to Rock 'n' Roll* (New York: Da Capo, 1993), 103.

30. Wolfe quoted in Larry Getlin, "A Mob Tale with a TWIST," *New York Post*, November 11, 2012, http://nypost.com/2012/11/11/a-mob-tale-with-a-twist/ (accessed July 25, 2017); Checker quoted in Smith, *Off the Record*, 196.

31. Jack Doyle, "Jackie & The Twist: First Lady History," *PopHistoryDig.com*, June 20, 2016, http://www.pophistorydig.com/topics/jackie-kennedy-the-twist/ (accessed July 25, 2017).

32. "Chubby Checker Interview," Library of Congress, October 30, 2015, https://www.loc.gov/programs/static/national-recording-preservation-board/documents/ChubbyChecker Interview.pdf (accessed July 28, 2017).

33. "Chubby Checker Interview," Library of Congress; Gabriel and the Angels, "Don't Wanna Twist No-More" (Swan, 1962). Composer: Kellis.

34. Joel Selvin, John Johnson Jr., and Dick Cami, *Peppermint Twist: The Mob, the Music, and the Most Famous Dance Club of the '60s* (New York: Thomas Dunne, 2012), 186.

35. The Silhouettes, "Get a Job" (Ember Records, 1958). Composers: Lewis and the Silhouettes.

36. Little Anthony and the Imperials, "Shimmy, Shimmy, Ko-Ko-Bop" (End, 1960). Composer: Smith.

37. Other memorable neo-doo-wop hits include: the Temptations "Barbara" (1960); Regents "Barbara Ann" (1961); Jarmels "A Little Bit of Soap" (1961); and Volumes "I Love You" (1962).

38. Ernie Maresca, "Shout! Shout! (Knock Yourself Out)" (Seville, 1962). Composers: Maresca and Bogdany.

39. The Rivingtons, "Papa-Oom-Mow-Mow" (Liberty, 1962). Composers: Frazier, White, Wilson Jr., and Harris.

40. Little Caesar and the Romans, "Those Oldies But Goodies" (Del-Fi, 1961). Composers: Politi and Curinga.

41. Mark Voger, "Jay Siegel of the Tokens Interview," *NJ.Com*, November 26, 2010, http://www.nj.com/entertainment/index.ssf/2010/11/jay_siegel_of_the_tokens_inter.html (accessed April 28, 2018).

42. Margo's quote comes from Kyler, "He's in Town: An Interview with Phil Margo," *Rare Rockin' Records*, May 23, 2011, https://rarerockinrecords.blogspot.com/2011/05/hes-in-town-interview-with-phil-margo.html (accessed April 27, 2018).

43. Voger, "Jay Siegel of the Tokens Interview"; Richard Aquila, interview with Jay Siegel (May 2, 2018).

44. Aquila, interview with Jay Siegel; Chris Wolf, "The Lion King Himself: Jay Siegel," *Penobscot Bay Pilot*, April 29, 2013, http://www.penbaypilot.com/article/lion-king-himself-jay-siegel/13322 (accessed April 30, 2018).

45. Aquila, interview with Jay Siegel.

46. Linda's original recording is available on YouTube, https://www.youtube.com/watch?v=mrrQT4WkbNE (accessed May 1, 2018); Rian Malan, "In the Jungle: Inside the Long, Hidden Genealogy of 'The Lion Sleeps Tonight,'" *Rolling Stone*, May 14, 2000, https://www.rollingstone.com/music/features/the-lion-sleeps-tonight-genealogy-what-you-dont-know-w474059 (accessed April 27, 2018).

47. Bill DeMain and Lydia Hutchinson, "The Story of Solomon Linda and The Lion Sleeps Tonight," *Performing Songwriter* 95, (July/August 2006), http://performingsongwriter.com/lion-sleeps-tonight (accessed April 27, 2018).

48. Malan, "In the Jungle;" DeMain and Hutchinson, "The Story of Solomon Linda." Following Linda's death in 1962, music publishers avoided payments to the singer's family. In 2006, the courts finally awarded Linda's three surviving daughters millions of dollars in royalties dating back to 1987.

49. Aquila, interview with Jay Siegel.

50. Barry Mann, "Who Put the Bomp" (ABC-Paramount, 1961). Songwriters: Mann and Goffin. In 1963 two other records focused on the doo-wop genre: Johnny Cymbal, "Mr. Bassman," and Lou Christie, "Mr. Tenor Man."

51. Gabriel and the Angels, "That's Life (That's Tough)" (Swan, 1962). Songwriter: Kellis.

52. Richard Aquila, interview with Bobby Vee (October 17, 1990); Paul Freeman, "The Shirelles . . . Interview with Founding Member Beverly Lee," *Pop Culture Classics*, October 2011, http://popcultureclassics.com/shirelles.html (accessed July 22, 2021).

53. Gene Chandler, "Duke of Earl" (Vee-Jay, 1962). Composers: Dixon, Edwards, and Williams.

CHAPTER 2. "WHAT DOES A GIRL DO?"

1. The Shirelles, "What Does a Girl Do?" (Scepter Records, 1963). Composer: Townsend.

2. Paul Freeman, "The Shirelles . . . Interview with . . . Beverly Lee," *Pop Culture Classics*, October, 2011, http://popcultureclassics.com/shirelles.html (accessed June 3, 2017).

3. Richard Aquila, interview with Bo Diddley for NPR's *Rock & Roll America* (January 21, 1998).

4. Freeman, "The Shirelles."

5. Shirelles, "Tonight's the Night" (Scepter Records, 1960). Composers: Owens and Dixon. Shirelles, "Will You Love Me Tomorrow" (Scepter Records, 1961). Composers: King and Goffin.

6. Ally Karsyn, "Shirley Alston Reeves Still Singing . . . Hits of the Shirelles," *Sioux City Journal*, April 2, 2015, https://siouxcityjournal.com/entertainment/arts-and-theatre/shirley -alston-reeves-still-singing-doo-wop-s-hits-of/article_d27f9d70-397c-5121-975e-e9ed12ca74dd .html (accessed August 28, 2018).

7. In 1960 a California group named the Chiffons (not to be confused with NY's Chiffons of "He's So Fine" fame) covered the Shirelles' "Tonight's the Night." Other girl groups influenced by the Shirelles include the Pearlettes, Charmettes, Cookies, and Ribbons.

8. Artie Wayne, "Hangin' In: Hank Medress," *Spectropop.com*, http://spectropop.com /HankMedress/index.htm (accessed June 7, 2017); Chiffons, "He's So Fine" (Laurie Records, 1963). Composer: Mack.

9. Richard Aquila, interview with Jay Siegel of the Tokens (May 2, 2018).

10. Chiffons, "One Fine Day" (Laurie Records, 1963). Composers: King and Goffin; Martin Luther King Jr., "I Have a Dream," August 28, 1963, https://www.americanrhetoric .com/speeches/mlkihaveadream.htm (accessed November 3, 2020).

11. Jaynetts, "Sally, Go 'Round the Roses" (Tuff Records, 1963). Composers: Sanders and Stevens. Arranged and conducted by Artie Butler.

12. Richard Aquila, interview with Artie Butler (June 12, 2017).

13. Ibid.

14. Ibid.

15. Examples include Pixies Three, Caravelles, Murmaids, Dixiebelles, and Secrets. After 1963 the Shangri-Las continued the white girl group tradition with "Leader of the Pack" (1964) and other hits.

16. For information about the Angels, see Jay Lustig, "My Boyfriend's Back: The Angels," *NJArts.net*, January 6, 2015, https://www.njarts.net/350-jersey-songs/my-boyfriends-back -the-angels/ (accessed May 6, 2018).

17. The Angels, "My Boyfriend's Back" (Smash Records, 1963). Composers: Feldman, Goldstein, and Gottehrer.

18. Charlotte Greig, "The Paris Sisters Interview," *Spectropop.com* (1990) , http://www .spectropop.com/ParisSisters/ (accessed January 9, 2019).

19. Ibid.

20. Paris Sisters, "He Knows I Love Him Too Much" (Gregmark Records, 1962). Composers: Goffin and King.

21. Russ Titelman quoted in Mark Ribowsky, *He's a Rebel: Phil Spector, Rock and Roll's Legendary Producer* (New York: Da Capo, 2006), 56.

22. Hermione Hoby, "Ronnie Spector Interview . . . ," *Telegraph*, March 6, 2014, http://www.telegraph.co.uk/culture/music/rockandpopfeatures/10676805/Ronnie-Spector-interview-The-more-Phil-tried-to-destroy-me-the-stronger-I-got.html (accessed July 13, 2017).

23. Love's comments appear in Mike Westfall, "He's a Rebel: The Darlene Love Story," *The American Worker*, October 15, 2005, http://michaelwestfall.tripod.com/id130.html (accessed July 7, 2017).

24. Ribowsky, *He's a Rebel*, 101–3.

25. The Crystals, "Uptown" (Philles Records, 1962). Composers: Mann and Weil.

26. Pitney quoted in Ribowsky, *He's a Rebel*, 118.

27. Anna H. Graves, *My Boyfriend's Back! The Story of the Girl Groups* (New York: Friedman/Fairfax, 1995), 43; Ribowsky, *He's a Rebel*, 114, 115, 120.

28. Kyle Long, "If Vikki Carr Is Happy, We're Happy," *Nuvo: Indy's Alternative Voice*, January 20, 2016, http://www.nuvo.net/music/a_cultural_manifesto/if-vikki-carr-is-happy-we-re-happy/article_da1b1670-c907-50f8-952f-f0f9af3100fd.html (accessed July 4, 2017); Ribowsky, *He's a Rebel*, 125.

29. Crystals, "He's a Rebel" (Philles Records, 1962). Composer: Pitney.

30. Love's comments appear in Westfall, "He's a Rebel."

31. Crystals, "Da Doo Ron Ron (When He Walked Me Home)" (Philles Records, 1963). Composers: Spector, Greenwich, and Barry.

32. Crystals, "Then He Kissed Me" (Philles Records, 1963). Composers: Spector, Greenwich, and Barry.

33. Spector quoted in Ribowsky, *He's a Rebel*, 150; Ellie Greenwich quoted in David P. Szatmary, *A Time to Rock: A Social History of Rock 'N' Roll* (New York: Schirmer Books, 1996), 77.

34. Ronnie's quote appears in Dave Simpson, "How We Made the Ronnettes' 'Be My Baby,'" *Guardian*, November 17, 2015, https://www.theguardian.com/culture/2015/nov/17/how-we-made-the-ronettes-be-my-baby-ronnie-spector-phil (accessed May 19, 2018).

35. Kristin Anderson, "Talking Style With Ronnie Spector . . . ," *Vogue*, October 20, 2016, http://www.vogue.com/article/ronnie-spector-style-ronettes-fashion-interview (accessed July 13, 2017); Hoby, "Ronnie Spector Interview."

36. Love quoted in Ben Sisario, "A Life of Troubles Followed a Singer's Burst of Fame," *New York Times*, February 16, 2009, http://www.nytimes.com/2009/02/17/arts/music/17rone.html

(accessed July 13, 2017); Allison Stewart, "Ronnie Spector's Christmas starts in September," *Chicago Tribune*, December 4, 2014, http://www.chicagotribune.com/entertainment/music/chi -interview-with-ronnie-spector-20141204-story.html (accessed July 13, 2017).

37. Ronettes, "Be My Baby" (Philles Records, 1963). Composers: Greenwich, Barry, and Spector; Ken Sharp, "Behind the Beehive: An Interview with Ronnie Spector," *Rockcellar Magazine*, October 25, 2013, http://www.rockcellarmagazine.com/2013/10/25/beyond-the -beehive-interview-with-ronnie-spector/ (accessed July 14, 2017).

38. Ronnie Spector quoted in Szatmary, *A Time to Rock*, 77.

39. For more on Spector, see "Phil Spector," *Biography.com*, https://www.biography.com /people/phil-spector-9489973 (accessed July 15, 2017); Ribowsky, *He's a Rebel*, 2–7, 230, 354–99.

40. Jerry Leiber and Mike Stoller with David Ritz, *Hound Dog: The Leiber and Stoller Autobiography* (New York: Simon & Schuster, 2009), 170, 177; Sill quoted in Ribowsky, *He's a Rebel*, 128. For Pitney's comments, see Alexis Petridis, "Phil Spector and the Myth of the 'Mad' Record Producer," *Guardian*, April 14, 2009, https://www.theguardian.com/music /musicblog/2009/apr/14/phil-spector-record-producers (accessed July 15, 2017).

41. Spector quoted in Mick Brown, "Pop's Lost Genius," *Telegraph*, February 4, 2003, http://www.telegraph.co.uk/culture/music/rockandjazzmusic/3589445/Pops-lost-genius.html (accessed July 5, 2017).

42. https://www.rockhall.com/inductees/phil-spector (accessed July 15, 2017).

43. Freeman, "The Shirelles."

44. For the album cover, see Michael Ochs, *1000 Record Covers* (New York: Taschen, 1996), 240; Shirley Owens is quoted in Karsyn, "Shirley Alston Reeves."

45. Ochs, *1000 Record Covers*, 239, 242, 243.

46. Karsyn, "Shirley Alston Reeves."

47. John Liberty, "Dick Clark Remembered: The Velvelettes . . . Share Memories of 1964 Tour," *Michigan Live*, April 20, 2012, https://www.mlive.com/entertainment/kalamazoo/index .ssf/2012/04/dick_clark_remembered_the_velv.html (accessed August 31, 2018).

48. Dick Clark and Richard Robinson, *Rock, Roll and Remember* (New York: Popular Library, 1978), 316–18.

49. Leo Shull, "Neither Heat, Bombs, Nor Birmingham Cops Shall Stop the Show . . . ," *Show Business* 23, no. 32 (August 10, 1963): 1, 10; Glen Whitcroft, "R&B Entertainers . . . Involved in the Civil Rights Movement," *U.S. Studies Online*, June 1, 2015, http://www.baas.ac .uk/usso/rb-entertainers-didnt-take-too-long-to-get-involved-in-the-civil-rights-movement/ (accessed August 31, 2018).

50. Tris McCall, "Passaic's Shirelles An Influential, Groundbreaking Pop Act," *Inside Jersey*, April 25, 2011, https://www.nj.com/entertainment/music/index.ssf/2011/04/passaics _shirelles_an_influent.html (accessed August 29, 2018).

51. *Life*, January 20, 1961, 17.

52. Karsyn, "Shirley Alston Reeves."

53. Santiglia's recollections appear in Mary Carole McCauley, "The Jersey Girl: Peggy Santiglia Davison . . . ," *Baltimore Sun*, October 1, 2009, http://articles.baltimoresun.com/2009 -10-01/entertainment/0909300074_1_frankie-valli-davison-jersey-boys (accessed May 6, 2018); and "Gary James' Interview with Peggy Santiglia Davison of the Angels," *classicbands .com*, http://www.classicbands.com/AngelsInterview.html (accessed May 6, 2018).

54. Sherrell Paris's recollection comes from Greig, "The Paris Sisters Interview."

55. Santiglia quotes come from "Interview With Peggy Santiglia Davison of The Angels: Part One," *Jersey Boys Blog*, February 25, 2009, http://jerseyboysblog.com/jbb-exclusive -interview-with-peggy-santiglia-davison-of-the-angels-part-one/3414 (accessed May 6, 2018).

56. Percells, "What Are Boys Made Of " (ABC-Paramount, 1963). Composers: Linde and Antell.

57. Angels, "My Boyfriend's Back" (Smash, 1963). Composers: Feldman, Goldstein, and Gottehrer; Four Pennies (a.k.a. Chiffons), "When the Boy's Happy (the Girl's Happy Too)" (Rust, 1963). Composers: Barry and Greenwich.

58. Cookies, "Chains" (Dimension, 1962). Composers: Goffin and King.

59. Crystals, "Please Hurt Me" (Philles Records, 1962). Composers: Goffin and King; Crystals, "He Hit Me (And It Felt Like a Kiss)" (Philles Records, 1962). Composers: Goffin and King; Gillian G. Garr, *She's a Rebel: The History of Women in Rock & Roll* (Seattle: Seal Press, 1992), 44–45; Sill quoted in Mark Ribowsky, *He's a Rebel*, 114.

60. Ribbons, "Ain't Gonna Kiss Ya" (Marsh Records, 1963). Composer: J. M. Smith.

61. Cookies, "Girls Grow Up Faster Than Boys" (Dimension 1964). Composers: Goffin and Keller.

62. Starlets, "Better Tell Him No" (PAM Records, 1961). Composer: Williams; Charmettes, "Please Don't Kiss Me Again" (Kapp, 1963). Composer: Young.

63. Bobbettes, "Mr. Lee" (Atlantic Records, 1957). Composers: E. Pought, Gathers, J. Pought, Webb, and Dixon; Bobbettes, "I Shot Mr. Lee" (Triple X, 1960). Composers: E. Pought, Gathers, J. Pought, Webb, and Dixon.

64. Shirelles, "Stop the Music" (Scepter Records, 1962). Composers: McCoy and Denson.

65. Dixie Cups, "Going to the Chapel" (Red Bird, 1964). Composers: Spector, Greenwich, and Barry.

66. Shirelles, "Soldier Boy" (Scepter Records, 1962). Composers: Dixon and Green.

67. Susan J. Douglas, *Where the Girls Are: Growing Up Female with the Mass Media* (New York: Times Books, 1994), 97.

68. David W. Chen, "A Shirelle, From Passaic High To the Rock Hall of Fame," *New York Times*, November 5, 1995, http://www.nytimes.com/1995/11/05/nyregion/in-brief-a-shirelle -from-passaic-high-to-the-rock-hall-of-fame.html (accessed June 6, 2017).

CHAPTER 3. "HEAT WAVE"

1. Martha & the Vandellas, "Heat Wave" (Gordy, 1963). Composers: Holland, Dozier, and Holland.

2. Richard Aquila, interview with Martha Reeves for NPR's *Rock & Roll America* (March 8, 1998).

3. Peter Benjaminson, *The Story of Motown* (Los Angeles: A Barnacle Book, 2018), 19–23.

4. Suzanne E. Smith, *Dancing in the Street: Motown and the Cultural Politics of Detroit* (Cambridge, MA: Harvard University Press, 1999), 66, 67; Berry Gordy, *To Be Loved: The Music, The Magic, The Memories of Motown* (New York: Warner Books, 1995), 12, 14–18, 20, 25.

5. Gerald Posner, *Motown: Music, Money, Sex, & Power* (New York: Random House, 2002), 9, 10; Gordy, *To Be Loved*, 12, 18–20.

6. Mick Brown, "Berry Gordy: The Man Who Built Motown," *Telegraph*, January 23, 2016, https://s.telegraph.co.uk/graphics/projects/berry-gordy-motown/index.html (accessed July 24, 2019); Posner, *Motown*, 10, 11; Benjaminson, *Story of Motown*, 29; Gordy, *To Be Loved*, 50–56, 61.

7. Gordy, *To Be Loved*, 68, 69; Posner, *Motown*, 15.

8. Posner, *Motown*, 14, 15; Gordy, *To Be Loved*, 63–65.

9. Benjaminson, *Story of Motown*, 30, 31; Gordy, *To Be Loved*, 65–75.

10. Posner, *Motown*, 18; Benjaminson, *Story of Motown*, 31–32; Gordy, *To Be Loved*, 75, 76.

11. Gordy, *To Be Loved*, 76, 77; Gareth Murphy, *Cowboys and Indies: The Epic History of the Record Industry* (New York: Thomas Dunne, 2014), 115. For Roquel Davis, see John Broven, *Record Makers and Breakers: Voices of the Independent Rock 'n' Roll Pioneers* (Urbana: University of Illinois Press, 2009), 319–21, 330–40.

12. Gordy, *To Be Loved*, 79.

13. Posner, *Motown*, 21; Gordy, *To Be Loved*, 89–92; Smith, *Dancing in the Street*, 71; Roquel Davis later wrote advertising jingles, e.g. Coke's "It's the Real Thing" and "I'd Like to Buy the World a Coke."

14. Touré, "Enter the Miracle Man: Smokey Robinson," *AARP: The Magazine*, December 2018, 42–44; Posner, *Motown*, 24, 25; Joe Smith, *Off the Record: An Oral History of Popular Music* (New York: Warner Books, 1988), 165–66.

15. Nelson George, *Where Did Our Love Go? The Rise and Fall of the Motown Sound* (Urbana: University of Illinois Press, 2007), 22–24; Posner, *Motown*, 25, 26.

16. Gordy, *To Be Loved*, 107, 115; Gilbert Cruz, "A Brief History of Motown," *Time*, January 12, 2009, http://content.time.com/time/arts/article/0,8599,1870975,00.html (accessed July 24, 2019); Dorian Lynskey, "How We Made Motown," *Guardian*, March 22, 2016, https://www.theguardian.com/music/2016/mar/22/how-we-made-motown-records -berry-gordy-smokey-robinson-stevie-wonder-interview (accessed July 24, 2019).

17. Gordy, *To Be Loved*, 116.

18. Miracles, "Bad Girl" (Motown Records, 1959). Composers: Gordy and Robinson.

19. Gerri Hirshey, "The Sound That Changed the World," *AARP: The Magazine*, December 2018, 47; Brown, "Berry Gordy"; Gordy, *To Be Loved*, 122–24.

20. Lynskey, "How We Made Motown."

21. Lisa Robinson, "It Happened in Hitsville," *Vanity Fair*, December 13, 2008, https://www.vanityfair.com/culture/2008/12/motown200812 (accessed July 24, 2019); Brown, "Berry Gordy"; Murphy, *Cowboys and Indies*, 116; Clay Latimer, "At Motown, Berry Gordy's Assembly Line Of Talent Remade Pop Music," *Investor's Business Daily*, July 11, 2016, https://www.investors.com/news/management/leaders-and-success/at-motown-berry-gordys -assembly-line-of-talent-remade-pop-music/ (accessed July 24, 2019).

22. Gordy, *To Be Loved*, 128, 129; See also Maxine Johns, "I Call Myself A Hunter: Conversation with Mickey Stevenson, Motown's First A&R Man," *Howl and Echoes*, March 12, 2016, http://howlandechoes.com/2016/03/interview-mickey-stevenson/ (accessed August 23, 2019); Gordy, *To Be Loved*, 128, 129.

23. Hirshey, "The Sound That Changed the World," 47; Gordy, *To Be Loved*, 129–30.

24. Gordy, *To Be Loved*, 129–30, 163.

25. Aquila, interview with Martha Reeves.

26. Daniel Kreps, "Al Abrams . . . Dead at 74," *Rolling Stone*, October 5, 2015, https://www .rollingstone.com/music/music-news/al-abrams-motown-records-pioneer-dead-at-74-161907 (accessed August 20, 2019).

27. Barrett Strong, "Money (That's What I Want)" (Tamla/Anna Records, 1960). Composers: Bradford and Gordy.

28. Gordy, *To Be Loved*, 127, 128.

29. Gordy, *To Be Loved*, 134–37.

30. Adam White with Barney Ales, *Motown: The Sound of Young America* (London: Thames and Hudson, 2016), 78; Gordy, *To Be Loved*, 138.

31. Miracles, "Shop Around" (Tamla, 1961). Composers: Robinson and Gordy; Smokey's quote comes from Michael Lydon, "Smokey Robinson: Meet the Reigning Genius of the Top 40," *Rolling Stone*, September 28, 1968, https://www.rollingstone.com/music/music-news /smokey-robinson-meet-the-reigning-genius-of-the-top-40-81354/ (accessed August 26, 2019).

32. Stu Hackel, liner notes, *Smokey Robinson & the Miracles: The Ultimate Collection* (Motown Records, 1998), 3.

33. Miracles, "Shop Around" (Tamla, 1961). Composers: Robinson and Gordy.

34. White and Ales, *Motown*, 32, 79, 85, 86; Brown, "Berry Gordy."

35. Smith, *Dancing in the Streets*, 106; Gordy, *To Be Loved*, 149, 181–83; White and Ales, *Motown*, 89.

36. Gordy, *To Be Loved*, 155; Brown, "Berry Gordy."

37. Benjaminson, *Story of Motown*, 43; Latimer, "At Motown"; Gordy, *To Be Loved*, 155–57.

38. Gordy, *To Be Loved*, 158.

39. Peter Lindblad, "The Marvelettes . . . A Trailblazing Girl Group," *Goldmine*, April 8, 2010, https://www.goldminemag.com/articles/motown-at-50-the-marvelettes-were-a -trailblazing-girl-group (accessed August 28, 2019); Anna H. Graves, *My Boyfriend's Back! The Story of the Girl Groups* (New York: Friedman/Fairfax, 1995), 52–55.

40. Marvelettes, "Please Mr. Postman" (Tamla, 1960). Composers: Dobbins, Garrett, Bateman, Holland, and Gorman.

41. Mary Wells, "The One Who Really Loves You" (Motown, 1962). Composer: Robinson.

42. Robinson quoted in David Chiu, "Smokey Robinson on the Legacy of Motown," *Medium.com*, February 19, 2015, https://medium.com/@davidchiu/smokey-robinson-on-the -legacy-of-motown-3b0d71b66753 (accessed October 26, 2020); Pete Lewis, "Smokey Robinson Classic Motown Interview," *Blues and Soul.com*, December 1992, http://www .bluesandsoul.com/feature/379/smokey_robinson__motown_classic_interview_-_dec_1992 (accessed September 15, 2019).

43. Mary Wells, "You Beat Me to the Punch" (Motown, 1962). Composers: Robinson and White.

44. Contours, "Do You Love Me" (Gordy, 1962). Composer: Gordy.

45. Marvelettes, "Beechwood 4-5789" (Tamla, 1962). Composers: Gaye, Stevenson, and Gordy.

46. George, *Where Did Our Love Go*, 39–41; https://www.rockhall.com/inductees /holland-dozier-and-holland (accessed September 4, 2019).

47. George, *Where Did Our Love Go*, 32–36.

48. Gordy, *To Be Loved*, 150, 151, 165.

49. John Walsh, "Mary Wilson: In the Name of Love," *Independent*, May 14, 2008, https://www.independent.co.uk/arts-entertainment/music/features/mary-wilson-in-the -name-of-love-827634.html (accessed September 6, 2019); George, *Where Did Our Love Go*, 80–84; Gordy, *To Be Loved*, 151, 152.

50. Benjaminson, *Story of Motown*, 65–71; Gordy, *To Be Loved*, 160–62.

51. George, *Where Did Our Love Go*, 44–48; Gordy, *To Be Loved*, 161, 162.

52. Aquila, interview with Martha Reeves; David Sheff, "Interview: Berry Gordy," *Playboy* 42, no. 8 (August, 1995), 129; Gordy, *To Be Loved*, 171, 172.

53. Gordy, *To Be Loved*, 174.

54. Ibid., 122, 182, 183; "Rock and Roll; Respect; Interview with Beans Bowles [Part 2 of 2]," WGBH Media Library & Archives, http://openvault.wgbh.org/catalog/V_7C8DFBE2FE6 24161A387BF83E0A62DF0 (accessed September 10, 2019); Gene Demby, "Remembering the

Woman Who Gave Motown Its Charm," *All Things Considered*, NPR, October 15, 2013, https://www.npr.org/sections/codeswitch/2013/10/15/234738593/remembering-the-woman -who-gave-motown-its-charm (accessed August 18, 2019). See also "Rock and Roll; Respect; Interview with Maxine Powell [Part 1 of 2]," WGBH Media Library & Archives, http://openvault .wgbh.org/catalog/V_6224956EC9BB49C080C966A79D547F2D (accessed August 18, 2019).

55. Bob Gulla, *Icons of R&B and Soul: An Encyclopedia of the Artists who Revolutionized Rhythm* (Westport, CT: Greenwood Press, 2008), 296, 297; George, *Where Did Our Love Go*, 87–89.

56. Demby, "Remembering the Woman"; "Rock and Roll; Respect; Interview with Maxine Powell [Part 2 of 2]," WGBH Media Library & Archives, http://openvault.wgbh.org /catalog/V_E38984D33CF24BE2BFD167F2B0A1ACF9 (accessed August 18, 2019). Gordy's comment comes from Graham Reid, "Mary Wilson of the Supremes Interviewed . . . ," *Elsewhere*, March 1, 2009, https://www.elsewhere.co.nz/absoluteelsewhere/2206/mary-wilson -of-the-supremes-interviewed-2009-the-dreamgirl-goes-on (accessed September 6, 2019).

57. Demby, "Remembering the Woman;" "Rock and Roll; Respect; Interview with Martha Reeves [Part 2 of 2]," WGBH Media Library & Archives, http://openvault.wgbh.org /catalog/V_38B4E344B4B34969A5BEA2ED170A1000 (accessed September 10, 2019).

58. Karen Schoemer, *Great Pretenders: My Strange Love Affair with '50s Pop Music* (New York: Free Press, 2006), 166; Demby, "Remembering the Woman Who Gave Motown Its Charm."

59. Mary Wells, "Two Lovers" (Motown, 1963). Composer: Robinson.

60. Chiu, "Smokey Robinson;" Lewis, "Smokey Robinson Classic Motown Interview."

61. Touré, "Enter the Miracle Man: Smokey Robinson," 74.

62. Gordy, *To Be Loved*, 169.

63. Joe Smith, *Off the Record: An Oral History of Popular Music* (New York: Warner Books, 1988), 173, 174; Gordy, *To Be Loved*, 164.

64. Gordy, *To Be Loved*, 169.

65. Gordy, *To Be Loved*, 153; Jack Doyle, "Fingertips—Pt.2, 1963," *PopHistoryDig.com*, April 21, 2008, https://www.pophistorydig.com/topics/stevie-wonder-fingertips/ (accessed September 12, 2019).

66. Little Stevie Wonder, "Fingertips—Pt 2" (Tamla, 1963). Composers: Paul and Cosby.

67. https://www.rockhall.com/inductees/stevie-wonder (accessed September 13, 2019).

68. Lynskey, "How We Made Motown"; Robinson, "It Happened in Hitsville."

69. Jon Landau, "The Motown Story: How Berry Gordy Jr. Created the Legendary Label," *Rolling Stone*, May 13, 1971, https://www.rollingstone.com/music/music-features /the-motown-story-how-berry-gordy-jr-created-the-legendary-label-178066 (accessed September 26, 2019).

70. https://www.rockhall.com/inductees/berry-gordy-jr (accessed September 23, 2019).

71. Chuck Yarborough, "Smokey Robinson . . . Interview with a Legend," *The Cleveland Plain Dealer*, November 7, 2015, https://www.cleveland.com/entertainment/2015/11/smokey _robinson_on_dreams_and.html (accessed March 8, 2019).

72. Gordy, *To Be Loved,* 174–76; "Rock and Roll; Respect; Interview with Martha Reeves [Part 2 of 2]."

73. White and Ales, *Motown*, 40; Robinson, "It Happened in Hitsville."

74. "Smokey Robinson Interview," *Art of the Song*, December 20, 2020, http://artofthesong .org/smokey-robinson-interview/ (accessed January 6, 2022); Hirshey, "The Sound That Changed the World," 47; Gordy, *To Be Loved*, 7; Danyel Smith, "Mighty Motown: A Conversation with Berry Gordy," *Essence*, February 26, 2013, https://www.essence.com/celebrity/mighty -motown-conversation-berry-gordy/ (accessed July 24, 2019).

75. Eric Althoff, "Gordy: Dr. King was on Motown's payroll," *Washington Times*, December 3, 2015, https://www.washingtontimes.com/news/2015/dec/3/berry-gordy -motown-records-had-martin-luther-king-/ (accessed September 19, 2019); David Szatmary, *A Time to Rock: A Social History of Rock 'n' Roll* (New York: Schirmer Books, 1996), 152.

76. Jeff Karoub, "1st Motown Records Publicist Alan Abrams Dies at 74," *AP*, October 5, 2015, https://www.detroitnews.com/story/obituaries/2015/10/04/motown-records-publicist -obit/73347594/ (September 24, 2019).

77. Gordy, *To Be Loved*, 158; Robinson, "It Happened in Hitsville"; Benjaminson, *Story of Motown*, 57.

78. Gordy, *To Be Loved*, 179; Szatmary, *Time to Rock*, 151.

79. Lionel Richie quoted in Robinson, "It Happened in Hitsville."

80. White and Ales, *Motown*, 70, 85; Brown, "Berry Gordy."

81. George, *Where Did Our Love Go*, 201

82. Sheff, "Interview: Berry Gordy," 128, 131; George, *Where Did Our Love Go*, 76, 78, 86, 107, 149, 151, 152, 161.

83. White and Ales, *Motown*, 380; Julian Bond quoted in Lisa Robinson, "It Happened in Hitsville."

CHAPTER 4. "SURFIN' SAFARI"

1. Beach Boys, "Surfin' Safari" (Capitol, 1962). Composers: Wilson and Love.

2. Frank Bergon and Zeese Papanikolas (eds.), *Looking Far West: The Search for the American West in History, Myth, and Literature* (New York: New American Library, 1978), 2.

3. "The Mad Happy Surfers, A Way of Life on the Wavetops," *Life*, September 1, 1961, 47–53.

4. See https://www.movieart.com/beach-party-1963-16434/ (accessed July 14, 2020).

5. Richard Sandomir, "Bruce Brown, 80, Dies: His 'Endless Summer' Documented Surfing," *New York Times*, December 12, 2017, https://www.nytimes.com/2017/12/12

/obituaries/bruce-brown-documentarian-of-surfing-is-dead-at-80.html (accessed August 10, 2018).

    6. Richard Aquila, interview with Dick Dale for NPR's *Rock & Roll America* (July 2, 1998); Margaret Rhodes, "The Fascinating Evolution of the Surfboard," *Wired*, February 25, 2016, https://www.wired.com/2016/02/fascinating-evolution-surfboard (August 23, 2020).

    7. Aquila, interview with Dick Dale.

    8. Sandomir, "Bruce Brown;" Mat Arney, "A Final Conversation with Bruce Brown," *SurfSimply.com*, 2017, https://surfsimply.com/surf-culture/a-final-conversation-with-bruce-brown (August 8, 2020).

    9. For more on surf groups, see Steve Otfinoski, *The Golden Age of Rock Instrumentals* (New York: Billboard Books, 1997), 137–44.

    10. Aquila, interview with Dick Dale.

    11. Ibid.

    12. Ibid.

    13. Ibid.

    14. Ibid.

    15. Ibid.

    16. Ibid.

    17. Aquila, interview with Dick Dale. See also Zach Weisberg, "Interview: Dick Dale," *The Inertia*, November 22, 2010, https://www.theinertia.com/music-art/interview-dick-dale-king-of-surf-guitar (accessed August 7, 2020).

    18. Aquila, interview with Dick Dale; Otis Hart and Anastasia Tsioulcas, "Dick Dale, Surf Guitar Legend, Dead At 81," *NPR Music*, NPR, March 18, 2019, https://www.npr.org/2019/03/18/704329806/dick-dale-surf-guitar-legend-dead-at-81 (accessed August 24, 2020); Amanda Petrusich, "Dick Dale, the Inventor of Surf Rock . . . from Boston," *New Yorker*, March 18, 2019, https://www.newyorker.com/culture/postscript/dick-dale-the-inventor-of-surf-rock-was-a-lebanese-american-kid-from-boston (accessed August 23, 2020).

    19. Dave Simpson, "The Beach Boys' Mike Love . . . ," *Guardian*, July 4, 2013, https://amp.theguardian.com/culture/2013/jul/04/beach-boys-mike-love-interview (accessed June 16, 2020); Jacob Uitti, "Mike Love Shares Beach Boys Stories . . . ," *American Songwriter*, May 7, 2020, https://americansongwriter.com/mike-love-this-to-shall-pass-beach-boys (accessed June 23, 2020).

    20. Mike Love, quoted in Joe Smith, *Off the Record: An Oral History of Popular Music* (New York: Warner Books, 1988), 175; James B. Murphy, *Becoming the Beach Boys, 1961–1963* (Jefferson, NC: McFarland & Co, 2015), 84–86.

    21. Murphy, *Becoming the Beach Boys*, 84–86; Lee Cotton, *Twist & Shout: The Golden Age of American Rock 'n Roll, Vol. III, 1960–1963* (Sacramento, CA: High Sierra Books, 2002), 561.

22. Cotton, *Twist & Shout,* 560–64; Murphy, *Becoming the Beach Boys,* 91–102.

23. Carl Wilson quoted in Geoffrey Himes, liner notes, *The Beach Boys:1962–1967* (Time-Life Music CD, 1986).

24. Liner notes, Beach Boys, *Surfin' Safari* (Capitol, 1962).

25. Brian Wilson, liner notes, Beach Boys, *Surfin' Safari/Surfin' USA* (Capitol, 1990), 3.

26. Ibid.; Beach Boys, "Surfin' U.S.A." (Capitol, 1963). Composers: Wilson and Berry.

27. Beach Boys, "Shut Down" (Capitol, 1963). Composers: Wilson and Christian.

28. Wilson, liner notes, 3.

29. Ibid., 22; David Leaf, liner notes, Beach Boys, *Surfin' Safari/Surfin' USA* (Capitol, 1990), 7.

30. Brian's quote at https://frankievallifourseasons.com/bio (accessed June 29, 2020).

31. Wilson, liner notes, 22; Beach Boys, "Lana" (Capitol, 1963). Composer: Wilson.

32. Brian Wilson with Ben Greenman, *I Am Brian Wilson: A Memoir* (New York: Da Capo Press, 2016), 82, 83.

33. Beach Boys, "Little Deuce Coupe" (Capitol, 1963). Composers: Wilson and Christian.

34. Bob Shannon and John Javna, *Behind the Hits: Inside Stories of Classic Pop and Rock and Roll* (New York: Warner Books, 1986), 144.

35. Brian Wilson, liner notes, Beach Boys, *Surfer Girl/Shut Down, vol 2* (Capitol, 1990), 3.

36. "Walter Cronkite on the Assassination of John F. Kennedy," *NPR Special Series: The Kennedy Assassination, 50 Years Later,* NPR, November 22, 2013, https://www.npr.org /transcripts/246628793?storyId=246628793?storyId=246628793 (accessed July 9, 2020).

37. David Browne, "The Assassination Blues . . . JFK Death Songs," *Rolling Stone,* March 27, 2020, https://www.rollingstone.com/music/music-features/assassination-history-jfk-death-songs -974198 (accessed July 9, 2020); "Brian Wilson on 'The Warmth of the Sun,'" https://www .youtube.com/watch?v=JXPjUV6H2Wc (accessed July 9, 2020); Mike Love quoted in Cathy Wurzer, "The Beach Boys Write a Song on the Day JFK Died," *MPR News,* November 22, 2013, https://www.mprnews.org/story/2013/11/22/music (accessed July 9, 2020).

38. Beach Boys, "Surfers Rule" (Capitol, 1963). Composers: Wilson and Love; 4 Seasons, "No Surfin' Today" (Vee Jay, 1964). Composers: Gaudio and Crewe.

39. Brian Wilson quoted in liner notes, Beach Boys, *Surfer Girl/Shut Down,* 11.

40. Beach Boys, "Fun, Fun, Fun" (Capitol, 1964). Composers: Wilson and Love.

41. Wilson, liner notes, *Surfer Girl/Shut Down,* 22.

42. Beach Boys, "Don't Back Down" (Capitol, 1964). Composer: Wilson.

43. Alison Beard, "Life's Work: An Interview with Brian Wilson," *Harvard Business Review* (December 2016), https://hbr.org/2016/12/brian-wilson (accessed January 27, 2022); David Leaf, "Paul McCartney Comments," *AlbumLinerNotes.com,* 1990, http://albumlinernotes .com/Paul_McCartney_Comments.html (accessed July 16, 2020).

44. Beard, "Life's Work;" Jordan Runtagh, "The Beach Boys in Their Own Words. . . ." *People*, June 8, 2018, https://people.com/music/the-beach-boys-stories-behind-songs-royal -philharmonic-album (accessed June 15, 2020).

45. Mike Love quoted in Runtagh, "The Beach Boys."

46. Chet Cooper and Gillian Friedman, "Brian Wilson: A Powerful Interview," *Ability Magazine*, 2006, https://abilitymagazine.com/past/brianW/brianw.html (accessed June 8, 2020).

47. https://www.kennedy-center.org/artists/w/wa-wn/brian-wilson/ (accessed July 25, 2020).

48. Examples include: King Curtis & the Noble Knights, "Beach Party"; Tornadoes, "Bustin' Surfboards"; Lively Ones, "Miserlou"; Sentinals "Latin'ia"; and Centurians, "Bullwinkle Part II."

49. Aquila, interview with Dick Dale.

50. Dean Torrence quoted in Dave Osborn, "Beach Boys' Influence: Dean Torrence Discusses Surf Music Origin" *Naples Daily News*, January 18, 2018, https://www.naplesnews .com/story/entertainment/music/2018/01/18/beach-boys-influence-dean-torrance-discusses -surf-music-origin/1039506001 (accessed July 27, 2020).

51. Osborn, "Beach Boys' Influence;" David Fricke, "Dean Remembers Jan," *Rolling Stone*, April 2, 2004, https://www.rollingstone.com/music/music-news/dean-remembers-jan -254891 (accessed January 7, 2021).

52. Jan & Dean, "Dead Man's Curve" (Liberty, 1964). Composers: Berry, Wilson, Christian, and Kornfeld.

53. Dean Torrence quoted in Steve Kolanjian, CD liner notes, *Surf City: The Best of Jan and Dean* (Liberty/EMI, 1990).

54. Dean Torrence quoted in Fricke, "Dean Remembers Jan."

55. Dean Torrence quoted in Osborn, "Beach Boys' Influence."

56. Richard Aquila, interview with Bob Spickard (Chantays) for NPR's *Rock & Roll America* (August 12, 1998).

57. Ibid.

58. Ibid.

59. Richard Aquila, interview with Jim Pash (Surfaris) for NPR's *Rock & Roll America* (July 27, 1998).

60. Surfaris, "Surfer Joe," (Dot, 1963). Composer: Wilson.

61. Richard Aquila, conversation with Dan Sawers (August 19, 2020).

62. Aquila, interview with Jim Pash.

63. Other surf records charted nationally or regionally in 1963, e.g.: Chubby Checker, "Surf Party"; Duane Eddy, "Your Baby's Gone Surfin'"; Al Casey, "Surfin' Hootenanny"; Lively Ones, "Surf Rider"; Rip Chords, "My Big Gun Board"; and Breakers, "Surfin' Tragedy."

64. Other surf songs by Black artists did not chart, e.g.: Chubby Checker, "Let's Surf Again" (1963); Bo Diddley, "Surfers' Love Call" (1963); Orlons, "Mr. Surfer" (1963); Dee Dee Sharp, "Riding the Waves" (1963). Jim Washburn, "Pyramid Power . . ." *Los Angeles Times*, March 31, 1995, https://www.latimes.com/archives/la-xpm-1995-03-31-ca-49218-story.html (accessed August 25, 2021).

65. Trent quoted in Janna Irons, "Sexism in Big-Wave Surfing Isn't Dead Yet," *Outside*, February 8, 2018, https://www.outsideonline.com/culture/opinion/sexism-big-wave-surfing -isnt-dead-yet/ (accessed August 24, 2021).

66. Kathryn Romeyn, "L.A.'s Ugly Jim Crow History: When Beaches Were Segregated," *The Hollywood Reporter*, August 5, 2016, https://www.hollywoodreporter.com/lifestyle/style /los-angeles-history-jim-crow-916441 (accessed October 26, 2021); John J. Bukowczyk, "California Dreamin', Whiteness, and the American Dream," *Journal of American Ethnic History* 35, no. 2 (Winter 2016): 92.

67. Bukowczyk, "California Dreamin'," 99.

68. The Surfaris, "Surfer Joe" (Dot, 1963). Composer: Ron Wilson.

69. Gary James, "Interview with Tony Andreason of the Trashmen," *ClassicBands.com,* http://www.classicbands.com/TrashmenInterview.html (accessed August 3, 2020).

70. Examples include tracks on Beach Boys' *All Summer Long* (1964), and the Rip Chords' "One Piece Topless Bathing Suit" (1964) and Sunrays' "I Live For the Sun" (1965).

71. The Rivieras, "California Sun" (Riviera, 1964). Composer: Glover.

72. Aquila, interview with Bob Spickard.

73. Chris Riemenschneider, "Minnesota's 'Surfin' Bird' Makers the Trashmen are Riding Another Wave," *Star Tribune*, January 23, 2015, https://www.startribune.com/minnesota-s -surfin-bird-makers-are-riding-another-wave/289476861 (accessed August 15, 2020).

74. Tradewinds, "New York's a Lonely Town" (Red Bird, 1965). Composers: Andreoli and Poncia.

75. Neil Morgan, *Westward Tilt: The American West Today* (New York: Random House, 1963), 12.

76. Dick Clark and Richard Robinson, *Rock, Roll & Remember* (New York: Popular Library, 1978), 323.

77. James Ford, "Interview: Mike Love Discusses the Legacy of The Beach Boys," *C-VILLE Weekly Magazine*, August 28, 2013, https://www.c-ville.com/interview-mike-love -discusses-the-enduring-legacy-of-the-beach-boys (accessed August 15, 2020).

78. Ibid.

79. Beach Boys, "Summers Gone" (Capitol, 2012). Composers: Wilson, Bon Jovi, and Thomas.

CHAPTER 5. "ON BROADWAY"

1. The Drifters, "On Broadway" (Atlantic, 1963). Composers: Weil, Mann, Leiber, and Stoller.

2. Peter Guralnick, "Ray Charles," in Jim Miller (ed.), *The Rolling Stone Illustrated History* (New York: Random House, 1980), 109–12; Arnold Shaw, *The World of Soul: Black America's Contribution to the Pop Music Scene* (New York: Cowles, 1970), 284.

3. Carin T. Ford, *Ray Charles: "I Was Born with Music Inside Me"* (Berkeley Heights, NJ: Enslow Publishers, 2008), 78.

4. Charles's recollection comes from "Ray Charles Takes Country Music to . . . the Pop Charts," *This Day in History*, June 2, http://www.history.com/this-day-in-history/ray-charles -takes-country-music-to-the-top-of-the-pop-charts (accessed May 7, 2017); Ray Charles Robinson Jr. with Mary Jane Ross, *You Don't Know Me: Reflections of My Father, Ray Charles* (New York: Harmony Books, 2010), 169.

5. Robinson Jr., *You Don't Know Me*, 169–70.

6. Shaw, *World of Soul*, 286.

7. Berry Gordy, *To Be Loved: The Music, The Magic, The Memories of Motown* (New York: Warner Books, 1995), 92.

8. Richard Aquila, interview with Dick Clark for NPR's *Rock & Roll America* (August 4, 1998).

9. Wexler quoted in Paul Friedlander, *Rock and Roll: A Social History* (Boulder, CO: Westview Press, 1996), 165.

10. Don Paulsen, "Interview with Sam Cooke," *sgco.biz*, July 1964, http://www.sgco.biz /DonPaulsenTribute3.html (accessed May 12, 2017).

11. Guralnick quoted in David Cantwell, "The Unlikely Story of 'A Change is Gonna Come,'" *The New Yorker*, March 17, 2015, http://www.newyorker.com/culture/culture-desk /the-unlikely-story-of-a-change-is-gonna-come (accessed May 6, 2017).

12. Sam Cooke, "A Change is Gonna Come" (RCA Victor, 1965). Composer: Cooke. For details, see David Cantwell, "The Unlikely Story;" Peter Guralnick, "How Martin Luther King Jr. Influenced Sam Cooke's 'A Change Is Gonna Come,'" *Daily Beast*, December 28, 2014, http://www.thedailybeast.com/articles/2014/12/28/how-martin-luther-king-jr -influenced-sam-cooke-s-a-change-is-gonna-come (accessed May 15, 2017); "Sam Cooke and the Song that 'Almost Scared Him,'" *All Things Considered*, NPR, February 1, 2014, http://www.npr.org/2014/02/01/268995033/sam-cooke-and-the-song-that-almost-scared -him (accessed May 12, 2017).

13. Joe McEwen, "Sam Cooke," in Anthony DeCurtis and James Henke (eds.), *Rolling Stone Illustrated History of Rock & Roll* (New York: Random House, 1992), 135–38. See also Peter Guralnick, *Dream Boogie: The Triumph of Sam Cooke* (New York: Little Brown &

Company, 2005) and Ed Gordon, "'Dream Boogie': The Life and Death of Sam Cooke," *News and Notes*, November 16, 2005, http://www.npr.org/templates/story/story.php?storyId =5014891 (accessed May 15, 2017).

14. Dick Clark and Richard Robinson, *Rock, Roll & Remember* (New York: Popular Library, 1976), 173–76; "Sam Cooke and the Song that 'Almost Scared Him."

15. Miller, *Rolling Stone Illustrated History*, 51. Other New Orleans singers include: Joe Jones, "You Talk Too Much" (1960); Clarence "Frogman" Henry, "I Don't Know Why I Love You (But I Do)" (1961); Lloyd Price, "Lady Luck" (1960).

16. Richard Aquila, interview with Dave Bartholomew for NPR's *Rock & Roll America* (July 2, 1998).

17. Ibid.

18. Billy Diamond quoted in Rick Coleman, "Seven Decades of Fats Domino," *Offbeat Magazine*, February 1, 1998, http://www.offbeat.com/articles/seven-decades-of-fats-domino (accessed May 2, 2017).

19. Gospel-influenced hits include Roy Hamilton's "You Can Have Her" (1961) and Clyde McPhatter's "Lover Please" (1962).

20. Other examples include Chuck Berry's "Let It Rock" (1960) and Bo Diddley's "You Can't Judge a Book by the Cover" (1962).

21. Dee Clark, "How About That" (Abner Records, 1960). Composers: Payne and Augustus; Dee Clark, "You're Looking Good" (Vee-Jay, 1960). Composers: Carter and Oliver.

22. Dee Clark, "Raindrops" (Vee-Jay, 1961). Composer: Clark.

23. Jerry Leiber and Mike Stoller with David Ritz, *Hound Dog: The Leiber and Stoller Autobiography* (New York: Simon & Schuster, 2009), 69.

24. Stoller quoted in Randy Poe, liner notes, *The Very Best of the Coasters* (Rhino Records, 1994).

25. "Rock and Roll; In The Groove; Interview with Jerry Leiber and Mike Stoller [Part 5 of 7]," WGBH Media Library & Archives, http://openvault.wgbh.org/catalog/V_39F7BDB454 EC4D469ABAC35DD51AB40A (January 17, 2019).

26. https://www.rockhall.com/inductees/coasters (accessed January 17, 2019).

27. Joe Smith, *Off the Record: An Oral History of Popular Music* (New York: Warner Books, 1988), 125; Leiber and Stoller, *Hound Dog*, 159.

28. Leiber and Stoller, *Hound Dog*, 159, 160.

29. "Rock and Roll; In The Groove; Interview with Ben E. King [Part 1 of 3]," WGBH Media Library & Archives, http://openvault.wgbh.org/catalog/V_99E8D2E3047E418AAC69 6DD4CCE0F126 (accessed January 18, 2019).

30. Rudy Lewis sang lead on seven hits: "Some Kind of Wonderful," "Please Stay," and "Sweets for My Sweet (all in 1961), "When My Little Girl is Smiling" (1962), and "Up on the Roof," "On Broadway" and "I'll Take You Home" (in 1963). After Lewis's death in 1964

Johnny Moore sang lead on the Drifters' last big hits: "Under the Boardwalk," "I've Got Sand in My Shoes," and "Saturday Night at the Movies" (all in 1964).

31. Charlie Thomas quoted in Ken Emerson, *Always Magic in the Air: The Bomp and Brilliance of the Brill Building Era* (New York: Viking, 2005), 122.

32. Other veteran R&B rock groups include Mickey & Sylvia, Falcons, Jayhawks, Olympics, and Ike & Tina Turner.

33. The Impressions, "Gypsy Woman" (ABC-Paramount, 1961). Composer: Mayfield.

34. Steve Huey, "The Impressions," *AllMusic.com*, https://www.allmusic.com/artist/the-impressions-mn0000082013/biography (accessed October 23, 2017); Mayfield quoted in Robert Pruter, *Chicago Soul* (Urbana: University of Illinois Press, 1991), 140.

35. Impressions, "It's All Right" (ABC-Paramount Records, 1963). Composer: Mayfield.

36. Johnny Pate quoted at http://www.curtismayfield.com/biography.html (accessed January 22, 2018).

37. Ibid.

38. Ibid.

39. https://www.rockhall.com/inductees/impressions (accessed March 3, 2018).

40. Shaw, *World of Soul,* 142.

41. Brown quoted in *Musicians Guide.com*, http://www.musicianguide.com/biographies/1608004017/The-Isley-Brothers.html (accessed December 14, 2017).

42. Marc Myers, "How the Isley Brothers Created 'Shout,'" *Wall Street Journal*, November 8, 2015, http://www.jazzpromoservices.com/jazz-news/how-the-isley-brothers-created-shout-wsj-3/ (accessed December 15, 2017).

43. Ron Isley's recollections appear in Marc Myers, *Anatomy of a Song: The Oral History of 45 Iconic Hits That Changed Rock, R&B and Pop* (New York: Grove Press, 2016), chapter 3.

44. Geoffrey Himes, "Isley Brothers: Positive Influence," *Washington Post*, September 20, 1996, https://www.washingtonpost.com/archive/lifestyle/1996/09/20/isley-brothers-positive-influence/37e28bcf-6b84-4828-8349-ff4f7f0358e7 (accessed January 14, 2018).

45. Isley Brothers, "Twist and Shout" (Wand Records, 1962). Composers: Russell and Medley.

46. U.S. Bonds, "New Orleans" (Legrand, 1960). Composers: Guida and Royster.

47. U.S. Bonds, "Quarter to Three" (Legrand, 1961). Composers: Barge, Guida, Anderson, and Royster.

48. Anderson denied the profanity, pointing out his mother was in the studio. See Bob Greene, "The Final Word On 'Quarter To Three,'" *Chicago Tribune*, September 7, 1994, http://articles.chicagotribune.com/1994-09-07/features/9409070038_1_mr-bonds-phrase-rumor (accessed May 22, 2017).

49. Jen McCaffery, "'Norfolk Sound' Creator Changed Rock 'n' Roll," *The Virginian-Pilot*, May 20, 2007, https://groups.google.com/forum/#!topic/alt.obituaries/k2Q27dVgg1g (accessed May 16, 2017).

50. The quote comes from "Gary 'U.S.' Bonds—This Little Girl is Mine," *Paste Magazine*, November 25, 2000, https://www.pastemagazine.com/articles/2007/04/gary-us-bonds-this -little-girl-is-mine2.html (accessed May 24, 2017).

51. Jimmy Soul, "If You Wanna Be Happy" (S.P.Q.R., 1963). Composers: Guida and Royster.

52. Ernie K-Doe, "Mother-In-Law" (Minit Records, 1961); Chris Kenner, "I Like It Like That" (Instant, 1961); Lee Dorsey, "Ya Ya" (Fury, 1961). Other examples include: Billy Bland, "Let the Little Girl Dance" (1961); Ron Holden, "Love You So" (1961); and Chuck Jackson, "I Don't Want to Cry" (1961) and "Any Day Now" (1962).

53. Leiber and Stoller, *Hound Dog*, 174; Emerson, *Always Magic in the Air*, 129.

54. Examples include: Solomon Burke, "Just Out of My Reach" (1961); Otis Redding, "These Arms of Mine" (1963); and Wilson Pickett, "It's Too Late" (1963).

55. Doris Troy, "Just One Look" (Atlantic Records, 1963). Composers: Troy and Carroll.

56. Jan Bradley, "Mama Didn't Lie" (Chess Records, 1963). Composer: Mayfield. Other hits by African-American women include: Damita Jo, "I'll Save the Last Dance for You" (1960) and "I'll Be There" (1961); Carla Thomas, "Gee Whiz" (1961); Barbara George, "I Know (You Don't Love Me No More)" (1962); Barbara Lynn, "You'll Lose a Good Thing" (1962); Betty Harris, "Cry to Me" (1963).

57. Ruby Nash quoted in David Barnett, "A Racial Divide, Diminished: What Was On the Radio in 1963," *All Things Considered*, NPR, July 10, 2013, https://www.npr.org/2013/07 /10/200465359/a-racial-divide-diminished-what-was-on-the-radio-in-1963 (accessed August 30, 2018).

58. Other pop-influenced groups include: Exciters, "Tell Him" (1962); Orlons, "The Wah Watusi" (1962), "Don't Hang Up" (1962), and "South Street" (1963); Tymes, "So Much in Love" and "Wonderful! Wonderful!" (both 1963).

59. Examples include: the Spinners, "That's What Girls Are Made For" (1961); Corsairs, "Smoky Places" (1962); Garnett Mimms and the Enchanters, "Cry Baby" (1963).

CHAPTER 6. "LET'S HAVE A PARTY!"

1. Melena Ryzik, "Rockabilly Queen Prolongs Her Party," *New York Times*, January 21, 2011, https://www.nytimes.com/2011/01/23/arts/music/23wanda.html (accessed October 29, 2020).

2. Rick Kienzle, liner notes, *Vintage Collections: Wanda Jackson* (Capitol Nashville Records, 1996).

3. Holly George-Warren, "Hard Headed Woman," *Offbeat Magazine*, May 1, 2009, http://www.offbeat.com/articles/hard-headed-woman (accessed January 7, 2020); Kienzle, liner notes.

4. George-Warren, "Hard Headed Woman."

5. Peter Lewry, "Interview with Bob Moore," *Art of Slap Bass*, April 6, 2020, https://www.artofslapbass.com/interview-with-bob-moore (accessed September 11, 2020).

6. David E. James, *Rock 'n' Film: Cinema's Dance with Popular Music* (New York: Oxford University Press, 2016), 111; Peter Guralnick, *Careless Love: The Unmasking of Elvis Presley* (Boston: Back Bay Books, 1999), 75.

7. Elizabeth McKeon and Linda Everett, *Elvis Speaks: Thoughts on Fame, Family, Music, and More in His Own Words* (Nashville: Cumberland House, 2004), 113, 114; *Elvis Commemorative Edition* (Lincolnwood, IL: Publications International, 2002), 113–16.

8. Siegel quoted in Chris Hodennfield, "Elvis Presley: Shake, Rattle and Roll 'Em," *Rolling Stone* (September 22, 1977), https://www.rollingstone.com/music/music-news/elvis-presley-shake-rattle-and-roll-em-49190/ (accessed January 30, 2022).

9. McKeon and Everett, *Elvis Speaks*, 137; Guralnick, *Careless Love*, 122. Some of Elvis's hits were solid rock & roll, including "(Marie's the Name) His Latest Flame" (1961), "Little Sister" (1961), and "Follow That Dream" (1962).

10. McKeon and Everett, *Elvis Speaks*, 126; Guralnick, *Careless Love*, 134.

11. Kurt Loder, "Everly Brothers: The *Rolling Stone* Interview," *Rolling Stone*, May 8, 1986, https://www.rollingstone.com/music/music-news/the-everly-brothers-the-rolling-stone-interview-110028 (accessed October 26, 2019).

12. Colin Escott, "Everly Brothers," in Paul Kingsbury (ed.), *Encyclopedia of Country Music* (New York: Oxford University Press, 1998), 167, 168; Phil Everly in Joe Smith (ed.), *Off the Record: An Oral History of Popular Music* (New York: Warner Books, 1988), 115, 116; Loder: "Everly Brothers."

13. Loder, "Everly Brothers"; Dave Simons, "That's Old Fashioned: Capturing the Sound of the Everly Brothers," *BMI Music World*, November 20, 2012, https://www.bmi.com/news/entry/thats_old_fashioned_capturing_the_sound_of_the_everly_brothers (accessed October 26, 2019).

14. Everly Brothers, "Bye Bye Love" (Cadence, 1957). Composers: Boudleaux and Felice Bryant.

15. "How Music Row & Acuff-Rose Killed the Everly Brothers," *savingcountrymusic.com*, https://www.savingcountrymusic.com/how-music-row-acuff-rose-killed-the-everly-brothers (accessed October 29, 2019); Loder, "Everly Brothers"; Phil Everly quoted in Franklin Bruno, "The Honeymooners," in Alex Ross, ed. *Best Rock Writing 2011* (New York: DaCapo Press, 2011), 204, 205.

16. Loder, "Everly Brothers"; Boyce Rensberger, "Amphetamines Used by a Physician to Lift Moods of Famous Patients," *New York Times*, December 4, 1972, https://www.nytimes

.com/1972/12/04/archives/amphetamines-used-by-a-physician-to-lift-moods-of-famous
-patients.html (accessed October 29, 2019).

17. Everly Brothers, "Cathy's Clown" (Warner, 1960). Composers: Don and Phil Everly; Don's quote appears in Loder, "Everly Brothers."

18. Everly Brothers, "Crying in the Rain" (Warner, 1961). Composers: Greenfield and King.

19. Loder, "Everly Brothers."

20. Ray Connolly, "Why DID the Everly Brothers hate each other?" *DailyMail.com*, January 5, 2014, https://www.dailymail.co.uk/tvshowbiz/article-2534400/Why-DID-Everly -Brothers-hate-RAY-CONNOLLY-reflects-little-concord-singing-duos-relationship.html (accessed November 2, 2019); Loder, "Everly Brothers."

21. "Don's Illness," *It Lasted.com*, n.d., https://itlasted.com/dons-illness (retrieved November 2, 2019); Loder, "Everly Brothers."

22. Loder, "Everly Brothers."

23. Everly Brothers, "Nancy's Minuet" (Warner, 1963). Composer: D. Everly.

24. Chris Talbott, "Don Everly Receives 'Special Spiritual Message,'" *Associated Press*, January 4, 2014, https://www.yahoo.com/entertainment/news/don-everly-receives-39-special -spiritual-message-39-181017985.html (accessed November 2, 2019).

25. Jon Pareles, "Phil Everly, Half of a Pioneer Rock Duo That Inspired Generations, Dies at 74," *New York Times*, January 4, 2014, https://www.nytimes.com/2014/01/05/arts /music/phil-everly-half-of-pioneer-rock-duo-dies-at-74.html?_r=0 (accessed November 2, 2019); Escott, "Everly Brothers," 167.

26. Berry quoted in Arnold Shaw, *The Rockin' 50s: The Decade That Transformed the Pop Music Scene* (New York: Hawthorn Books, 1974), 187–88.

27. "Brenda Lee: the Lady, the Legend," press packet sent by Jackie Monaghan of Brenda Lee Productions Inc. to NPR's *Rock & Roll America* (1995); Irwin Stambler and Grelun Landon, *Country Music: The Encyclopedia* (New York: St. Martin's, 1997), 250, 251.

28. Bradley quoted in Joseph Sweat, "The Brenda Lee Story," *Billboard*, May 28, 1966: BL-10

29. Brenda Lee, "Sweet Nothin's" (Decca, 1960). Composer: Self.

30. Richard Aquila, interview with Brenda Lee for NPR's *Rock & Roll America* (October 17, 1995).

31. Bradley in Sweat, "The Brenda Lee Story," BL-22; Aquila, interview with Brenda Lee.

32. Bradley in Sweat, "The Brenda Lee Story," BL-22.

33. Aquila, interview with Brenda Lee.

34. Bradley in Sweat, "The Brenda Lee Story," BL-22.

35. Brenda Lee, "Dum Dum" (Decca, 1961). Composers: DeShannon and Sheeley.

36. Brenda Lee, "Let's Jump the Broomstick" (Decca, 1959). Composer: Robins.

37. Aquila, interview with Brenda Lee.

38. Ibid.

39. Ibid.

40. Jonathan Bernstein, "Inside the Life of Brenda Lee, the Pop Heroine Next Door," *Rolling Stone*, February 20, 2018, https://www.rollingstone.com/music/music-features/inside-the-life-of-brenda-lee-the-pop-heroine-next-door-205175/ (accessed November 8, 2019); Ken Morton, "Brenda Lee: A Sparkling Interview with Little Miss Dynamite," *Highwire Daze*, May 6, 2017, https://highwiredaze.com/2017/05/06/brendaleeint1 (accessed November 5, 2019).

41. Aquila, interview with Brenda Lee.

42. Aquila, interview with Brenda Lee; Krause quoted in J. Bernstein, "Inside the Life of Brenda Lee."

43. Aquila, interview with Brenda Lee.

44. John Lennon quote from https://www.rockhall.com/inductees/brenda-lee (retrieved November 10, 2019).

45. Eric Westervelt, "Roy Orbison: A Great Voice, A Lonely Sound," *All Things Considered*, NPR, May 3, 2010, https://www.npr.org/templates/story/story.php?storyId=126475636 (accessed October 19, 2019); Al Rudis, "Roy Orbison's Career Rocketed from 1 Note," *Chicago Tribune*, February 24, 1987, https://www.chicagotribune.com/news/ct-xpm-1987-02-24-8701150683-story.html (accessed October 23, 2019).

46. Colin Escott with Martin Hawkins, *Good Rockin' Tonight: Sun Records and the Birth of Rock 'n' Roll* (New York: St. Martin's Press, 1991), 148; "Roy Orbison: Biography," *sunrecords.com*, https://www.sunrecords.com/artists/roy-orbison (accessed December 12, 2019); Bruce Eder, "The Teen Kings," *AllMusic.com*, https://www.allmusic.com/artist/the-teen-kings-mn0000476539/biography (accessed December 14, 2019); Orbison quoted in Smith, *Off the Record*, 100.

47. Escott, *Good Rockin' Tonight*, 149; Roy Orbison interview in "Chuck Berry: Hail! Hail! Rock 'n' Roll" (dir. Taylor Hackford, 1987), https://www.youtube.com/watch?v=j492RhfRt7Y (accessed February 1, 2022); Eder, "Teen Kings."

48. Escott, *Good Rockin' Tonight*, 151; Ari Surdoval, "Sweet Dreams: Roy Orbison and the Birth of the Pop Masterpiece," *Music World*, February 24, 2009, https://www.bmi.com/news/entry/sweet_dreams_roy_orbison_and_the_birth_of_the_pop_masterpiece (accessed October 23, 2019); "Roy Orbison: Biography"; Rick Kennedy and Randy McNutt, *Little Labels—Big Sound: Small Record Companies and the Rise of American Music* (Bloomington: Indiana University Press, 1999), 145, 146; Rachel DiGregorio, "Talk Thursday to Me: Fred Foster," *Postcard Elba* (blog), April 28, 2011, https://postcardelba.wordpress.com/2011/04/28/talk-thursday-to-me-fred-foster/ (accessed October 19, 2019).

49. Roy Orbison, "Up Town" (Monument, 1960). Composers: Orbison and Melson.

50. DiGregorio, "Talk Thursday to Me: Fred Foster."

51. Roy Orbison, "Only the Lonely (Know the Way I Feel)" (Monument, 1960). Composers: Orbison and Melson.

52. Roy Orbison, "Running Scared" (Monument, 1961). Composers: Orbison and Melson.

53. DiGregorio, "Talk Thursday to Me: Fred Foster"; Foster interviewed in *Country Music: A Film by Ken Burns* (dir. Burns, 2019), https://www.thirteen.org/programs/country -music/producer-fred-foster-runnin-scared-f5q3jb (accessed October 19, 2019).

54. Orbison quoted in Rudis, "Roy Orbison's Career Rocketed"; Fred Foster quoted in Erick Trickey, "Roy Orbison Revealed," *clevelandmagzine.com*, October 31, 2006, https:// clevelandmagazine.com/entertainment/music/articles/roy-orbison-revealed (accessed October 19, 2019).

55. Foster quoted in John Broven, *Record Makers and Breakers: Voices of the Independent Rock 'n' Roll Pioneers* (Urbana: University of Illinois Press, 2010), 413; Porter quoted in Steve Sullivan, *Encyclopedia of Great Popular Song Recordings, Vol. 1* (Lanham, MD: Scarecrow Press, 2013) and Michael Fremer, "Interview with Elvis Presley's Sound Engineer, Bill Porter," *Elvis Australia*, April 1, 2017, https://www.elvis.com.au/presley/interview-with-elvis-presleys -sound-engineer-bill-porter.shtml (accessed October 23, 2019).

56. DiGregorio, "Talk Thursday to Me: Fred Foster."

57. Jim Sullivan, "Roy Orbison: 'My voice is a gift,'" *Guardian*, December 4, 2013, https://www.theguardian.com/music/2013/dec/04/roy-orbison-rocks-backpages (accessed October 19, 2019); Dion quoted in "100 Greatest Singers of All Time," *Rolling Stone*, December 3, 2010, https://www.rollingstone.com/music/music-lists/100-greatest-singers-of -all-time-147019/?list_page=2 (accessed November 15, 2019).

58. Roy Orbison, "Pretty Paper" (Monument, 1964). Composer: Willie Nelson.

59. Orbison quoted in Steve Pond, "Roy Orbison's Triumphs and Tragedies," *Rolling Stone*, January 26, 1989, https://www.rollingstone.com/music/music-news/roy-orbisons -triumphs-and-tragedies-103421 (accessed January 12, 2020).

60. The video of Orbison is available on YouTube, https://www.youtube.com/watch?v =KfHPie6cLx8 (accessed January 12, 2020); Orbison quoted in Smith, *Off the Record*, 101.

61. Trickey, "Roy Orbison Revealed."

62. Roy Orbison, "In the Real World" (Virgin, 1989). Composers: Jennings and Kerr.

63. Fendermen, "Mule Skinner Blues" (Soma, 1960). Composer: Rodgers.

64. Examples include: Conway Twitty, "Lonely Blue Boy"; Donnie Brooks, "Mission Bell"; Alvie Self, "Nancy" (all 1960); and Johnny Cash, "Ring of Fire" (1963).

65. Scott quoted in Paul Rigby, "Jack Scott: A Struggle with Stardom," *The Audiophile Man*, December 20, 2019, https://theaudiophileman.com/jack-scott-rock-interview-bear -family (accessed January 16, 2020).

66. Richard Aquila, interview with Jerry Allison (Crickets) for NPR's *Rock & Roll America* (January 5, 1999).

67. McCartney quoted in Nicholas Mojica, "Buddy Holly 80th Birthday . . . ," *International Business Times*, September 7, 2016, https://www.ibtimes.com/buddy-holly-80th-birthday-11 -quotes-lyrics-remember-peggy-sue-singer-2412512 (accessed October 12, 2020).

68. Richard Aquila, interview with Johnny Tillotson for NPR's *Rock & Roll America*, (January 21, 1998).

69. Ibid.

70. Ibid.

71. Ibid.

72. Ibid.

73. https://dos.myflorida.com/cultural/programs/florida-artists-hall-of-fame/johnny -tillotson (accessed December 15, 2020); Aquila, interview with Johnny Tillotson.

CHAPTER 7. "A TEENAGER IN LOVE"

1. Richard Aquila, interview with Dion for NPR's *Rock & Roll America*, (October 19, 1995); Dion DiMucci with Davin Seay, *The Wanderer: Dion's Story* (New York: Beech Tree Books, 1988), 75.

2. Ken Emerson, *Always Magic in the Air: The Bomp and Brilliance of the Brill Building Sound* (New York: Viking, 2005), 48.

3. Dion and the Belmonts, "A Teenager in Love" (Laurie Records, 1959). Composers: Pomus and Shuman.

4. DiMucci and Seay, *The Wanderer*, 55, 56, 92.

5. Emerson, *Always Magic in the Air*, 49, 50.

6. Ibid., xii, 17.

7. Ibid., 267–68.

8. Richard Aquila, interview with Pat Boone for NPR's *Rock & Roll America* (June 12 and 25, 1998).

9. Ibid.

10. Ibid.

11. Ibid.

12. Ibid.

13. Joel Selvin, *Ricky Nelson: Idol for a Generation* (Chicago: Contemporary Books, 1990), 60, 66, 67; liner notes, *Ricky/Ricky Nelson* (Imperial Records/Capitol Records, 2002).

14. Jeremy Roberts, "James Burton Interview: Rick Nelson—and Elvis," *Elvis Information Network*, April, 2011, https://www.elvisinfonet.com/interview_james_burton_rick_nelson .html (accessed January 24, 2020).

15. Ricky Nelson, "Travelin' Man" (Imperial, 1961). Composer: Fuller.

16. Haskell quoted in James Ritz, liner notes, *Rick Nelson: Greatest Hits* (Capitol Records, 2002): 5.

17. Roberts, "James Burton Interview."

18. For details about Nelson's sound, see Bruce Bartlett, "In the Studio: Detailing the Techniques Used to Record Rick Nelson," *HistoryofRecording.com*, https://www .historyofrecording.com/Rick_Nelson.html (accessed February 18, 2020); Fogerty quoted in Selvin, *Ricky Nelson*, 8.

19. Paul Anka with David Dalton, *My Way: An Autobiography* (New York: St. Martin's Press, 2013), 49.

20. Anka's quotes come from the official Paul Anka website, from www.paulanka.com (accessed February 24, 2020); and Robert Kiener, "Teen Idol," *Readers Digest Canada*, July, 2011: 74.

21. Paul Anka, *My Way*, 78.

22. Ibid., 50–51.

23. Jerry Osborne, "An Interview with Connie Francis," *DISCoveries Magazine*, September 1991; Karen Schoemer, *Great Pretenders: My Strange Love Affair With '50s Pop Music* (New York: Free Press, 2006), 175.

24. Osborne, "An Interview with Connie Francis"; Michael Shore with Dick Clark, *The History of American Bandstand* (New York: Ballantine Books, 1985), 31.

25. Micki Siegel, "Look! She Reminds Me of Me," *TV Radio Mirror*, October, 1962: 38, 89–90.

26. Connie Francis, liner notes, *More Italian Favorites* (MGM Records, 1961).

27. Al DiOrio, *Borrowed Time: The 37 Years of Bobby Darin* (Philadelphia: Running Press, 1986), 49–51.

28. Dick Clark and Richard Robinson, *Rock, Roll & Remember* (New York: Popular Library, 1976), 217, 218.

29. Quotes come from Bobby Darin website www.bobbydarin.net, and Jimmy Mc-Donough, *Shakey: Neil Young's Biography* (New York: Anchor Books, 2003), 65, 66, 716.

30. Emerson, *Always Magic in the Air*, 66, 67, 71–75, 77, 104; Patricia Romanowski and Holly George-Warren, *The New Rolling Stone Encyclopedia of Rock & Roll* (New York: Rolling Stone/Fireside, 1995), 880, 881; Bruce Pollock, *When Rock Was Young* (New York: Holt, Rinehart, and Winston, 1981), 149, 150.

31. Emerson, *Always Magic in the Air*, 107.

32. Ibid.

33. Mark Marymont, "Frankie Avalon," liner note, *The Very Best of Frankie Avalon, Venus* (Collectibles Records, 1999); John A. Jackson, *American Bandstand: Dick Clark and the Making of a Rock 'N' Roll Empire* (New York: Oxford University Press, 1997), 62, 63.

34. Avalon quoted in Shore and Clark, *History of American Bandstand*, 29, 30.

35. Schoemer, *Great Pretenders*, 159, 165, 167.

36. Ibid., 166.

37. Clark, *Rock, Roll & Remember*, 210, 211.

38. Fabian quoted in Shore and Clark, *History of American Bandstand*, 28.

39. Richard Aquila, interview with Bobby Rydell (August 6, 2013). See also Bobby Rydell with Allen Slutsky, *Teen Idol On The Rocks: A Tale of Second Chances* (Cherry Hill, NJ: Doctor Licks Publishing, 2016).

40. Aquila, interview with Bobby Rydell.

41. Ibid.

42. Ibid.

43. Ibid.

44. Rydell quoted in Jeff Tamarkin, "The Bobby Rydell Story," liner notes, *The Best of Bobby Rydell: Cameo-Parkway, 1959–1964* (Cameo-Parkway Records, 2005), 3–4.

45. Aquila, interview with Bobby Rydell.

46. Ibid.

47. Ibid.

48. Ibid.

49. Ibid.

50. Ibid.

51. Jeff Tamarkin, "The Cameo Parkway Story," liner notes, *Cameo Parkway, 1957–1967* (ABKCO Industries, 2005), 2–19.

52. Jackson, *American Bandstand*, 148, 149; Clark, *Rock, Roll & Remember*, 224, 227.

53. Clark, *Rock, Roll & Remember*, 324.

54. Clark, *Rock, Roll & Remember*, 324–27; Richard Aquila, interview with Dick Clark for NPR's *Rock & Roll America* (August 4, 1998).

55. Dodie Stevens, "No" (Dot Records, 1960). Composers: Pockriss and Vance.

56. Examples include: Four Preps, "More Money for You and Me" (1961), "The Big Draft" (1962); Danny & the Juniors, "Twistin' U.S.A." (1960); Skyliners, "Pennies from Heaven" (1960); Crests, "Step By Step" (1960), "Trouble in Paradise" (1960); Diamonds, "One Summer Night" (1961).

57. DiMucci and Seay, *The Wanderer*, 74.

58. Casey Chambers, "Interview: Gary Troxel," *thecollegecrowddigsme.com* (blog), July 26, 2016, https://www.thecollegecrowddigsme.com/2016/07/interview-gary-troxel -fleetwoods.html (accessed March 12, 2020).

CHAPTER 8. "TAKE GOOD CARE OF MY BABY"

1. Bobby Vee, "Take Good Care of My Baby" (Liberty Records, 1961). Composers: King and Goffin.

2. Richard Aquila, interview with Bobby Vee for NPR's *Rock & Roll America* (February 14, 1995).

3. David P. Szatmary, *A Time to Rock: A Social History of Rock-and-Roll* (New York: Schirmer Books, 1996), 61, 62; John Broven, *Record Makers and Breakers: Voices of the Independent Rock 'N' Roll Pioneers* (Urbana: University of Illinois Press, 2009), 484; data for number of births comes from https://www.cdc.gov/nchs/data/statab/natfinal2003.annvol1 _01.pdf (accessed June 27, 2021).

4. Dion DiMucci, "The Dion Interview," provided by Dion's talent agent, Howard Silverman of Paradise Artists, Inc., to NPR's *Rock & Roll America* (October, 1995).

5. Richard Aquila, interview with Dion for NPR's *Rock & Roll America*, (October 19, 1995).

6. Dion, "Runaround Sue" (Laurie, 1961). Composers: DiMucci and Maresca; Aquila, interview with Dion; Dion DiMucci with Mike Aquilina, *Dion the Wanderer Talks Truth* (Cincinnati, OH: Servant Books, 2011), 55.

7. Aquila, interview with Dion; Dion DiMucci with David Seay, *The Wanderer: Dion's Story* (New York: Beech Tree Books, 1988), 106.

8. Scott Kempner, "Kickin' Child: Dion at Columbia, 1965," liner notes, *Dion: Kickin' Child: The Lost Album, 1965* (Norton Records, 2017), 3; DiMucci and Seay, *The Wanderer*, 132–34.

9. DiMucci and Aquilina, *Dion the Wanderer*, 62–67; DiMucci and Seay, *The Wanderer*, 144; Aquila, interview with Dion.

10. Aquila, interview with Dion; DiMucci and Seay, *The Wanderer*, 142, 149.

11. Dion, "Donna the Prima Donna" (Columbia, 1963). Composers: DiMucci and Maresca; DiMucci and Seay, *The Wanderer*, 150.

12. Aquila, interview with Dion.

13. Ibid.

14. Aquila, interview with Dion; liner notes, *Donna the Prima Donna* (Columbia, 1963).

15. Aquila, interview with Dion; DiMucci and Aquilina, *Dion the Wanderer*, 54.

16. DiMucci and Aquilina, *Dion the Wanderer*, 109.

17. Aquila, interview with Dion; DiMucci and Aquilina, *Dion the Wanderer*, 37.

18. Dion with Paul Simon, "Song for Sam Cooke (Here in America)" (Keeping the Blues Alive Records, 2020). Composers: DiMucci and Aquilina. https://www.youtube.com/watch?v =pA2AyRi7MuA (accessed June 28, 2021).

19. DiMucci, "The Dion Interview"; Lou Reed in liner notes, Dion, *King of the New York Streets* (Arista, 1989).

20. Bud Buschardt, "Interview: Bobby Vee," in Bob Celli, *Friends of Bobby Vee Newsletter* (September 1994): 8.

21. Aquila, interview with Bobby Vee (1995).

22. Aquila, interview with Bobby Vee (1995); Bobby Vee, liner notes, *Bobby Vee and the Shadows: The Early Rockin' Years* (Cema/Capitol, 1995), 4.

23. Aquila, interview with Bobby Vee (1995); Bobby Vee, liner notes, 12; Richard Aquila, interview with Snuff Garrett for NPR's *Rock & Roll America* (March 13, 1998).

24. Aquila, interview with Bobby Vee (1995); Richard Aquila, interview with Bobby Vee (October 17, 1990).

25. Aquila, interview with Snuff Garrett.

26. Bobby Vee, liner notes, 7; Aquila, interview with Bobby Vee (1995).

27. Richard Aquila, interview with Bobby Vee (July 25, 2006); Aquila, interview with Bobby Vee (1995); Aquila, interview with Bobby Vee (1990).

28. Aquila, interview with Bobby Vee (1995); Buschardt, "Interview: Bobby Vee," 9.

29. Aquila, interview with Bobby Vee (1995); Buschardt, "Interview: Bobby Vee," 9. Studio musicians on Vee's hits include Red Callender, Earl Palmer, Barney Kessel, James Burton, Glen Campbell, Tommy Allsup, and Leon Russell.

30. Aquila, interview with Bobby Vee (1995); Aquila, interview with Bobby Vee (1990).

31. Aquila, interview with Bobby Vee (1990); Aquila, interview with Bobby Vee (1995).

32. Aquila, interview with Bobby Vee (1995).

33. Ibid.

34. Alexis Petridis, "Life After Tulsa," *Guardian*, May 14, 2003, https://www.theguardian.com/music/2003/may/14/artsfeatures.popandrock (accessed April 13, 2020).

35. "Gene Pitney Biography," http://www.genepitney.com/printerbio.html (accessed April 10, 2020); Jim Liddane, "Gene Pitney," *Songwriter Magazine*, http://www.songwriter.co.uk/page71.html (accessed April 11, 2020).

36. Liddane, "Gene Pitney"; Ken Burke, "Gene Pitney Biography," *Musicianguide.com*, https://musicianguide.com/biographies/1608003442/Gene-Pitney.html (accessed February 3, 2020).

37. Gene Pitney, "Twenty Four Hours from Tulsa" (Musicor, 1963). Composers: Bacharach and David; Liddane, "Gene Pitney."

38. Spencer Leigh, "Gene Pitney . . . ," *Independent*, April 6, 2006, https://www.independent.co.uk/news/obituaries/gene-pitney-6104462.html (accessed April 18, 2020); Bob Greene, "Does It Hurt to Be Gene Pitney?" *Chicago Tribune*, September 14, 1997, https://www.chicagotribune.com/news/ct-xpm-1997-09-14-9709140455-story.html (accessed April 18, 2020).

39. Greene, "Does It Hurt to Be Gene Pitney;" Graham Keal, "Still Giving It All He'd Got," *Northern Echo*, April 6, 2006, https://www.thenorthernecho.co.uk/news/7160711.still-giving-got (accessed April 9, 2020).

40. Dawn Eden, "I've Never, Ever Been Away," *National Review*, April 7, 2006, https://www.nationalreview.com/2006/04/ive-never-ever-been-away-dawn-eden (accessed April 19, 2020); Karen Price, "Pitney Dies After 'Fine Performance,'" *Wales Online*, April 6, 2006, https://www.walesonline.co.uk/news/wales-news/pitney-dies-after-fine-performance -2342618 (accessed November 13, 2020).

41. Del Shannon, "Runaway" (Bigtop, 1961). Composers: Shannon and Crook.

42. Joe Smith, *Off the Record: An Oral History of Popular Music* (New York: Warner Books, 1988), 112.

43. "Interview with Max Crook," *Nightwaves Magazine*, http://nightwaveswebsite.tripod .com/id30.html (accessed April 4, 2020); Crook also quoted in Brian C. Young, "The Making of 'Runaway,'" *delshannon.com*, http://www.delshannon.com (April 7, 2020).

44. Buschardt, "Interview: Bobby Vee," 8.

45. Shannon quoted in Bob Celli, *Friends of Bobby Vee Newsletter* (February, 1994): 2; Richard Bak, "Del Shannon's 'Runaway' Success Led to His Downfall," *Hour Detroit Magazine*, June 30, 2011, https://www.hourdetroit.com/community/del-shannons-runaway -success-led-to-his-downfall (accessed April 7, 2020).

46. Jim Clash, "Rocker Dion DiMucci on . . . Del Shannon," *Forbes*, February 15, 2019, from https://www.forbes.com/sites/jimclash/2019/02/15/rocker-dion-dimucci-on-his-big-hit -the-wanderer-del-shannon/#73ce35296d4d (accessed April 6, 2020); Buschardt, "Interview: Bobby Vee."

47. Del Shannon, liner notes, *Little Town Flirt* (Bigtop, 1963); Aquila, interview with Dion; DiMucci and Seay, *The Wanderer*, 102; Clash, "Rocker Dion DiMucci."

48. Bak, "Del Shannon's 'Runaway Success,'"

49. Johnny Preston, "Running Bear" (Mercury, 1960). Composer: Richardson; Richard Aquila, interview with Johnny Preston for NPR's *Rock & Roll America* (January, 1998).

50. Mark Dinning, "Teen Angel" (MGM, 1960). Composer: Surrey.

51. Brian Hyland later earned several Top 30 hits, including two number 3 records— "Sealed With a Kiss" (1962) and "Gypsy Woman" (1970). Tommy Roe scored major hits such as "Everybody" (1963), "Sweet Pea" (1966), and "Dizzy" (1969). Bobby Vinton racked up thirty Top 40 hits, including two additional number 1 records—"Mr. Lonely" (1964), and "There! I've Said It Again" (1964).

52. Examples from 1961 include: Troy Shondell, "This Time"; Ral Donner, "You Don't Know What You've Got"; Kenny Dino, "Your Ma Said You Cried in Your Sleep Last Night"; Tony Orlando, "Bless You"; Buzz Clifford, "Baby Sittin' Boogie." Hits in 1962 include: Mike Clifford, "Close to Cathy"; Larry Finnegan, "Dear One"; Chris Montez, "Let's Dance"; Kris Jensen, "Torture"; Ernie Maresca, "Shout! Shout! (Knock Yourself Out)." In 1963 hits included: Paul Petersen, "My Dad"; Johnny Cymbal, "Mr. Bass Man." And in 1964, Terry Stafford, "Suspicion."

53. Ray Peterson, "Tell Laura I Love Her" (RCA-Victor, 1960). Composers: Barry and Raleigh.

54. Dickey Lee, "Patches" (Smash, 1962). Composers: Mann and Kolber.

55. Carla Stockton, "Get Real: Lightnin' Keeps Strikin'—An Interview with Lou Christie," *Columbia Journal*, February 20, 2016, http://columbiajournal.org/get-real-lightnin-keeps -strikin-an-interview-with-lou-christie (accessed April 23, 2020).

56. Gaudio quoted in Terry Gross, "How the Four Seasons Clashed, Dealt with the Mob and Made Lasting Hits," *All Things Considered*, NPR, September 9, 2014, https://www.wbur .org/npr/346988513/how-the-four-seasons-clashed-dealt-with-the-mob-and-made-lasting -hits (accessed April 24, 2020).

57. Richard Aquila, interview with Bob Gaudio for NPR's *Rock & Roll America* (October 1999); David Cote, *Jersey Boys: The Story of Frankie Valli and the Four Seasons* (New York: Broadway Books, 2007), 33, 34.

58. Aquila, interview with Bob Gaudio.

59. Ibid.

60. Ibid.

61. The 4 Seasons, "Big Girls Don't Cry" (Vee Jay, 1962). Composers: Gaudio and Crewe.

62. Aquila, interview with Bob Gaudio; 4 Seasons, "Walk Like a Man" (Vee Jay, 1963). Composers: Gaudio and Crewe.

63. Aquila, interview with Bob Gaudio; 4 Seasons, "Dawn (Go Away)" (Phillips, 1964). Composers: Gaudio and Linzer.

64. Aquila, interview with Bob Gaudio.

65. Ibid.

66. Ibid.

67. Ed Masley, "Frankie Valli: Jersey Boy looks back on Four Seasons, Broadway Hit that Revived his Career," *AZCentral*, December 6, 2016, https://www.azcentral.com/story /entertainment/music/2016/12/06/frankie-valli-interview-four-seasons-jersey-boys/95006166 (accessed May 4, 2020); Cote, *Jersey Boys*, 9.

68. Valli quoted in Ed Masley, "Frankie Valli;" Gaudio quoted in Gross, "How The Four Seasons Clashed."

69. Gaudio quoted in Gross, "How The Four Seasons Clashed."

70. Aquila, interview with Bob Gaudio.

71. Aquila, interview with Bob Gaudio; Gross, "How The Four Seasons Clashed."

72. Cote, *Jersey Boys*, 152.

73. Lettermen, "Come Back Silly Girl" (Capitol, 1962). Composer: Mann.

74. Richard Aquila, interview with Tony Butala for NPR's *Rock & Roll America* (February 17, 1998).

75. Kingsmen, "Louie Louie" (Wand Records, 1963). Composer: Berry.

76. The letter may be viewed in *FBI Records: The Vault*, 13, https://vault.fbi.gov/louie-louie-the-song/louie-louie-the-song/view (accessed May 10, 2020) [hereafter cited as *FBI Records*].

77. Dave Marsh, *Louie Louie: The History & Mythology of the World's Most Famous Rock 'n' Roll Song* (New York: Hyperion, 1993), 124–26, 128; Will Higgins, "That Time Indiana Teens Ratted Out Dirty 'Louie Louie' Lyrics, and the FBI Got Involved," *Indy Star*, January 2, 2019, https://www.indystar.com/story/entertainment/2019/01/02/kingsmen-louie-louie-richard-berry-song-lyrics-dirty-version-fbi-investigation-indiana-teens/2240339002 (accessed May 8, 2020); Peter Blecha, *Sonic Boom: The History of Northwest Rock, from "Louie Louie" to "Smells Like Teen Spirit"* (New York: Backbeat Books, 2009), 152.

78. Higgins, "That Time Indiana Teens . . ."

79. *FBI Records*, 7.

80. *FBI Records*, 62.

81. Documents related to complaints filed in 1964–65 are sprinkled throughout the FBI's 119-page file; Berry's original lyrics are on p. 37, the obscene lyrics are on p. 22.

82. *FBI Records*, 45, 46.

83. Gary Graff, "Rock and Roll Hall of Fame Inducts . . . 'Louie Louie,'" *Billboard*, April 14, 2018, https://www.billboard.com/articles/columns/rock/8333912/rock-and-roll-hall-of-fame-inducts-songs-born-to-be-wild-louie-louie (accessed May 10, 2020).

84. Carl Wiser, "Kenny Vance," *Songfacts.com*, April 3, 2008, https://www.songfacts.com/blog/interviews/kenny-vance (accessed June 28, 2021).

85. The Lafayettes, "Life's Too Short" (RCA, 1962). Composers: Bonner and Huth.

86. Dick and Deedee, "The Mountain's High" (Liberty, 1961). Composer: St. John.

87. Paul and Paula, "Hey Paula" (Philips, 1963). Composer: Hildebrand.

88. Timi Yuro, "What's a Matter Baby" (Liberty, 1962). Composers: Otis and Byers.

89. Shelley Fabares, "Johnny Angel" (Colpix, 1962). Composers: Duddy and Pockriss.

90. Joanie Sommers, "Johnny Get Angry" (Warner Brothers, 1962). Composers: Edwards and David.

91. Carole King, *A Natural Woman: A Memoir* (New York: Grand Central, 2012), 106–8; Carole King, "It Might as Well Rain Until September" (Dimension, 1962). Composers: Goffin and King; Carole King, "He's a Bad Boy" (Dimension, 1963). Composers: Goffin and King.

92. Little Peggy March, "I Will Follow Him" (RCA, 1963). Composers: Altman, Gimbel, Stole, and Roma.

93. Richard Aquila, interview with Peggy March for NPR's *Rock & Roll America* (March 1998).

94. Lesley Gore, "It's My Party" (Mercury Records, 1963). Composers: Wiener, Gluck, and Gold.

95. Lesley Gore, "Judy's Turn to Cry" (Mercury, 1963). Composers: Ross and Lewis.

96. Margaret Farrell, "The Teenage Wisdom of 'Lesley Gore Sings of Mixed-Up Hearts,'" *NPR Music Reviews*, August 30, 2017, https://www.npr.org/2017/08/30/546386766/forebears -the-teenage-wisdom-of-lesley-gore-sings-of-mixed-up-hearts (accessed May 15, 2020).

97. Gary James, "Interview with Lesley Gore," *classicbands.com*, http://www.classicbands .com/LesleyGoreInterview.html (accessed May 15, 2020).

98. Lesley Gore, "You Don't Own Me" (Mercury, 1964). Composers: White and Madara.

99. Dave Davies, "Fresh Air Remembers Lesley Gore . . . ," *Fresh Air*, NPR, February 20, 2015, https://www.npr.org/2015/02/20/387769267/fresh-air-remembers-lesley-gore-who -sang-hits-including-you-dont-own-me (accessed May 15, 2020).

100. Gore quoted in Jon Kutner, "You Don't Own Me (Lesley Gore)," *Jonkutner.com*, December 27, 2015, https://www.jonkutner.com/you-dont-own-me-lesley-gore (accessed May 20, 2020).

101. Marcie Blane, "Bobby's Girl" (Seville, 1962). Composers: Hoffman and Klein.

102. Aquila, interview with Bobby Vee (1995).

103. John Beland quoted in Paul Freeman, "Rick Nelson: Rock 'n' Roll Pioneer" *Pop Culture Classics*, http://popcultureclassics.com/rick_nelson.html (accessed on February 3, 2020).

CHAPTER 9. "WILD WEEKEND"

1. Richard Aquila, interview with Tom Shannon for NPR's *Rock & Roll America* (June 17, 1998).

2. For information about Top 40 radio, see Ben Fong-Torres, *The Hits Just Keep on Coming: The History of Top 40 Radio* (San Francisco: Miller-Freeman Books, 1998).

3. Aquila, interview with Tom Shannon.

4. Aquila, interview with Tom Shannon; the theme can be heard at https://www.youtube .com/watch?v=EUkH7_GSD9A (accessed July 5, 2021).

5. Ibid.

6. For information about the Rebels, see *colorradio.com*, http://www.colorradio.com /rebels.html (accessed September 13, 2020). "Wild Weekend" was later covered by numerous bands and influenced John Fogerty's "Rock and Roll Girls" (1985), which featured "Wild Weekend's" distinct guitar riffs and blaring sax, as well as lyrics that mentioned Buffalo and listening to the radio.

7. Richard Aquila, interview with Duane Eddy for NPR's *Rock & Roll America* (August 12, 1998).

8. Aquila, interview with Duane Eddy. The Sharps became the Rivingtons and had a hit with "Papa Oom Mow Mow" (1962).

9. Aquila, interview with Duane Eddy.

10. Ibid.

11. Aquila, interview with Duane Eddy; Dan Forte, liner notes, *Twang Thang: The Duane Eddy Anthology* (Rhino Records, 1993), 23.

12. Aquila, interview with Duane Eddy.

13. Ibid.

14. Ibid.

15. Ibid.

16. Other examples include: Bill Black, "White Silver Sands"; Johnny & the Hurricanes, "Beatnik Fly"; Chet Atkins, "Teensville" (all in 1960); Royaltones, "Flamingo Express"; Bob Moore, "Mexico" (both in 1961); Champs, "Limbo Rock"; Ace Cannon, "Tuff"; Dave "Baby" Cortez, "Rinky Dink"; Virtues, "Guitar Boogie Shuffle Twist" (all in 1962).

17. Don Wilson quoted in Del Halterman, with Josie Wilson, Bob Bogle, and Don Wilson, *Walk—Don't Run: The Story of the Ventures*, 2nd edition (Raleigh, NC: Lulu Press, 2009), 16.

18. Steve Otfinoski, *The Golden Age of Rock Instrumentals* (New York: Billboard Books, 1997), 52–54; Halterman, *Walk—Don't Run*, 40.

19. Bob Shannon and John Javna, *Behind the Hits* (New York: Warner Books, 1986), 102; Otfinoski, *Golden Age,* 52–54.

20. Lisa Torem, "Ventures Interview," *Pennyblackmusic Magazine*, October 27, 2011, http://www.pennyblackmusic.co.uk/MagSitePages/Article/6228/Ventures-Interview (accessed September 8, 2020).

21. Torem, "Ventures Interview."

22. Dennis McLellan, "Bob Bogle/ Co-Founder and Lead Guitarist of 1960s Rock Band the Ventures," *Pittsburgh Post-Gazette*, June 17, 2009, https://www.post-gazette.com/news/obituaries /2009/06/17/Obituary-Bob-Bogle-Co-founder-and-lead-guitarist-of-1960s-rock-band-the -Ventures/stories/200906170178 (accessed September 8, 2020); Torem, "Ventures Interview."

23. Halterman, *Walk—Don't Run*, 68, 70; Torem, "Ventures Interview."

24. https://www.rockhall.com/inductees/ventures (accessed September 7, 2020).

25. Two of the Mar-Keys, Steve Cropper and Donald Dunn, later became members of Booker T. and the MG's.

26. Other popular instrumentals included: Frogmen, "Underwater" (1961); King Curtis, "Soul Twist" (1962); Lonnie Mack, "Memphis" (1963).

27. Aquila, interview with Duane Eddy.

28. Ibid.

29. Ibid.

30. "Wonderland by Night" was not the first pop instrumental to attract rock & roll fans, as evidenced by earlier hits: Perez Prado, "Patricia" (1958); Martin Denny, "Quiet Village" (1959); Andre Previn, "Like Young," (1959).

31. Adrian Kimberly, "Pomp and Circumstance" (Calliope, 1961). Composer: Elgar, adapted by Kimberly. Hits about exotic locales such as Arthur Lymon's "Yellow Bird" (1961) and Herb Alpert and the Tijuana Brass's "Lonely Bull" (1962) also interested young listeners.

32. White House Historical Association, https://www.whitehousehistory.org/collections /the-kennedys-and-the-arts (accessed on September 15, 2020).

33. Other jazz hits from 1962 include: Bent Fabric, "Alley Cat"; Stan Getz/Charlie Byrd, "Desafinado"; Jimmy Smith, "Walk on the Wild Side."

34. Other teen-oriented pop songs include: Tina Robin, "Dear Mr. D.J. Play It Again" (1961); Frank Ifield, "I Remember You" (1962); Richard Chamberlain, "Theme from *Dr. Kildare*" (1962).

35. Peggy Lee, "I'm a Woman" (Capitol, 1963). Composers: Leiber and Stoller. See Jerry Leiber and Mike Stoller with David Ritz, *Hound Dog: The Leiber and Stoller Autobiography* (New York: Simon & Schuster, 2009), 234–36.

36. "Singer Trini Lopez," *American Profile*, August 21, 2005, https://americanprofile.com /articles/trini-lopez-singer/ (accessed May 22, 2020).

37. Lonnie Donegan, "Does Your Chewing Gum Lose Its Flavor" (Dot, 1961). Composers: Rose, Breuer, and Bloom.

38. Other examples include: Stan Freberg, "Heartbreak Hotel" (1956); Playmates, "Beep Beep" (1958); Lou Monte "Lazy Mary" (1958); Homer & Jethro, "The Battle of Kookamonga" (1959); Bob and Dor McFadden, "The Mummy" (1959).

39. Examples include: Bobby "Boris" Pickett, "Monster Mash"; Chipmunks, "The Alvin Twist"; Phil McLean's "Small Sad Sam" (all in 1962); Allan Sherman, "Hello Muddah, Hello Fadduh" (1963).

40. Liner notes, Vaughn Meader, *The First Family* (Cadence, 1962).

41. Bill Adler (ed.), *The Kennedy Wit* (New York: Bantam Books, 1964), 110.

42. Larry Verne, "Mr. Custer" (Era Records, 1960). Composers: DeLong, Darian, and Van Winkle. Other songs mocked minorities or different cultural traditions, e.g.: Larry Verne, "Mr. Livingston" (1960); Charlie Drake, "My Boomerang Won't Come Back" (1962); Rolf Harris, "Tie Me Kangaroo Down, Sport" (1963).

43. Associated Press, "Bill Dana . . . dies at 92," *Los Angeles Times*, June 26, 2017, https:// www.latimes.com/local/obituaries/la-me-bill-dana-20170626-story.html (accessed February 13, 2022); Kliph Nesteroff, "Interview with Bill Dana," *Classic Television Showbiz*, February 18, 2011, http://classicshowbiz.blogspot.com/2011/01/interview-with-bill-dana.html (accessed February 7, 2022).

44. Ray Stevens, "Ahab, the Arab" (Mercury, 1962). Composer: Stevens; Richard Aquila, interview with Ray Stevens for NPR's *Rock & Roll America* (February 5, 1999).

45. Richard Aquila, interview with Casey Kasem for NPR's *Rock & Roll America* (November 25, 1996); Aquila, interview with Ray Stevens.

46. Claude King, "Wolverton Mountain" (Columbia, 1962). Composers: Kilgore and King. Country songs about love gone wrong include: Faron Young, "Hello Walls"; Patsy Cline, "I Fall to Pieces" and "Crazy"; Bobby Edwards, "You're the Reason" (all in 1961); Jimmy Elledge, "Funny How Time Slips Away" (1962); Bill Anderson's "Still" (1963). Other country songs with teenage appeal include: Johnny Bond, "Hot Rod Lincoln" (1960); Bobby Helms, "Jingle Bell Rock" (charted in 1957 and 1960–62).

47. Hank Locklin, "Please Help Me, I'm Falling" (RCA, 1960). Composers: Robertson and Blair. Other country hits about infidelity include: Jim Reeves, "He'll Have to Go" (1960); Leroy Van Dyke, "Walk on By" (1961); Bobby Bare "Shame on Me (1962).

48. Ferlin Husky, "Wings of a Dove" (Capitol, 1961). Composer: Ferguson.

49. Bob Luman, "Let's Think About Livin'" (Warner, 1960). Composer: B. Bryant.

50. Ron Eyerman and Scott Barretta, "From the 30s to the 60s: The Folk Music Revival in the United States," *Theory and Society* 25, no. 4 (August 1996): 501–43, at 501.

51. Richard Aquila, interview with Pete Seeger for NPR's *Rock & Roll America* (May 13, 1994).

52. Seeger's HUAC testimony (August 18, 1955) is available on George Mason University's *History Matters* website, http://historymatters.gmu.edu/d/6457 (accessed September 23, 2020).

53. Aquila, interview with Pete Seeger

54. Ibid.

55. Kingston Trio, "Where Have All the Flowers Gone?" (Capitol, 1962). Composer: Seeger.

56. Aquila, interview with Pete Seeger.

57. John Stewart, album liner notes, Kingston Trio, *New Frontier* (Capitol, 1962); Kingston Trio, "The New Frontier" (Capitol, 1962). Composer: Stewart.

58. Aquila, interview with Pete Seeger.

59. Ibid.

60. Liner notes, Peter, Paul, and Mary, *Peter, Paul and Mary* (Warner Brothers, 1962).

61. "Peter Yarrow . . . talks 'Puff the Magic Dragon,'" *Sounds of the Times*, Decades TV Network, November 19, 2018, https://www.youtube.com/watch?v=mTfO0VKKxSM (accessed September 25, 2020).

62. Ibid.

63. Ibid.

64. Richard Aquila, interview with Mary Travers for NPR's *Rock & Roll America* (October 8 and 9, 1998).

65. Peter, Paul, and Mary, "If I Had a Hammer (The Hammer Song)" (Warner Brothers, 1962). Composers: Seeger and Hays.

66. Aquila, interview with Mary Travers. TV's blacklisting of Seeger continued until 1967, when the Smothers Brothers convinced CBS to let him perform on their top-rated program.

67. Aquila, interview with Mary Travers.

68. Ibid.

69. Ibid.

70. Ibid.

71. Ibid.

72. Ibid.

73. JFK quoted in Marc J. Selverstone, "John F. Kennedy: Campaigns and Elections," Miller Center of the University of Virginia (2019), https://millercenter.org/president/kennedy /campaigns-and-elections (accessed September 27, 2020).

74. Aquila, interview with Mary Travers.

75. Bob Dylan, liner notes, Peter, Paul, and Mary, *In the Wind* (Warner Brothers, 1963).

CHAPTER 10. "GOD, COUNTRY AND MY BABY"

1. Johnny Burnette, "God, Country and My Baby" (Liberty, 1961). Composers: Dolan and Holiday; Richard Aquila, interview with Snuff Garrett for NPR's *Rock & Roll America* (March 13, 1998).

2. For more information about anticommunism in American society and culture, see: Douglas T. Miller and Marion Nowak, *The Fifties: The Way We Really Were* (New York: Doubleday & Co., 1975); Elaine Tyler May, *Homeward Bound: American Families in the Cold War Era* (New York: Harper Collins, 1988); Stephen J. Whitfield, *The Culture of the Cold War* (Baltimore: Johns Hopkins University Press, 1991).

3. Whitfield, *Culture of the Cold War*, 53; hits by non-Americans typically were pop instrumentals or novelty songs.

4. Jerry Osborne (ed.), *Elvis: Word for Word* (New York: Gramercy Books, 2006), 116. Other singers who wore uniforms while performing include the Essex, Angelo D'Aleo of Dion and the Belmonts, and the Fleetwoods' Gary Troxel.

5. Dallek quoted in Jon Goodman et al, *The Kennedy Mystique: Creating Camelot* (Washington, DC: National Geographic Society, 2006), 59.

6. Kennedy quoted in Bill Adler (ed.), *The Kennedy Wit* (New York: Bantam Books, 1964), 73.

7. Paige Sutherland, "Superman Artwork of JFK Makes it to His Library," *The San Diego Union Telegram*, March 20, 2014, https://www.sandiegouniontribune.com/sdut-superman -artwork-of-jfk-makes-it-to-his-library-2014mar20-story.html (accessed June 4, 2012).

8. Bo Diddley, "Mr. Khrushchev" (Checker, 1962). Composer: McDaniel (a.k.a. Bo Diddley). Songs that opposed the military didn't resonate in Cold War America, as evidenced by two Motown records that flopped in 1961: the Valadiers' "Greetings (This is Uncle Sam)" and Mickey Woods' "Please Mr. Kennedy (I Don't Want to Go)."

9. For Kennedy's comments, see "The Moon Decision," Smithsonian National Air and Space Museum, https://airandspace.si.edu/exhibitions/apollo-to-the-moon/online/racing-to -space/moon-decision.cfm (accessed June 5, 2021).

10. Prior to the early 1960s, records about space focused mostly on UFOs and aliens, e.g.: Buchanan and Goodman, "Flying Saucer" (1956); Sheb Wooley, "Purple People Eater" (1958); Jesse Lee Turner, "The Little Space Girl" (1959). Pat and the Satellites (note their name) found success in 1959 with "Jupiter-C", which was a prototype for early 60s songs inspired by US space program.

11. Miller and Nowak, *The Fifties*, 90.

12. May, *Homeward Bound*, 3.

13. Sammy Salvo, "A Mushroom Cloud" (Hickory Records, 1961). Composer: Bryant.

14. Ann-Margret, "Thirteen Men" (RCA Victor, 1962). Composer: Thompson.

15. Richard Aquila, interview with Pat Boone for NPR's *Rock & Roll America* (June 12 and 25, 1998).

16. Jimmy Cross, "I Want My Baby Back" (Tollie, 1965). Composers: Botkin and Garfield.

17. The number of baby boomers in the early 60s is based on data from the National Center for Health Statistics, https://www.cdc.gov/nchs/data/statab/natfinal2003.annvol1_01 .pdf (accessed June 27, 2021).

18. Richard Aquila, interview with Brenda Lee for NPR's *Rock & Roll America* (October 17, 1995).

19. Bobby Vee's comment appears in *New Musical Express*, February 17, 1961.

20. For more examples, see Richard Aquila, *That Old Time Rock & Roll: A Chronicle of an Era, 1954–1963* (New York: Schirmer/Macmillan, 1989), 17–31, 63–141.

21. The Beach Boys, "Be True to Your School" (Capitol, 1963). Composers: Wilson and Love.

22. Robert von Bernewitz, "The Chantels—An interview with Lois Harris . . . ," *music-guy247* (blog), May 12, 2014, http://musicguy247.typepad.com/my-blog/2014/05/the-chantels -an-interview-with-lois-harris-from-the-pioneering-girl-group.html (accessed May 8, 2018).

23. Steve Knopper, "Racism on the Road: The Oral History of Black Artists Touring in the Segregated South," *Billboard*, November 10, 2020, https://www.billboard.com/articles/news /features/9474793/oral-history-black-artists-touring-segregated-south/ (accessed June 16, 2021).

24. Ibid.

25. Richard Aquila, interview with Duane Eddy for NPR's *Rock & Roll America* (August 12, 1998).

26. Sonny Turner quoted in Knopper, "Racism on the Road."

27. Richard Aquila, interview with Bo Diddley for NPR's *Rock & Roll America* (January 21, 1998).

28. Bob Abrahamian interview with Jan Bradley, *Sitting in the Park*, WHPK-FM, December 28, 2008, http://www.sittinginthepark.com/interviews/janbradley-12-28-2008 .mp3 (accessed March 25, 2018).

29. Richard Aquila, interview with Dion for NPR's *Rock & Roll America* (October 19, 1995); Dion DiMucci with Mike Aquilina, *Dion the Wanderer Talks Truth* (Cincinnati: Servant Books, 2011), 36.

30. Joel Whitburn, *Pop Singles Annual, 1955–1990, Compiled from Billboard's Pop Singles Charts* (Menomonee Falls, WI: Record Research, 1991), 79–84, 131–37.

31. Paul Freeman, "The Shirelles . . . Interview with Founding Member Beverly Lee," *Pop Culture Classics* (blog), October 2011, http://popcultureclassics.com/shirelles.html (accessed July 22, 2021); "Rock and Roll; Respect; Interview with Martha Reeves [Part 1 of 2]," WGBH Media Library & Archives, http://openvault.wgbh.org/catalog/V_E841408868F24736BC6597 230D8EC462 (accessed September 13, 2019).

32. Knopper, "Racism on the Road."

33. Knopper, "Racism on the Road;" Dion's story appears at the end of the official music video, "Song for Sam Cooke (Here In America)," recorded with Paul Simon in 2020, https://www.youtube.com/watch?v=pA2AyRi7MuA (accessed June 19, 2021).

34. John A. Jackson, *American Bandstand: Dick Clark and the Making of a Rock 'N' Roll Empire* (New York: Oxford University Press, 1997), 205.

35. Knopper, "Racism on the Road."

36. Lewis quoted in Danny Goldberg, "Rock Against Racism," *Dissent*, June 2, 2014, https://www.dissentmagazine.org/online_articles/rock-against-racism (accessed March 31, 2018).

37. For information about the post–World War II cult of domesticity, see Sara M. Evans, *Born for Liberty: A History of Women in America* (New York: Free Press, 1989), 238, 239, 245–46. Jackie Kennedy quoted in Mark Mooney, "Jacqueline Kennedy 'Would've Winced' at Her Anti-Feminist Comments," *ABC News*, September 14, 2011, https://abcnews.go.com/Politics /jacqueline-kennedys-victorian-views-shocked-grandchildren/story?id=14519045 (accessed June 21, 2021).

38. Bo Diddley, "You Can't Judge a Book by the Cover" (Checker, 1962). Composer: Dixon.

39. Aquila, interview with Dion.

40. Whitburn, *Pop Singles Annual*, 79–84, 131–37, 313–18.

41. Anita Bryant, "Wonderland by Night" (Carlton, 1961). Composers: Neumann and Chase.

42. Jackie DeShannon, "Needles and Pins" (Liberty, 1963). Composers: Nitzsche and Bono.

43. Harold Dorman, "Mountain of Love" (Rita, 1960). Composer: Dorman.

44. Roy Orbison, "Crying" (Monument, 1961). Composers: Orbison and Melson.

45. Bruce Springsteen, *Born to Run* (New York: Simon and Schuster, 2016), 46.

CHAPTER 11. "THIS MAGIC MOMENT"

1. The Drifters, "This Magic Moment" (Atlantic Records, 1960). Composers: Pomus and Shuman.

2. Bob Dylan, "The Times They Are A-Changin'," (Columbia Records, 1964). Composer: Dylan.

3. Anthony F. C. Wallace, "Revitalization Movements: Some Theoretical Considerations for Their Comparative Study," *American Anthropologist* 58 (1956): 264–81, at 264–65. See also Richard Aquila, "Why We Cried: John Lennon and American Culture," *Popular Music and Society 10*, no.1 (October 1985): 33–43. Sawers' quote appears in Aquila, "Why We Cried," 39.

4. Carl Belz, *The Story of Rock*, 2nd edition (New York: Harper Colophon, 1973), 119.

5. Richard Aquila, interview with Pat Boone for NPR's *Rock & Roll America* (June 25, 1998).

6. Richard Aquila, interview with Don McLean for NPR's *Rock & Roll America* (January 18, 1999).

7. Don McLean, "American Pie" (United Artists, 1971). Composer: McLean; Raymond I. Schuck and Ray Schuck (eds.), *Do You Believe in Rock and Roll? Essays on Don McLean's "American Pie"* (Jefferson, NC: McFarland, 2012).

8. Aquila, interview with Don McLean; Robert McParland, "A Generation Lost in Space," in Schuck and Schuck (eds.), *Do You Believe in Rock and Roll*, 153.

9. Betrock quoted in Paul Friedlander, *Rock and Roll: A Social History* (Boulder, CO: Westview Press, 1996), 70; Reebee Garofalo, *Rockin' Out: Popular Music in the USA* (Boston: Allyn and Bacon, 1997), 160–64.

10. Larry Lehmer, *The Day the Music Died: The Last Tour of Buddy Holly, the "Big Bopper," and Ritchie Valens* (New York: Schirmer Books, 1997), 167; Glenn C. Altschuler, *All Shook Up: How Rock 'n' Roll Changed America* (New York: Oxford University Press, 2004), 160, 176.

11. Greg Shaw, "The Teen Idols," in Anthony DeCurtis and James Henke (eds.), *Rolling Stone Illustrated History of Rock & Roll* (New York: Random House, 1992), 107.

12. Todd Leopold, "The Day the Music Died? Hardly," CNN, February 2, 2009, http://www.cnn.com/2009/SHOWBIZ/Music/02/02/day.music.died (accessed December 10, 2016).

13. Evidently, Twain actually said, "The report of my death was an exaggeration." *This Day in Quotes: May 31, 2015*, http://www.thisdayinquotes.com/2010/06/reports-of-my-death-are-greatly.html (accessed October 5, 2016).

14. Richard Aquila, interview with Brenda Lee for NPR's *Rock & Roll America* (October 17, 1995).

Index

Abrams, Al, 71, 88, 92

"Ahab the Arab," 288, 289, 320

"Ain't Gonna Kiss Ya," 60

Ales, Barney, 74, 93

Alexander, Arthur, 160

"All Alone Am I," 180

Allison, Jerry, 191, 193, 235, 236. *See also* Crickets

American Bandstand: diverse playlists, 2; payola scandal, 15, 223; and record sales, 49, 199, 208, 210, 215–18, 223, 234; and the Twist, 20–21; and young audience, 2, 318, 329. *See also* Clark, Dick

American Century, 131, 340

American Dream, 82, 130–31, 135, 255, 269

American Exceptionalism. *See* Cold War culture

"American Pie," 2, 193, 335–36. *See also* McLean, Don

American West: and Cold War culture, 279, 309; Garden of Eden, 97; heroic figures, 105, 127, 131, 240; images in popular music, 96–98, 115, 121, 240, 274, 279; as land of opportunity, 97; mythic West, 97, 117, 121–22, 125, 129, 290; and surf music, 96–98, 104–10, 113, 115, 125, 130;

and traditional myths, 97, 309. *See also* California Dream

"Angela Jones," 197, 325

"Angel Baby," 261

Angels, 42, 57–59

Anka, Paul, 201, 208–9, 220, 337

Annette (Funicello), 98, 126, 224, 313

"Apache," 279

Apollo Theater, 49, 80, 153, 229

ASCAP (American Society of Composers, Authors and Publishers), 14–15

"Astronaut, The," 287, 289, 312

A-Team, The, 198. *See also* Nashville Sound

Atkins, Chet, 169, 171, 198, 276

Atlantic Records, 52, 93, 136, 147–48, 214

Avalon, Frankie, 98, 215–18, 222, 337

B. Bumble and the Stingers, 281

"Baby Blue," 27

baby boomers: characteristics and number of, 4, 229, 316; and Cold War, 339; collective memory, 132, 158, 217, 256, 269, 284, 329, 336; and consensus behavior, 117, 240, 314, 317–18, 339–40; and consumer culture, 24, 72, 222, 314; diversity of, 6; enter high school, 2–4, 35, 330; and generational solidarity, 5–6, 32,

baby boomers (*continued*)
96, 318, 335; and help from the Beatles, 114, 331–33; impact on music, 3; and innocence, 7, 112, 215, 222, 239, 340; and lost innocence, 117, 331–35, 340; and record sales, 229, 261, 280–82, 316; and rock & roll, 5–6, 38, 72, 114, 222, 316, 331. *See also* youth culture
Baby It's You, 59, 325
Bacharach, Burt, 202, 240–41, 282
Baez, Joan, 295, 300, 323
Ballard, Hank, 19–21
Bartholomew, Dave, 89, 144, 145
"Bashful Bob," 237, 328
"Battle of New Orleans, The," 290, 309
Bay of Pigs, 23, 131
Beach Boys: California and the mythic West, 103, 106–11, 113–15, 117; car songs, 105, 107–8, 110–11, 114–15; decline, 116–18; early career, 96, 103–4, 106; formula for success, 105–6, 109–10, 121; influence of Beatles, 114; influence of 4 Seasons, 109, 113–14; Kennedy's assassination, 112–14; later success, 113–18; legacy, 118, 130–32; members, 104, 116; sound, 97, 104–9, 112–13, 115–16; surf music, 96, 105–10, 118–19; and youth culture, 106–8, 111–12, 114, 117–18, 132
Beach Party (movies), 98, 126
Beatles: arrival on the American charts, 2, 112–13, 331; British Rock Invasion, 113, 129, 332–33; as cultural revitalization figures, 331–32; impact on American rock & roll, 2, 112–13, 222, 280, 332–33; impact on American youth culture, 113, 331–32; Kennedy's assassination, 94, 333
"Because They're Young," 273, 280

"Beechwood 4–5789," 59, 78
Beland, John, 269
"Believe Me," 249
Belmonts, 5, 199–201, 225, 229. *See also* Dion and the Belmonts
"Be My Baby," 49–51, 53
Benton, Brook, 145
Berlin Crisis, 61, 294, 307, 311
Berry, Chuck, 13, 89, 108, 110, 114
"Be True to Your School," 317–18
Big Bopper (J.P. Richardson), 3, 13, 191, 234, 245–46, 338
"Big Girls Don't Cry," 249, 250–51
Binnick, Bernie. *See* Swan Records
Biondi, Dick, 5
Blane, Marcie, 268, 325
Bleyer, Archie, 160, 171–72, 195–96
Blossoms. *See* Love, Darlene
"Blowin' In the Wind," 141, 300–301, 323
Blue Hawaii, 167
"Blue Moon," 26–27
BMI (Broadcast Music International), 14–15, 17, 19
"Bobby's Girl," 268, 325
Bogle, Bob. *See* Ventures
Bond, Julian, 95
Bonds, Gary U.S., 156–58
Booker T. and the MGs, 279, 379n25
Boone, Pat, 203–5, 315, 334, 337
Bradley, Jan, 161–62, 320
Bradley, Owen, 176–78
"Breaking Up is Hard to Do," 215
Brill Building Sound, 173, 201–3, 338
British Rock Invasion, 2, 222, 280, 332–33. *See also* Beatles
Britz, Chuck, 109
Brooks, La La, 47. *See also* Crystals

Brothers Four, 295, 312

Brown, Bruce, 98–99

Brown, James, 139, 145, 153, 323

Brubeck, Dave, 281

Bryant, Anita, 327

Bryant, Boudeleaux and Felice, 169–71, 314

Buddy Holly Story, The, 191–93. *See also* Holly, Buddy

Burnette, Johnny, 190, 307–8, 311, 317

Burton, James, 206–7

Butala, Tony. See Lettermen

Butler, Artie, 40–42

Butler, Jerry, 145, 150

"Bye Bye Love," 169

Byrnes, Edd "Kookie," 282

Cadence Records. *See* Bleyer, Archie

California car culture, 108, 110–11, 121, 128

California Dream: and Beach Boys, 104–10, 113, 117; and Jan & Dean, 121; and surf music, 97, 125, 131

"California Sun," 128–29

Cameo-Parkway Records, 20–22, 216–22

Cannon, Freddy, 223, 254

capitalism. *See* Cold War culture

Caravan of Stars. *See* Clark, Dick

Carawan, Guy, 296

Carr, Vikki, 46

Carrelli, Justine, 6

car songs, 5, 110, 269, 279, 285, 295, 317, 338. *See also* Beach Boys; surf music

Cascades, 260, 317

Cash, Johnny, 184, 291, 308, 369n64

"Cathy's Clown," 172

"Chains," 59

Chancellor Records. *See* Marcucci, Bob

Chandler, Gene, 33, 309

"Change is Gonna Come, A," 142–43, 324

Chantays, 97, 123–24, 129

Chantels, 36, 54, 58–59, 318

"Chapel of Love," 61, 313

Charles, Ray, 136–39, 154, 314, 322

Checker, Chubby, 19–24, 108, 218, 337

Chiffons, 39, 40, 54, 337

Chipmunks, The, 285–86

Christie, Lou, 247, 348n50

civil rights and popular music: anthems, 142, 295–97, 301, 324; images in music, 33, 45, 135, 152, 301; and integration, 33, 35, 40, 163, 275, 279, 321–23; and performers, 38, 53, 56, 90–91, 145; and racial cooperation, 33, 221, 233–34, 238, 274, 291, 319–21; and racial prejudice, 221, 233–34, 238, 274, 291, 319–20; significance of, 25, 91, 95, 153, 324

Clanton, Jimmy, 224, 314, 326

Clark, Dee, 146, 326, 329

Clark, Dick: Caravan of Stars bus tours, 33, 55, 221, 319, 323; and payola scandal, 15–17; and racial issues, 33, 55, 221, 319, 323; and record sales, 19, 21, 24, 210, 215, 218–19, 223; and youth culture, 6. See also *American Bandstand*

classical music influences, 281

Clayton, Bob, 5–6

Coasters, 89, 147–48, 202, 324

Cold War culture: American Exceptionalism, 1, 97, 131, 279; anxieties, 314–16; capitalism and consumerism, 72, 74, 194, 314; marriage and the family, 61, 74, 262, 268, 313–14; nuclear fears, 294, 307, 314–15; patriotism, 1, 61, 211, 309–10, 317–18; politics, 294, 302, 307–8, 311, 317; religion, 62, 152, 238, 264, 283, 290,

Cold War culture (*continued*)
313, 317; space program, 311–12;
traditional myths, 97, 105, 131, 309,
314; traditional values, 7, 173, 182, 211,
308, 313; ubiquitous Cold War culture,
2, 7, 308, 317, 339
Cold War tensions, 307, 309, 311. *See also*
Cold War culture
Cole, Nat King, 28, 282–83
"Come Back, Silly Girl," 255
"Come Back When You Grow Up," 238
"Come Softly to Me," 225–26
"Come to Me," 68
communists, 285, 289–90, 292, 308, 311, 313
consumerism. *See* Cold War culture
Cooke, Sam, 141–43, 233–34, 324
country music, traditional: 138–39, 176,
178, 196–97, 289–91
country rock: 3, 164–65
Cramer, Floyd, 171, 180, 198, 275
Crests, 25, 28
Crewe, Bob, 114, 223, 249–52, 254. *See also*
4 Seasons
Crickets, 191, 193, 236, 313. *See also* Holly,
Buddy
"Crying," 187, 189–90, 329
"Crying in the Rain," 173–74, 329
Crystals, 44–48, 54–55, 59, 324, 337
Cuban Missile Crisis, 131, 197, 240, 260,
294, 315
Curtis, Sonny, 193. *See also* Crickets

Daddy G and the Church Street Five,
156–58
"Da Doo Ron Ron," 47
Dale, Dick, 99–103, 118–19, 130
Dana, Bill, 287, 312, 320

dances: 7, 19, 23–25, 27, 129, 314. *See also*
the Twist and other specific dances
Danny and the Juniors, 22, 266
Darin, Bobby, 208, 213–14, 220
David, Hal, 202, 240, 263, 282
Davis, Skeeter, 197, 290, 314
"Dawn," 251–52
"day the music died, the," 2–3, 330, 336.
See also McLean, Don
"Dead Man's Curve," 121–22
Dean, Jimmy, 290, 309–11, 317
"Dear Ivan," 290, 311
death rock, 315–16
Dick and Deedee, 261–62
Diddley, Bo: Cold War themes, 309, 311;
macho image, 309, 311, 326; and "Soldier
Boy," 38; sound, 84, 146, 169
Dion (DiMucci): attitude, 199; authentic
sound, 200, 229–30, 232, 234; and blues
music, 231–32; and country music,
231–32; embarks on solo career, 229; and
folk music, 231–32; and gender stereotypes, 231–32, 326–28; and other singers,
27, 187, 233–34, 245; and pop music,
231; and racial issues, 233–34, 320, 323;
relationship to audience, 5, 201, 225,
232–33; relationship to the times, 232–33;
and rock & roll, 199–200, 225, 229–32;
success, 234. *See also* Dion and the
Belmonts
Dion and the Belmonts, 5, 199–201, 225,
229. *See also* Belmonts; Dion (Dimucci)
Dixon, Luther, 37, 39, 89. *See also* Shirelles
"Does Your Chewing Gum Lose Its Flavor,"
285
"Dominique," 313
"Don't Go Near the Indians," 291

"Don't Worry, Baby," 114

Domino, Fats, 89, 143–45, 159, 309, 333

doo-wop: early doo-wop, 25–26; neo-doo-wop, 26–34

Douglas, Susan J., 62

Dovells, 23, 314, 323

"Down Home," 206

"Do You Love Me," 23, 78

Drifters, 1, 135–36, 148–50, 330, 340. *See also* King, Ben E.

"Duke of Earl," 27, 33, 309

Dylan, Bob, 141, 182, 300–301, 303, 311, 331

"Easier Said than Done," 162

Echoes. *See* "Baby Blue"

Eddy, Duane, 272–75, 277, 279–80, 319, 333

Endless Summer (Beach Boys' album), 117–18, 130

Endless Summer, The (Bruce Brown's movie), 99, 117

"End of the World, The," 197, 314

Ertegun, Ahmet, 3, 136–37, 148. *See also* Atlantic Records

Essex, 162, 325

ethnicity, 233, 284, 288, 320–321, 339

Everly Brothers, 104, 169–70, 172–76, 313

Fabian, 216–17, 222, 326

fallout shelters, 307, 314

fashions: females, 58, 81, 91, 246, 267, 314; males, 106, 216–17, 219, 221, 332

FBI (Federal Bureau of Investigation), 258–59, 377n76

Feminine Mystique, The, 36, 266, 339.

Fender, Leo, 100–104

Fendermen, 190

"Fingertips-Pt 2," 87–88

Fireballs, 192, 259, 276, 326

First Family, The, 286–87, 311

Fleetwoods, 201, 225–26, 337

Fogerty, John, 207, 278, 378n6

Folk music, 291–303

"Footsteps," 29

Foster, Fred, 184–87

Four Freshmen, 104, 107, 250

4 Seasons: background, 249; Bob Crewe's role, 114, 249–51, 254; decline, 252–53; influence on Brian Wilson, 109, 113; *Jersey Boys,* 253; later hits, 253; members, 249, 253; number 1 hits, 249–53; reasons for success, 253–55; rivalry with Beach Boys, 113–14; Rock & Roll Hall of Fame, 253

Francis, Connie, 210–13, 261, 308–9, 327, 337

Franklin, Aretha, 139, 142, 160–61, 231

Freed, Alan, 15–18

Friedan, Betty. *See Feminine Mystique, The*

"Fun, Fun, Fun," 114, 116–17

Funk Brothers, 70–71, 79

Fuqua, Harvey, 79, 81

Gabriel and the Angels, 24, 33

Garrett, Snuff, 5, 45–46, 160, 235–37, 307

Gaudio, Bob, 114, 248–55. *See also* 4 Seasons

Gaye, Marvin, 76, 79–80, 82, 84–86

gender. *See* women and popular music

gender stereotypes: females, 126, 159, 231, 238, 251, 263, 265, 326; males, 146, 173, 251, 265–66, 325–26, 328–29

Generation Gap, 339

Gibson, Bunny, 5

Gibson, Don, 139, 289

Gidget, 98–99

Gilmer, Jimmy. *See* Fireballs

girl groups: and advice, 58–59; background, 36; and civil rights, 38, 53–56; female perspectives, 36, 38, 40, 62; gender equality, 35–36, 56–57, 62, 268; images on album covers, 54; as pioneer women singers, 35, 57; racial integration, 35–36, 53–55; as role models, 36, 38, 58, 327; and sex, 60–61; and social change, 35–36; sound, 35, 62

"Go Away Little Girl," 282

"God, Country and My Baby," 307–8

Goffin, Gerry, 3, 32, 135. *See also* King and Goffin

"Good Timin'," 159

"Good Vibrations," 115–16

Gordy, Berry, Jr. (Motown Records): Background, 64–67; civil rights movement, 73, 76, 80, 82, 90–93, 95; decline of Motown, 94–95; Hitsville, U.S.A., 69, 72, 90; marketing and promotion, 71, 74, 91, 93; Motown artist development program, 81–82; Motown assembly line and quality control, 70, 75; Motown family, 70, 90–91; Motown Sound, 63, 70–71, 88–89; as music publisher, 68, 71; as producer, 67–68, 71–72; as record company owner, 68–69, 88–90, 93; significance, 88, 90, 95; as songwriter, 67–68, 72–73; Sound of Young America, 88–89, 90, 92; staff, 71, 74–75, 89–90; white artists at Motown, 93

Gore, Lesley, 264–68, 326, 337

Grant, Janie, 262, 326

Greenfield, Howie, 202, 214

Greenwich, Ellie, 47–48, 202

Grossman, Albert, 297, 301

Guard, Dave. *See* Kingston Trio

Guida, Frank, 157–59

"Guided Missiles (Aimed at My Heart)," 308

"Gypsy Woman," 150

Hammond, John, 231

"Handy Man," 159, 244

"Happy Birthday, Sweet Sixteen," 214, 317

"Hark is that a Cannon I Hear," 237

"Harlem Nocturne," 279

Haskell, Jimmie, 204, 207

Hays, Lee, 291–92, 299

"Heat Wave," 63

"He Hit Me (and it Felt Like a Kiss)," 59, 326

"Hello Mary Lou," 206–7

"Hello Walls," 382n46

"He's a Bad Boy," 264

"He's a Rebel," 45–48, 52, 239, 241

"He's So Fine," 39

"Hey Paula," 262, 268, 324

Highlander Folk School, 296

"Hit the Road, Jack," 136, 138, 329

Holland, Dozier, and Holland, 78–79, 94

Holly, Buddy, 3, 13, 191–95, 209, 235

Hootenannies, 295, 312

Horton, Johnny, 290, 309, 317

Horton, Zilphia, 296

HUAC (House Un-American Activities Committee), 292, 381n52

Hugo and Luigi, 29–30, 154

"I Can't Stop Loving You," 136, 138–39

"If I Had a Hammer," 291, 295, 297, 299

"If You Wanna Be Happy," 158–59, 326

"I Left My Heart in San Francisco," 282

"I'll Never Dance Again," 220

"I Love How You Love Me," 43, 60

"I'm a Woman," 283

"I'm Gonna Be Strong," 241–42, 326

Impressions, 145, 150–53, 324

"I'm Sorry," 177–78

"I Need Your Loving," 163

"In My Room," 111

innovations, 7, 135, 201–3

instrumental music: jazz, 281–82; rock instrumentals, 272–80; traditional pop instrumentals, 280–82

interviews, 343–44

"I Shot Mr. Lee," 60

Isley Brothers, 153–55

"It Doesn't Matter Anymore," 191, 195, 209, 235

"It Keeps Right On A-Hurtin'," 195–96

"It's All Right," 151, 152

"It's My Party," 265, 326, 329

"It's Over," 187, 189

"Itsy Bitsy Teenie Weenie Yellow Polka Dot Bikini," 246

"I've Told Every Little Star," 262, 325

"I Will Follow Him," 264, 268, 325

"I Wish I Knew What Dress to Wear," 267

"I Wonder Why," 225

Jackson, Wanda, 164–65, 315

Jamerson, James, 70–71, 94

"Jamie," 78

Jan & Arnie, 119

Jan & Dean, 97, 119–22, 128

Jay and the Americans, 1, 202, 260, 309

Jaynetts, 40, 41

Jersey Boys, 253, 255

JFK. *See* Kennedy, John F.

Jimenez, Jose. *See* Dana, Bill

Joey Dee and the Starliters, 22, 154, 221, 259

"Johnny Angel," 263, 268

"Johnny Get Angry," 263, 325

Johnson, Marv, 68–69

Jones, Jimmy, 159

Jones, Landon Y., 6

Jones, Quincy, 265

Jordanaires, 11, 168, 206–7

"Just One Look." *See* Troy, Doris

Kaempfert, Bert, 280, 327

Kasem, Casey, 289

"Keep on Pushing," 152, 324

Kennedy, Jackie (Mrs. John F. Kennedy), 23, 57, 324

Kennedy, Jacqueline. *See* Kennedy, Jackie

Kennedy, John F. (JFK), 7–8, 310–12, 330, 340; New Frontier, 3, 136, 185, 188, 291, 294–95, 302

Kennedy's assassination: and British Rock Invasion, 51, 331–33; and music, 94, 112–14, 122, 127, 232, 252, 257, 331–33; and youth culture, 39, 94, 112, 129, 182, 329, 333–35. *See also* Beatles

Khrushchev, Nikita, 307, 311

King, Ben E., 148–49, 159,

King, Carole, 3, 30, 135, 173, 202, 264. *See also* King and Goffin

King, Martin Luther, Jr., 55, 91, 142, 152, 232

King and Goffin, 40, 43, 59, 149, 160–61, 227, 239, 282

Kingsmen, 256–59

Kingston Trio, 293–95, 311–12

"Kookie, Kookie (Lend Me Your Comb)," 282

Krupa, Gene, 101–2, 218

Lafayettes, 260

Lance, Major, 23, 152, 160

"Last Kiss," 316

"Last Night," 279

Lawrence, Steve, 29, 282

"Leader of the Pack," 316

Lee, Beverly, 33, 37–38, 53, 56, 321. *See also*
Shirelles

Lee, Brenda: authenticity, 181, 316;
background, 176; and changing musical
tastes, 182, 333; and country music, 176,
178, 180, 182; and pop music, 180; and
producer Owen Bradley, 176–78, 181;
and rock & roll songs, 177–80; self-
confidence, 176, 181–82, 327; significance, 165, 181–83, 327; sound and style,
178, 180–81; and youth culture, 177–79,
181, 316, 339

Lee, Peggy, 283

Leiber and Stoller: and Ben E. King, 45, 159;
and Coasters, 147–48; and Drifters, 135,
148–49; and Jay and the Americans, 1,
260; and Peggy Lee, 283; significance of,
135, 149, 202

Lennon, John, 183, 193, 245, 332. *See also*
Beatles

"Let's Go Trippin'," 102, 118

"Let's Have a Party," 3, 164–65

"Let's Jump the Broomstick," 179–80

Lettermen, 255–56

Lewis, Barbara, 161

Lewis, Jerry Lee, 13

"Life's Too Short," 3, 260

Linda, Solomon, 31, 32, 348n48

"Lion Sleeps Tonight, The," 27, 29–32

Little Anthony and the Imperials, 25–26,
320

"Little Deuce Coupe," 110–11

Little Richard, 13, 203, 237, 280

"Little Town Flirt," 244, 326

"Loco-Motion, The," 23, 161

"Lonely Sea, The," 109

"Lonely Teardrops," 67, 140, 153

Lopez, Trini, 284

Loudermilk, John D., 197

"Louie Louie," 3, 256–59, 314

Love, Darlene, 44, 46–47, 49–50, 126, 161,
275, 325

Love, Mike, 104–5, 111–12, 114, 116.
See also Beach Boys

Lowe, Bernie. *See* Cameo-Parkway Records

Mabey, Richard, 5

"Mama Didn't Lie," 161–62

"Mama Said," 61, 313

Mammarella, Tony. *See* Swan Records

Mann, Barry, 1, 32, 45, 135, 202, 241

"Man Who Shot Liberty Valance, The," 240,
309

Marcels, 26–27

March, Peggy, 264, 268

March on Washington, 40, 56, 83, 91, 152,
295, 301

Marcucci, Bob, 82, 215–17

Maresca, Ernie, 27–28, 230–31

Mar-Keys, 279, 379n25

marriage. *See under* Cold War culture

Martha & the Vandellas, 63–64, 79, 86, 94.
See also Reeves, Martha

Marvelettes, 59, 62, 75–76, 78

Matassa, Cosimo, 136, 143

Mathis, Johnny, 56, 283–84

Mauldin, Joe B. *See* Crickets

Mayfield, Curtis. *See* Impressions

McCarthyism, 292–93, 302, 308

McCartney, Paul, 115, 175, 193, 245. *See also* Beatles

McDaniels, Gene, 160

McLean, Don, 12, 193, 335–36. *See also* "American Pie"

McPhatter, Clyde, 56, 148, 363n19

Meader, Vaughn. *See First Family, The*

"Midnight in Moscow," 281

military, the, 162, 268, 311, 382n8

Miracles, 68, 72–74, 76, 78, 84, 85–86. *See also* Robinson, Smokey

"Miserlou," 103, 118–19, 130. *See also* Dale, Dick

Modern Sounds in Country and Western Music, 139

"Money (That's What I Want)," 72, 314

"Moody River," 204, 315

"Moon River," 145, 240, 282

Motortown Revue, 80, 91

Motown Records. *See* Gordy, Berry, Jr.

Motown Sound, 7, 63, 70–71, 88–89

"Mountain of Love," 328

"Mr. Blue," 226

"Mr. Custer," 287, 320

"Mr. Khrushchev," 311

"Mr. Lonely," 328

"Mule Skinner Blues," 190

"My Block," 54

"My Boyfriend's Back," 42, 59, 325

"Nancy," 369n64

Nashville Sound, 178, 198

"Navy Blue," 268

"Needles and Pins," 328

Nelson, Ricky, 205–7, 269, 321, 326

Nelson, Sandy, 275–76

New Frontier, 136, 291, 294–95, 302, 311–12, 333

"New Orleans," 156–57

New Orleans Sound, 144, 159

"Night Has a Thousand Eyes, The," 236–37

Nitzsche, Jack, 52, 125

Norfolk Sound, 157–58

"Norman," 197

"No Surfin' Today," 113–14

"Not Fade Away," 195

Novelty and comedy records, 2, 280, 285–89

"Oh Dio Mio," 225, 313

"On Broadway," 135–36, 149, 309

"One Fine Day," 39–40

"One Who Really Loves You, The," 76–77

"Only in America," 1–2, 260, 309

"Only Love Can Break a Heart," 240–41

"Only the Lonely," 185

Orbison, Roy, 183–90

"Our Day Will Come," 162

Owens, Shirley, 36, 38, 54–55, 57, 62. *See also* Shirelles

"Palisades Park," 223

"Papa-Oom-Mow-Mow," 28, 128

Paris Sisters, 42–43, 58, 60, 62

Parker, Tom (Colonel), 11–12, 166–68

Pash, Jim, 124–25. *See also* Surfaris

"Patches," 247. *See also* death rock

Patriotism. *See Cold War culture*

payola, 12, 14–19, 24, 217, 223, 229

Peace Corps, 30, 310

"Peggy Sue," 191, 194

"Pepino the Italian Mouse," 288–89, 320

Peppermint Lounge, 22, 25, 154

"Peppermint Twist, The," 22, 259

Peter, Paul, and Mary, 291, 294–303, 312, 323

Peterson, Ray, 43, 246–47, 315

Pet Sounds, 115

Petty, Norman, 183, 192, 284

Petty, Tom, 190, 245

Philadelphia Pop Rock, 215

Phillips, Sam, 183, 337

"Pipeline," 123–24, 129, 278

Pitney, Gene, 43, 45–46, 207, 239–42

Platters, 146, 162, 319

"Please Don't Kiss Me Again," 60

"Please Hurt Me," 59

"Please Mr. Postman," 75, 76

"Poetry in Motion," 196, 326

Pomus and Shuman, 135, 149, 199–202, 282

Pony, 23, 24, 218

pop music (traditional), 2, 282–84

pop rock: experienced pop rockers, 199–201; second wave of pop rock, 227–28

Powell, Maxine, 81–82

Presley, Elvis: and early 60s America, 13, 166, 309, 313–14; and movies, 13, 166–69; and rock & roll, 3, 11, 165, 168, 366n9

Preston, Johnny, 245–46, 315, 320

"Pretty Blue Eyes," 29

"Pretty Little Angel Eyes," 27, 43

"P.T. 109," 290, 310, 317

"Quarter to Three," 156–58, 329

quiz show scandal, 14–15

race and popular music: equality, 33, 82, 91–92, 319, 321–24, 339; racism, 38, 55, 142, 233, 318–20, 324; record album covers, 54; stereotypes, 291, 320–21; tour

buses, 33, 55, 80, 233, 275, 319, 322–23. *See also* civil rights and popular music

"Rag Doll," 252

"Raindrops," 146, 329

"Rainin' in My Heart," 145

R&B rock and rhythm and blues: 3, 63, 135–36. *See also* Gordy, Berry, Jr.

Randolph, Boots, 180, 184, 196, 198, 279

"Rave On," 191

"Rebel Rouser," 273–75

Rebels (the Buffalo Rebels). *See* "Wild Weekend"

record sales, 19, 228–29, 318

Reeves, Martha, 71–72, 82, 86, 90, 319, 321

religion. *See* Cold War culture

"Remember Then," 27

"Rhythm of the Rain," 260, 317

Rivingtons, 28, 128. *See also* Sharps

Robbins, Marty, 98, 210, 214, 290

Robinson, Smokey, 69, 75, 84, 88, 90–92, 318, 323. *See also* Miracles

rockabilly, 19, 164–65, 169, 177–79, 184–85, 190–92, 207, 235

rock & roll, historical and cultural significance: and consensus behavior, 7, 125, 274, 289, 308, 317–19, 338–40; as a cultural binding force, 318; problems in 1960, 12; promoted racial equality, 25, 279, 322–24; quality of the music, 338; and rebellious behavior, 27, 146, 155, 164, 247, 257, 261–62, 274; relationship to the times, 4–5, 7–8, 269, 308, 329, 338–40. *See also* baby boomers; Cold War culture; race and popular music; women in popular music

Rock & Roll Hall of Fame, 337

"Rockin' Around the Christmas Tree, 180

Roe, Tommy, 192, 246, 337

Ronettes, 44, 49–51, 54, 58, 327

Rose, Wesley, 169, 171, 184

"Roses Are Red (My Love)," 246

Royal Teens, 249

"Rubber Ball," 192, 236, 239

"Runaround Sue," 229–31, 234, 326–27

"Runaway," 242–43, 245

"Running Bear," 245–46, 315, 320

"Running Scared," 186–88

"Run to Him," 236

Russia (Soviet Union), 197, 282, 285, 290, 307, 308, 311. See also Cold War culture

"Russian Bandstand," 285

Rydell, Bobby, 218–22, 313, 333, 337

"Sally, Go 'Round the Roses," 40. See also Butler, Artie

"Salute to Freedom, 1963," 56

Santiglia, Peggy. See Angels

"Save the Last Dance for Me," 149

Sawers, Dan, 332, 360n61, 385n3

Schroeder, Aaron, 45, 239, 241

"Scotch and Soda," 293

Scott, Jack, 165, 190–91

Scott, Linda, 262, 325

Sedaka, Neil, 202, 214–15, 313, 337

Seeger, Pete, 31–32, 291–96, 299. See also Weavers

Self, Alvie. See "Nancy"

Seville, David, 285. See also Chipmunks

sex: dances, 19, 22–25; lyrics, 26, 38, 60, 77–78, 138, 146, 155, 315; sexy image, 49–50, 58, 85, 140, 164, 217; sound, 43, 77, 177–79, 188, 256, 279, 281

Shadows, The. See Vee, Bobby

Shangri-Las, 62, 316, 349n15

Shannon, Del, 242–45, 326, 329

Shannon, Tommy. See "Wild Weekend"

"Sharing You," 237

Sharp, Dee Dee, 23, 161, 323

Sharps, 273, 275, 378n8

"She Cried," 202, 260

"Sheila," 192, 246

"She Loves You," 224

"Sherry," 109, 249–50, 254

"Shimmy, Shimmy, Ko-Ko-Bop," 25–26

Shirelles: authentic sound and style, 35, 37–38; background, 36; and Cold War culture, 61–62, 311; and gender, 36, 38–39, 57, 59–61, 324–25, 327; group's demise, 39; members, 36; and producer Luther Dixon, 37, 39; and race, 33, 38–39, 53–56, 321–22; significance of, 35–36, 39, 62, 161, 261; and youth culture, 35–36, 38, 59–61

Shirley, Don, 281

"Shop Around," 73–75

"Shout," 154–55

"SHOUT! SHOUT! (Knock Yourself Out)." See Maresca, Ernie

"Shut Down," 107, 108

Siegel, Jay. See under "Lion Sleeps Tonight, The"; Tokens

Sill, Lester. See Spector, Phil

Sinatra, Frank, 12, 15, 208, 284

"Soldier Boy," 35, 38, 61, 311, 324

"Song for Sam Cooke (Here in America)," 234, 384n33

Soul, Jimmy, 158–59, 326

"Sound Off," 311

Sound of Young America, The, 88, 92

space program, 287, 311, 312

"Spanish Harlem," 45, 49, 159

Spector, Phil: auteur producer and Wall of Sound, 42–46, 48–49, 51, 338; demise of, 51–53; dubious ethics, 44–47, 52; and girl groups, 42–51; and Lester Sill, 42, 44, 46, 52, 59; significance of, 52–53; as singer, 42; as songwriter, 45, 47

Spector, Ronnie (Veronica Bennett). *See* Ronettes

"Speedy Gonzales," 204–5, 320

Spickard, Bob, 123–24, 129. *See also* Chantays

Springsteen, Bruce, 158, 189, 329

"Stand By Me," 159–60

"Stay," 26

stereotypes, racial and ethnic, 246, 287–89, 320–21

Stevens, Connie, 282–83

Stevens, Ray, 286, 288–89, 320

Stevenson, Mickey, 70, 75, 86, 92

"Stripper, The," 281

"Stroll, The," 19

Strong, Barrett, 72, 314

"Sukiyaki," 283

"Summer's Gone," 132

Supremes, 79–80, 91, 94

Surfaris, 97, 124–25, 127

"Surf City," 120, 121, 326

"Surfer Girl," 110

"Surfer Joe," 124–25

"Surfers Rule," 113. *See also* "No Surfin' Today"

"Surfin' Bird," 127–28

"Surfin' Safari," 96

"Surfin' U.S.A.," 107–10, 119

surf music: and California Dream, 97, 104–5, 108, 110, 117, 125, 128; and car culture, 97, 106, 108, 110, 128; and Cold War, 317–18; demise, 128–30; lack of diversity, 126–27; later surf music, 130; and movies, 98; and mythic West, 97–98, 106–8, 110, 125, 127–28; and new technology, 99, 101; performers, 118–19, 123–25, 360n48, 360n63; pioneers, 99–100; significance of, 96–97, 112, 130–32; styles and sound, 97, 102–3, 106, 110; and surfing, 97, 99, 106, 115; and youth culture, 108, 111, 118, 125, 132. *See also* Beach Boys; Dale, Dick; Jan & Dean

"Suzie Baby," 235

Swan Records, 222–24

"Sweet Nothin's," 177, 316

"Take Good Care of My Baby," 227, 236

"Tallahassee Lassie," 223, 254

"Teenager in Love," 199–200

teenagers. *See* baby boomers; youth culture

"Teen Angel," 246. *See also* death rock

teen idols, 195, 205–9, 215–20, 222–24, 227, 234, 243, 313

"Tell Laura I Love Her," 246–47. *See also* death rock

"Telstar," 279, 312

"That'll Be the Day," 191, 194

"That's Life (That's Tough)," 33

"Then He Kissed Me," 47–48

"There Goes My Baby," 148–49

"There's a Moon Out Tonight," 26, 260

"Thirteen Men," 315

"Thirteen Women," 308, 315

"This Magic Moment," 330, 340

"Those Oldies But Goodies (Remind Me of You)," 28

"Thousand Stars, A," 26, 261

Tillotson, Johnny, 195–97, 337

"Times They Are A-Changin', The," 331

Tokens, 27, 29–32, 39, 40

"Tom Dooley," 293

"Tonight's the Night," 36, 38, 60, 329

Top 40 radio, 270, 272, 280, 302, 338

Torrence, Dean, 119–20. *See also* Jan & Dean

"Town Without Pity," 240–42

Traditional values. *See* Cold War culture

"Travelin' Man," 206–7

Travers, Mary, 299–302; 327. *See also* Peter, Paul, and Mary

"Triangle," 262

Troy, Doris, 161–62

"Twenty Four Hours from Tulsa," 241

"Twist, The," 19–25

"Twist and Shout," 155

"Two Lovers," 83

"Uptown" (Crystals), 45, 324

"Uptown" (Roy Orbison), 184–85

Valens, Ritchie, 3, 13–14, 191

Valli, Frankie, 248–49, 252–53, 255. *See also* 4 Seasons

Vee, Bobby: authenticity, 234, 237–39, 316–17; background, 234–35; and Cold War values, 238; and gender attitudes, 33, 238, 268; and Buddy Holly, 191–93, 234–36; observations about music, 2, 236, 238–39; and pop rock, 12, 227–28, 236–37; and race relations, 33, 238, 322; role in recording process, 236–37; significance of, 236–39, 337; sound and style, 227, 235–37; and teen idols, 195, 221, 227, 234; and youth culture, 237–39, 316–17, 328

Velvelettes, 55

Ventures: background, 276–77; distinct sound, 277–78; focus on albums, 277–78; members, 276; significance, 278; and surf music, 100, 128, 278

"Venus in Blue Jeans," 224, 314, 326

Videls, 328

Vinton, Bobby, 246

"Wake Up Little Susie," 170

"Walk—Don't Run," 276–77

"Walking to New Orleans," 144

"Walk Like a Man," 249, 251, 326

"Walk Right Back," 172, 193

Wall of Sound. *See* Spector, Phil

"Wanderer, The," 230–31, 326–27

"Warmth of the Sun, The," 112

Warwick, Dionne, 282–83

"Washington Square," 282

"Way You Look Tonight, The," 255

Weavers, 29, 31–32, 292–93, 299, 301

Weil, Cynthia, 1, 45, 135, 202, 241, 282

Wells, Mary, 76, 83–84, 327–28

"We Shall Overcome," 295–96, 323

"West of the Wall," 311

Wexler, Jerry, 52, 136, 141, 148

"What About Us," 147, 324

"What'd I Say," 138

"What's Your Name," 163

"When I Fall in Love," 255

"Where Have All the Flowers Gone," 294

White, Dave, 266. *See also* Danny and the Juniors

"Who Put the Bomp," 32

"Why Do I Love You So," 195

"Wild Weekend," 270–72, 378n6

Williams, Andy, 282

Williams, Hank, 138, 180, 183, 231, 245

"Will You Love Me Tomorrow," 35–36, 38, 60, 202

Wilson, Brian, 104, 108–9, 113, 115, 248. *See also* Beach Boys

Wilson, Don. *See* Ventures

Wilson, Jackie, 140–41, 149, 153

"Wings of a Dove," 290

Winter Dance Party (tour), 13. *See also* "day the music died, the"

"Wipe Out," 124–25

WKBW. *See* "Wild Weekend"

"Wolverton Mountain," 290

Women and popular music: assertive, 266–68, 327–28; as dependents, 264, 268, 324–25; double standard, 35, 74, 126, 326–27; as equals, 36, 161–62, 181, 267, 328; fashions, 49–50, 58, 246, 267, 314; objectified, 25–26, 146, 196, 238, 246, 326; stereotypes, 238, 263, 324–29; as trailblazers, 35–36, 76–77, 165, 176–78, 210–12, 265–67; as victims of abuse, 57, 59, 165, 225, 265, 325. *See also* girl groups

Wonder, Stevie, 86–87, 94

"Wonderful Summer," 267

"Wonderful World," 141

"Wonderland by Night," 280–81, 327–28

Wrecking Crew, 237

"You Are My Destiny," 209

"You Beat Me to the Punch," 77, 328

"You Better Move On," 160

"You Don't Own Me," 261, 266–68, 283, 327

"Young World," 206, 269

youth culture: boundaries of, 5–6; and coming of the Beatles, 331–33; evolving youth culture, 51, 333–34; and Kennedy's assassination, 114, 331; and rock & roll, 5–7, 131, 182, 316–17. *See also* baby boomers

"You've Really Got a Hold on Me," 84

Yuro, Timi, 262, 268

"Zip-a-Dee-Doo-Dah," 49